THE LETTERS OF SYLVIA BEACH

The
Letters
of
Sylvia Beach

Edited by
Keri Walsh

With a foreword by Noel Riley Fitch

COLUMBIA UNIVERSITY PRESS   NEW YORK

Columbia University Press
Publishers Since 1893
New York   Chichester, West Sussex
Copyright © 2010 Columbia University Press
Paperback edition, 2012

The author and Columbia University Press gratefully acknowledge the support
of Claremont McKenna College in the publication of this book.

Library of Congress Cataloging-in-Publication Data
Beach, Sylvia.
[Correspondence, Selections]
The letters of Sylvia Beach / edited by Keri Walsh ; with a foreword by Noel Riley Fitch.
p. cm.
ISBN 978-0-231-14536-7 (cloth)—ISBN 978-0-231-14537-4 (pbk)— ISBN 978-0-231-51784-3
(e-book)
1. Beach, Sylvia—Correspondence. 2. Publishers and publishing—France—Correspondence.
3. Booksellers and bookselling—France—Correspondence. 4. Americans—France—Paris—
Correspondence.   I. Walsh, Keri. II. Title.

Z305.B33A3   2010
070.5092—dc22
[B]   2009045434

Designed by Lisa Hamm

For Deirdre and John Walsh

CONTENTS

The Letters of Sylvia Beach

LIST OF ILLUSTRATIONS

FOREWORD

Noel Riley Fitch

SYLVIA BEACH was the midwife of literary modernism. Certain people are meant to be midwives—not mothers of invention. Sylvia was one. Through her Paris bookshop, Shakespeare and Company, she published James Joyce's *Ulysses*, running interference with the printer so that he could rewrite and add at least a third more of his novel to the renewable proofs. She spent a decade promoting and caring for his business and reprints of the novel, and presented him to the leading men of letters in France.

Beach's contribution to modernism went far beyond what she did for Joyce, for she created and presided over a literary center, serving as librarian, promoter, and sometimes banker and broker for many established and aspiring writers. She introduced William Carlos Williams to Valery Larbaud, F. Scott Fitzgerald to André Chamson, and Eugène Jolas to James Joyce. In short, she orchestrated many of the transactions between English and French literature during the first half of the twentieth century.

She was a missionary to the arts or a midwife, though Sylvia herself usually used masculine and business terms, calling herself a "businessman." Despite her self-designation, her casual bookkeeping and generosity made her anything but a keen moneymaking "commercial" businessman. For twenty-two years, like a Geneva Calvinist, she worked in the arts and lived over the store. She also called it "my literary welfare work" and once she indeed called the shop "my missionary endeavor." In my experienced opinion as a minister's child myself, I see her as a good minister's daughter (if you discount her atheism). She knew how to keep a secret; knew how to take up a collection—from the wealthy, for the poor (artists); and devoted her life to something greater than herself.

Before my *Sylvia Beach and the Lost Generation* was published, few people had studied the women artists who lived and worked in Paris in the first half of the twentieth century, and no one had told the story of the woman and bookshop that presided over this literary crossroads. Literary history had ignored her.

One of the early discoveries I made—and I think that *Sylvia Beach and the Lost Generation* helped to shift critical interpretation in this direction— was that it was the modernist women who as pioneers led the way to Paris: Natalie Barney in 1902, Gertrude Stein in 1903, Edith Wharton in 1912, Beach in 1916. It was the women who stayed the longest (three of these four died there). It was the women who made a room of their own, learned the language, and occasionally wrote in French. Wharton wrote a short story in French, all of Barney's poetry was written in French, Beach translated Henri Michaux' *Barbare en Asie* into English. Modernism was at least as much a creation by the women as by the men, and certainly it was the women who nurtured the new.

In the twenty-five years since Beach's story was published, numerous books about the women of modernism have appeared, from monographs on Barney and Stein to such sweeping studies as Shari Benstock's *Women of the Left Bank.*

Shakespeare and Company and Sylvia Beach were one and the same. Their success and endurance resulted primarily from the force of her personality, which was characterized as much by her hospitality and loyalty (the quality Ernest Hemingway most admired) as by her sharp wit and verbal playfulness. Her friends told me that in her speech she tripped through and delightedly combined the English and French languages.

This personality and wit stand revealed in the letters contained in this book, especially in the earlier letters to family and friends before she became so busy that her correspondence was chiefly business. The letters in this volume reveal her personal voice, the important role her family played in establishing the bookshop, the details of her "bootlegging" of *Ulysses,* and her working relationship with Adrienne Monnier.

This first collection of her letters, carefully edited by Keri Walsh, completes the story of Beach's missionary zeal and her role in modernism. She—and the company of notables foregathered at Shakespeare and Company—altered the course of modern literature.

ACKNOWLEDGMENTS

*M*Y FIRST thanks go to Sylvia Beach's nephew, Fred Dennis, with whose permission Beach's letters appear here. Don Skemer, Princeton's Curator of Manuscripts, welcomed me into the Sylvia Beach Papers and shared his deep knowledge of expatriate Paris. Archivists seem universally to share my love of Sylvia Beach, and working with them was one of the greatest pleasures of this project. AnnaLee Pauls and Meg Rich, two extraordinary research librarians, facilitated this edition and became friends in the process, as did Linda Bogue, Mary George, Charles Greene, Chris Kitto, John Logan, Aaron Pickett, Jane Snedeker, and Sylvia Yu. Thanks to Peter Nelson at Amherst College; Naomi Saito at the Beinecke Rare Book and Manuscript Library (Yale University); Erika Ledermann and Michael Basinski at SUNY Buffalo; Elizabeth Garver and Richard Workman at the Harry Ransom Center (University of Texas at Austin); the British Library; Georgetown University; Houghton Library (Harvard University); the Historical Society of Pennsylvania; the Lilly Library (Indiana University); the Huntington Library; and the Zurich International James Joyce Foundation, as well as Mauro Piccicinni and Charles Amirkhanian for assistance with George Antheil materials.

I was lucky to be surrounded by a circle of inspiring mentors at Princeton, including April Alliston, Dan Blanton, Daphne Brooks, Anne Cheng, Maria DiBattista, Jeff Dolven, Diana Fuss, Simon Gikandi, Jason Klugman, Uli Knoepflmacher, Meredith Martin, Deborah Nord, Jeff Nunokawa, Starry Schor, P. Adams Sitney, Susan Stewart, Kerry Walk, Tim Watson, Torey Wilson, Tamsen Wolff, Susan Wolfson, and Michael Wood. Pat Guglielmi made many resources available through her creativity and skill as graduate administrator.

Fellow scholars of modernist literature and culture also helped to bring this book into being. Noel Riley Fitch and Bonnie Kime Scott were especially essential to its success, and my thanks also go to Briallen Hopper, Kevin Dettmar, Christine Froula, John Kelly, Kevin Lamb, Daniel Larlham, Saikat Majumdar, Neil Maybin, Carol Loeb Shloss, Mark Wollaeger, David Yaffe, and all those who shared their ideas about Beach's role in modernism with me. Research assistance and time to undertake this collection came from the Mrs. Giles Whiting Fellowship, the Center for Human Values at Princeton, the Princeton University Preparatory Program (PUPP), the Princeton English Department, the Princeton Writing Program, and Claremont McKenna College. For assistance with translation, transcription, annotations, permissions, and other details, I am grateful to Garaudy Etienne, Siya Kapur, Evan Kindley, Jonathan Mann, Gerri O'Shea, Tiffany Otoya, Ritika Puri, Casey Reck, Livia Romano, Ashley Vinson, Martin Vivas-Valdez, and Melanie Walsh. Rashi Jhunjhunwala and Aisha Shaikh deserve special mention for their labors on the manuscript.

I have benefited tremendously from the expertise of Jennifer Crewe, Afua Adusei-Gontarz, Roy Thomas, and the entire staff at Columbia University Press, and I am also delighted to thank my colleagues in the Literature Department at Claremont McKenna College for their encouragement as I completed the project. In addition to the pleasures of Sylvia Beach's company, these letters were assembled, transcribed, and edited in the company of John Bugg, *my* Adrienne Monnier. His genius for drawing a story out of an archive is the reason this volume exists.

My parents, Deirdre and John Walsh, enabled my own expatriate experiences while always giving me a place to call home. This book is dedicated to them with love.

INTRODUCTION

"No one that I ever knew was nicer to me," recalled Ernest Hemingway of Sylvia Beach. When he was a young and unknown writer, he was given a library card on his first visit to Shakespeare and Company, even though he did not have enough money to pay the subscription fee:

> There was no reason for her to trust me. She did not know me and the address I had given her, 74 rue Cardinal Lemoire, could not have been a poorer one. But she was delightful and charming and welcoming and behind her, as high as the wall and stretching out into the back room which gave onto the inner court of the building, were shelves and shelves of the wealth of the library. (*A Moveable Feast* 35–36)

He was an obscure and impressionable young man, but she was just months away from becoming world-famous as the first publisher of James Joyce's *Ulysses*. In the early 1920s, as she dispensed membership cards to newly arrived writers, Beach was working round the clock to serve not only her customers but also James Joyce and the broader cause of international modernism. Her letters from 1922 reveal that she was negotiating with Marianne Moore for the placement of Joyce's "Work in Progress" (later *Finnegans Wake*) in *The Dial*, overseeing the French translation of *Ulysses* and battling its piracy in America, organizing French teachers for American friends in Paris, and hosting the French literary elect for roast chicken dinners.

Beach's facility for nurturing talent and promoting the avant-garde has long been recognized by scholars of modernism. Yet because she so infrequently wrote for publication, her own perspective on the legendary events she presided over has never been widely heard. In this collection of her correspondence, we become privy to Beach's public and private worlds, witnessing her day-to-day dealings as bookseller and publisher. After its opening in 1919, Shakespeare and Company quickly became a hub where English-speaking writers and readers could satisfy their hunger for books and gossip from home. European writers including André Gide, Simone de Beauvoir, Walter Benjamin, and Paul Valéry also appeared at Beach's shop, pursuing their interest in English and American literature. One of the most well-connected and influential women in modernism, Beach makes cameo appearances in Joyce's *Finnegans Wake*, Stein's *Painted Lace*, and William Carlos Williams' *Autobiography*. Her correspondence with writers including Ernest Hemingway, Gertrude Stein, James Joyce, H.D. (Hilda Doolittle), Marianne Moore, Valery Larbaud, and Richard Wright, among others, provides a rich window on transatlantic networks of modernist production, and on French expatriate life from the 1920s to the 1960s.

In these letters we see Beach issuing praise, advice, and generous criticism to her valued friends, patrons, and colleagues. Beach's incoming correspondence shows the extent to which writers and publishers relied on her judgment. In 1936, André Breton sought help with English-language selections for his *Anthology of Black Humor*, and a year later the Vanguard Press wrote from New York in search of "current French literature—especially of the Left," and requesting Beach's help in rescuing one of their novels from censorship.[1] Meanwhile, Robert McAlmon sent Beach an account of his "new idea for the Jazz Opera; Too Cosmic if I describe it, but not as I think it; episodic like a review; the History of the World Toward Machinery; the original stage set being a dinosaurs egg hatching everything."[2] And Marianne Moore confessed to Beach that, "It is enheartening to us that you should value The Dial. I also feel the benefit of your confidence in my own work and thank you for telling me of it."[3] Beach's responses to requests for advice were kind and encouraging, but consistently discerning and straightforward. She encouraged Bryher (Annie Winifred Ellerman) not to neglect her own writing in favor of promoting others,[4] and to her friend and sometime tenant, the American composer George Antheil, she confessed: "I am glad you are off the Neo Classic. Where does it lead?"[5] Writing to Joyce's assistant Paul Léon, Beach suggested Joyce's mistake in declining Yeats's invitation to be a Founding Member of the Academy of Irish Letters: "it seems to me it would have done no harm to accept, and that it might have been the first step towards lifting the ban on 'Ulysses.'"[6] A tireless advocate for the writers she believed in, perhaps more importantly she pressed them to advocate for themselves. She had wit, vision, diplomacy, resourcefulness, and a talent for human relations, all of which she shared abundantly.

* * *

Beach was "so American and so French at the same time," according to Adrienne Monnier ("Americans in Paris" 413). She fell in love with Paris and with books at a young age. Bibliophilia permeates her early correspondence, which is full of reviews and recommendations, from Hugo's *Les Misérables* to American sentimental fiction. The daughter of a Presbyterian minister, Beach was born in 1887 and grew up in Bridgeton and Princeton, New Jersey, in comfortable middle-class surroundings. She lived in Paris with her family in 1902 and returned to Europe again in 1907 and 1914 to travel and learn languages in Italy, Spain, and France. Her correspondence from 1901 to 1919 reveals that action and adventure appealed to her. Like many women of her generation, Beach took advantage of the shortage of male labor during the First World War to become a volunteer agricultural worker in France and a member of the American Red Cross staff in Belgrade. Her views on the conflict, which erupted while she was living in America, developed from a quizzical outburst in August 1914 ("isn't it all mad and bloody! Those rowdy German barbarians!")[7] to distressed comments about Paris's ubiquitous amputee veterans. As a farm worker in the countryside surrounding Tours, she harvested crops alongside wounded *poilus* (French infantrymen) and German prisoners of war. It was during this period that she developed her preference for male attire, shocking the provinces with her Khaki suit and eschewal of side-saddle horse-riding, not to mention her zest for physical labor. Letters to her sister Cyprian reveal excitement at escaping from the companionship of proper young ladies, but also an urbanite's frustration with rural life. The farm communities of the Touraine seemed happy enough to put up with her masculine flair, and she enjoyed her experiences of horse-riding and harvesting a safe distance from the front. It was at her next job, working with relief efforts in Serbia, that Beach learned the true cost of war: skeletons of horses by the roadside ("I don't know whether the war killed them or just hunger") and "a continual stream of returning prisoners from Germany and Austria."[8] Beach quickly became frustrated with the hierarchy of the Red Cross, complaining to her parents about

> seeing men doing all the managing and helping themselves to all the pleasant things that come along—[while] the women are subjected to humiliations that American women are not at all accustomed to when they are at

home—they rank as buck privates—are ordered hither & thither, forced to obey unquestioningly.

Beach proclaimed that this edict to obey "has made a regular feminist of me."[9] Her wartime correspondence offers a fresh first-person account of American women's activities in Europe from 1914 to 1919. The suffering she witnessed contributed to her transformation from a pleasure-seeking tourist to a woman determined to do something useful with her life.

SHAKESPEARE AND COMPANY

At the war's end, several callings beckoned to Beach. Her mother suggested that they open a business for importing fine European goods to America, while Beach briefly flirted with the idea of a career in journalism. Through all this, she recalled that reading was her first love, and in 1916, with very little idea of how to proceed, she visited the publisher Ben Huebsch in New York, seeking his advice with her "vague plan for a bookshop" (*Shakespeare and Company* 8). Her first idea was to open a French-language bookstore in New York or London, but she found herself increasingly pulled toward a life in France, especially as she realized the prohibitive cost of doing business in dollars or pounds. Beach found both inspiration and practical advice in Paris when she met the French bookstore-owner Adrienne Monnier, who would become her lifelong personal and professional partner. They met in Monnier's La Maison des Amis des Livres— a "house for the friends of books"—where Beach had traveled in search of materials for her study of contemporary French poetry. Beach's predilection for exploring the quiet avenues of Paris was rewarded, and she was only slightly exaggerating when she guessed, "I was the only American to discover the rue de l'Odéon and participate in its exciting literary life at that time" (14). Of their early romance, Beach reminiscences, "During the last months of the war, as the guns boomed closer and closer to Paris, I spent many hours in the little gray bookshop of Adrienne Monnier" whose light blue eyes "reminded me of William Blake's" (13). Their relationship would grow into a lifelong mutual devotion, one rooted in a shared commitment to writing, reading, and serving the artistic community of Paris. It was an attraction of opposites, with the bustling, chain-smoking Beach complementing the more reflective but nonetheless more outspoken Monnier.

It was with substantial help from Monnier, and with funds contributed by her mother, that the 32-year-old Beach opened her own bookstore, Shakespeare and Company, in 1919. But while she followed her mentor's advice on most business matters, she was determined to cultivate a distinctly different atmosphere from Monnier's monastic retreat. Beach sought to create a lively, approachable, and cozy bookshop. Describing her plans for the décor of Shakespeare and Company to her mother, she insists that "Monnier is not going to have anything to say in that part. She wants me to have that hard battleship grey that she has in her place—but never a-bit, say I! I'm going to have a paint called 'Matolin'—its dull finish—and some beige and yellow."[10] Beach covered the floors with rugs she had purchased in Serbia, and rather than filling the shop with shelves, she restricted them to the perimeter of the walls, giving the interior space the feeling of a comfortable living room. In its first incarnation, Shakespeare and Company was not located at its famous address on the rue de l'Odéon, but in a discreet cubby hole on the rue Dupuytren. It was in 1921 that Beach moved her shop across the street from Monnier's, inaugurating the shared geography where French and English-speaking writers could meet and mingle freely. Encountering Shakespeare and Company after its move to the rue de l'Odéon, Beach's friend Morrill Cody suggested that its intimacy stemmed from her talent, like that of a set designer, for creating "a 'character' store, the brown burlaped walls, the grotesque Chinese goldfish, the pair of brass scales (just as tho books were sold by the pound as they were in the olden days), and the feeling of old wood, homeliness, comfort, always clean without being shiny" (Cody 1261). For Edward Alden Jewell, who worked for Eugène Jolas' journal *transition* when it was published out of Shakespeare and Company in the 1930s, the place "seemed ensnared, *a merveille*, an 'atmosphere.'"[11]

The debut of this "merveille" at the end of the First World War closely coincided with the opening of the American Library in Paris, marking the first time in the city's history that English and American books, magazines, and newspapers could be read cheaply and conveniently.[12] In 1920, nearly five hundred patrons visited the American Library in Paris each day, one-third of them French. The American Library had 30,000 books in its collection, covering "the development of American literature, history, life, and affairs" (Kelly 48). Meanwhile, Beach's shelves were stocked with books from the secondhand bookstores of Paris, American books sent by her sister Cyprian, and British books she purchased herself on trips to London. She found that lending books in Paris was more successful than selling them—money was tight at the end of the war, and few English titles were available in cheap editions (*Shakespeare and Company* 21). Never methodical, Beach confesses that her style of keeping track of her holdings "would have horrified an American librarian, with her catalogues and card indexes and mechanical appliances": at Shakespeare and Company there "was no catalogue . . . no card index" (21). But *New York Times* journalist Marjorie

Reed, overcome by the charm of Shakespeare and Company in 1922, promised Beach's prospective patrons:

> She is almost invariably helpful. She is ready to serve you in her multiple
> capacities and out of a long experience. I have known her called upon to
> produce not only the latest books and periodicals and lend or sell them to
> her customers, but also jobs, places to live, introductions and reliable infor-
> mation on a diversity of subjects. (Reed 69)

Beach joked about her lack of formal education, but she became a teacher
out of necessity, offering impromptu lectures to French clients on the lives
and works of American authors. Despite her growing expertise, she consistently identified herself, as Virginia Woolf did, as a "common reader," not an
academic. Downplaying analytic skills, she made clear her sense of the pri-
macy of the artist: "Good writers are so rare that if I were a critic, I would
only try to point out what I think makes them reliable and enjoyable. For
how can anyone explain the mystery of creation?" (*Shakespeare and Company* 83). Beach's notion that criticism was a derivative activity may help to
account for her mistrust of some of the scholars who came knocking at her
door seeking access to Joyce manuscripts (and anecdotes) later in her life.

Along with praising Beach's helpfulness and knowledge, the *Times* columnist Reed offered a sense of Shakespeare and Company's eclectic stock:

> the works of contemporary English and American writers, modern German,
> French and Russian literature, conservative, radical, realistic, impressionis-
> tic, erotic: Yeats, Dreiser, Hardy, Henry James, F. Scott Fitzgerald, Joseph
> Hergesheimer, Tagore, Tolstoy, Nietzsche, Schopenhauer, Gertrude Stein,
> side by side with the Tauchnitz and Everyman editions and the classics. It is
> a varied collection, showing throughout a high taste in selection. Magazines,
> sedate and flippant, are included—everything from the Dadaists' journal to
> the London Mercury, the Atlantic Monthly, the New Republic, the Freeman,
> the Dial, Broom, Today, the Little Review, Harvard Parabalou, the Chap-
> book, Poetry Magazine and the N.R.F.[13] Nowhere in Paris is there a more
> complete collection. (Reed 69)

Shakespeare and Company was more contemporary and more experimental in its holdings than the American Library in Paris. One notable borrow-
ing card shows the diversity of Beach's collection: while he was working on
The Sun Also Rises and then *A Farewell to Arms*, Hemingway's program
of reading included Stendhal's *The Charterhouse of Parma*, Gide's *Strait is*

the Gate, Lawrence's *Lady Chatterley's Lover*, the journals *This Quarter* and *The Dial*, *The Adventures of Sir Walter Raleigh*, Wilder's *Bridge of San Luis Rey*, Andrew Lang's *Yellow Fairy Book*, Carl Sandburg's *Collected Poems*, plays by Eugene O'Neill, Bertrand Russell's *Problems of Philosophy*, and several volumes of *Sportsman's Sketches*.[14] Beach's own favorite writers were "my associate 'Bill' Shakespeare, William Blake and James Joyce," and close behind she placed Thomas De Quincey and Herman Melville.[15] She collected photographs as well as books, and autographed portraits of the artists who patronized her store lined the walls, with Malcolm Cowley standing alongside Aaron Copland, and D. H. Lawrence keeping company with George Gershwin.

* * *

Beach spent much of her time in the 1920s organizing the publication of *Ulysses* and acting as a promoter, assistant, and general manager for Joyce, his family, and their affairs.[16] This was a project of love, one that made Shakespeare and Company world-famous, and that turned Beach into a culture-hero of the avant-garde. Ultimately, as a result of their disputes over publishing rights for *Ulysses*, Beach and Joyce's relationship soured. Beach ceded the rights to *Ulysses*, and in the 1930s Joyce turned to other friends and supporters, including Eugène Jolas and Paul Léon, to render the services Beach had once performed. The dynamic of the Beach/Joyce relationship, which had initially made them successful as a team—Joyce demanding everything for the sake of his art, and Beach willing to give it, no matter what the personal cost—proved unsustainable over the long term. After Joyce's death, Beach remained in touch with his family through another of his major supporters, Harriet Weaver. The letters from Beach to Weaver in this volume show that their friendship was strong and lasting, but also riddled with tensions, especially in later years.

Beach's role in bringing modernism's masterwork to the public meant that after 1922 her opinions commanded respect and her circle of influence grew. She continued to shape the taste for experimental writing through translations, participation in avant-garde reviews, and recommendations to editors and publishers. Beach and Monnier published the first French translation of T. S. Eliot's "The Love Song of J. Alfred Prufrock" in Monnier's journal *Le Navire d'Argent* (*The Silver Ship*). She was also determined to make Yeats available to French readers: "Yeats, Irish poet and the greatest poet in the English language of our time," she writes in a letter to Monnier. "His daughter, Miss Ann Yeats, was shocked last year, when she asked for the works of her father translated into French and they told her that they don't exist except in magazines."[17] She counseled that Dorothy Richardson and Norman Douglas should be introduced to French readers (though she admitted the problem posed to any venture of translation by the sheer bulk of Richardson's thirteen-volume *Pilgrimage*). Long after her store closed, Beach retained her eye for the gem and the dud: in 1961 she sent no new French books to her friend Carlotta Welles Briggs, concluding that the year's "prize winners are hopeless."[18]

Translations, exhibitions, and advising consumed Beach alongside book-selling, but as a publisher her career was singular. The success of *Ulysses* in 1922 meant that Shakespeare and Company might easily have gone on to become a publishing dynamo like Virginia and Leonard Woolf's Hogarth Press, but Beach was only interested in bringing out Joyce's book. Among the many manuscripts turned down in its wake was D. H. Lawrence's *Lady Chatterley's Lover*: "It was all preaching, preaching," Beach later recalled. "It's nobody's duty to go in for sex if he doesn't want to, is it?"[19] Not every author who offered her a manuscript was seeking protection from obscenity laws: in some cases, authors brought her politically controversial material. In 1923 she received a letter from a writer named G. A. Bena requesting that she publish a book that "English publishers are prejudiced against" because they think it might "stir up trouble in India."[20] It was with regret that Beach declined many of the works she was offered. The only ones she seemed to enjoy refusing were the "hot books" that she passed along to Jack Kahane's Obelisk Press, which specialized in erotica.[21]

Beach put the full weight of her opinion behind only one other writer, Henri Michaux. She spent several years engaged in translating Michaux's 1931 *Un barbare en Asie* (*A Barbarian in Asia*) for New Directions, an achievement for which she won the Denyse Clairouin Memorial Award for Translation in 1950.[22] Beach's enthusiasm for the work of Michaux looks surprising now (his reputation has not worn well), though it is one she shared with Joyce's biographer Richard Ellmann, who also translated some of Michaux's work, and who declared in the *Kenyon Review* in 1949 that he was "one of the most original and important writers of his generation" ("Ductile Modernism" 188). *A Barbarian in Asia*, Michaux's poetic and prophetic narrative of travels in India, China, and Japan, bears certain stylistic affinities with Henry Miller's *Tropic of Cancer*, published in 1934, but Michaux's mescaline-induced, hallucinatory style perhaps most anticipates the Beat writers. Beach's letters of the late 1940s reveal the time and effort she spent promoting Michaux, whom she insisted "must not be lost sight of."[23]

BEYOND SHAKESPEARE AND COMPANY

If Beach's letters are rich in details about early twentieth-century liter-ary culture, they also offer detailed information about her daily activities, especially in letters to two close female friends in America, Carlotta Welles and Marion Peter. Beach met Marion Peter in Paris in 1910, when both were in their early twenties. Their mothers had arranged for them to travel together to Florence to board with an Italian family. "Our friendship began, slowly and cautiously at first," Peter explained, "but soon develop[ed] into a completely happy, sympathetic and devoted relationship."[24] The Beach/Peter correspondence, full of gossip about mutual friends and inquiries about Peter's suitors, began upon Peter's return from Florence to Paris to resume her training as a singer. With this kindred spirit Beach shared her infatuations for the Italian actress Lida Borelli ("such lovely looks and tall graceful figure")[25] and a "craze for Eve Lavallière,"[26] the Montmartre music hall star. When Peter married and returned to Chicago, she helped Beach smuggle copies of *Ulysses* into America.[27] In 1937 she sent her daugh-ter Sylvia, named for Beach, to work at Shakespeare and Company as an assistant.

Another lifelong American friend was Carlotta Welles (1889–1979), who was born on the Italian Riviera while her American parents were abroad. Beach recalls Welles as an "independent, rather sarcastic little girl in a gingham dress" (*Shakespeare and Company* 6). Beautiful and widely trav-eled, she came to the attention of Mark Twain, who was besotted with her on board the S.S. *Minneapolis* during its 1907 transatlantic voyage.[28] Like Beach, Welles came from a Presbyterian family engaged in war relief efforts in Europe. In 1914 she worked at the anti-typhoid lab of a French military hospital. Her parents opened their home in Bourée (Loir-et-Cher) as a hos-pital, and later as headquarters of the American Expeditionary Forces dur-ing the First World War. It was to their house that Beach came to escape Paris during the Second World War. Beach described the Welles estate at Bourée as overflowing with books and wine, a "chateau above the winding little Cher" in a setting "that was like an old French tapestry" (*Shakespeare and Company* 5).

During the Second World War, Beach was taken prisoner by German soldiers of the Occupation and sent to an internment camp at Vittel along with a number of her American friends, including the sculptor Mabel Gardner and the painter Katherine Dudley. The American women were imprisoned alongside a group of English nuns, and in another part of the camp were Jewish prisoners from Eastern Europe, many of whom later died in Auschwitz. Before Beach was captured, she had hastily closed her bookstore, painted over the Shakespeare and Company sign, and hidden all of her books upstairs. Beach's memoir tells of how Hemingway arrived in uniform in 1944 to "liberate" her and her books, but she never reopened the store. Writing to Dorothy Pound in 1949, Beach was matter-of-fact about the sufferings she faced at mid-century: "Shakespeare and Company has gone, but I still live at No. 12, was interned during the Occupation, was lucky enough to save my library, but bookshop went under."[29]

A further strain on Beach in later years was Monnier's declining health. In 1955 we find Beach writing to Marion Peter that work on her book *Shakespeare and Company* was interrupted by "much anxiety over Adrienne" who "has a distressing trouble with her ears and head called Ménière's Disease. She hears noises continually day and night and suffers from them terribly."[30] Monnier's ailment led her to commit suicide later that year. Though she lost both Monnier and Shakespeare and Company, Beach continued to be sought out by newly arrived expatriates, and in the postwar years she cultivated relationships with a younger generation of Americans, including Richard Wright. Beach was also gratified during these years to see her work on behalf of Joyce vindicated by his critical ascendance. After Joyce's death in 1941, Beach and his literary executor, Harriet Weaver, continued to work to serve the interests of the Joyce family, particularly Joyce's daughter Lucia.

Outliving many members of her generation, Beach enjoyed great prestige as the guardian of the memory of 1920s Paris. She coined the term "Bloomsday" to describe the day on which *Ulysses* is set, and she traveled to Ireland for the first time in her life to be present for the opening of the James Joyce Tower and Museum at Sandycove. She was honored by various exhibitions and tributes, and she was granted an honorary doctorate by SUNY–Buffalo, where many of her Joyce manuscripts now reside. She inspired affection and protectiveness in the younger generation, including friends like Maurice Saillet, Jackson Mathews, James Laughlin, and Morrill Cody. Beach died in her apartment in Paris in 1962, at the age of 75. After a funeral service in Paris, her remains were brought to America, and her grave is in Princeton, New Jersey, near her childhood home and the campus of Princeton University. A portrait of her by Monnier's brother-in-law, Paul-Emile Bécat, hangs in Princeton University Library,[31] which now holds most of Beach's papers, a substantial archive of modernism from which many of the letters in this collection are drawn.[32]

* * *

Today, a small specialty shop called Moi Cani inhabits Shakespeare and Company's premises at 12 rue de l'Odèon, and just across the street, on Monnier's side, one finds the Librairie Rieffel. Aside from a commemorative plaque, no trace of Beach's shop remains today. On the rue de la Bucherie, however, just around the corner from Notre Dame, the spirit of Shakespeare and Company lives on. George Whitman, an expatriate American who arrived in Paris after the Second World War, founded a bookstore of his own, Le Mistral, in 1951. He later renamed the shop in honor of Beach's, and this second "Shakespeare and Company" has been serving Parisians and international visitors for over fifty years. Now run by Whitman's daughter, Sylvia Beach Whitman, the new Shakespeare and Company offers readings of poetry and fiction, creative writing groups, and a Sylvia Beach memorial library. Beach's original plan for a bookstore in Greenwich Village has also been fulfilled in the form of another Shakespeare and Company in the neighborhood of New York University. Beach has been called the patron saint of independent bookstores. "She surrounded herself with the books and the background and the atmosphere she wanted, and it was just that quality of individuality Sylvia expressed that other book-lovers wanted," said Marjorie Reed, who commented on her "idealism," and on the shop's placing of a love of reading over a quest for profit (69).

In her last years, Beach was sought out by readers and booksellers, all striving to re-create the model of her shop. Visiting her apartment, teeming with books, in 1960, *Guardian* reporter Peter Lennon was happy to discover that Beach's legendary energy had persisted into her old age: her eyes were "alert and quick as a teenager's" and "You had the feeling that if you asked her to do a jig, she'd be up like a shot" ("Bloomsday Wake" 5). We also have this feeling when we read Beach's letters and encounter firsthand the alacrity and wit that drove one of the singular careers of modernism.

NOTES

1. Sylvia Beach Papers (hereafter, SBP), Manuscripts Division, Department of Rare Books and Special Collections, Princeton University Library (box 187, folder 3; box 86, folder 3).
2. SBP, June 23, 1924 (box 214, folder 3).
3. August 26, 1926, Yale University, Beinecke Rare Book and Manuscript Library, YCAL MSS 34 (hereafter YCAL).
4. When she received a copy of Bryher's journal *Life and Letters To-Day* with contributions by André Gide, Havelock Ellis, H.D. and Mary Butts, Beach urged: "The only disappointment is that there is nothing of yours in this number. I was hoping to see

some of your new work. That's a pity. But there will be something in the next No., won't there?" (September 21, 1935) (letter #145, this volume: for full text of letters cited by dates in the following notes, follow the chronological sequence of letters and recipients).

5. December 22, 1927.
6. September 24, 1932.
7. August 14, 1914.
8. March 11, 1919.
9. April 18, 1919.
10. August 27, 1919.
11. Jewell, Edward Alden. "Whichness of the What: Concerning the 'Revived' *transition* and various Thorny Problems of the Day." *New York Times*, July 12, 1936, X7.
12. The American Library was founded as part of an effort to supply books to American servicemen abroad. It opened its doors at 10 rue de l'Élysée in 1920 under the directorship of Charles Seeger, with Edith Wharton as a trustee (today the Library is located at 10, rue de Général Camou, near the Eiffel Tower).
13. *Nouvelle Revue Française*, the journal founded by André Gide in 1909.
14. SBP (box 201, folder 2).
15. Letter, no date, c. 1940.
16. The story of the initial publication of *Ulysses* can be found in Richard Ellmann's biography *James Joyce*, as well as in Noel Riley Fitch's *Sylvia Beach and the Lost Generation*.
17. Letter, no date, c. 1940.
18. That year, the Prix Goncourt went to Jean Cau's *La Pitié de Dieu*, the French Academy's novel prize to Pham Van Ky's *Perdre la demeure*, the Prix Femina to Henri Thomas' *Le Promontoire*, and the Prix de Deux Magots to Bernard Jourdan's *Saint-Picoussin*.
19. Lennon, Peter. "Bloomsday Wake." *The Guardian Miscellany*, April 9, 1962, 5.
20. SBP, April 16, 1923 (box 86, folder 4).
21. See Beach, *Shakespeare and Company*, 90–97.
22. The award commemorated the translator Denyse Clairouin, who died in Ravensbrück concentration camp. Clairouin's French translation of DuBose Heyward's *Porgy* (1926) appeared posthumously in 1947.
23. Letter from Sylvia Beach to John Slocum, American scholar and foreign service officer, February 22, 1950 (James Joyce Collection, Yale University, Beinecke Rare Book and Manuscript Library).
24. Marion Peter to archivist Howard Rice, March 21, 1966. SBP (box 60, folder 4).
25. Undated letter, 1911.
26. Undated letter, 1912.
27. See Beach's letter of August 7, 1922, for details of Peter's role in getting *Ulysses* to buyers in New York.
28. Welles and Twain developed a short-lived friendship and correspondence (her notes to Twain are held in the Mark Twain Papers at Berkeley).
29. SBP (box 224, folder 4).
30. SBP, January 7, 1955 (box 60, folder 4).
31. The portrait can be seen hanging behind Adrienne Monnier in figure 16.
32. The Beach archive at Princeton and elsewhere holds more treasures than this book can contain, and pieces of her story remain to be told. Not all of Beach's letters to Monnier and Monnier's assistant Maurice Saillet (held at the Harry Ransom Center for the Humanities) are included here. Nor are the 108 letters she wrote to James

Joyce which form part of the Jahnke Bequest at the Zurich International James Joyce Foundation. As of the publication date of this volume, the Beach letters in the Jahnke Bequest are closed to scholars indefinitely.

REFERENCES

Banta, Melissa and Oscar A. Silverman, eds. *James Joyce's Letters to Sylvia Beach, 1921–1940*. Bloomington: Indiana UP, 1987.

Beach, Sylvia. *Shakespeare and Company* (1959). Lincoln: U of Nebraska P, 1991.

Benstock, Shari. *Women of the Left Bank: Paris, 1900–1940*. Austin: U of Texas P, 1986.

Berry, James, Frances May Dickinson Berry, and Walter Lyon Blease. *The Story of a Red Cross Unit in Serbia*. London: J. and A. Churchill, 1916.

Brown, John L. "A Report from Paris." *New York Times*, July 7, 1946, 101.

Cody, E. Morrill. "Shakespeare and Company—Paris: Successfully Selling English Books on a French Side Street." *Publishers Weekly* 12 (April 12, 1924): 1261–63.

Ellmann, Richard. "The Ductile Modernism of Henri Michaux." *Kenyon Review* 11.2 (1949): 187–98.

——. *James Joyce* (1959). Rpt., Oxford: Oxford UP, 1982.

Fitch, Noel Riley. *Sylvia Beach and the Lost Generation: A History of Literary Paris in the Twenties and Thirties*. New York: Norton, 1983.

Hemingway, Ernest. *A Moveable Feast* (1964). New York: Scribner, 2003.

Huddleston, Sisley. *Bohemian Literary and Social Life in Paris: Salons, Cafes, and Studios*. London: Harrap, 1928.

Imbs, Bravig. *Confessions of Another Young Man*. New York: Henkle Yewdale House, 1936.

Joyce, James. *Letters of James Joyce*. Vols. 1 and 2. Edited by Stuart Gilbert. London: Faber, 1957.

Joyce, Stanislaus. *My Brother's Keeper: James Joyce's Early Years*. New York: Viking, 1958.

Kelly, Florence Finch. "American Literature in France." *New York Times*, December 26, 1920, 48.

Larbaud, Valery. *Letters to Adrienne Monnier and Sylvia Beach*. Edited by Maurice Saillet. Paris : Institut Mémoires de l'édition contemporaine; [Malakoff]: Distribution Distique, c. 1991.

Laughlin, James. "Introduction." *Shakespeare and Company*. Lincoln: U of Nebraska P, 1991.

Lennon, Peter. "Bloomsday Wake." *The Guardian Miscellany*, April 9, 1962, 5

Lidderdale, Jane. *Dear Miss Weaver: Harriet Shaw Weaver, 1876–1961*. New York: Viking, 1970.

Maddox, Brenda. *Nora: A Biography of Nora Joyce*. London: Hamilton, 1988.

Maurat, Laure. *Passage de l'Odéon : Sylvia Beach, Adrienne Monnier et la vie littéraire à Paris dans l'entre-deux-guerres*. Paris: Librairie Artheme Fayard, 2003.

McAlmon, Robert. *Being Geniuses Together, 1920–1930*. Garden City: Doubleday, 1968.

Michaux, Henri. *A Barbarian in Asia*. Trans. Sylvia Beach. New York: New Directions, 1949.

Monnier, Adrienne. "Americans in Paris." In *The Very Rich Hours of Adrienne Monnier*, 308–311. Trans. Richard McDougall (1976). Lincoln: U of Nebraska P, 1996.

Reed, Marjorie. "Shopkeeper of Shakespeare and Company." *New York Times*, December 3, 1922, 69.

Scott, Bonnie Kime. *Joyce and Feminism*. Bloomington: Indiana UP, 1984.

Shloss, Carol Loeb. *Lucia Joyce: To Dance in the Wake*. New York: Farrar Straus and Giroux, 2003.

Sweeney, James Johnson. "For Browsers There Was 'Ulysses.'" *New York Times*, September 13, 1959, BR1.

Wickes, George. *Americans in Paris*. Garden City: Doubleday, 1969.

Williams, William Carlos. *The Autobiography of William Carlos Williams*. New York: New Directions, 1948.

Wineapple, Brenda. "Introduction: Odéonia." *The Very Rich Hours of Adrienne Monnier*, 3–66. Trans. Richard McDougall (1976). Lincoln: U of Nebraska P, 1996.

CHRONOLOGY

1887   In Baltimore, Maryland, Eleanor Thomazine Orbison and her husband, Presbyterian minister Sylvester Woodbridge Beach, welcome their second of three daughters, Nancy Woodbridge Beach, who would later take the name Sylvia, on March 14.[1] In Paris, assembly of the Eiffel Tower begins.

1892   Adrienne Monnier is born on April 26.

1899   *Blackwood's Magazine* publishes Joseph Conrad's *Heart of Darkness*, and Freud's *Interpretation of Dreams* appears in German. Ernest Hemingway is born in Oak Park, Illinois.

1900   Oscar Wilde dies in Paris.

1902   The Beach family moves to France when Sylvester Beach is appointed as the assistant minister of the American Church in Paris.

1904   James Joyce courts Nora Barnacle on June 16, a date he will immortalize in *Ulysses*.

1905   The Beach family moves to Princeton, New Jersey, when Sylvester Beach takes the position of minister at the First Presbyterian Church of Princeton.

1907   Beach takes her first trip as an adult to France and Italy.

1908   Gertrude Stein publishes *Three Lives*.

1909   André Gide founds the *Nouvelle Revue Française*.

1911   Charles Osgood, professor of English at Princeton University, employs Beach as a research assistant for his *Concordance to the Poems of Edmund Spenser* (1915). She begins to use the name "Sylvia."

---

1. Details of Beach's life are drawn from Noel Riley Fitch's *Sylvia Beach and the Lost Generation: A History of Literary Paris in the Twenties and Thirties* (New York: Norton, 1983).

1912   Woodrow Wilson, a friend of the Beach family, is elected president of the United States. Thomas Mann releases *Death in Venice*. The Balkan Wars begin.

1913   Beach becomes active in the women's suffrage movement.

1914   World War I begins. The Panama Canal opens. Beach meets with the publisher Ben W. Huebsch in New York to discuss her career, and then leaves on an extended trip to Europe, spending two years in Spain with her mother. James Joyce publishes *Dubliners*.

1915   Adrienne Monnier becomes one of the first French women to establish herself as a bookseller when she opens La Maison des Amis des Livres in Paris. T. S. Eliot's *The Love Song of J. Alfred Prufrock* appears in *Poetry* magazine.

1916   Beach's mother returns to Princeton. Beach settles in Paris to study French poetry. James Joyce publishes *A Portrait of the Artist as a Young Man*.

1917   All three Beach sisters, Holly, Cyprian, and Sylvia, are living in Europe. Beach joins the Volontaires Agricoles and spends two months grape picking, wheat bundling, and tree grafting in the Loire as part of the American Ambulance Field Service's war-relief efforts. Her article on the Rodin Museum in Paris appears in the July edition of the *International Studio: An Illustrated Magazine of Fine and Applied Art*. The Russian Revolution begins. Beach decides to stay permanently in Europe and meets Adrienne Monnier at La Maison des Amies des Livres.

1918   The signing of an armistice between Germany and the Allied nations ends World War I on the western front on November 11.

1918–   Beach and her sister Holly serve in Serbia with the Balkan Commission
1919   of the American Red Cross.

1919   In November, Beach opens an English-language bookshop and lending library, Shakespeare and Company, on the Rue Dupuytren in the St.-Germain-des Prés quarter of Paris. The League of Nations is created.

1920   The American Library in Paris opens. Edith Wharton publishes *The Age of Innocence*. In March Beach meets Gertrude Stein and Alice B. Toklas; in July she meets James Joyce. Women are given the right to vote in the United States with the passing of the nineteenth amendment.

1921   As James Joyce becomes acquainted with French intellectuals, his professional relationship with Beach grows. Shakespeare and Company relocates to 12 rue de l'Odéon, across from Monnier's Maison des Amis des Livres. The Harlem Renaissance begins in the United States. Jane Heap and Margaret Anderson are put on trial for obscenity for publishing installments of *Ulysses* in the *Little Review*.

1922   Modernism's *annus mirabilis*. Shakespeare and Company gains prestige when Beach publishes the first edition of *Ulysses* in its entirety. T. S. Eliot publishes *The Waste Land*.

1923 After a feud over finances and careers, Beach's sister Cyprian informs her that she never wishes to speak to her again, ending their relationship. The two see each other only once again in Pasadena, California, in 1936.

1924 Premiere of George Antheil's *Ballet mécanique*.

1925 Josephine Baker makes her Parisian debut at the Théatre des Champs-Élysées. Beach and Monnier translate T. S. Eliot's *The Love Song of J. Alfred Prufrock* for the first edition of Monnier's journal *Le Navire d'Argent* (*The Silver Ship*). Shakespeare and Company opens its Walt Whitman Exhibition. Beach publishes two more editions of *Ulysses*.

1927 Beach takes time off to cope with the death of her mother. Virginia Woolf's *To the Lighthouse* appears.

1928 Beach introduces F. Scott Fitzgerald to James Joyce. William Butler Yeats writes *The Tower*. In England, Radclyffe Hall's *The Well of Loneliness* is prosecuted for obscenity.

1929 Shakespeare and Company publishes a volume of studies on Joyce titled *Our Exagmination Round his Factification for Incamination of Work in Progress*. The collection features a contribution from Samuel Beckett. A pirated edition of *Ulysses* is published in New York. The beginning of the Great Depression is signaled by the stock market crash on Black Tuesday.

1930 Beach catches pneumonia. Joyce takes 13,000 francs in overdrafts from Shakespeare and Company and becomes increasingly estranged from Beach and Monnier. Beach leaves Shakespeare and Company for three months to travel with Monnier.

1931 Beach receives information that a pirated edition of Joyce's *Pomes Penyeach* is being distributed in Cleveland, Ohio. Her father aids her in securing a copyright for the work. The Depression worsens. After a dispute over the *Ulysses* contract, Beach resigns as Joyce's publisher.

1933 In *United States v. One Book Called Ulysses*, U.S. District Judge John M. Woolsey overturns the decision to ban *Ulysses*. He rules the book is neither pornographic nor obscene. Adolf Hitler takes power in Germany and establishes the first concentration camps.

1934 Random House sells 35,000 copies of *Ulysses* in the United States between January and April, a total exceeding the combination of all sales from Shakespeare and Company. On "bloody Tuesday," thousands of people in France are provoked by the Depression to protest French taxes, political corruption, and rising living costs.

1935 Beach struggles to keep Shakespeare and Company open through the Depression.

1936   The Spanish Civil War begins. Beach's fears that Shakespeare and Company will go out of business come to an end when André Gide organizes a small group of writers to deliver fundraising readings at the shop. Later that year, Gide leaves Paris for Russia in support of communism. Beach returns to Princeton in July to visit her family, traveling with her father to Pasadena, California. Beach undergoes a hysterectomy in Long Island. Upon her return to Paris, she finds that photographer Gisèle Freund is living in the apartment she had shared with Monnier. She moves into the rooms above Shakespeare and Company.

1937   Beach holds a reception in honor of Bryher and her journal *Life and Letters To-Day*. She begins to write her memoirs.

1939   Germany invades Poland in September, marking the beginning of World War II. Beach disregards her family's urgings to return to the United States.

1940   In May the German army occupies France. Winston Churchill becomes the British prime minister, Charles de Gaulle leads the Free French forces and Samuel Beckett joins the Resistance. Walter Benjamin dies while trying to escape from Spain. Richard Wright publishes *Native Son*. Beach's father dies at age 88.

1941   James Joyce dies in Zurich. Pearl Harbor is bombed, bringing the United States into the war. Beach sells her last books at Shakespeare and Company.

1942   Beach hides the bookstore's stock in her apartment. She is arrested as a result of her American nationality and spends six months in an internment camp at Vittel. Albert Camus publishes *The Stranger*.

1944   Hemingway returns in uniform to "liberate" Shakespeare and Company, which never reopens for business.

1945   The United States drops atomic bombs on Hiroshima and Nagasaki. World War II formally ends. The United Nations and Arab League form.

1943–   Beach does volunteer work with veterans and others in war-ravaged
1950   France. She lends out books from her collection and becomes friends with Richard Wright when he joins the expatriate community. French literary culture booms. Beach devotes more time to her memoirs. Jean-Paul Sartre publishes *Being and Nothingness*.

1946   The Cold War begins.

1947   André Gide wins the Nobel Prize in Literature.

1948   T. S. Eliot wins the Nobel Prize in Literature.

1949   Simone de Beauvoir publishes *The Second Sex*.

1950   Beach wins the Denyse Clairouin Memorial Award for her translation of Henri Michaux's *A Barbarian in Asia* (*Un barbare en Asie*), published by New Directions.

1951   Cyprian Beach and Nora Joyce die. George Whitman opens the Parisian bookstore Le Mistral, which he later renames Shakespeare and Company.

1953   Beach travels to Greenwich, Connecticut, to visit her last remaining family member, Holly. She goes to London with Monnier and Bryher for the coronation of Queen Elizabeth II.

1954   Ernest Hemingway wins the Nobel Prize in Literature.

1955   After years of illness, Monnier dies from an overdose of sleeping pills on June 19.

1956   Beach publishes her memoir, *Shakespeare and Company*, containing stories of her experiences with writers such as Joyce, Gide, Eliot, Stein, and Hemingway. The First Congress of Black Writers meets in Paris.

1957   Samuel Beckett publishes *Endgame*.

1958   The Algerian War for Independence begins.

1959   In June, Beach travels to the United States to receive an honorary doctorate of letters from the State University of New York at Buffalo. She makes her final visit to Princeton in the fall.

1961   The United States enters the Vietnam War. Ernest Hemingway commits suicide. H.D. and Harriet Weaver die. John F. Kennedy becomes president of the United States.

1962   Beach is threatened with the loss of her Paris apartment, but friends and supporters come to her aid. She travels to Ireland for the first time to be present at the opening ceremonies of the James Joyce Tower and Museum at Sandycove, and then vacations in Greece, the Middle East, and Egypt. On October 6, she dies at home in Paris.

THE LETTERS OF SYLVIA BEACH

I

FRIENDSHIP AND TRAVEL

1. To Holly Beach[1]　　　　　　　**November 8, 1901**

Bridgeton[2]

Dear Holly,

You owe me a letter but I thought I would write and tell you the news. We have a smallpox scare here now and every body has been vaccinated, or is being. There is a case on Pine Street and four houses are quarantined with a policeman there all the time. There are two more cases one of which is on Vine Street.

The little Robinsons are not allowed to play with Anna Thompson because her father attends the case on Pine Street. Eleanor is not allowed to either. Mr Elmer Shoemaker across the street vaccinated his whole family including the cook last Sunday with his razor. The day before yesterday I asked Allen if his vaccination had taken. He said, "no its going to take tomorrow and I spect to die." Yesterday he said to Eleanor, "I was going to die tomorrow but Mama wouldn't let me."

On Saturday Mother, Eleanor, and I are going to drive over to Vineland to get a rug. It takes two hours and half to drive over and the same to come back of course so we will have a long drive. Did you know that little Virginia Spresher has broken her leg? Did you know that dear cute Chummy is never going to be well of the rheumatism? Miss Julia said so.

Item. The Hitshoner baby has a new crib.

---

1. Beach's sister, born Mary Hollingsworth Morris Beach in 1884.
2. The New Jersey parsonage where Beach's father was serving.

Item. I am reading the "Old Gentleman of the Black Stock," by Thomas Nelson Page.[3]

Item. Bobby is coming in a week or less. Mrs Beach and Mrs Smith have scrap about him. Question. Shall affore said gentleman stay at Mrs Smith's all the time or will Mrs Smith be generous and allow him to go to Mrs B's for some of the time. Private.

I hear that you are sick. Take Pink Pills for Pale People.[4]

With much love, Nancy Beach[5]

Sylvia Beach Papers, Manuscripts Division, Department of Rare Books
and Special Collections, Princeton University Library (manuscript)

* * *

2. To Holly Beach   1904

206 Bd. Raspail
Paris

Chére Celine,

Mother could not possibly write to you this morning on account of Mrs Brandenburg being here and this afternoon she had to go with Cousin Bessy to the Bon Marché to try on her dress. She was very anxious to write to you too. Perhaps you will accept a letter from me as a substitute though but a poor one. We read in the Herald that your boat had arrived. Monday was an exciting day for us. We were eating an early dinner (we had to meet the Somervilles on the 6-45 train) when a dispatch from Popsin came saying he would be at the St Lazare at 9-30, so after we had seen Cousins Bessy and Alan to their hôtel, we went to meet Father. We were mighty glad to see him. He brought Bidsy's Benita in a box-stall, and a great many packages of chewing gum, a present from a chewing-gum King Father met on the board as our German friend calls it.

I am in a great hurry Höllychen. Last night Father had to get out of his bettchen at 2 and go to see a young architect who was dying. I had a singing lesson this morning and some kind treatment. Wasn't it nice

---

3. Thomas Nelson Page (1853–1922), Virginia-born writer of "plantation fiction" idealizing the pre–Civil War era in the American South. He also served as the American ambassador to Italy. The novel Beach refers to appeared in 1897.
4. A nineteenth-century headache and cold medicine.
5. Beach went by her birth name, Nancy, until she was a teenager.

that you could see Marguerite before she left for school? Give her much love from me.

There was a crazy woman on the stairs the other day and three strong policemen came and carried her off amid cries and screams. We miss you awfully. Do you understand this joke?

The Thurbers went home this morning. F. and M. went to say good-bye yesterday.

Cousin B. brought Moundy[6] a pretty center-piece, Bidsy and one each a pin.

Give our love to Cousin Mary and everybody

Much to yourself

    Deine Onghrir

Sylvia Beach Papers, Manuscripts Division, Department of Rare Books and Special Collections, Princeton University Library (manuscript)

*   *   *

3. To Holly Beach   **December 7, 1904**

         206 Bd. Raspail.

         Paris

Dear Holly,

Just a line (but not a very straight one) to acquaint you with my condition. I think I may safely say that this last is no longer critical. The Welleses arrived home last Saturday and today Carlotta and I had a conversation in the telephone.[7] She asked Bidsy and me to come over tomorrow.

The other day Mother and Father went with Mrs Rainer to see Emma Nevada[8] and her daughter Mignon. They are very nice people. Mignon is very bright. You knew that she had composed an opera did you not. At Ms Nevada's they met Loïe Fuller[9] who is also lovely. She

---

6. A nickname for Beach's mother.

7. Beach's friend Carlotta Welles, later Carlotta Welles Briggs. Letters to her are well-represented in this volume. See the introduction for more details.

8. Emma Nevada, born Emma Wilson (1859–1940). American opera singer and her daughter Mignon (1886–1971).

9. Loïe Fuller (1862–1928), American dancer who performed regularly at the Folies Bergère and other Paris venues after beginning her career in American vaudeville and burlesque. She was a pioneer of stage lighting and one of the founders of modern dance. Yeats's poem "Nineteen Hundred and Nineteen" includes the tribute: "When Loïe Fuller's Chinese dancers enwound / A shining web, a floating ribbon of cloth, / It seemed that a dragon of air / Had fallen among the dancers" (ll. 49–52).

asked us to go and see her yesterday so Father took Bids and me. She stays at the Hôtel Bedford. When we went into her drawing-room we found Nevada and her daughter, a Greek lady with her little girl and an <u>English</u> neice,—and others. Loïe had some radium and showed us a piece of her dancing dress with it. The little Greek girl danced the cake walk and recited some pieces in French and in Greek. When it was time to go, Loïe presented us with a card on which she had written an order for a loge at the Moulin Rouge where she dances now. We went last night.

I must hurry. Mother can not possibly write today either as the house is all upside down. We go to London on Thursday. Mother says to tell you she is afraid you will think she neglects you. You understand how it is don't you?

We enjoyed your letter <u>so much</u>

much, much love,

Went to Faust, Lindsey,

Cousin Bessy.

Nancy

Sylvia Beach Papers, Manuscripts Division, Department of Rare Books
and Special Collections, Princeton University Library (manuscript)

* * *

4. To Eleanor Orbison Beach[10] No date

Högestad[11]

Dear Mummy:

We were homesick for the family on Christmas but we had a fine time. The day before Christmas we trimmed a tree for the servants and one for ourselves and wrapped up and sealed all the presents which they always have Christmas-eve in Sweden. After dinner in the evening the Count took them one by one out of a clothes basket and presented them with a bow. Holl and I got a pin from Lilly and Thommy, a book, and some pretty Swedish things from Mrs Piper but we liked

---

10. Beach's mother (1864–1927).
11. A town in Sweden.

the book you sent, better than anything else. The girls were delighted with the collar etc. When we had opened our presents we all took hands and danced around the tree, Ullsohn the butler and some of the other servants did it with us. The other morning Thomazine and I took presents to some of the tenants and Gustaf and Manu came too. I never saw such a wretched little house as those the tenants live in and the tenants themselves look like people in the slum of a city. The Pipers told me that so many people go to America because they get higher wages, and that it was a great pity. No wonder they go. I am getting perfectly sick of seeing these poor tenants and how they bow to kiss your hand.

The cake-walk is greatly in demand, and they make me do it all the time. I can't dance it but I just jerk around like a hen on a hot griddle and they think thats the real cake-walk. I had to do it for the Baron Wrangel von Something, last night. He is an officer who has a monocle in one eye and stays here nearly all the time. He is about eight feet tall and most uninteresting but the Pipers adore him. We are going horse back riding this afternoon. We have a gorgeous time here. Dear little cute moundy, I am so glad we will see you soon!

With much love to elegant Bidsy and dear Mr Beach

Your loving
Nancy

Cher Pére,

This morning we went skating on a big marsh about a mile from the house and the ice could not have been worse. Nearly every step we took, we broke through but as the water was only an inch or so deep, we escaped drowning. After lunch we went out driving in a big wagon with four horses. We went to see a house and estate that used to belong to the Piper family. It is very cold here now but we still spend a great deal of time out of doors. We are going soon to Copenhagen. The other day when we were out hunting Thomazine and I got cold so we went to the house of Count Piper's "chasseur," an old man who takes charge of the hunt and who, with the aid of a cross yellow dog, keeps poachers out of the forest. His wife is a typical old Swedish peasant woman. She wears a coarse white shirt, over this a sort of knitted bodice, and a very short skirt. I never saw such hands as her's, all gnarled and wrinkled as if she had worked very hard all her life. She brought us into her sitting-room bed-room and dining-room combined. We sat down on a bench and she on the bed. Then she told us, always rocking herself to and fro, about her son in America whom she had not heard from for two years. When last he wrote he was getting four dollars a day in . . . [12]

Sylvia Beach Papers, Manuscripts Division, Department of Rare Books and Special Collections, Princeton University Library (manuscript)

* * *

5. To Marion Peter   February 1, 1911

7 Via Palestro
Florence

Dearest Marion,

It was so nice to get your interesting letter telling me all about everything. I could see you writing it on your well known blotter-book-arrangement and with your nice fountain pen (inferior to mine however).

Are'nt you a good child to be so abstemious about Mr Why!

Are'nt you having a grand old time in Paris?

Wasn't it nice about those flowers (not from America)!

I think tho, that you had better move to some more comfortable place the "Villa Coperique" or that place where the Brakets stayed, near our apartment. It is on Rue Chalgrin. You must surely move. You ought to have good things to eat in Paris.

Have you read "Jean Christoffe"? I forget who it is by.[13]

Miss Craik has left for the Hague the night before last at half past ten via Genoa and two days at Monte Carlo. She was invited by some cousins to spend a month, with all expenses paid. Her mother and sister are coming today to take the "double-bedded room".

Last evening at dinner were present among others the Avocato, father of Pete, and a Professoressa cousin of the Michelis, very learned and dull. Maddalena handed some Pasta to Signora. Pietrino noticed a letter for himself and blushed and blushed and held out his hand for it. The Avocato who was sitting next to Signora took the letter instead and proceeded to open it while Pietrino held out his hand and implored and

---

12. The rest of this letter is missing from the archive.
13. Romain Rolland's *Jean Christophe* (1910), like Joyce's *Portrait of the Artist as a Young Man* (1914–15), is a novel about an artist's alienation from society.

beseeched his father to let him have it. He blushed more than you even. The old cuss calmly got out the letter and read it through taking hours to do it then he passed it to Pietrino. I don't see why that boy didnt use the nut cracker on his old father.

Signora told me that when Pietro was staying two years in a professors family here, a sister in law much older than himself got him in her clutches. She writes to him and asks him to send her things. This was a birthday day letter and she sent "thousands of kisses" and other silly things.

Miss Lucy is here!!! She is a dear but a great care to me she is so fussy. She plays your piano and warms herself at your stove (I mean trys to). She likes Signora and everything but complains of the cold pretty constantly.

I envy your being in *the* Spot in the World.[14]

Signora got a Femina[15] this morning.

How is your family and cat?

Remember me to

Mr Why.

> Lots of love
> Sylvia

Sylvia Beach Papers, Manuscripts Division, Department of Rare Books and Special Collections, Princeton University Library (manuscript)

✳   ✳   ✳

6. To Marion Peter   February 24, 1911

> 7 Via Palestro
> Florence

Dearest Marion,

O such a rush I have been in since your letter came and I was going to answer it immediately! Mrs Brandenbourg is going to Rapallo on Monday for two weeks.

---

14. Paris.

15. Feminist newspaper.

Yesterday Miss Lucy, Miss Craik and I went to Pistoia and had a good time and got all worn out. Every afternoon we take a long walk with hot chocolate in a thermos and no rest for anyone.

I was very glad to hear you were moving away from the Wagner home. You did well. What an awful place it must have been. Why didn't you tell me more of the details? Your mysterious hints made me anxious to know all. Write me about the pension you are in now.

Wasn't it nice to hear Mr Clark again, but you haven't said how his concert turned out. I was awfully interested in all those lovely songs you are doing with Lapierre. The Michelis are as well and nice as ever. You made a mistake to leave them. The other evening Ada bounded into my room and told me to mount to Signora directly, she had cut off her finger. I found Signora pale and uneasy with her finger all bloodying up a basin of water so I wrapped two or three handkerchiefs around it and then remembered something about a tourniquet. I took a pencil and twisted it in the knot of the handkerchief like anything. Signora seemed to think it hurt her some but I didn't pay any attention to that. I twisted and twisted. Next we hurried to a pharmacy and they told us to go to a doctor so I supported the patient to Dr Piccinini's. He said when you make a tourniquet you don't make it on the wound but above it. I should have made it on the arm. He said it was a wonder that finger didn't drop off when I twisted the pencil. He bound it up and now it is well.

How are the Paris styles? Do you wear those striking trousers? Do you hear much Debussy and others.

Miss Cécile Craik is visiting in Holland and has been presented at Court and the whole family in a great state of excitement as usual. They are awfully nice about wanting me to take a house in Siena with them this summer. Mrs Branderbourg and I are perhaps going to Rome in April and Hill Towns on the way back to Siena.

How is all your family and how are "Eleanor Smoot," "Bessie Smith," "Hazel Page" and "Helen and Margaret" and "tad" and "Ad"?[16] How is Mr Why?

When do you sail?

Lots of love
Sylvia

I am going to ask a great favor of you and awfully merry it is to do it. Would it be too much trouble sometime when you are in the Printemps

---

16. American singers and actresses.

or Galeries to get me a book of powder like this I enclose. It is 45 centimes. Don't go out of your way to do it. I will send the money.

Signora meant to write today but was too busy. She says please she would like flowers instead of the bag. Those delicate roses at the <u>Printemps</u>. She is afraid it will be a bother to send them.

Sylvia Beach Papers, Manuscripts Division, Department of Rare Books and Special Collections, Princeton University Library (manuscript)

* * *

7. To Marion Peter   **No date**

7 Via Palestro
Florence

Dearest Marion,

Now I am going to ask another great favor of you and you will be perfectly horrified at such news and won't want to be friends any more. Mr Bburg is to stop in Paris on his way to America. He is taking for me a small package which I wonder if you would take to America? I hate to ask you and if you mind at all you must just leave it at the Clarks. Now comes an annoying thing. You will have the awful bother of going way over to Bd Montparnasse 135 to the hotel des Etats Unis and asking the concierge for the package. I think 135 is the number and anyhow it is just opposite rue de Chevreuse where the Girls' Club is. Is it awfully out of your way and you will be all worn out getting there. It is a filet pillow case and perhaps you could get it through by using it as a clothes bag or something and stuffing it away with your things. If you dont want to take it just tell me so and I will understand perfectly. In that case would you mind asking Mrs Clark to keep it for me till I can get it? It looks now as if I should be arriving in Paris in the fall to stay with sister Eleanor[17] for the winter. They think they will send her over to go on with her music and I must take care of her. Mother wants us to stay at Mme Callot's near Place Victor Hugo, recommended by friends in Princeton. Of course Eleanor will study with

---

17. Eleanor Beach, an aspiring performer, went by the name of Cyprian. See the introduction for more details.

Mr Clark. Holly may come to Italy this summer to stay with me. We have been gay here lately. Mr & Mrs Micheli, Miss Camilla Miss Craik and I went to the Politeana[18] twice. Both times it was to see Lida Borelli a perfectly beautiful young actress. The plays were "Le Bois Sacré" and "L'Aventurier"[19] translated into Italian. The first is very clever and funny and it was given extremely well. It was running all last year in Paris. I wish you could see la Borelli. She is has such lovely looks and tall graceful figure.

We have a pleasant bunch in the house now. The Craiks are very good to Signora but they do keep a hot fire in the salottino[20] and all the drafts turned on burning up coal by the ton. It must be expensive for Signora. They have the room so hot no one else can sit in it. They are probably going to take a villino in Siena for the summer and I am going to live in it with them, paying of course my share of the expenses. Jean Craik and I are going to Siena tomorrow to look at a villino which we heard of through Adolfo at the Vieusseux. It is twenty minutes outside the walls and supposed to have a lovely view. We must spend the night in Siena and come back to Florence next day. Wasn't it a pity you and I didnt get there? When do you sail? Do you think you will come back to Europe soon again? You dont know how I have missed you since you left.

Probably when you are married you will come back.

With very much love
Sylvia

Excuse this annoying thing I ask you to do. Mr BBurg would take it to u.s.a but a man is not allowed anything of the sort.

In America I am afraid I must ask you to trouble to do it up in a package and register it to 26 Library Place
Princeton
N.J.

* * *

18. The National Politeama Theatre, Florence.
19. Gaston Armand de Caillavet's *The Sacred Wood* (1910) and *The Adventurer*, an unidentified French play.
20. Bedroom.

8. To Marion Peter   May 28, 1911

Pensione May
183 Via Cavour
Rome

Dearest Marion,

I was so glad to get your letter especially the extra sheet for me only. You are the best dear that ever lived to take home that lace for me and I never will forget it. Marion, I paid eighteen francs for that and your mother can have it for anything she wants. It is awfully nice of her to like it so. The things you helped to get arrived all right and were a great success but the duty was terrible. At first they only charged a reasonable sum but then they changed their minds and sent a huge extra bill out of all proportion. Mother had to ask large prices for the things but it is coming out very well.

There must have been great excitement at your house when you arrived and all your experiences to tell and friends pouring in from morning to night. I can imagine how nice it was.

My sister Holly suddenly came over to Italy with no warning but a telegram and she and I went to Venise and came down to Rome by way of Ancona as Mrs Brandenbourg was too rheumatic to take the hill-town trip. Next week we are going to Capri to stay until Holly goes home and after that I hope to be in Siena with the Craiks. They have taken such a lovely little villa for the summer and are awfully nice about wanting me to go there.

How is your sister? Is she still crazy about the University of Chicago? Didn't we have a good time together at Signora's house all winter? Didnt we have fun going to such excitements as the cinematografo[21] and do you remember Pietro's "tired cow"?

Capri, May 28
Villa Cercola

I began this letter in Rome several weeks ago but never had a minute to finish it. Marion, you know how it is when you are trying to see everything in Rome in two weeks. We never even had time to eat lunch. I am so sorry not to have answered your letter sooner but you must forgive me.

---

21. Cinema.

We are at Mrs Neville's lovely villa in Capri and it is the place to spend your tired old days in. The garden is !!! and we have breakfast in it and such a view of the sea. The rest of the day we read and go in bathing. I wish you were here but I suppose you are enjoying home too much to think of being anywhere else.

Do you hear often from Signora? I expect to go to Siena about the middle of June so if by any chance you write to me the address is To Miss Craik

> Villa Montecelso
> Siena

O Marian do write to me soon and tell me lots of things. I don't forget you for a minute.

Thankyou very much for taking care of the lace.

You must enjoy doing all the songs you know with your mother. When shall I see you again.

With lots of love

Please give my love to your mother and sister

> Sylvia

How is Sweet Annie?

Eleanor is coming to Paris in the fall and we will be there together. You had better come too.

Sylvia Beach Papers, Manuscripts Division, Department of Rare Books and Special Collections, Princeton University Library (manuscript)

✳ ✳ ✳

9. To Marion Peter

June 27, 1911

> Villa Monte
> Celso

Dearest Marion,

O dear you never got my nice letter and you don't love me any more. It was written in Naples some time ago. I received yours of June 5 a day or two after I came to Siena and was so excited at getting it. Isn't it wonderful about making all that money singing in a choir? My nice business doesnt compare with it.[22] Also Marion I don't see why you don't come over here immediately on that money. You have been home long enough now. I wrote to Eleanor the news of Miss Munn's strange doings. I don't think she had heard about it at all.

I arrived here on the fifteenth of this month, the day Holly sailed. We stayed together until the last minute but I didn't see her boat leave. She wouldn't let me. This villa is a great success and I enjoy being with the Craiks so much. We stay in the garden all day long and eat all our meals under the trees, on a stone table with two beautiful lucerne lighted at dinner and lots of fire flies.

Our villa is about three miles outside the gates of Siena and we are always so glad to get back to our cool place. We rent an angel donkey, small and grey with a stylish cart with red cushions and a basket behind for when we do the marketing. The donkey wears one of those tall feathers, also some gay bells.

Cecile and I are going to Paris together as she is going to spend the winter there learning French. The others are going to sail the last of August.

Wasn't it sad but fortunate, the death of Signora's baby. She is a wreck. Friends of the Craiks that were staying there at the time said Signora came to every meal even the very day and looked like a ghost. The Craiks invited her to come here for a visit and she may come in July. Now she has been taken to Carrara by Pietro's sister to visit them for a while. This Annina was staying with Signora during May and June. I left before she came. They say she is a pill but Signora seems very fond of her.

I saw Signor Micheli's portraits of Mrs Piccinini and Pete in Rome. They were hung so well, in such a good room.

My nice business is so so.

See how well this fine fountain pen still writes. I know you never cared for it but I couldn't help seeing that was jealousy on account of yours not being half so good. You never say how your cat Nino is. I hope all your family is well. Give them my love. Were they much startled at the Dolciana?[23]

With lots and lots of love

As ever
Sylvia

Yes I received your theater postal. I would like to see that play.

---

22. Beach was experimenting with an import/export business of European goods.
23. A dulciana is a type of organ stop.

Marion I think of you every minute and look out not to forget me please. How is your Line a Day?

Are you staying in Highland Park all summer?

Our maid of all work is an orphan.

Sylvia Beach Papers, Manuscripts Division, Department of Rare Books and Special Collections, Princeton University Library (manuscript)

* * *

10. To Marion Peter   **August 22, 1911**

3, ave MacMahon
Paris

Dearest Marion,

You are such a very dear friend that I must write to you again. What kind of a fine summer did you have? You must be happy to be with your family. I would like so much to be with my nice family that I havent seen for a year exactly.

The leaves are beginning to turn here and you can imagine if Paris isn't going to be looking lovely the next two months but oh dear its been hot. My being in Paris is a surprise to everybody I know as I am not supposed to come till next month but I have been here since the seventh. Mrs Craik was so desperately ill they had to take her home the first of August. It was very sad. Those poor Craiks were worried awfully. Jean went home with her mother and Cecile is now studying French at Grenoble and will come to Paris later to study it some more. I like Jean much the best. You never met her did you? She is the nicest thing. Cecile wants to go into a French family here. I hope it won't be like your experience at Mme Wagner's. That was ghastly wasn't it?

I came on to Paris because I didnt care to spend the rest of the summer in Italy. Signora invited me to come to their Villa del Amico at the sea for a visit in September, but I thought I would just hurry up here. Signora's villa is at Massa near Viareggio. Cecile and I passed through your Levanto on our way up. We came by Genoa. O I forgot to thank you for sending that filet to mother. She wrote me about it long ago. She was delighted with it, Marion, thank you very much for all the trouble you took.

How is your nice voice? I would give anything to hear you sing again, especially the Chansons de Bilitis[24] which are my favorite songs I ever heard and goodness you sang them well! Do you ever hear from your Lapierre?[25] Do you sing in Church still? How are Rondinella and Guilia Gentil and Babbo mon viole?[26] See how my nice fountain pen writes as exquisitely as ever and at last that pad of thick blue paper like yours gave out. Now I bought this at the Louvre and isn't it nicer? Do you think I am wasting any of it? How is beautiful Miss Helen Messenger?

With lots and lots of love

Sylvia

Sylvia Beach Papers, Manuscripts Division, Department of Rare Books and Special Collections, Princeton University Library (manuscript)

❀   ❀   ❀

11. **To Marion Peter**   **August 29, 1912**

Concarneau
Bretagne

Dearest Marion

You don't know how glad I was to get your letter. Please write oftener to me. You know I have a feeling that you aren't interested in my nice fountain pen any more still you may be glad to hear that its still as good as new.

Signora spent an hour or two in Paris on her way to London. We were very anxious to have her spend the night with us but she would hurry on. Wasnt it mean of her? Eleanor and I went to meet her at the Gare de Lyon and we went to the Gare St Lazare together and breakfasted in a little café nearby. Signora was as lovely as ever which is saying a lot. We talked about you and wished for you like anything. She didn't seem to be very well. I hope her trip did her good. She was as pretty as ever although she wrote and warned me that she was looking awfully changed. I think it must be a relief to her not to have the baby any more.

---

24. Debussy's musical setting of the poet Pierre Louÿs' Sapphic verse.
25. Lapierre: one of Peter's music teachers.
26. Music pieces Peter was working on.

Think of your brother living in Paris all summer and coming to see me at the Avenue Victor Hugo when we never lived there in our lives! We live on Avenue Carnot 16. We have been in Brittany since the 1st of July. Did your brother come to Paris before then? We must see him when we go back if he is still there. I would love to hear him sing. We left the day the Clarks arrived so we never saw them.

I was so excited to hear that Miss Helen Messenger was married now. I remember her perfectly and how good-looking and interesting she was. So you were the Maid of Honor. You were away for all your other friends' weddings weren't you?

I hope we will see Mrs Edmond Henry Eitel[27] in Paris. We have been until the last week at St Jean du Doigt, a sweet little place where it never stops raining and you never stop freezing. It was a sweet place anyhow with a neat little plage and everything so quaint in the town.

Concarneau is wonderful. All the fishing boats have red and blue and yellow and brown sails and the sardine nets are a lovely shade of blue. Everything is adorable.

Marion why dont you come over and see me soon?

With very much love

Sylvia

Sylvia Beach Papers, Manuscripts Division, Department of Rare Books and Special Collections, Princeton University Library (manuscript)

* * *

12. To Marion Peter   **No date, 1912**

3 Avenue Mac. Mahon
Paris

Dearest Marion,

Isnt it outrageous that I have never written to thank you for that lovely photograph and it was so sweet of you to send it. You must just forgive me because I am awfully sorry. I had a long dream about you night before last and all your friends were present too. O Marion I enjoyed your letter so much. You must have had a lovely Christmas, all

---

27. Edmund Henry Eitel (1886–1960), author and nephew of the writer James Whitcomb Riley.

the family together. I envy you the opera you are hearing. Eleanor and I are wild about Mary Garden[28] too. What matter about her voice. Isn't she an artist! I cant help thinking how the Italians would kiss her.

Spring has come to Paris today. I have just come back from St Germain where I spent a week getting some good air. This winter in Paris has run me down, you never saw the like. You wouldn't know me.

Did you see Gaby Deslys[29] when she was in America? Simone doesnt seem to have made a success does she? Did you see her? The other day Eleanor went to see Sara in La Dame aux Camélias.[30] She is doing it twice and not a seat to be had. We have a craze for Eve Lavallière[31] and so has everybody else in Paris. She is the most popular actress here now. I never saw such a fascinating creature.

Isnt it funny; every time I write I ask you about your Dolciana, and never get an answer. Every time you write you ask if I ever got that postal of George Arliss[32] in Disraeli and another of some cottages and words in a strange handwriting that "might have been my sainted mother" and I always forget to tell I got them.

Don't you suppose Signora is happier now that the baby is gone. I would like to know wouldn't you.

Very much love

Sylvia

Sylvia Beach Papers, Manuscripts Division, Department of Rare Books and Special Collections, Princeton University Library (manuscript)

* * *

---

28. Mary Garden (1874–1967), Scottish soprano who sang in the Paris debut of Debussy's *Pelléas et Mélisande* and in Strauss's *Salome*.

29. French music hall dancer whose 1911 performance caused Yale students to rush the stage in the wake of the November Yale-Princeton football game.

30. French actress Sarah Bernhardt (1844–1923) in the famous role created by Alexandre Dumas, fils.

31. Eve Lavallière, a Montmartre dancer and actress who later became a recluse.

32. George Arliss (1868–1946), British actor. Louis Napoleon Parker's play *Disraeli* was written for him, and he performed it on tour for five years and eventually became the first British actor to win an Academy Award for his film performance in the role.

13. To Marion Peter　　　　　　　　**November 9, 1913**

> Green Hill
> Overbrook[33]

Dearest Marion,

Its quite a long time I think since I was going to answer your nice interesting letter but didn't. Please excuse me and let me know whether you still consider you should have me for a friend or not.

I was awfully sorry to hear about your mother having such a break-down last winter and I hope that Western trip this summer did her lots of good. I got your postal and envied you like anything for being able to go to such a grandiose spot.[34] Mother was in Paris a few weeks ago and the Clarks told her that your family was planning to go to Europe again soon. Also that your brother was now living in Paris. How are your pupils in singing coming on?

My sister Holly happens to be in Cincinnati just now. We were all in Princeton a month ago, mother just back from Europe where she spent the summer with Eleanor, Holly from Nantucket, I from Jamestown etc etc etc. Marion, I have just about given up my nice business. My health is so poor[35] I have to be taking some violent treatment called Naprapathy (!) Its on the order of osteopathy but even less mild I think. I am staying with a cousin of mine near Philadelphia.

Marion, did you ever know Jean Craik? I dont remember. Well she is married suddenly now. Yours with lots of love as usual

　　Sylvia

Sylvia Beach Papers, Manuscripts Division, Department of Rare Books and Special Collections, Princeton University Library (manuscript)

* * *

---

33. The farm of Beach's Pennsylvania cousins.
34. The Grand Canyon.
35. Beach suffered from migraines.

14. To Cyprian Beach   January 30, 1914

Green Hill Farm

Dear Lenore[36]

Still I must mention what a steady good time I have from those tango
Rose and roses d'orsay & card case and Richepin The Paste and The Sea.[37]

Yesterday I had a letter from you with complaints about the "drauma"
in Paris. Isnt it too bad. They need a Hauptmann or a BShaw badly.[38]
Theres nothing sweety pie about Hauptmann is there? All bitter and hideous and big and disagreeable. I love him.

Well I took my lovely Venetian card case and joined Marguerite in a
call on Morris' inamimatato Mrs Greice. She lives in a hotel and has a
sitting room and two bed rooms. From the sitting you look into the bed
room and see a toilet table containing a giant powder puff sticking in a
holder. In the sitting is a hired piano and an other with an electric player
which Morris has bought on the installment plan. Mrs Greice played
Too Much Mustard (Tres moutarde) and other things for us. The two
little children came in in middy suits. The little girl with very beautiful
black eyes with lashes like this,[39] the boy eight yrs old, such a funny fella
not a tooth in the front row, just vacancies, and a humorous expression.
His mother tried to force him not to smile so that his gums wouldnt be
seen but it was no use. The mother looks so little & young and is awfully
pretty with hair as curly as yours but dark red. Shes a regular man killer.
One side swipe from those half closed eyes and they'd _ _ _ _ well, they'd
_ _ _ _ _ _ _! Morris will be her 3rd husbande but I think the hundredth
man ready to pass in his checks for her as the vulgar say.

Morris has the chicken pox.

My skin is fine now but I still take the neck snap and back bounce
and lie in the "baashulaay" as the Faust and her attendant call it. Dr.
Faust asked me if I had ever tried chewing gum for sticking purposes in
clothes. And she showed me her hat with the feather firmly pasted on
with a piece of chewing gum. She said she always uses it an has told lots
of people and they had found it such a helpful thing. Somehow I was all

36. Beach gave her sister Cyprian a number of nicknames, including "Lenore."
37. Jean Richepin (1849–1926), controversial French writer, playwright, and sailor. Beach
mentions his books *La Glu* (1881) and *La Mer* (1886).
38. Playwrights Gerhart Hauptmann (1862–1946) and George Bernard Shaw (1856–1950).
39. At this point in the letter Beach supplied a drawing of a curled-up eyelash.

upset at that and at hearing a girl on the train telling a friend that she was teaching little boys at a downtown mission to make soup, and they were playing with a sponge and it fell right in the soup and she made them eat it just the same, the soup.

Morris has a trained nurse and high temperature and has to stay 3 weeks in his room. We haven't had anything to do with him so we aren't quarantined but we can't go to Marguerite's for fear of the baby getting it. The baby's been ill for a day but is well again. She s a little dear of a baby, a regular Valentine cherub.

I'm hearing Titta Ruffo[40] in Pagliacci next Monday eve. I'll probably get all irritated. Mary Garden I also have a seat for in Manon next Sat the 7th

Very much love from your loving sister Sylvia

Sylvia Beach Papers, Manuscripts Division, Department of Rare Books and Special Collections, Princeton University Library (manuscript)

* * *

15. To Sylvester Woodbridge Beach   No date[41]

Green Hill Farm   Tell mother I sent back all the
                                    Bontril & Teller underwear
                                    but <u>one</u>.

Dearest Father

Indeed its very pleasant to know that you are thinking of me at times and are desirous of opening up a correspondence. Indeed, I thought your letter was very interesting too.

We have a great yellow sign on the front door now.

Chicken Pox.

No admittance except on business.

The Mr Morris, in a scrape as usual. He woke up one day feeling despondent and in another minute he was covered inside and out with pocks. The doctor didn't seem sure of its not being small pox for a day but in some hours pronounced it chicken. Nan Hay decided she would leave when they thought it was small pox but I had about decided to stay

---

40. Titta Ruffo (1877–1953), Italian baritone.
41. Beach was working as secretary at Green Hill Farm in 1914.

and have it. So Morris has a nurse who must never leave his room for three weeks and Miss Smith waits on her. The library has all the furniture taken out of it and is kept closed up because its near Morris' room and Cousin Mary has moved all her bedroom appurtenances from next to Morris back to her old room. He had nearly 104 temperature but is all well now and soon can get up and wear an old suit of clothes he was going to give to a tramp. His fiancée talks to him all day by telephone and has sent flowers and a book and wants to see him. Cousin Mary was having a long talk with him from the study when he let the telephone fall on his nose and it bumped it severely.

You must let me know how Miss Lily Paxton was getting along. Mother told me about that dreadful spell she had and I am anxious to know how she is. I'm going to the opera tomorrow evening, Pagliacci with Titta Ruffo. Marguerite and Logan & Helen Wood are sitting in $3.00 seats and I mount to the top which I arranged specially to do so as not to hear their "Grand Opera" talk, although they offered to help me out with the price of one like theirs. So Joseph takes us all in.[42]

I was going so so so glad Aunt Agnes was stout and well. Indeed (I've got that from Nan Hay) indeed a potato baked in its skin twice a day is wonderful if increased obesity is desired. Thats whats brought my size up so that its scarcely healthy.

Andrew Bowden is Cousin Mary's gardener, a strong Ulster man. His wife was ill in bed and she caught sight of her husband spanking one of her babies to make it go to sleep so she burst to tears and was soon in such a state, she had to be hurried to the Homeopathic Hospital in an ambulance. So Andrew let go of himself completely and while on his way to see his wife in the hospital yesterday he jumped out of the automobile while it was going at great speed and sprained his knee and thumb and bruised himself all over. But he is better today and Mrs Andrew is home again. Wasnt it too bad Nan couldnt go to Princeton.

Mary <u>broke</u> her wrist.

> Very much love from yours
> NB

Sylvia Beach Papers, Manuscripts Division, Department of Rare Books and Special Collections, Princeton University Library (manuscript)

---

42. To Philadelphia.

* * *

16. To Marion Peter   **April 21, 1914**

Green Hill Farm
Overbrook,
Pennsylvania

Did you vote? You are fortunate to live in a State where they aren't still in the Back Ages.[43]

Dearest Marion,

I wonder if you remember sending me a calendar years ago at Christmas 1913. I am now at last, writing to thank you for it and I deserve to have you forget you ever knew me. It was a lovely calendar and I really did appreciate your sending it to me although I was so rude as never to thank you for it till about a year later. But you must be used to the idea of my being a rude barbarian, by this time.

Marion, I wonder what has become of you by this time, whether you are in Europe or just making for Europe, or perhaps you've just come from Europe. I had a nice long letter from Sofia. She said that you were not married yet, which I was much relieved to hear. She seems to think there's only one thing a woman can do, and that is to get married. I wonder why she's so enthusiastic about marriage.

I have been secretary to my cousin here for about a year now and she is so good to me. I wish I could keep up my artistic objects business but tariff got so high and capital was badly needed to really make a good start.

How is your work coming on? Do you have a studio? I wish I could see you again and hear all about what you've been doing since we last met! Isnt it a long time!

Eleanor is working hard in her operatic studies and loves it. She is coming to spend the summer on this side with her family.

Doesn't your brother Norman live in Paris now? How is your brother Archie? and how is Blanche? I noticed that a <u>Lapierre</u> was playing

---

43. The 1914 senatorial election occurred in the middle of Woodrow Wilson's first presidential term. Peter lived in New Jersey.

with someone, I forget who, in America this winter. What that <u>your</u> Mr Lapierre?

I heard quantities of music this winter, Ysaye, Paderewski, Kreisler, Homer, Heinck, Culp, Goodson, and dear knows what all, besides a few operas with Gardens and things.[44] Isnt it exciting!

With much love
     ever yours
        Sylvia

Sylvia Beach Papers, Manuscripts Division, Department of Rare Books
and Special Collections, Princeton University Library (manuscript)

* * *

17. To Marion Peter　　　　　　**August 14, 1914**

26 Library Place
Princeton N.J.

Dearest Marion,

It was so exciting to get your letter from such a nearby place! It was forwarded from Overbrook and arrived here just now and we are really going to see each other again! Isnt it fun!

We are spending the summer in Princeton (all of us but Holly who is at Nantucket) and now Marion, if you can stand the absolute deadness of Princeton in summer you must make a nice visit here. Our extra room is being inhabited by some relations and friends until next Wednesday at noon and would that be too late for you Marion to come and stay as long as ever you can?! O you <u>must</u>! It you cant arrange for that date we'll fix another, any you say. This is a chance of a lifetime for me to see you again!!! Write me instantly whether Wednesday August 19 suits you. I wish it was to be right away! Those tiresome creatures—!

You must be worried at not hearing any word from your brother but of course its almost impossible to get calls through, especially from Germany.[45] Fortunately Eleanor came over here for the summer. She is crazy to go back

---

44. Eugène Ysaÿe (1858–1931), Belgian violinist; Ignacy Paderewski (1860–1941), Polish pianist and composer; Fritz Kreisler (1875–1962), Viennese violinist and composer; and other lesser-known classical musicians.

45. Britain had declared war on Germany on August 4, 1914.

and nurse the soldiers or something and I would love to be in the midst of it myself. But isnt it all mad and bloody! Those rowdy German barbarians!

Hoping to hear from you in a minute or two

As ever

Sylvia

The whole family is looking forward to seeing you.

Sylvia Beach Papers, Manuscripts Division, Department of Rare Books and Special Collections, Princeton University Library (manuscript)

* * *

18. To Marion Peter   **No date, September 1914**

26 Library Place
Princeton

Dearest Marion,

Never never in the world should you have done such a thing! That beautiful book so expensive! It was dreadfully extravagant of you Marion dear, but it certainly was exciting to have this great package with a note stuck in, handed to me yesterday morning as I sat on the porch the trustees built for us![46] And when I opened that lovely book—! O it as a dear of you Marion!!! I am specially interested in Récamier,[47] and arent those fine pictures of her all through the book! Eleanor likes the one of Napoleon with such soulful eyes.

Wasnt it interesting to meet the Carlton Hacketts in New York and hear all about their experiences on the other side.

Marion, we miss you so and wish you could have stayed longer although we made you work like a day-laborer.[48]

You must plan another trip to the East very soon again.

I am returning your little paper-cutter (?) which you left on the bureau. I hope it will arrive safely.

---

46. The Trustees of Beach's father's church.
47. Jeanne-Françoise Julie Adélaïde Récamier (1777–1849), French salonnière and friend of writer Germaine de Staël.
48. See letter of June 3, 1916, in which Beach reminds Peter how she made her work as a "cook and general house-maid with light gardening."

Will you write and tell me how Drusilla and Martha were, and whether you had a good time in Detroit with your brother and Baedecker?[49]

And whether Mrs Mason[50] was displeased that you never saw the Death Masks & Library?[51]

Thank you <u>very</u> <u>very</u> much for my <u>wonderful</u> book!

> Lots of love
> from
>   Sylvia

Sylvia Beach Papers, Manuscripts Division, Department of Rare Books and Special Collections, Princeton University Library (manuscript)

* * *

19. To Marion Peter   June 3, 1916

Madrid

Dearest Marion,

I hope you notice that I have let some time relapse before answering your letter containing such unkind allusions to my fine fountain pen, and such falsehoods to the effect that you had not heard from me for so long! What about this nice pen father gave me only two Christmases ago and that hasnt begun to wear out yet and is filled automatically by me every day and is a self-starter and all. . . . .? . . ? What about the perfect letter, long and interesting I went and took the trouble to write you last summer, explaining my absence from America and telling you to come on over. . . . ?! It was at the time you were out West I think, you and your sister were taking a trip in the "typewriter" and I sent the letter to Highland Park with requests to forward. I cant think what could have happened to it! Either you gave orders before leaving not to forward <u>third</u> <u>class</u> <u>matter</u>, or on receiving it you gave a glance at the superscription and then tossed the thing into the Grand Canyon unopened. Perhaps it was never sent off from the town I was in because I had failed to

---

49. Baedeker: travel guide.
50. Marion Peter's mother.
51. In 1897, the writer Laurence Hutton presented Princeton University Library with a collection of sixty death masks of prominent figures, including Coleridge, Wordsworth, and Keats.

tip the Post-Master! They never would deliver any of our mail without holding us up for a pesota or two.

Marion, what are you doing this summer? I was awfully glad to hear you had such a successful musical season! And your brother's wife up among the stars . . . !

And Marion, you came to New York and we werent in Princeton to have a visit from you! Its infuriating, that it is! Perhaps you consider it a fortunate escape with the memories you have of the last one when you had to be a cook and general house-maid with light gardening, and during your time off after your domestic duties you were made to ride out in the town watering cart.

What a pity Holly didnt know you were in town! She is just finishing a course of stenography at the Miller School where she is star pupil if we do say it and has won all the honors besides aplying herself to all the Russian Ballets, operas, plays, movies, dances, and races that friends kept taking her to!

As for Eleanor, she is working hard with Jean Perier[52] and a répétituer[53] or whateveryoucallit and lives in a studio in Bd. Raspail with a marmoset that a California girl friend gave her and two birds and some gold-fish.

As for mother, she feels she ought to hurry home to father and the Parish but she is nervous about submarines, especially since our friends the Baldwins' mishap. She may go any minute tho, as people seem to cross all the time. But she wont take a Spanish boat which would be so much safer; it seems they are not too comfortable and the passage is very dear.

We are about decided to go to Saint Jean de Luz,[54] mother to go on to Bordeaux and I shall probably stay there all summer.

Depressed! I should say we are over this war! But ¡¿que vamos á hacer?![55] as the two senoritas we are living with would say. If you know anyone that wants to stay with a nice family in Madrid tell them that Srtas. Román de La Chica is the one for them. They are direct descendents of a Moorish King on one side and a Malaga grape on the other and are awfully nice in spite of it. I speak enough Moorish, I mean Spanish, to get about now, and mother can more than get about with what she's learned. The only thing is Madrid is a hell of

---

52. Jean Périer (1869–1954), French actor and singer who debuted the role of Pelléas in Debussy's opera.
53. *Répétiteur*: singing coach and musical accompianist.
54. A French fishing town close to the border with Spain.
55. "What is there to do?"

a town. Philadelphia translated into Spanish. It's the drearyest place and climate.

What do you hear from Sofia? What if "Alberto" has to join the army?! Dont you know of some fine thing for Sofia to do in Chicago?

Mother joins me in love

Yours with a hug
Sylvia

Spaniards manage to get almost everything if you only give them time. Now they are having the Russian Ballet for the first time, and the Comedie Française is coming this month to give four performances. The opera here is anything but good and I never dared to go to a concert. Their theaters are fine though and Maria Guerrero[56] a great old girl!

But no one really wakes up except at a bullfight or going to and coming from one, the Senoritas of every age in their best "mantillas" and Manila shawls, and the gents in runabouts. But the joke is all on the poor horses so not having enough Moorish blood in my veins to make me enjoy the sight, I don't go.

Sylvia Beach Papers, Manuscripts Division, Department of Rare Books and Special Collections, Princeton University Library (manuscript)

* * *

20. To Marion Peter   **October 5, 1916**

13, rue de Beaujolais
Palais Royal[57]
Paris

Dearest Marion,

So for some reason, no doubt a good one, you never write to me at all. Not even a post card like that one about George Arliss you sent me

---

56. Maria Guerrero, Spanish actress. The Teatro Maria Guerrero in Madrid is named for her.
57. Beach recalled that her rooms, shared with sister Cyprian, were in the theatrical neighborhood near the Palais Royal Theatre, "where the naughtiest plays in Paris were put on" but that "in spite of the theatre and one or two bookshops dealing mostly in erotica, the Palais Royal was at this time fairly respectable. It had been otherwise in the old days" (*Shakespeare and Company* 9). Beach and her sister watched air raids of the First World War from the balcony of their hotel (11).

once. When are you coming to Paris again? not till after this detestable war?

As for me, I am living in the quaintest room imaginable and my window looks out over the gardens of the Palais Royal and the nice fountain and Rodin statue and so forth and so forth and so forth. Eleanor lives in a studio furnished à la Bakst,[58] Martine with a friend and 'way across the river, and they have a little green parrot that imitates the metro whistle which he hears under the house, and they have a monkey or two.

Me, I am doing some studies at the Bibliothéque[59] around the corner. But oh how sad this war!

Marion, the last time I ever heard from you was last Feb when I was in dreary Madrid. I was learning all kinds of Spanish in a family of Moorish origin and the bullfight season was just beginning . . .

I had to stop for a minute to fill my fine fountain-pen, you remember the one father gave me to replace that fine old one you used to admire so much . . . well, oh yes, you wrote that you had been having a great winter, you and Miss Precilla Carver. I wonder what you were doing last summer. Mother determined she must go somewhere where there was something fit to eat, and I felt I couldnt exist out of France any longer so we spent the summer at St Jean de Luz, (do you know the nice quiet little plage?) and then moved up here. Mother has gone home now and she and father and Holly are in Princeton this minute.

Lots of love

As ever

Sylvia

Write to me immediately!!!

Sylvia Beach Papers, Manuscripts Division, Department of Rare Books
and Special Collections, Princeton University Library (manuscript)

❅ ❅ ❅

---

58. Léon Bakst (1866–1924), Russian modernist painter, costume, and set designer; his best-known designs were for Sergei Diaghilev's Ballets Russes.
59. Library.

21. **To Marion Peter**   **November 29, 1916**

One of awful passport photos![60]

a punishment I'm inflicting on you for never writing!

> 15, rue de Beaujolais
> Paris

Dearest Marion,

Merry, merry Christmas! How are you? I always write to my friends at Xmas whether they are deserving or not! For example how do I know that all your letters didnt strike a mine or something on the way over, or that the censorship didnt permit <u>them</u> to pass its office!?..!!??!!!?!???!!!!????!!!!?? (theres no news over here so I fill up space with these things.)

Are you all together and at Highland Park this Christmas?

We are not very united, as usual. Holly is living in New York and will go to Princeton to be with father and mother and the new black cook and white poodle mother has been fortunate enough to pick up (in Princeton, both.) As for Eleanor and me we shall spend a coal-less, sugar-less butter-less Christmas with no tree but the stumps of the poor old "grands blessés"[61] of which there's no scarcity! Pardon the melancholy pun.

Are you giving concerts this winter again Marion? How I should like to be a regular attendant of them! What is your sister Blanche writing at present? Is your brother Archie still living on a raft? Isnt that where you joined him after paying us an all-too-short visit in Princeton (and the spongy ride we took!)

I'm so glad not to be in Madrid this winter! Marion, never spend a winter or a summer, or a spring, or a fall, or a month, or a week, or even a day and a night, or a day, or a night in Madrid. An hour will do if at any time you want to go there to see the Prado[62] which certainly is worth the trip there and back from anywhere.

Were you glad when Woodrow Wilson was reelected?[63] We were so happy! A Frenchman at the front wrote to me a few months ago when

---

60. Beach included an extra copy of her passport picture in the letter.
61. Wounded veterans.
62. The Museo del Prado is Madrid's museum of fine arts.
63. Woodrow Wilson (1856–1924): Democratic president of the United States from 1913 to 1921 and friend of the Beach family.

an American boat of some kind got sunk, and said, "I suppose more ink will be wasted in another message!" I replied to that contemptuous remark "Yes, probably. Thank the Lord its ink-shed Wilson believes in, not blood-shed!"

Marion, excuse this mess! It looks like a letter from a cat to a dog or something.

Have you, for example, ever read Les Misérables?[64] I never have till now and am at Vol. 2. It pays to read it, even if you wear out two or three pairs of glasses in doing so.

Goodbye, much love, a very merry Christmas

from yours as ever
Sylvia

Sylvia Beach Papers, Manuscripts Division, Department of Rare Books
and Special Collections, Princeton University Library (manuscript)

*   *   *

22. To Cyprian Beach   August 22, 1917[65]

August 22
Hotel du Palaisa
Poitiers

Dearest Gilles

I got them to change the name of one of their bridges here and call it after you in case you ever wanted to take a look at Poitiers. At a little village where Suzanne and I lunched day before yesterd such a good green parrot. Would fly at all but 2 people 1 little girl & 1 domestic. You never say how my little bird keeps, whether well or pining![66] Superb sun today. I hope to be a profit-bird. My 2 Boys are well.[67] Spent a good night and don't give much trouble, thank the lord! Little drinking cup I use con-

---

64. *Les Misérables* (1862), Victor Hugo's lengthy chronicle of French life from the defeat of Napoleon until the uprising of 1832.

65. Beach was working in the summer of 1917 as a volunteer farmhand while many French men were at the front.

66. Beach's parrot Guappo.

67. Beach's nickname for her feet.

tinually & what I should have done without it lord knows. Elder, elder and elder. I breakfast at 7 each morning, roam the town and country wrote yesterday to mother.

Love

Sylvia Beach Papers, Manuscripts Division, Department of Rare Books and Special Collections, Princeton University Library (manuscript)

* * *

23. **To Cyprian Beach** August 25, 1917

Dearest Gilles,

Well just a few minutes after sending off an appeal to Holly for news, appears the fem de ch.[68] with a letter from Holly herself! You, likely as not have one too old Snyps. Well I was relieved to hear that H was still on board and her life hadn't begun to be too hard as yet.[69] Lord knows whether they've begun to receive some wounded up there, Holly is so secretive and Miss Terious all over again!

After I finish this letter I'm going to announce to the lady-behind-the-desk a stay-over till Monday. And this is why. This afternoon I went to the Manège[70] outside of Poitiers ½ hr. and took out Bébé, a lovely mare with long long eyelashes and a lot of go in her. She has more charm yes charm than anyone I've ever known and loves a good time above all. As an example, she would stop to look at the sunset, which tho good was nothing remarkable; but she didn't care to miss it. She screwed and screwed her neck to the left till I thought it was getting twisted right off the shoulders!! Well besides her pleasure-loving disposition she has a gait worth at least 25 quinnies the half hour! Her long trot is indescribably pleasant and she hasnt a fault as far as I can see. An officer owns her and has left with M. Verron-du-Manège-St. Georges for the present. I rode to Ligugé famous abby where still more famous Huysmans[71]

---

68. *Femme de chambre:* housekeeper.
69. Holly was about to begin working for the American Red Cross.
70. Riding school.
71. Joris-Karl Huysmans (1848–1907), author of the Decadent classic *À Rebours* (*Against Nature*). Husymans lived near the Benedictine Abbey Ligugé from 1899 to 1901, and it was the setting for his 1903 novel *L'Oblat* (*The Oblate*).

loitered, now full of Belgians, wounded & otherwise so you can imagine how insupportable. My trows[72] made the usual stir. Aren't people easily stirred? I never saw the like of so much of the regul*a*r as this old world contains! And seeing me all alone in my travellings. . . . that's enough to make everyone perspire at every pore . . . !

The Poiteirns are so provincial but so polite. They all have light blue eyes, bulging, and thin well-shaped noses & nice mouths. Their complections are pleasant owing to the humidity in the air. In fact all they lack is temperament or deep feeling or something. What & how are you doing? That letter from Guiot you sent me—in no time I had answered it saying exactly the truth about the Peuroux affaire (they are friends of hers too) and that professors of bonne education begin to terrify me not a little . . . !!! The other girls werent going to say a thing, but you bet I'm not going to pass by such a scandal without a squeak from any mouse of us!

Another ride tomorrow and Monday at 9 something I leave for Tours. How I wish we could ride that Bébé every day for 60 years. It makes dull care whip away in the opposite direction!

P.S. Yes that it does.

P.S. a gnome, smallest size gnome is stable man at my manège!! Isn't it fine! He has on a little bit of an apron, a few inches his trousers are, & little green woolen socks. How fine he is!

Father seems to have enjoyed getting his book.

Sylvia Beach Papers, Manuscripts Division, Department of Rare Books and Special Collections, Princeton University Library (manuscript)

* * *

24. To Cyprian Beach   **No date [1917]**

La Poste, Poitiers

Dearest Gilles

Pardon the pencil (not that there's anything particularly insulting in using a pencil as far as I can see.) Please send my letters to <u>Tours</u> <u>Poste</u>

---

72. Trousers.

<u>Restante</u> till I let you know to the contrary. I've given up Angoulême. These little towns are so treest[73] after their 4 sights are once seed and instead of Angoulême followed by Limoges followed by Paris I shall settle at Tours and look at some the chateaux for a while. I hope to find a cheaper hotel there than here. These towns are the dickens of an expense to stop over in! In tours I'll leave my (your) basket at the station and look up a nice place, not too dear and not too dingy. Poitiers is the finest little city but a cloud of deadly dullness & melancholy has been settled directly over it since about twelve hundred and something.

And this war has achevé'd it!

> Very much love
> Sylvia

Sylvia Beach Papers, Manuscripts Division, Department of Rare Books and Special Collections, Princeton University Library (manuscript)

---

73. Sad (triste).

II

WORLD WAR I

25. To Cyprian Beach   **August 4, 1917**

Dearest Gilles,

I sent you a postal from the station in Paris when we left but by mistake it was sent here. You must be tired waiting to hear from your farmer sister but tomorrow I shall have a min. for writing. We've been Busy I can tell you! You'll soon know all the details. Meanwhile I'm well and happy, work not too awful, people all fine, little old Dog sweet, bed fine, country sweet, sheep, duck pond

My clothes only ones successful!!! Mr & Mrs fine, girls fine
    Lots of love dearest Cnyps and write me soon, I'm so anxious to hear how you are & Guappo[1] & 2 birds and Ciné
    Much much much

            Love

Address me chez Mme Joyeux-Laffuie

            PEUROUX d'Asnois par Charroux Vienn

* * *

1. Beach's pet parrot.

26. To Cyprian Beach   **August 20, 1917**

> Hotel du Palais
> Poitiers August 20

Dear Gilles,

I hope you received my letter asking for my mon in a lettre char-gée. I'm so comfortably fixed at this hotel and the town is fine, particularly the walks around it. We arrived yesterday. Suzanne[2] stayed over and leaves tonight. It was nice for me to have her instead of being left all alone. My Khaki suit is gaped at something awful in the streets. The townsmen have never before seen the like. They've never seen anything before anyhow of its kind, so dead is the little town. I think I'll see if a horse to ride can be had and then won't they be petrified with my pants!

> Much love, Sylvia

Were you surprised to hear of our sudden displacement from Peuroux?

Sylvia Beach Papers, Manuscripts Division, Department of Rare Books and Special Collections, Princeton University Library (manuscript)

* * *

27. To Cyprian Beach   **September 5, 1917**

> 2 rue Traversière
> Tours Sept 5

Dear Gilles,

How are you for ex.? How successful you're being in films! Its proved to be as self-supporting as can be that it has! Me I'm loitering about Tours, absolutely all there is this summer in the way of Tourists and I'm not even that, I'm a farm-hand. My famous Khaki uniform is now in the hands of a competent-I-hope washing establishment and will reappear looking like old in a handful of days. Meanwhile the green suit and tammy are what I put on for town and country. Comme shoes—

---

2. Unidentified.

those tan stouts from Hanans' are now reduced to skin and bone, they fairly flap as I pass along. So this morning I did Tour-les-Shoes. Oh là-là! You never saw so pitiful and ridiculous a display—and not one shoery had my size anywhere nears. No Touranquelle but puts on a shoe 41 at lowest estimate. The situation was hopeless. I was forced to get some café-au-lait colored tennis-as-you-might-say foot wear, elevated by means of an extra piece and a round rubber ball at the heel. (!!!) This will suffice for walks to the châteaux de la Loire and back and don't look so large neither which is the bright side of it, but I should like to get hold of another pair from Hanans like these ones I got in the spring. They were 34 frs. Its probable they've sold them all by this time isn't it? Oh dear! C'te vie . . . !³

As I wrote to Holly this dear Serb officer and his friend Serb No 2 a little Jewish looking I can't imagine why, promenaded me to Chenonceau & and Amboise⁴ in 1st Class wagons and a fine lunch etc and refused point blank to let me pay for a thing. Such Don Quijolèryness!⁵ We had such fun, you can't figure to yourself!

Would you mind my asking if you ever took Back "Europe" and the other book

You won't forget to mention it in your next will you old Cnyps. And I owe you a considerable sum which you neglected to subtract from my stipend. Jeanne Montbrial of the Equipe borrowed 10 frs off me which was cheeky of her considering I had next to nothing to keep me going in Poitiers till my money came and she knew it. Instead of sending it to me she wrote that it might get lost in the mail . . . I wrote to her to give it to you as I owed it to you. Mrs B'burg stunt but if you knew Jeanne a Lillian all over again. cheekiest little thing.

Did you ever receive Enfer⁶ I sent you? I'm sending you a Ch. dows Phiqqrs I picked up here.

> Very best
> love
> Sylvia

---

3. "This is life!"
4. Châteaus in the Loire.
5. Chivalry (a reference to Cervantes's *Don Quixote*).
6. Possibly a reference to Arthur Rimbaud's 1873 volume *Une saisone en enfer* (*A Season in Hell*).

The women at this pension are a set of real cats if ever! It makes one squirm to hear and see them.

Sylvia Beach Papers, Manuscripts Division, Department of Rare Books and Special Collections, Princeton University Library (manuscript)

* * *

28. To Cyprian Beach   **September 7, 1917**

> Friday Sept 7
> 2 rue Traversière
> Tours

Dearest Gilles,

Once more I'm going to put you to so much trouble! Here's what. Next Wed or Thur the 13th or 14th I'm off to Joué-Les-Tours four kilometers or so from here to do the vintage on the place belonging to an important grapeicst, Hertault his name. They've a nice big house and Mme. A nice big women puts me up for the two weeks the vintage goes on. Its quite a Lark. Martin prof. d'agriculture (I told you about him) gave me a card to Heurtault, great viniculturist in the direction of St Pierre des Corps (you know where tout le monde[7] descend generally for Tours) so yesterday I went out to see the party and his wife. They are fine fat prosperous creatures with lots of acres of grapes etc and a little boy and dog as well. After a few minutes and the astonishment & chock had passed off somewhat they accepted the offer of one of these eccentric Americans to help with their vendages and I'm to be on the same footing as a poilu[8] who has lost an arm and who has arranged to be there.

I wish you could see people's faces when I spring the agriculturist surprise, oh how deverting. They lay it all down to Indian blood, it helps them to understand. Well as I'm going to leave here just before the time I get my monthly all from Paris and I must get myself a sweater for these coldish days on a farm could you possibly send me about fifty frs. tout de suite[9]

---

7. Everyone.

8. Slang term for a French infantry soldier, meaning "hairy one." Used similarly to the British term "Tommies."

9. Right away.

(if it doesn't put you in too much of a hole) for that and a little over for expenses! I shan't need as much as fifty but don't like to run too short. Its too too inconvenient that the vintage starts just a day before my money is due. I don't think there's any way of getting a lettre chargée except by coming to Tours, perhaps Sunday if we don't work that day!

I don't like to ask you to lend me this sum and wouldn't need to if weren't for this damn vintage beginning two or three days too soon! But once there I shall save a lot! Don't fail to subtract the 50 <u>and other large sums I owe you</u>, otherwise I shall have the trouble <u>and expense of sending you from here the amount I owe you</u>!!! Perhaps a mandat[10] for the fifty would be best and my bank money after the 15th in a lettre chargée if it isn't too awfully much trouble!

Very much love and thanks for all the trouble!!

Sylvia

Sylvia Beach Papers, Manuscripts Division, Department of Rare Books and Special Collections, Princeton University Library (manuscript)

* * *

29. To Cyprian Beach   September 13, 1917

Tours Sept 13

Dearest Gilles,

Papers came just now and thanks very much. You must be back in Paris. What wretched weather you had for Fontainebleau![11] I don't see how you could accomplish anything. Well I'm now settled for a little time at this pension which is the Booby prize one of France if I'm not mistaken. The room I have is superb but oh là-là! how moyen age[12] the toilet and scarce the food! I supplement outside so fill up all right. The other guests must have to do likewise. There are now about 7 of us. Two officer's wives, a jewish officer (next to me (!!!!!)), a Serb officer, a travelling sales lady etc all seated at a table d'hôte.[13] I got the address of a

---

10. Money order.
11. Château de Fontainebleau, a tourist destination on the outskirts of Paris.
12. Medieval.
13. The table shared by guests at an inn or hotel.

certain professor of agriculture here and paid him a visit. His wife is sweet. M.D. q'uelle est gentile![14] He the prof is going to sent me to some farm for the vintage, to start in 2 weeks or so and meanwhile he may hurry me to a place belonging to a friend of his to graft young fruit trees. It interests me a great deal, the idea. You've no idea how interesting these farms are and getting right next to the peasants! I shall never regret the Peuroux experience. The fun far exceeded the annoyances even though it was so upsetting to discover the depths of unreliability of our sweet Fr.[15] people.

How lovely your white hotel at Fontainebleau and nice for you to have a change even though so little, old Elder. How goes the Phinances? I find these provincial towns the hell of an expense to live in! Paris is cheaper as far as rooms & meals are concerned. Blois[16] yesterday. How I wished for you!

Poor old Elder you took it much too hard about my bird! That distressed me much more than elopement of Bird I can tell you! Is Mrs Hott back? Give her my love. I got your postcard and letter at the Poste Restante all right. What are your plans for the winter? Nice? I hope so you would be able to keep a little warm at least. Answer this question and don't forget

Much love from
loving sister S

My 2 boys keep the femme de chamber weak with their pranks!

Sylvia Beach Papers, Manuscripts Division, Department of Rare Books and Special Collections, Princeton University Library (manuscript)

✳ ✳ ✳

---

14. "Mon Dieu [My God] she is sweet."
15. French.
16. Another château in the town of the same name.

30. To Cyprian Beach   September 16, 1917

Hotel de la Boule d'Or
Tours
Sept. 16 1917

Dearest Gilles,

This is the 1st minute I've had off the Vendanges to write and thank you for "letting me have" seventy frs last Sunday (a week ago!) Today being Sunday I came off the property to Tours, lunched at the Gold Ball where I spent the first day & night when arriving from Poitiers and where the proprietor & his wife are on such terms with me they said they'd adopt me, and am now sitting to write you in the ptit[17] saloon with a view on the Sunday attired Touranqeaux. You were mignonne[18] as can be to lend me in such a hurry and what I would do in this life without you to fall back on at a time like these I don't Know indeed I don't! fine Elder. And You Never Can Tell! What a nice surprise for me! I've brought it out with me today to read on the banks of the Cher on this lovely afternoon in place of yourself which would be jolly too!

The Vendanges.[19] . . . I've done 5 days now and with great success. Suddenly on Monday I received word from Mme. Heurtault to come in the evening to begin Tuesday. It was several days sooner than I expected so I had to make quite a good deal of haste to get off, champong, shopping etc all pushed into an hour or two and arrangements made for my wash which I left at the pension and some superfluous articles they were kind enough to keep for me. Fortunately you were so trouble taking & worthy as usual & had hurried the seventy to me which arrived in time! I arrived at Joué by train late but not too late for dinner on a French farm which is at any hour after 9 P.M. Mme Heurtault is fine fine fine, so kind, so stout, stumps about the place from morning till night in sabots attending to the cows, chickens, geese, horses, servants, children of the servants etc. Its a big place, 60 or 70 hectares I forget what the difference between an acre and an hectare. Mr. Heurtault a tall stout Tamany-Sew-profiteur[20] for looks very kind man au fond[21], little boy of 7 the only child and

---

17. "Petite"; small.
18. Cute.
19. Grape harvesting.
20. *Profiteur:* opportunist.
21. *Au fond:* fundamentally.

excessively clever & naughty and wild manners. They've a big house & big rooms in it. Mine is lovely with a huge window and huge bed. Its the son's by Heurtault's first marriage. He's at the front I believe. I'm treated like a member of the family. They are so nice. Such good-natured, such sloppy people, what housekeeping. Its a "handsome" house and they keep it looking like a barn-yard. They howl at table, the little maid-of-all-work hurls down the dishes and as for table manners_ _ _ Lucy Henry'd better not come around! They press wine on me, fine old vintages of all soils and are disappointed that I can't use but a glass a meal.

At 630 breakfast in the kitchen with Le Père Louis, the cook, her sister a vendangeur,[22] her brother a poilu on leave. They have wine, garlic & cheese, bread & coffee. At 7 we start work in the grape yards. There are over 20 of us, counting the German prisoners and its very hard work till 12, knock off till 1, very hard work till 730 (yes 730.) The first day you think is your last positively! The second you think is your last after your last day and the third you begin to take notice again slightly and find you're not dead after all. The fourth day is much easier, your legs & back stop hurting so and by the 5th, if you're going to be a vendangeur ever you're one on the 5th day. I'm delighted with my experience and intend to continue it. My health is fine. I keep along with the first ones the whole time which isn't bad for an amateur I can tell you. As for that bunch of bourgeoisies misses I was with at Peuroux, thank the Lord its the real thing in the équipe[23] I'm in at present. No jeune-fille talk[24] to drive you mad, no Tyrol mountain marching songs or Thèodore Botrel[25] ditties, but real peasant, unartificial goings on. The work is directed with a regular idea of order & method, we don't rush from pillar to post dropping one thing in half an hour to start another, there's nothing inefficient about Heurtault I can tell you. When there's work to be done give me that kind of management every time. I always have the same partner for my row. She works rapidly and never talks which is so refreshing for the nerves. I always get as far as I can from La Mère[26] Potel who jabbers without cease all the eleven hours and a half and her little dog barks and catches poor little bunnies and mice along the rows. I think I've bored people talking so much all my life but at least during work I'm silent.

---

22. Grape picker or harvester.
23. Team.
24. Girlish chatter.
25. Patriotic Breton songwriter of the First World War.
26. The mother.

I must go to the pension rue Traversiere, 2 now to see if I've letters and about my wash. They were kind enough to lend me a little handsatch to take to the Joué. I wish I had taken mine which is at Paris. It would have exactly done with your basket which has been very very useful. You're sure you don't need it now? Be sure and let me know. As for my money this month you needn't draw it till I get back to Tours after the vintage. I don't know how long exactly it will be before the vintage is over, there are about 21 days I believe, usually.

Well lots and lots of love dearest fella

from Sylvia

What's that about Holly being at Chaumont!?[27] Not the one in Touraine, but Vosges isn't it. So little mother's picture is lovely. I must see it directly. I haven't time to write to the family this week so you must send a little word sure. You are busy too but a little less, I think.

Sylvia Beach Papers, Manuscripts Division, Department of Rare Books
and Special Collections, Princeton University Library (manuscript)

* * *

31. To Cyprian Beach   **September 27, 1917**

La Bouchardière
Chez M. Heurtault
Joue-les-Tours
Sept 27 Thurs.

Dearest Gilles,

Never a minute to answer your nice letters and the questions a propos of Greek letter *y* which is *g* and hand writing of Hol. lady which will do later.[28] How are you? How fine to have all balcony together next winter. I'm staying on a few days here so could you send my money along here? if not too much of a bother for you. I do seem to make your life a bur-

---

27. A nearby town in Tours. Holly was stationed in various places during her Red Cross duties.
28. Beach was interested in the analysis of handwriting.

den with my errands and things in every letters and you never make a complaint. Well I'll be glad to see you after a summer among these fr.[29] people that I've learned to mistrust utterly I'm afraid . . . rotten in every way. Mme is the only nice person I've seen this trip except the cook and her sister. I'm afraid I'll have to ask you to send me my satchel which I can't leave Tours for Paris without possibly. So glad you got yourself the clothes you needed. You earned them I should say so and are the best sport in the family no matter how you look at it. Do you find the fr. wear well? Won't we tell ourselves a lot of things when we get together? I'm staying here over Sunday only, then to Tours back to the 2 rue Traversière pens. then Paris probably. Must write to Holly. Lots of love and thanks for doing so many tiresome things for me

S.

Sylvia Beach Papers, Manuscripts Division, Department of Rare Books and Special Collections, Princeton University Library (manuscript)

* * *

32. **To Cyprian Beach** September 29, 1917

Chez M. Heurtault
La Bouchardière
Joué-les-Tours

Dearest Gilles,

So sorry to be giving you so much trouble the whole enduring time and just when you're on such a rush! I enclose check and a bon de poste I should think would do to send me the money. I'll be at Tours 2 rue Traversière on Monday so there's no use sending it here. Gilles you know how I think you've been to be always sending me things!!! Please subtract the exact sum I owe you from different debts otherwise I shall send it to you. Now as to that room next to mine . . . I hadn't exactly decided what day I would go back to Paris but I see you have to know on account of keeping the room. On Monday morning I'll be in Tours and shall stay just long enough to have a little washing done, my Khaki suit, its cheaper

---

29. French.

than in Paris and if possible shall get off by <u>Wednesday</u>. But in case the money doesn't arrive in time . . . I'll have to wait. I'll be strapped.

The 3rd October then and I'll let you know what train and all but don't stop off filming to meet me I should be angry as the dickens and you know I don't mind you're not being there when you've business on hand.

Much love

Sylvia

I hope you sent the valise to Tours, but it doesn't matter. I can get it here and so much the better. I'm "assommante"[30] with my errands!

Sylvia Beach Papers, Manuscripts Division, Department of Rare Books and Special Collections, Princeton University Library (manuscript)

* * *

33. **To Cyprian Beach**   **No date**

This hotel is a peach.

Dearest Gilles,

I'm waiting for my bag to leave for Paris. When I got to Tours today I found at the pension your letter saying you had had Mrs Hottinger send my valise to Joué so as the Chef de Gare there doesn't answer the telephone judging by the failure of the Mme at this hotel to get him on the line I may have to hasten to Joué tomorrow to fetch the affair. It's all my fault giving you so much trouble when you're on duty at the Movie-Works all day and poor dear Mrs Hottinger taking the trouble_ _ ! So sorry. But I <u>did</u> say the station at Tours in my letter I think. You've but to consult it if you've still got it. The 250 frs have come but I was out at the 330 delivery so will step in at the Post Office towards five, that is to say in ½ hr from now. Thank you is too inadequate a word in return for what stacks of a bother I've caused you old Elder!! So we're to have Hollyberry on the 15th of this very month! Isn't that capital! It means a steady grind for our poor tongues for a period.

30. Overwhelmed.

I lingered on at La Bouchardière to see the distillery of eau de vie[31] yesterday. The Heurtaults pressed me to. But would you believe it, the bottle of Noble Joué Mme Heurtault mentioned she was going to give me to take you never materialized all owing I'm positive to that old Père Grandet of an Heurtault. I didn't like to remind Mme. They're people that wouldn't forget a thing like that and I'd rather they be under obligations to me, which they are, than to owe them anything whatsoever. How I regret the Noble Joué for you tho. The fr. are so very close I've discovered. They're the original They himself.

I can't tell what train to take till the bag arrives and all. There's a train in the afternoon at about 3 that reaches Paris at 6 something but I doubt if I can get off on that. I'm investing in a fourneau à petrole[32] did you ever! Its 21 frs but will save that much in alcohol which is so dear and scarce and will save expense in lunch outside besides. The Heurtaults have one & so convenient. It doesn't smoke or smell and cooks the coffee and grills toast rapidly. The special kind can only be had here at Tours. How can I wait to see you in your roll at Gaumonts!! Every time I see the Judex[33] posters here (Tours just is getting Judex!!) I think of how strange it will be to see up posters with you on them. Bertini films,[34] 2 of them have just been tried on the Touranqeaux, Fédora and a detective one. I saw the photos but alas not the films. Its pearls before swine here believe me. I hope you'll never have to appear here you'd faint from off the screen.

Best love Sylvia aurevoir till a day or so.

I've just had a telephone talk with M. le Chef de G. at Joué. He's got the valise & it'll reach here tomorrow morning. Probably I'll leave Thurs. I don't know what train.

Sylvia Beach Papers, Manuscripts Division, Department of Rare Books and Special Collections, Princeton University Library (manuscript)

* * *

---

31. Fruit brandy.
32. Petrol oven.
33. Cyprian played "Belles Mirettes" in the French silent film series *Judex*.
34. Francesca Bertini (1892–1985), Italian silent film actress.

34. To Sylvester Woodbridge Beach   January 29, 1919[35]

Belgrade, January 29, 1919.

Dearest Father:

We are old Belgradians by this time, Holly and I and can really find our way from Red Cross Head Quarters to the place where we spend our nights. Everything seems to be on one street, the Main and just about only street, you begin to descend immediately to the river, so you have to think things over carefully before taking such a step. It is very sad indeed to see the town in such a state of ruin as it has been left by the wars. It is quite a scene of desolation, the last touch being a miserable kind of wind that blows over from the Black Sea and stays with us for a week or so. Its something on the order of the Sirocco, but cold instead of hot. It has the effect of ruffling everybody's feathers up the wrong way somewhat.

Holly went to the Embassy this morning. They requisitioned her from here to do some translating, they seem to be hard up for someone that can do that sort of thing. We are able to make good use of any languages we have learned. Very few of the others can speak anything but American.

A courier took our mail yesterday to Paris, so this will have to wait till the next one, a week or two perhaps, no one knows. Mail goes when it goes—that's all any can say. The Serbian Post Office is working slightly now but only for the Interior. You've no idea how everything in Serbia was at a standstill—still is of that matter. No schools, few shops, no factories, no constructing nor rec onstruction, no water supply nor lighting nor heading nor nuthin'.

The Serbsky tongue is most difficult to learn, but we are trying to master some of the more important words such as—please—how many—cream puffs etc. Just so that we can manage to get about.

The Red Cross is beginning to get busy now distributing the "Stuff" as they always seem to call it, which arrived by the car-load yesterday or day before and has to be all gotten over from across the Danube. Its

---

35. From January to June 1919, Beach and her sister Holly worked in Serbia as secretaries and translators for the Balkan Commission of the American Red Cross. Beach dispatches the Serbian period quickly in her memoirs: "my sister Holly managed to get me a job in the American Red Cross. We went to Belgrade, where for nine months I distributed pajamas and bath towels among the valiant Serbs. In July 1919, I was back in Paris" (*Shakespeare and Company* 14).

at Semlin, the Jersey City of Belgrade. You have to first strike Semlin if you're on the way to Belgrade, and then be transported over the water in a large sort of ferry, and my but its a cold trip. The prospect, as you come in to Belgrade is rather dreary, at least at this season. It was quite a feat getting all the supplies here intact. The next step is to investigate the Needy and Seedy to see if they are really as needy and seedy as they say they are. The men canvas all the small towns within reach, the nurses look into impoverished homes, "Stuff" is doled out, work-rooms are started and orphanages and hospitals opened. Every one in this party is more or less of a specialist—or pretends to be. Things fairly hum.

We have met some interesting Scotch women who have opened a hospital for children here, M.D.s they are.

Well, we are still in suspense about Cyprian and her goings and comings but letters are bound to come through some day. You must not send any to us here for by the time they get to Belgrade we will probably be else where. Our mail can be addressed Care of the American Red Cross, Hotel Regina, Paris, which is going to be kept posted as to our whereabouts and get our letters to us somehow. I have written to Mrs. Hottinger, 15 Rue Beaujolais, too to send our mail to that Red Cross place. By the way, why did you always spell it "Beaujolaif"? I never have found out. Not that the postman seemed to care one way or another.

Good bye, Father dear and lots & lots of love & so forth.

> From ever devtd.
> Yours,
> Sylvia

P.S. Holly is such a favorite with everybody, in fact the most popular person in the entire Forces. German turns out to be the language you have to use on the Serbs, the ones in shops and restaurants and the People in general, so Holly with her ever-ready German is greatly in demand. Its thanks to her and that Boche tongue that we get anything to eat or a shoe-shine or pins.

Sylvia Beach Papers, Manuscripts Division, Department of Rare Books and Special Collections, Princeton University Library (manuscript)

* * *

35. To Eleanor Orbison Beach   February 2, 1919

Belgrade, February 2, 1919.

Dearest Little Mother:

I have to get off letters in a hurry to-day. I have just heard that the courier is taking them to Paris at Three—in one hour from now, in fact. He is a Peace-Conference courier who is kind enough to carry our mail too.[36] Holly sends lots of love but hasn't the time to write to-day. She has to attend 2 teas this afternoon and I am going to one myself. Col. Farman always asks us to high-tea on Sundays at six-thirty, when we have sort of hot beans and large slices of bread and ham or bread-alone and the thing winds up with a slice of chocolate cakesy. Mother dear, I fear you wouldn't be able to digest this 'igh tea meal. It's all washed down with copious draughts of ice-water. Everyone in the party has indigestion on Monday, thanks to the Col. and his hospitality.

Belgrade is beginning to have Belgrade weather and it's going to last till April at that. It snows nearly all the time, Sundays as well as week-days. It's a dry snow and not disagreeable, as snows go. The few conveyances turn into sleighs, the drivers wear stylish sheepskins all embroidered in good colours and they have very fine serbishe blanketviches. The Serbs have the most handsome costume, with embroidered designs and colours and classic-looking shoes. Serb faces are good-looking, the dark ones particularly

I learned to run the mimeograph yesterday. Quite a lot of ink got all over me but I managed to turn out some ten hundred copies of a thing the nurses have to make out in their visits.

There are now three parties arrived from Rome making in all about—I don't know how many—and don't care either. I went to the Movies last Sunday and there who should I see but John and Flora Bunny-Finch![37] Think of it. Way off in Serbia. And John Bunny dead these 20 years or so and Flora Finch perhaps as well, for all I know.

We don't work on Sundays here but the office is open all day and we come and write our letters on the machines. There's no use trying to do anything at our rooms with five people in a room and fifty more coming

---

36. The Paris Peace Conference was convened by the victors of the First World War in January of 1919 and lasted for one year.
37. John Bunny (1863–1915) and Flora Finch (1867–1940) were the first comedy team to become famous in American silent films. Popularly known as the "Bunnyfinches," the pair starred in a hit series of shorts produced by the studio Vitagraph.

in and out and besides the nurses always give a tea on Sunday afternoons in the parlour of the establishment- namely our bed-room. Which leaves you with the alternative of attending a tea (!!!) or passing all of a Sunday afternoon at the office- which I am doing, personally.

Mother dear, I hope you are all keeping that awful "Flu" in its proper place.[38] It makes me quite anxious to hear that its back again at home. The last people from home brought letters—but none for Holly and me. I hope you are all as well as well can be and that Cyprian is there and not too thinned out by the voyage.

We shall probably be dropping in on our family by next June or so—so brace yourselves.

Give my love to Daisy Paxton—you and she must be great friends. Give my love to different others too—Jessie Frothingham and so forth. And love to Maggie who takes such good care of you, tho it comes dear.

I only wish there was more time to write letters. I have to write one to Cousin Mary[39] and to a few others, but when, I ask you, do we get time? We are busy here from 9 AM to 1230 and ensuite from 130 PM up to after six, what with all the relief we have to bring to these Serbs. I think they will some of them be very much relieved when we go away too.

This Serb language is a hard nut to crack. The daily paper is a sealed book to us and we live in darkness like the Mountain Whites[40] as to happenings in the outside world. We don't even know what is going on in Serbia in politics or murders or Society, only that a certain quantity of blankets are needed and that we must rush 3 million car-loads of condensed milk to them Serbs. I have not seen a paper once since I came from Rome (Jan.15).

Good bye P.L.M.[41] and hugs—the ones that come in a large size—and very much love,

From very loving,

Sylviskyevitch

---

38. The influenza epidemic of 1918 killed approximately fifty million people—over three times the number who died in the First World War. One-quarter of the American population was afflicted, but the Beach family was spared.

39. Beach's cousin on her mother's side, Mary Morris.

40. A reference to inhabitants of the Appalachian region of the United States. On the stereotypes surrounding Appalachian life in the late nineteenth and early twentieth centuries, see John Inscoe's *Appalachians and Race: The Mountain South from Slavery to Segregation*.

41. Poor Little Mother.

Please send our mail to the American Red Cross, Hotel Regina, Paris. They see forwarding it to us wherever we are, that is when they don't lose it.

Sylvia Beach Papers, Manuscripts Division, Department of Rare Books and Special Collections, Princeton University Library (manuscript)

* * *

36. To Eleanor Orbison Beach February 6, 1919

Belgrade, Feb. 6th, 1919.

Dearest Little Mother:

This is about the third letter I've written home since coming here. I hope they get over to you all right. It's a gamble. Parties or persons (single) leave for home or Paris every once in a while and act as postman for us.

We are having a lot of snow just now—all drifted up by the kind of wind they have here and which I wrote you all about in my last. All of us have splendid boots issued to us and wool socks and stockings and I have got through so far without chilblains of any kind. The Red Cross looks after its people as to clothes and keeps them nice and warm (or cold as the case may be.)

After lunch today I took a sort of walk in the Public Park, a place with some parts of trees in it, a fountain (ice-bound) and the rest snowsky. A few paces and you come to a high open space whence you look out over and down the Danube which is a queer Slavish colour—between Tiber brown and the Spanish kind. The river makes a lovely curve just below the town and the prospect must be quite nice in reasonable weather. All the houses down along the wharf are blown off a great deal by the bombardments. Their roofs are mostly gone. Also top walls. You can see further along the river the bridge, or what is left of it, and a partly destroyed pontoon. Also down there is the place where you land when ferried over from Semlin, (where they have such good cream puffs)

The cakes in Belgrade are such corking ones that our walk to and from homesky looks like a Virginia Reel, what with so many cake-shops on the way.

The work here is going on like a great factory would be conducted at home. There's a noise like glass-blowing towards eleven AM or four PM when the personnel gets to pouring in and out and filing and relieving cases and typing. I see to the Head Nurse's work and she is nice as she can be to me. Her name is Leete, Harriet. I keep a list of supplies given out and file away about one million names of worthy poor. The nurses have been unable to find any unworthy ones yet they tell me. Some of the individuals in a party like this are not so worthy when you start looking up their cases, I can tell you, though they may not be poor. They don't feel any hesitation in making a verdict on cases that come before them though, and take it very seriously at that. I'm not speaking of nurses though.

Holly is well and an Army Man is rushing her so fast she can't see the scenery as she goes by with him. He's in the Food Commission, and I must say Holly seems to get a great many little cakes and Slickaviches (Serbishe drinksky) offn him.

                    Lots of love from your very
                              loving
                                        Sylvia

Sylvia Beach Papers, Manuscripts Division, Department of Rare Books
and Special Collections, Princeton University Library (manuscript)

* * *

37. To Sylvester Woodbridge Beach   February 25, 1919

Belgrad, Feb. 25, 1919.

Dearest Father:

It seems as though we never got a chance to write in this little place— and we never hear from the family for that matter.

Holly and I are making out very well and are living comfortably with a lady & her dog & daughter. I think there is an old auntie somewhere as well. We are right in the French quarter and can get quite good Turkish coffee around the corner. Poilus & ourselves are the only frequentees of the Joint.

What are you all doing? H. (little) and I went over to Semlin on Sunday but it was such a Spring day and the air so bomby, we really couldn't take in some of the interesting things we were seeing. All I know is that there were some nicely typical weddings with dancing in the middle of the street and costumes quite good, and a performance in the Church where a cake was prayed over and presently distributed with a spoon to the congregation—specially little boys.

I forgot to say that the wedding party was in ox-carts pulled by horses. We came back to Belgrade in a boat filled to the scuppers with real Serb-skys and a few pigs in sacks—all squealing quite a good deal. Some fleas came over in the same boat.

We are relieving the Serbs—of a quantity of cakes. There are too many different kinds and they are all too really delicious, it's the only criticism I have to make.

Holly has been as good as requisitioned by the Minister (not clargy-man) to Serbia for she works at the Embassy early and late and most every day now. They make her stop with them to lunch as well and she is friends with the Daughter.

The Serbs have a long-dance, as you might call it, which they can always be roused long enough to take part in. They take hands & do little steps and it's the "Kola". It's what our A.R.C.ers[42] call dead easy—but they none of 'em can do it. They take hands with the Serbs and then they hop till the music stops. But "c'est pas ca".[43] The music for the Kola is one continual wail—just like a wake. The steps are more varied & twice as difficult as they look. We went to a dance at an orphanage where all but the orphans were present.

I must close now, so good by, wont you?

and with all sorts of love and some shipments of hugs-------------.-.-.- * ?

S. Beach,
Investigator to Serbia.

Sylvia Beach Papers, Manuscripts Division, Department of Rare Books and Special Collections, Princeton University Library (manuscript)

✳ ✳ ✳

---

42. A.R.C.: American Red Cross.
43. "That's not it."

38. To Eleanor Orbison Beach   March 6, 1919

Belgrade, Serbia, March 6, 1919.

Dearest Little Mother:

There's a mistake in the Serbian on this paper[44]—it ought to be three words instead of two—but its all right to use on your family and no questions asked.

Everyone has gone to Church this morning to hear Good Cardinal Bourne or something address them & a special service gotten up for all of us in the Catholic Church kindly loaned by its owner. I'm so glad to have a chance to write to the "Folks", its one in a life-time. But we never hear from you and father and Maggie and Cyprian at all for some reasons I spose.

I had such a splendid little trip this week to Obrenovatz. Holly had already been there and left a favorable impression among the Obrenovatz-ites—they were still talking of her visit. I went with Miss Leete. The journey takes about 3 to 4 to 5 hrs. under normal conditions but coming back there was such a drove of passengers getting on, the Captain of the little second-hand Austrian boat was afraid to put out lest we sink. We had left Obrenovatz in plenty of time and the Carry On of the A.R.C., for the place where you embark. Its some kilometers away from the town. We got there at Nine Thirty, waited till 12–30 for the boat to come down from Chabatz, and then, as you have already guessed, one thousand & 50 passengers not including pigs, turkeys & C all insisted on boarding the good schloop Willy-Nilly and she began to sink quite far under at least. The Captain confided his fears to us and said he had sent to Belgrade for an extra boat. All of us settled down and made ourselves uncomfortable. The costumes were perfect, embroidered leather vests edged with fur, Balkan colors, pointed astrakhan hats, Balkan shoes, old Gypsy ladies smoking their pipes and Serbian soldiers on leave from Zagreb & so forth. The usual Gypsy violinists were along and played for the dancing which begins when Serbs get up in the morning and keeps up till they fall into bed towards morning. The music is a repetition of mournful sounds and begins anywhere and ends anywhere. The men in their pointed astrakhan hats (see above) hold each other round the neck, jiggle in

---

44. Beach is referring to the Serbian-language Red Cross letterhead on which she wrote the letter.

time to the music, and seem to go into a sort of trance. Their faces loose all expression. It reminds you of Gorky stories[45] somehow too.

Well to make a short story long—that boat never left till nearly six and no other kind of a boat ever did arrive. There we were sitting on a thing about the size of a ferry boat all day dozing on camp stools in the pilot house and waking up to see the same dancing, hear the same sad music and smell the same sad garlic and other smelskys.

Well by the time we left the moon was up and the Save looking very fine but the Captain was too worried to enjoy anything. He was afraid (the machine is not working well) he wouldn't be able to navigate in the dark past the blown-up bridge to Belgrade and with the ship ready to sink with so many people and pigs aboard. And just as he feared, long towards 930 we had to make for the shore at a point where there was nothing to be seen but what was left of a blown-up house. The Capt. Invited us to stay on board all night but as all the best refugees were disembarking and were going to push on to Belgrade we decided to join them. In pitch darkness we climbed over a few barges between our ship and the shore and walked across a plank over some water and took to the railroad track where we strolled for some time. Then we struck a road and plodded along for several miles in company with all the refugees, packs on their backs, and it looked like the Serbian Retreat as seen in posters.[46]

We struck Belgrade about Ten o'clock.

End of a great day.

I may take a little trip to Bosnia, three days on a Torpilleur or something and on my return will let you know all that's worth knowing about it. We have such nice spring days here. Holly is well and we took a gallon on some Arab steeds last Sunday—I'm still decrepit from the good time we had.

I always wish for you & Cyprian & Father when we are having these interesting experiences. Cyprian should be here with those Arab Steeds and so forth.

---

45. Maxim Gorky (1868–1936), Russian writer. An English translation of his *Creatures That Were Once Men* had been released by Funk and Wagnall's in 1906, with an introduction by G. K. Chesterton. From 1906 to 1913 Gorky lived in exile on Capri, Italy.

46. In late 1915 and into 1916, Serbian soldiers were forced to retreat over the Albanian mountains. This became a well-known reference point for World War I, and a number of images of the movement were taken.

When shall we get news from home!
Lots & lots of love dear little M. to all

Sylvia Beach Papers, Manuscripts Division, Department of Rare Books and Special Collections, Princeton University Library (manuscript)

* * *

39. To Cyprian Beach   March 11, 1919

Belgrade, Serbia

Dearest Gilles:

Nearly 2 months and not a letter from you since the one you wrote announcing you were sailing the 24th or something. Its all very well— but I would like to know what has become of you know. Old Gilles. Do I suppose you are in Princeton all this time—if ever you reached there— or whether in New York seeing and interviewing the New Yorkskys, or what. Gilles if we could only be together and very soon—that's all I ask. I wonder how de max is getting along without us and how many times he has done "de Bells" since I saw him last. And as for you, you went and took a last look before leaving Paris—and you done right.

We are Balkan along here very remote, Holly and I, and took a motor spin over the mountains last Sunday the 9th of March. Skeletons of horses lay in the road-side all the way along. I don't know whether the war killed them or just hunger. All around Belgrade is a battle-field—its where a great deal of fighting took place and it looks it, it does that. And the people look it. And there's a continual stream of returning prisoners from Germany and Austria, poor everybody.

The architecture in Belgrade is worse than useless, but as soon as you get out into the landscape you begin to see such nice REAL houses with no modern improvements to spoil the Line. And the REAL people dress so nicely and use such good bullocks[47] and the sort of pigs we used to read about in the different-colored Fairy Books,[48] very fanciful. When

---

47. Castrated bulls (also known as oxen).
48. Andrew Lang's twelve-volume collection of *Fairy Books*, published from 1889 to 1910, featured translations of world fairy tales for children.

you leave town you get among hills and look back at Belgrade and the two rivers. The mountains are not cone-shaped like Spanish ones, but round Balkan looking things. There are plenty of trenches & barbed wire and other war-products to be seen, and everyone is making collections of battle-field souvenirs to take home. They all speak of It as of an awfully successful game of hare and hounds. xxxx x xxxxxxxxxxxxxxxxxxxxxxxx xxxxxxxxxxxx xxxx

Oh for some of the Lower Animals!

Somebody or other has a party every few days here—either they've moved in to a new home and are having what they call "open house" or its a birthday or a subscription ball or plain one. I go to all I can but not to the others. My love to the Girls.

I wonder whether you and P.L.M.[49] ever got our letters we have written at different times from here. Anyhow we told you all about our life and that sort of thing and how comfortably we were billeted on a lady & her daughter in a house smelling of incense on Sundays and just serbsky the rest of the week. A little boy belonging to the A.R.C. and named Stojadin with the accent on the last syllable, brings us a can of hot water in the morning and wood for the fire and he blacks our brown shoes till you wouldn't know them for such.

We are busy all day and of an evening take a Serbian lesson with the young lady of the house, which isn't so bad when you consider that she is out-&-out ONE OF US where the Emancipation of the Sex is concerned. She claims there are 14 Suffragettes in Serbia alone not counting Albania, Makedonia and female croats. Isn't it interesting.

I wonder how your old Guapo is, speaking of interesting. I miss him like fury as holly wd. say. Did he, or did he not, do lovely dental work for me and I never knew him to charge me a cent for it. He used to say he couldn't bring himself to charge a Clergymans family for "handling" their teeth.

Everything in the Organization is "handled". The question always is whether a thing is being handled right or not. So frequently the handling could be improved upon but as every speck of it is done by the men—no women control anything whatsoever in it—they have no one to blame but themselves when ALL goes wrong.

We are having such good weather. Are you casting around for to "locate" my Books Tore over there and do you think it sounds feasible

---

49. "Poor little mother."

now that you have looked over the situation.[50] I could stop in Paris and get a wagon-load of books for the French part of the Concern in June or so when we leave for home.

Well give much love to P.L.M. & P.A.F. de ma part,[51] as well as a set of embracements, and same to yourself from your specially loving

Sylvia

Sylvia Beach Papers, Manuscripts Division, Department of Rare Books and Special Collections, Princeton University Library (typescript)

* * *

40. To Eleanor Orbison Beach   April 18, 1919

Belgrade, April 18, 1919.

Dearest Little Mother:-

Perhaps very soon we shall be getting away from here—who knows. It's a pity not to have seen more of the Country, but we came to work and what else have we done?

This is Good Friday. The Serbs are all sinking down exhausted because they have cleaned house so frantically for the last days. Everything has to be tidy for Easter-Tide (!) in the land of Kroats & Slovenes.

We dined last evening in the Col's house way off up at the street. The Col. is away off down at Salonique just now and we were entertained by Major Edwards, the Almighty of the North Serbia Commission.

He is a M.D., and under normal conditions raises pigs & prickly pears in Florida and runs his home town. Mrs. Vorse (Mary Heaton or something) was also there for she is staying at the Col's till another suitable room can be found for her. She belongs to the A.R.C. temporarily and was sent out here to write up the Pyjamas and Bed Jackets in the Balkans. She is more interesting looking than her Work would lead one to suspect.

I wonder what Cyprian has cooked up by this time, and what you are all doing. Mrs. Hottinger wrote me a post card in which she

---

50. Before opening Shakespeare and Company in Paris, Beach contemplated opening a bookstore in Greenwich Village, New York City, or in London.
51. "On my behalf."

referred to Cyprian as "Cyperio." Wouldn't it be wise for her to take that as a permanent name rather than "Simplico" – tell her not to take any hasty steps in the matter however till I get there and can talk it over with her.

_____ had _____[52] Tomorrow is Easter—but so cold and rainy. We have our spring weather and now winter is coming on again by mistake.

You remember that lock that spells a word, which I got at the Rag Fair[53] in Madrid? I brought it down to the "Plant" yesterday. Some of the men thought they could open it with the help of a system all their own—but the systems were out of order or something. All kept on trying while the afternoon wore away and I was trying to make a faithful record of Leposava Milanovitch & C° for the Files. Finally when nightfall had fallen and still, inspite of having worked through the dictionary the thing still wouldn't unlock for some reason, a Capt. McAleavey, Dentist A.R.C., a man who has "slept by the roadside during the retreat through Albania" took down on paper every letter on the lock in the order they come in, and retreated to the Bulgarian Legation where he and others of the A.R.C. live. He said he was going to get that thing open UNLESS it was a "phoney". A Lieut. Anderson tried for a while to find the word then went away—he said, to throw himself in the Danube or the Save, I forget which. Anderson runs the "De-lousing Plant" here as it's universally called. Several hundred returning prisoners or soldiers on leave are run through it daily. They & their clothes bathed, baked and generally disinfected and all through the intervention of their noble American Allies.

My stars—what wet weather! Its enough to make a bolchevic[54] of me, if I was as easily influenced as all that. As it is, the r.c. has made a regular feminist of me. It's seeing men doing all the managing and helping themselves to all the pleasant things that come along—the women are subjected to humiliations that American women are not at all accustomed to when they are at home—they rank as buck privates—are ordered hither & thither, forced to obey unquestioningly. A mere nothing of a man is a Lt., but the women at the head of their departments rank as nothing whatsoever and haven't the slightest say about anything— even in their own department. Yet women are regular members of the

---

52. These words redacted from letter by unknown hand.
53. Beach is referring to El Rastro, Madrid's famous open-air flea market, held on Sundays and holidays.
54. Bolsheviks: Russian political party which later became the Communist Party.

organisation and are subject to its laws exactly the same as the men. These creatures are in the dark ages as regards women—but what can you expect.---------

Where are you going to spend next summer, you all?

> Very, very much love, P-L-M,
> from your loving,
> Sylvia

Sylvia Beach Papers, Manuscripts Division, Department of Rare Books and Special Collections, Princeton University Library (manuscript)

* * *

41. To Sylvester Woodbridge Beach   April 29, 1919

> Belgrade, Serbia
> April 29, 1919

Dearest Father:

Who knows if by the time you get this letter we wont be far from the Balkans and somewhere else or somepin. It's all most uncertain and will remain so till we know anything to the contrary—perhaps when the Col. gets back from Salonique.[55] He is coming tonight. Holly and I would like to go home by way of Salonique but may not be able to arrange the thing.

Major Edwards took an interesting little 2 days trip last Sat. & Sun. the 26th and 27th. All over hills and down into valleys and fording streams, in a Fiat that kept blowing up and busting on us. The roads were like bogs after the heavy rains Serbia has been having, and twice ox teams had to come to our rescue and draw us out of the depths of mud. We also had a blow-out etc. But the sun was shining so nicely and the meadows all green, and flocks of different colored sheep and pigs and people with a sprinkling of goats made good decorations. A little shepherd in: a white linen smock & tight pants to the ankles, of the same, a leather vest with Balkan Decoration on it, Serb turned-up-at-the-toes sandals, the whole topped off by such a good hat, was diverting his flocks by a weird air on a pipe. He parted with his pipe for 3 Dinara—but not the air that went with

---

55. City in Greece, more often known as Thessaloniki or Salonika.

it which was an air-loom I fear. We went way off to Kraguievatz talking in Palanka and so forth and spent the night in the former little place. I had a nice room at the back of the house. I got up so long before the 2 lady doctors or M.D.ettes the next morning, I had to climb out my window— careful to avoid the barrel of water which stood just below it. Sunday we came back—by way of Milanovatz. There was a Weddin' and the Party was dancing the Kolo in front of the Church. They had come in ox-carts from far out in the country. The Major's chauffeur has been a Serbo-Parisian taxi driver so the Major communicates with him in French. He calls the SPRINGS "les PRINTEMPS."[56] Les printemps de l'automobile.

I wish we could see P.-L.-M. in her nice new hat which she plucked out of Wait's window one day—or Cyprian did. Or somepin. And wish we could see her nice new suit she had made in Philadelphia that time. No one says a thing about your costumes, so we take them for granted as the last word in Class—as usual. What a delicious garden Mother and Cyprian must have planted. Were there any little onions? Write me c/o A.R.C., Hotel Regina, Balkan Commission, (Please Forward).

I wish Cyprian could get some work now in her own line, worthy of her skilled workmanship.[57] The whole family must now bend its energies to getting her started off once for all on something that she will be a great success in. Besides that, she has not written to me once since she sailed but I don't hold it up against her. I know that it is not her fault and that she could write but wont.

On how spring-like to-day—and rightly. Day after tomorrow, you must remember, is May-Day. The office-boy is not around so he must have left the premises for some open air recreation—and rightly. His name is Gena (Gayna). He has taught me to play Mica (Mitza) a Serb gamesky with black and white pebbles as the what-you-may-call-'ems. The only thing that's lacking is a little stick to prop open your eyelids while you play it, so as to keep awake.

What is Morris doing these days? I don't see how he gets along with Mildred. Why is Cousin Mary staying in bed now? I thought she was so well this spring. I heard once from Uncle Tom, just when I was coming out here. I hadn't time to answer his letter at that time and can't find his address anywhere now. I must have left it in Paris. As for Archie—he never wrote us at all and I've no idea where he is. Do you hear from Lilian sometimes? I wonder how she is.

---

56. The pun derives from the fact that "Printemps" is the French word for the season spring, not for the springs of a car.

57. Acting work.

Tell Cyprian she ought to write to Paul Fort.

Holly and I were invited to lunch by the Military Attachay and Mrs.[58]—a little young couple and charming brainless creatures—pronounced delightful to know. Her father is Sompin in the Red Cross and she is as pretty as a Movie Star—lovely!

With lots & lots of love from your ever loving

SB

Sylvia Beach Papers, Manuscripts Division, Department of Rare Books and Special Collections, Princeton University Library (manuscript)

* * *

42. To Eleanor Orbison Beach   May 14, 1919

Belgrade, May 14, 1919.

Dearest little Mother:

Holly is away for example. She went off in a great camion[59] yesterday at 8 A.M. sitting up in front with a Miss Mourot and the chauffeur. A chair was placed inside—and in the chair—a Parson. He was going for the trip and to see the country, Holly and Mourot also, and to take the mail. They are due at Mitrovitza by Friday or Saturday. They are having nice weather for the trip.

I had the last trip so am booked to remain at the "Plant"[60] this time and I have quite a little stack of reports and things to see to. I have so few to do lately that I am getting quite lollish. The work in this plant is not interesting unless you are interested in Philanthropic Enterprizes. And it's on the same order. Holly and I are going to stay longer than we thought when we wrote you last. More supplies I think are en route from Salonique and we shall probably have to stay till the 1st of July. We may leave sooner however—in this work one can never tell. Ask Cyprian whether she sits up reading G.B.S. much these days.[61]

I never read at all out here, and I don't study and I don't do anything that I ever used to do in my former existence. Except (tell Cyprian) I do

---

58. At this point on the letter someone (perhaps Holly Beach) has written: "Mr. and Mrs. Hamilton Fish Armstrong. They were divorced later and she is now Mrs. Walter Lipmann."
59. A truck, usually without sides, used for hauling heavy loads.
60. The "Delousing Plant," described in Beach's letter of April 18, 1919.
61. George Bernard Shaw.

read in M. Bergeret[62] her favorite, now and again. I discovered it by mis-
chance in one of the so-called book shops of this town.

One up to date feature they've got here is the nightingales—singing
every single evening in all the trees.

Yours in haste,

The Courier is leaving Lots of love Sylvia

Very very much love from your loving Sylvia

---

*Sylvia Beach Papers, Manuscripts Division, Department of Rare Books
and Special Collections, Princeton University Library (manuscript)*

* * *

43. To Eleanor Orbison Beach   May 24, 1919

Belgrade, Serbia, May 24th, 1919.

Dearest little Mother:

We have not heard from any of you birds for a number of weeks or
so and are most anxious as you can guess. I am using another machine
and always write *q* instead of *a* the keyboard being like that. Is Cyprian
still writing Father's letters of an afternoon, I wonder. Holly had a letter
from Father the other day but it wasn't written by his Secretary so I take
it she has been bounced for in officiousness. That letter was dated May
1st, 1919. It told of Cyprian planting a whole flower garden and she is
energetic, Holly and I think.

The nearest thing we come to flowers here is to buy them in the Market
for all sorts of Kronen and things. Clove pinks for ex. are 2 Kr. per clutch.
Roses are so so. Irises are 1 Kr. each. Pansies hors de prix.[63] There were
some rather good spoons at the market this morning, wooden, painted
in a sort of Russian style with certain subjects. I took 3 at a Dinar for all.
That's about 18 cents you know. The market is lacking in charm, the baskets being banal and the arrangement of the wares quite uninspired. The
choice of vegetables is limited to onions and garlic with here and there
a potato. Spinach however is awfully plentiful, and usually smothered

---

62. Anatole France's 1901 novel *Monsieur Bergeret à Paris*, based on the Dreyfus Affair.
France was a socialist and supporter of Alfred Dreyfus, the falsely convicted Jewish officer.
63. Priceless.

in garlic when served which is on a general average of twice a day. The people at the market are nice though, they have the jackets and aprons and belts and horn shaped buckles and classic shoes that help you to get over your disappointment at the baskets and other arrangements.

Holly has had her bed removed right out from under her for 2 Bishops who have come to stay a week in our house. They have on very smart sashes of a crimson and are dressed something on the same plan as some of Cyprian's costumes. They live in the Salon next to our room and this morning rose early to play a game of basket ball, to judge by the sound. It must be a great task to curry down their long shiny beards each day and their locks down to their knees, presque. The people in our house had a large sum of Kronen and Dinars stolen from them about 2 weeks ago, and we were afraid there were going to trace it back to us for a time, but it has all blown over I think. They haven't found the money yet but they think they know someone who knows someone whose cousin took it. They seem to be much calmer now over it all.

I wish Cyprian had the magnificent opportunities Holly and I have to ride these days. Such a nice little Grey is the one I use. He breathes fire out of his nostrils and acts so skittish when you are going to get up on him that he creates quite an atmosphere of dread around about: but it's all bluff and bluster. Once you're seated on his back he ambles along like old Dewitt or something. Holly likes to ride a certain Kiki a tall bay with a side step and a passo doble.[64] She looks like the Queen of all the Belgums[65] making entries in re-constructed flanders. The French and Serbs lend us these steeds and we do the rest. The country is fine for riding here, fairly made for it.

How are you poor little mother? I wish to. . . . I could leave Serbia and I won't say what, and see you again. We may go soon though. Perhaps another couple of weeks will see us clearing out of here.

Lots and lots of love from your loving,

Sylvia

Sylvia Beach Papers, Manuscripts Division, Department of Rare Books and Special Collections, Princeton University Library (manuscript)

---

64. *Pasodoble:* Spanish for "double step." Refers to a kind of music, or the dance based on it (often associated with bullfighting, since it is the kind of music played when the bullfighter enters the ring).
65. Belgians.

* * *

44. To Eleanor Orbison Beach   June 3, 1919

Belgrade, June 3, 1919.

Dearest Little Mother:

Nothing new to report this week except the non-arrivage of letters for some time and we don't know what they are about up there at the Paris end of the thing. Everyone is getting restless over it—no news from Mother and the Boys, nor from Joe since she left Base Hospital No.3: did or did not Elnore go out to see her folks in Seattle? As for Holly and me, we are on worse than tenterhooks to know how Cyperio's trip to New York resulted, and whether the new kitten has taken in Mousie yet or not, and why no mention was made of Father in your last letter (April 22nd). Wasn't that a tiresome lot of stuff you were having to do in D.O.P.[66] with one relief work after another! P.=L.=M.![67]

We have a lot that's tiresome here as well, what with one thing and another, but enjoy life say what you may. Last Sat. we took a great ride on our Jaguar and Kiki steeds. Those beasts can climb up regular per-pendiculars and slide down the other side. They can penetrate through the thickest kind of a thicket. The first thing we do when we get out of town is to gallop across a field on the top of a hill where we skirt a flock of sheep and avoiding shell holes and marking with one eye the view of Danube & Save rendez-vous and the storks nests of Semlin across the river, manage to have quite a nice time. The country smells good with acasciasa[68] and looks nice with its new poppies and primroses. There is a good supply of nightingales and larks not to mention the large parties of magpies ill-concealed by the foliage and so forth. Any No. of Gypsies are always among those present, always traveling and their baggage always a poultry farm and a violin, and their costume a few loud-colored rags, and a flower behind the ear.

Sunday we were to have another trot but the horses never showed up. I found out why as I was trotting out on foot to Toptchider. There were a French Sergeant and a sampla Poilu mounted on ours Jaguar & Kiki

---

66. "Dear Old Princeton."
67. "Poor little mother."
68. Acacias.

and trying to make them take trenches and other natural obstacles and with but small success as you have already guessed. I was so indignant that . . . . I never said a word but just simply took a walk and visited the British but uninhabited Veterinary Stables, in company with a Roughneck Private, Secora by name from the Food Commission but very nice, and some little Englishman probably from Surry.[69]

This concern is nearing its semi-finals and we are waiting for Col. Farnam to get back from Bucarest[70] with his publicity-man to know what the score is and who we are to challenge next. Meanwhile the weather is warmer and the sun has taken to appearing every once in so often.

The Serbs are so much like the Spanish except that they are better in some respects—agriculture, to give only one sample. But they are apt to rouse the very worst in one just like the S.S and all the while one feels so sorry for them.

Holly is well and will write sometime soon I am sure. We still live comfortably at the Toplicin Venatz place and are usually able to keep up our strength say what you may. But we are awfully homesick and would be glad to see the Family again as soon as arrangements can be made.

Mother dear I'm so glad your pictures turned out so well and I wish we could see them, odma as we say out here!

Lots and lots of the very best love from your loving,

Sylvia

Sylvia Beach Papers, Manuscripts Division, Department of Rare Books and Special Collections, Princeton University Library (manuscript)

*   *   *

45. To Sylvester Woodbridge Beach   July 1, 1919

Belgrade, July 1st ,1919.

Dearest Father:

I never hear from you so will write you a short letter. Holly and I, for example, moved from Toplicin Venatz where we had passed so many

---

69. Surrey (a county in southeast England, bordering on London).
70. Bucharest.

months of every sort, to the Anglo-American Rest House on Dobracina Ulica. The name doesn't mean anything—it's what the British always call their pensions for the Nursing Sisters. They are nice quiet places where the Sisters and Doctoresses and Canteensters come and go as they please and no questions asked: most of them have short hair and all are very busy—they've no time to chat. At 7 A.M. tea is brought to your bedside whether you want it or not, there's no use struggling. The meals are on the sideboard, everyone helping themselves to the tinned tongue or bully beaf,[71] the British boiled potatoes and the lettuce. There is an unlimited supply of bread & jam & butter, also Tea and coffee. When the sideboard begins to look a bit food-forsaken just press the button and the German prisoner sees to a fresh installment of eats. All the curtains and different covers throughout the house are a tasteful chintz or somepin, and there are assorted black arm chairs that you can regularly disappear into and places to put the tea cups on into the bargain. All the work in the plant is done by German prisoners—mostly former Professors I think. The bath is large and fine to fit the strapping British female and no end of hot water flows in and removes the Serbian National Bug (bed) and the different Cooties you pick up in trips about the country.

There is only one (1) rule in the house—you must on no account whatsoever go into the kitchen. That suits me very nicely. In fact the whole atmosphere is quite suffragette.

July 10th_

This letter was interrupted by an important trip we had to take to Sarajevo, thence to Ragusa, Holly and I. My contract done expired the 1st of July and the season being a slack one, owing to the absence of all our Colonels in Bucharest, we made Major Edwards give us papers authorizing us to travel from Belgrade to Sarajevo "on business for the Red Cross." The Serbs never let us pay a cent on their railroads or boats: they give us a special compartment with a guard detailed to accompany us all the way and to prevent people from coming in on you. Everyone calls you "Sestra" (Sister) and tells you how Wilson is Serbia's God,[72] and America the mother of Serbia. Every once in so often you meet a soldier who has lived 2 years in Los Angeles and "by Golly—I like live in the States!"

Sarajevo is the best town I ever inspected. Jammed with Turkish, I mean to say Mohamedan people in costumes that are regular Theatrical

---

71. Tinned corned beef.
72. Woodrow Wilson, U.S. president (1913–1921) and Princeton resident.

Props—Turkish pants, turbans, purple jackets with lots of nice gold or silver braid, the women with black veils over their faces and complete Turkish outfits, really too extreme for street wear. Minarets, white with sky blue tops are sprinkled all over the town. The houses are too satisfactory for words, say what you may.

We pushed onto Ragusa next day and you might think you were in Italy. White roads—black cypresses—turquoise sea and old walled-in town and fortress!

We went bathing in the nice warm cool sea, 2 performances—a morning and an afternoon one, and left next day, reporting last night in Belgrade according to schedule. I think we spent about 62 hours on the train altogether, We had to get along with a minimum of sleep and subsist on some quite weird eats, but neither of us were at all tired when we got back from our tour of inspection of Bosnia and Herzegovina not to speak of Dalmatia (coast of) and we saw a whole set of Montenegro mountains as we strolled along towards Ragusa.

The people in the fields, making hay while the sun shone were all in Turkish costume, the ladies hastening to cover their faces when the train passed. The hay was all piled on donkeys and everything very up-to-date you better believe. Fig trees were growing wild along some river of a good blue that accompanied us through Herzegovina.

We found a letter from P.L.M., dated June 15 when we got back to Belgrade. It was written in New York where she and Cyprian had flown for relief from Commencement activities. What a pity Yale won this year! It must have been a flook or whateveryoucallit. People that have been in Paris these days tell great tales of the new Perishing Stadium and the feats of our athletes. What is the Censor doing, to allow the Enemy to score like that! You know, enemy from an athletic point of view.

Mother touched very lightly on your doings with the boys of 76 but probably there was nothing slow about any of those Reunions this year. I do hope no one got "jazzed up" and that there were no "Phosphorescent Streaks" in the streets of Princeton at night.

Father dear, write to your devoted some time when you have the spare minute, and with lots of love, believe me yours.

(I hate to send such a bad specimen of my type writing to such an expert as you, but I have a brute of a machine just now.)

Sylvia Beach Papers, Manuscripts Division, Department of Rare Books and Special Collections, Princeton University Library (manuscript)

* * *

46. To Sylvester Woodbridge Beach   June 15, 1919

Belgrade, June 15, 1919

Another Mail in and no letters, as Mother would say.

Dearest Father:

This is Sunday as you have already guessed. We started the day at 6 A.M. with a gollop across country, taking in—entirely by mistake—a review of his Srbsky troops by the Crown Prince in his glasses and all.[73] It was on a large hillside and so were we at the time, so we had to review the troops from horseback. There were some flocks of sheep with Patriarchs at the head, and some wild horses wandering around. All the soldiers were in American uniforms sent to Serbia by the U.S.A. to replace the rags they had as sole outfits. They were the new troops swearing allegiance to the Flag, Srbsky Totem, while a voluptuously dressed Bishop bleated out all the pre-conceived prayers for this year's warriors. The band played too. I declare, these Serbian horses though, are the best things. The Spanish Arabs are nothing to them. All the Royal Guards mount grey stallions that stand up on their hind legs, their front ones swimming high in air, their manes and tails really exaggerated. They breathe fire and toss their heads and are not even half broken in.

Miss Leete whom I secretaried, has left Serbia and also left this mean little Corona [74] belonging to a certain Lt. Jimmie Reagan in my care. I hope not to write very often on it, I'm tellin' the World. Miss Leete and another nurse got Typhus down at Palanka while over-hauling the Military Hospital—which needed it; 20 to 30 patients a day was the death rate—the bodies piled one on top of another in a room and left till someone had a spare moment to put them away for ever in the ground. They were mostly Bulgarian prisoners so no one bothered much about it. The water supply came from a well containing a German prisoner which had fallen in some time ago and had not as yet been removed. There were 30 beds for 250 men and the patients were crowded together in layers on

---

73. Crown Prince George of Serbia (1887–1972). He had been forced to renounce his right to succeed to the throne in 1909 as a result of mental health problems.
74. Typewriter.

the floor, absolutely no nursing provided for them, their uniforms rotting on them. The dying men had their pockets looted by the prisoner attendants, who never attended to them except to perform this last little service for them.

Talk about—

How are you and P.L.M. and Simplico and some of the animals, father dear? WE are longing very much to see you and all get ensemble again. I would write to tom but have lost his address tell Mother. I wonder, is he still in France caring for the Shell-Shocked.

The purple off this type ribbon has gotten onto my face somehow and looks fierce. Do you know—every single afternoon that's fine, Gena the Office Boy comes in fresh from a swim in the Save and tells me all about the joys of it. I think it tactless of him under the circumstances, don't you. Specially this hot weather. But we make up in ices what we lack in baths, tell Cyprian. They are very nice ices under the circumstances— strawberry being a favorite among some of us. Then there are coffee ones with whipped cream on top and not bad considering.

Next Monday, that is to say tomorrow, is one of the dates set for the revelation to us all of what is to befall us in the way of a date set for departure. It will be in another fortnight if not ten days attenarate.[75]

So here' hopping, and meanwhile with much love father dear to you and some of the others,

From your loving,

SWB

Holly is considered the best dancer in Belgrade! And yet there are several very expert ones in the Commission. She gets complimented regularly on her work at the dances I can tell you.

Sylvia Beach Papers, Manuscripts Division, Department of Rare Books and Special Collections, Princeton University Library (manuscript)

* * *

75. "At any rate."

47. To Cyprian Beach   July 11, 1919

Belgrade, July 11, 1919

Dearest Cyprian,

Still another machine! We have to change every other few minutes and I ought to be able to write on anything after this Balkan experience.

We're still hanging on here, waiting for the Col.s to return from Bucharest. They were due in Belgrade long ago at that. Meanwhile it's a great state of uncertainty we're in. No one (I write it in 2 words now in order to please you) knows whether they are going to the U.S.A. or to Roumania. I should like to stay on in the Balkans another month—it's not a very good time to be going to Paris—I'll tell you why: There are no rooms to be had—there are no berths to be had on home-going boats—the town is crowded with noble allies and C°—(a grand Rejoicings over Victory has been organized by prominent actors and politicians, Firmin Gémier[76] had a whole mise-en-scène arranged for mourning the Dead, celebrating the Triumph, and on the third day a set of the most sensational N°s ever seen by the naked eye)—and for various other etc.s too numerous to mention I should like to be elsewhere. I can be saving a little money meanwhile out here. Do you know, Cyprian, I've practically decided to settle in London for my book plan. You suggested it yourself once—do you remember? There is much more interest in that sort of thing over there than there is anywhere at home, and besides that I like living on this side so much better. It's near Paris and I could keep in touch with the Situation. I know that anything but Business & Sport, plus Clothes in our country is a for-lorn hope. These are the Favorites and no one in their senses would put up any money on Art. I don't blame them for not taking an interest in a thing so passé-de-mode either. I wouldn't myself if I hadn't been cursed with a preference for the thing instead of good, practical horse sense. I envy these fine Americans, we see out here—so sportmanlike, so busi-nesslike, so keen and energetic, nicely well-to-do and useful. The world is "the Great Adventure" to them and I should worry. All the same someone has to do their thinking for them and I must have some books for those someone's. Social questions are interesting people at home, though I hear and it's an interesting world over there.

If only you were going to be in London to help me start—if I do start. I really don't know where I shall find the capital, and they say the town

---

76. French actor (1869–1933). He debuted the role of Père Ubu in Alfred Jarry's *Ubu Roi.*

is crammed at present—no rooms whatsoever. Holly is going along and hopes to find a job of some sort there. I hope her business experience will help me out and she is much interested in the big idea (Little h— Art—Books!!!) I will explain it all to you some day and you will see that any other arrangement is impossible. If I knew anyone over here that would be interested in going into it with me—but I don't. I know I shall love living in London—New York UH uh! And besides, you've never given me any information on the subject of prospects over there—I have been waiting in vain.

Capt. Armstrong of the Food Commission, a dear old fellow that looks like a horse and is another Bill Hart, has left me his little hat (overseas) and when you see a scout with a khaki colored cap with 2 bars on it, its me.

I wish we didn't have to wait so long to see P.-L.-M.'s photograph! It certainly is the deuce. But perhaps you all will have to come on over if we are planning a reunion, for Holly and I think of postponing the States-going trip for a little time (see above). But Gilles I have got to see you right away or I can't stand it any longer. You must come to London straight off. I have stood our separation about long enough so will get a room ready for you all in London town and you must see about booking a passage at once.

I wonder whether Mother couldn't come to London and help me start my books. She could meet me there in the early part of September. She probably wouldn't want to leave you or somepin, supposing you had your work going in California or New York by that time. I really think she would like living in England for a time.

She must hurry up and decide.

> With much love Gilles
> from your loving
> Sylvette

I got you (I can't wait to tell you) in Sarajevo from the Turks there, a little coffee set for 2 persons—little pot, 2 gold and white cups in holders, an ash retriever, on a tray—all in copper.

Sylvia Beach Papers, Manuscripts Division, Department of Rare Books and Special Collections, Princeton University Library (typescript)

* * *

48. To Eleanor Orbison Beach   July 14, 1919

Belgrade (for nearly the last time, perhaps)

Dearest Little Mother:

My but it's a time since I seen you last! I'm hoping somehow to start my books in London this fall if the worst comes to the worst. I think we have now decided to omit Bucharest this trip. Holly's friend, Peggy O'Leary stopped in Belgrade on her way to Paris from Bucharest where she has been for some time and advises us to laisser tomber[77] that town— which we shall probably do. As soon as we know any plans concerning ourselves we will advise family. (As the business man would say.) I took Peggy over to Semlin this morning to put her on the train for Paris. She is most attractive and a clever girl about getting about and getting interesting jobs for herself and friends all over the world. Her father is a brilliant lawyer and his daughter would make one of the same kind if she had a chance—she is a great sort. Holly finds her interesting and altogether she is a fine friend for her to have.

I was rushing to catch the boat back to Belgrade when Capt. Ramsay's camion[78] was held up by a couple of freight cars that had been left right on the piece of track that crosses the road. An English or Irish officer and myself had to assist the driver in shoving the cars along while Courfou, the chauffeur's Retreat dog barked with the loud pedal on and was a great help altogether considering his size (about oxo). I made the boat too—leaping on just as the toot was tooting. I lived to regret it—there was a former and chosen head waiter from the Grand Hotel, Belgrade, waiting to shake hands with me and to discuss the exchange in dinars, kronen and all. Holly is the one to go for that sort of thing. I never saw anything like the grasp she has on the financial situation out here—what exchange you can demand from day to day, week to week, hour to hour. Where to find the most advantageous offers for your money and is a regular confidence-man in the A.R.C. I can tell you!

July 16

I carried this letter around so much it seems to have got rather untidy in its appearance.

On Sunday afternoon I went with a crowd of the British out to Toptchider Park where they have a convalescent hospital for children that

---

77. To drop or abandon.
78. Truck.

have been done for in their Belgrade hospital for same. They are sent to try to recuperate on a hill-top fitted up by the British. The Doctor is a woman. We had tea in and out of a tent—Admiral Trowbridge, chief Naval man for the Orient, Captain Haggard Holly's friend also of the Navy out here—General Plunkett or "Plankett" as he is pronounced—Miss Picton, transportation man for the British and Serbian armies and starting out right now with a whole set of supplies on pack mules for distribution in out-of-the-way spots in the Balkans—and a few other delightful people that I really regret will have to be trimmed down by the "New Order of Things"—Cyprian or Eleanor will know what I mean unless she has already left for California.

Now there you see—it's raining again. Its the Sun's turn but everything is disorganized out here and will be till the League of Nations[79] is established and set going—meanwhile one must expect a state of great unrest among these smaller States and more or less irregularity in the fonctionnement du système solaire.

We saw the Crown Prince pass down the Kneza Mihailova of whatever you call the Main St. the other day on his way to Church. He was surrounded by his troops—all the new recruits—and altogether there was such a fuss that I think his church-going must be something like mine—only once in so often. He was on a white horse of a certain shape, and was wearing his glasses. With the new Order of Things, all that must go.

Holly and m'self are leaving upon the Orient Express for the Extreme West on Monday next. This is the 16th isn't it, so you can picture us arriving in Paris on Wednesday the 23rd, 1919 and going straight to Holly's sanitary little Red Cross pension on Rue Galilée. As long as I am affiliated with this business I had just as lief not try to mix Palais Royal with it. We are only going to stay long enough in Paris for me to unpack all Cyprian's and my things in the cellar of the Hottingers, and to re-pack them properly. I had to stow them away most hastily when I was scuttling the ship to make a getaway out here while the going was good. And it seems old Cyprian never went around to have a look in at our precious junk when she was around that neighbourhood. A great deal of it is in boxes (packing cases) sold me by Mme Martin that has a coffee shop and that I gave my poor Bamboula to. Alackaday. Some of it is just in

79. The League of Nations: an international organization founded in the wake of the war, with the aim of preventing future wars through diplomacy and collective security.

packages on the floor—what a time I had with it all and getting my Papers and equipment and English shorthand ready in plenty of _____ Monnier is keeping our Bakst for us. I'm going right around to see her and break the news that I'm going to London instead of New York and she won't like it. She was anxious for me to be in New York and fly back and forth between Jewville and Paris. She doesn't like English things. Still it can't be helped. I've decided to stay on this side and if one scheme doesn't work, another will. Holly wants to stay over too. She and Peggy are planning to find something interesting to do in one of these countries. I move that the whole family move across as soon as possible.

I hope we find some letters awaiting us in Paris—next best to finding some of the family awaiting us there. I must have a suit made but don't need anything else in the way of clothes I hope. The "Civies" I go back to are not very complicated thank the Lord or m'self.

Very very much love dearest little mother
Sylvia

Sylvia Beach Papers, Manuscripts Division, Department of Rare Books and Special Collections, Princeton University Library (manuscript)

III

SHAKESPEARE AND COMPANY: EXPATRIATES

49. To Eleanor Orbison Beach   August 27, 1919

Dearest Little Mother,

Yours of August 14th has just arrived. It went first to the Rue Galilée. Since you wrote it a great deal has transpired—my visit to London where one look was enough to show me that London was not the town to start my shop in—the return-trip to Paris, the discovery of the unheard-of yes unheard-of opening for an English & American book club in the very book center of Paris under the haut patronage of Monnier herself, the Pope-to-be-erè-long-throughout France in that Branch of art—and the cable I sent you in lots of trepidation—and a cable from you saying you were sending $3000 by mail[1]—well it left me as weak as a—French athlete we'll say. Oh mother dear, you never never have failed your undeserving children at a critical moment!!! and how can I tell you in a letter what a D.L.M.[2] you are but there are hugs & kisses O O O O + + + O O O + + +

O O + + O O + O + O + O + O +—

never did see such a mother and you must come over as soon as possible so that I can explain with a regular Hug how I feel!!!

---

1. Beach writes in her memoir that the cable said: "'Opening bookshop in Paris. Please send money,' and she sent me all her savings" (*Shakespeare and Company* 17). In the margin of this letter, she notes, "Your cable arrived last Friday the 22 nd."
2. Dear Little Mother.

Now you say in your letter that you think G. Village³ a good proposition and that any rate I should go home and talk it over a bit, but by this time you have had my letters explaining all the advantages of starting a shop in Paris and AT ONCE.

I'm sorry yours and Cyprian's letters describing prospects over there never came, and G. Village interests me very much. It would be far nicer being near my family & in my own country of course; but the scheme was all more or less in the air over there—whereas on this side they are fairly begging me to step in. Monnier and I have got it all mapped out so that success is well nigh or nie or ny a certainty—Get it now or never! That's why I can't go home and see you all as I wish wish wish I could do. Just wait till this thing gets going though, and we can all be a happy family together again, for what's a little ocean or two for me to cross now and again after I get successful! Think what luck!

Such a mother to give me the money to start just wherever I want to. And a friend like Monnier with all the ability and experience lacking in me. And interesting patrons all ready-in-hand. And a shop that's the only thing of its kind to be found in Paris—any number of people were after it. And least but not last the right to live in Paris which is enough to make anyone as happy as happy can be and life read like the Pink Fairy Book.

The best thing Holly & I could have done was to go to the Balkans just when we did. All this would have been impossible for me now if I had not been able to earn the money that I did out there. And it enabled me to be in Paris just at the right moment. I owe it to Holly that I do. She it was who got me into that remote spot where I could get a perspective of life and save up enough money and strength to start out this fall, all nice and new.

I'm now waiting for the son-in-law of the lady who owns the shop to come to town and arrange for the signing of the lease and the payment in advance of half a years rent—ins 750,00 which Holly is going to lend me is case yours doesn't come in time. Then comes the cleaning, the repairing, the painting and the furnishing of the shop. Monnier is going to see that they don't charge me American prices for all this. I only wish I had yours and Cyprian's artistic genius to help me with the color scheme! At least Monnier is not going to have anything to say in that part. She wants me to have that hard battleship grey that she has

---

3. Beach's mother proposed opening a bookstore in Greenwich Village, New York City.

in her place—but never a-bit, say I! I'm going to have a paint called "Matolin"—its dull finish—and some beige and yellow à la Cyprian mebbe. A painter, Barnett, told me about the nice shades you could get in Matolin and he wants me to have blue and orange. Well this will be continued, this story—

Very very much love mother dear,
Sylvia

Sylvia Beach Papers, Manuscripts Division, Department of Rare Books and Special Collections, Princeton University Library (manuscript)

* * *

50. To Gertrude Stein[4]　　　　May 5, 1920

Thursday
8 rue Dupuytren

Dear Miss Stein

It's a miserable business and I'm going to sell out to Mr Griggs and his mother or something if this keeps on! Now I can't dine at your pavilion nor spend the evening with you but have to sit with Workers from the ARC[5] picking out of catalogues travelogue books to be sent for. It's their blasted Permanent Supplies system. Already they've got Finland and the Finns and all the Oxford Alien pamphlets but they're calling for more. I'll come in the first evening they let go of me.

With loving homage
Sylvia Beach

Gertrude Stein and Alice B. Toklas Papers, Yale Collection of American Literature, Beinecke Rare Book and Manuscript Library, Yale University (manuscript)

4. Gertrude Stein, American writer who had arrived in Paris in 1903, where she and her brother Leo had become patrons of the arts. "Gertrude subscribed to my lending library, but complained that there were no amusing books in it," according to Beach (*Shakespeare and Company* 27–28).
5. American Red Cross.

* * *

51. To Gertrude Stein May 13, 1920

Wednesday

8 rue Dupuytren

Dear Miss Stein

Please pardon me. I thought you knew "Literature"—it has gone partly Dada but some of its elements are still quite Guillaume Apollinaire.[6] Anyhow I was going to see you again before taking any fatal steps. I had planned to call on you last evening but was prevented, and this evening there is Jules Romain's new piece at the Vieux Colombier.[7] Perhaps you would let me come tomorrow

Your affectionate

Sylvia Beach

Please don't trouble to reply. Just instruct your Alsatian to say not at home if anyone looking like me should ring.

Gertrude Stein and Alice B. Toklas Papers, Yale Collection of American Literature,
Beinecke Rare Book and Manuscript Library, Yale University (manuscript)

* * *

52. To Gertrude Stein July 13, 1920

Dear Miss Gertrude Stein,

Raymonde says she has written to you all about the great desolation.[8] She will not be free on Wednesday nor on Thursday and we are both very much down hearted not to be able to take advantage of your kind invitation.

---

6. Guillaume Appollinaire (1880–1918), French poet and art critic. Sometimes credited with the neologism "surrealism."

7. The poet and dramatist Jules Romains (1885–1972), the founder of the literary movement Unanisme, presented his poetic drama *Cromedeyte-Le-Vieil* at Jacques Copeau's Théâtre du Vieux-Colombier.

8. Raymonde Linossier (1896–1930), French writer and close friend of Beach and Monnier. Linossier was heavily involved in the type-scripting of *Ulysses.*

Did you see me turn in at "the Old Doves" the other evening?[9] I was disappointed not to see you and Miss Toklas there (pardon me if I haven't spelt it right.) It was the last night and literally thousands were turned away and a myriad of automobiles in different sizes were clogging up the streets of those "O.D.s".[10]

> Very regretfully,
> yours very affectionately
> Sylvia Beach

I'm sorry I forgot to give you Bibi the other day.[11] I've been keeping it some time for you

---

Gertrude Stein and Alice B. Toklas Papers, Yale Collection of American Literature, Beinecke Rare Book and Manuscript Library, Yale University (manuscript)

* * *

53. To Gertrude Stein   August 19, 1920

> Hotel Regina
> Rapallo

Dear Miss Gertrude Stein,

I wanted so much to go around to see you before I left but had become more and more tied down since the Christian Science Monitor published their now famous article on my stores. And something in an account of them in the Publishers Weakly July 17th must have called the attention of publishers of Devotional works and pamphlets as they have started corresponding with me something awful. I have to have a special Folder (like in the American Red Cross) for their communications. A young lady in Los Angeles with 50 years experience in a Library, Juvenile Dept., sent me a 5 cent American stamp with offers to assist me.

This Publishers Weekly says that among the eminent patrons of Shakespeare and Company is Miss Gertrude Stein.

I wonder if you are spending the month of August in Paris. Mother made me come to Italy so I let the employees go for a month and

---

9. The "Old Doves" was Stein's nickname for the Théâtre du Vieux-Colombier.
10. Initials of "Old Doves."
11. "Bibi-la-Bibiste," an idiosyncratic work of poetry by Linossier. Beach gave a copy to Ezra Pound as well, who had it published in *The Little Review*.

everything will reopen September 2nd. Brentanos and Smiths will remain open I understand.

We had six hours of a terrible storm last night. My bathing-suit was out and I was afraid it would get struck.

Please give my love to Miss Toklas and accept my affectionate homage

Sylvia Beach

Gertrude Stein and Alice B. Toklas Papers, Yale Collection of American Literature, Beinecke Rare Book and Manuscript Library, Yale University (manuscript)

* * *

54. To Gertrude Stein   October 2, 1920

Dear Miss Gertrude Stein,

Valerie Larbaud[12] is in town and accepts with plaisir if you should happen to invite him to dine. He will also write up "Two Lives"[13] in the Nouvelle Revue Française.[14] You know Larbaud is what they call "very capricious" so perhaps you had best beware of inviting another Frenchman. To 9 out of 10 Larbaud would behave very morosely while Spanish men, Englishmen and South Americans only excite him pleasantly.

Please excuse my suggesting anything at all!

You probably are thinking "she's gotta nerve."
Yours

Sylvia Beach

Valerie Larbaud
71 rue Cardinal Lemoine

Gertrude Stein and Alice B. Toklas Papers, Yale Collection of American Literature, Beinecke Rare Book and Manuscript Library, Yale University (manuscript)

---

12. Valery Larbaud (1881–1957), French writer and translator. He supervised the French translation of *Ulysses* and was also known for his work in translating and popularizing the nineteenth-century British writer Samuel Butler (author of *Erewhon* and *The Way of All Flesh*). Larbaud's letters to Beach and Monnier have been published in France under the title *Lettres à Adrienne Monnier et à Sylvia Beach, 1919–1933* (1991).
13. A reference to Stein's *Three Lives*, which Larbaud considered translating into French.
14. Literary journal founded by André Gide in 1909.

* * *

55. To Alice B. Toklas   October 16, 1920

Dear Miss Toklas

If I had only waited a little longer! But the coal supply in the kitchen was getting almost too damp to burn and the Société Litteraire de France saw my Othella[15] and wanted her no matter how many kittens. I think they burn wood. So I placed her there at once. Its not an active business like mine and they play with and feed my cat all day. M. Le Grix comes and tells me—"she had a whole petit suisse for her tea today, liver tant-qu'elle-voudra for lunch and the usual bassin of milk fresh from the cow as soon as she felt like getting up in the morning."

Valerie Larbaud is not coming back till the 21st or 22nd, in time for the Butler Séance.

Miss Toklas dear, I wonder if you have finished the pair of tomes you drew at the A.d.L. a while ago. It seems some of the Bunnies[16] are anxious to have a turn at them, but if you're not finished them its all right.

> Yours gratefully,
> Sylvia Beach

Gertrude Stein and Alice B. Toklas Papers, Yale Collection of American Literature, Beinecke Rare Book and Manuscript Library, Yale University (manuscript)

* * *

56. To Alice B. Toklas   October 27, 1920

Dear Miss Taklass

A young Irish person in a green sweater & tie, and a good poet I believe—his name is Austin Clarke—asked me how he could find James Stephens if he was still in Paris.[17] I knew that you and Miss Stein were the

---

15. Beach's cat.

16. Beach referred to her patrons as "Bunnies" because the French word for *subscriber* is *abonné*.

17. Austin Clarke (1896–1974), Irish poet, playwright, and novelist.

only people that could boast of having des relations étroitès[18] with him so I'm taking the great liberty of asking you if you could spare James Stephens'[19] address if it isn't too much trouble. Please pardon me the trouble I'm putting you to and don't hesitate not to pay any attention if you're too busy—he's just a child.

Your affectionate

Sylvia Beach

Gertrude Stein and Alice B. Toklas Papers, Yale Collection of American Literature,
Beinecke Rare Book and Manuscript Library, Yale University (manuscript)

* * *

57. To Gertrude Stein   No date, 1921

Shakespeare and Company

8 rue Dupuytren, Paris (6e)

Dear Miss Gertrude Stein,

Would you let me bring around Mr Sherwood Anderson of Poor White and Winesburg Ohio to see you say tomorrow evening Friday? He is so anxious to know you for he says you have influenced him ever so much & that you stand as such a great master of words.[20]

Unless I hear from you saying NO I will take him to you after dinner tonight

Yours affectionately

Sylvia Beach

Thursday

Gertrude Stein and Alice B. Toklas Papers, Yale Collection of American Literature,
Beinecke Rare Book and Manuscript Library, Yale University (manuscript)

---

18. A close relationship.

19. James Stephens (1882–1950), Irish novelist and poet.

20. Anderson and Stein would become friends. Anderson wrote the foreword to *Geography and Plays* (1922), for which Stein felt grateful, and moved her to write "A Valentine to Sherwood Anderson," later retitled, "A Portrait of Sherwood Anderson." *Sherwood Anderson/ Gertrude Stein: Correspondence and Personal Essays*, ed. Ray Lewis White (Chapel Hill: U of North Carolina P, 1972), offers an interesting look at their developing relationship.

* * *

58. To Gertrude Stein   **No date, 1921**

Shakespeare and Company
8 rue Dupuytren

Dear Miss Gertrude Stein,

Will you pardon me if I bring Mr Sherwood Anderson & Co this evening instead of tomorrow!?
They are leaving town suddenly.

Yours with apologies
Sylvia Beach

Thursday

Gertrude Stein and Alice B. Toklas Papers, Yale Collection of American Literature, Beinecke Rare Book and Manuscript Library, Yale University (manuscript)

* * *

59. To Holly Beach   **April 16, 1921**

Paris

Dearest Holly,

This is a beautiful little Corona[21] that was given me by Mrs Gibbons that we met in Paris you remember. Mother was asking them in Princeton the price of Coronas and they up and guv me this one. Its almost new and they only gave it to me because they had another. I think it was what Mrs Michaelides would call "very preeecious" of the Gibbonses, don't you Holly.

Well Holly my preecious you were so fine to write me such an encouraging letter about Ulysses and subscribing to a copy and just like you it is! Its all owing to your help and publicity work for Shakespeare and Company that I've been able to make such a success of the thing! And

---

21. Typewriter.

YOU know it. And the Tribune sent around their Miss Rosemary Carr[22] to interview me for a write-up which will appear ere very long. Your Misters Scull and Bryson were in just yesterday and also Major Stuart[23] who has a new baby now and a little girl he claims.

I am sending you a bulletin so that you can make out and sign the order form on the last page. Doesn't it remind you of the A.R.C.[24] papers we had to sign such a lot of? But you don't have to tell your age and experience this time. Just tear off the order page and keep the rest with the portrait of our dear Mr Joyce.

I wonder whether you are in Florence now. Mother and Cyprian are going to move into a delightful apartment not far from here. The first of June is the date fixed. It is all furnished in squisite taste and has a piano and lift and bathroom and Lord knows what I guess for I've not seen it. And lucky they are.

Cyprian says to tell you that Mr Lane told her and Mother this morning that you were the most remarkable girl in This World and that you did work that would kill the average person which you were far removed from the type of. They went to the A.R.C. to ask if anyone wanted to share the nice apartment with them as there's an extra room and the expenses would be cut down. They are sure to find someone to fill the bill—in fact a lady is contracting arrangements with them now.

Sofia came in one day but I was not in; Cyprian was keeping the shop as she is so kind as to do for me whenever help is pending.

Holly do get my husband[25] and some other guys to subscribe to Ulysses! I am sending you a few extras copies of the bulletin with that view in view.

Sylvia Beach Papers, Manuscripts Division, Department of Rare Books
and Special Collections, Princeton University Library (manuscript)

---

22. Rosemary Carr (1898–1962) was a foreign correspondent who worked for the *Chicago Tribune* and other periodicals, as well as writing verse. In Paris she met and married the Pulitzer Prize–winning writer Stephen Vincent Benét (1898–1943).
23. Unidentified friends of Holly Beach. It is possible but unlikely that "Major Stuart" refers to Stuart Gilbert (1883–1969), a friend of Beach's and of James Joyce. He assisted in the first French translation of *Ulysses*, but was still serving as a judge in Burma when this letter was written.
24. American Red Cross.
25. Possibly a reference to Holly's husband, Frederic Dennis.

* * *

60. To Holly Beach   April 23, 1921

8, rue Dupuytren
Paris (VI)

Dearest Holly

Once more I have let a few gallons of water flow under thems bridge since writing to you. And such a lot to tell too. In the 1st place you sent up by the Ottensooser qells those delicious little chocolates—1 box to each of us! And you are a little chocolate ducky yourself . . a daacky! Then in the 2nd place you sent up those bijou calendars 1 to each and we drew lots and she drew the red copy, and myself the speckled. And Adrienne wishes she had one, a speckled, and Larbaud, a speckled.

Holly I am about to publish Ulysses of James Joyce. It will appear in October—a thousand copies—subscriptions only.[26] 150 for the cheapest, 250 sur verge d'arche—350 frs on Hollande paper 100 copies signed by the author.[27] What do you think of that Holly!? You had better come to Paris soon to look after things don't you think so. And those Ottensoosers said you spoke of not coming till the fall . . . what does that mean?

Ulysses is going to make my place famous. Already the publicity is beginning and swarms of people visit the shop on hearing the news. I'm getting out a bulletin announcing the publication in October of the book and you will soon receive one. All American & Eng. subscriptions are to be sent to me and if all goes well I hope to make money out of it, not only for Joyce but for me. Aren't you excited!

Most business houses in Paris are facing failure at present but Shakespeare and Company is taking in more every day. Today we made 236 frs. Cyprian helps me to cope with the crowds and with the work on Ulysses. I don't know what I would have done without her. Adrienne helps with publishing details in which I am perfectly inexperienced, and everyone is interested in subscribing to Ulysses and in bringing me names of likely subscribers. Marjorie Reed is going to give me a write-up in the New

---

26. Beach's prediction that *Ulysses* would appear in October 1921 proved optimistic. It did not come out until Joyce's fortieth birthday, February 2, 1922. In order to fund the publication of the novel, Beach sold advance copies to Joyce's admirers, as well as her own family and friends.

27. To maximize her profits while keeping the volume accessible, Beach decided on an escalating scale of prices to correspond with increasingly luxurious volumes.

York Sunday Herald with a sketch of Joyce and me in the shop and other publicity is promised. I'm sending a copy of the London Observer with a word by Sisley Huddleston[28] on Ulysses.

Well loads of love Holly dear to you and your bear[29]

from your loving sister Sylvia

Sylvia Beach Papers, Manuscripts Division, Department of Rare Books and Special Collections, Princeton University Library (manuscript)

* * *

61. To Marion Peter   May 23, 1921

Dearest Marion,

Mother has just showed me the nice letter you wrote her not long ago about the baby's dress. I'm glad you got it before the girls were quite grown-up and married which I feared they would be if mother & Cyprian put off much longer the sending of it.[30] You know I got it over a year ago here . . . yes indeed I did.

Your father and his wife came to see me and my shop several times and by this time you must have heard all about it from them. Norman dropped in also not long ago. I have wanted to write you all about my shop ever since I opened it but I never had the time to write even to my family. But I think of you all the time and if there anything in this wireless business you must have got many a message from me. Little old Sylvia's picture is up in the shop and she is the mascot that has brought me any amount of luck. Your father described her and Phyllis to me to the best of a man's ability but to see them and you in flesh and blood . . . en chair et en os[31] . . . would be better still. I wish I could fly to Chicago and see you all in your nice new house!

---

28. Sisley Huddleston (1883–1952) was a British journalist living in France. During the Second World War, he became a Vichy sympathizer who published in collaborationist journals and promoted Marshal Pétain.

29. References to the "bear" are a recurring private joke in Beach's letters to her sister.

30. Marion Peter had two daughters, one of them named Sylvia to commemorate her friendship with Beach. Sylvia Peter (later Preston) worked as an assistant at Shakespeare and Company in the 1930s.

31. "In flesh and bone."

Mother and Cyprian are in splendid spirits over being in Paris once more. They are taking an apartment for the summer and Cyprian is going to do something in the moving picture line soon.

My shop is a great success and self supporting and all that sort of thing and just think I am publishing a book now. Ulysses by James Joyce, the greatest book and author of the age. . . . ! You probably saw in the papers the uproar caused by the trial of the Editors of the Little Review for printing some of Ulysses in it, and how they were fined $100 and their thumb prints taken.[32] Nine stenographers gave up the typing of the last episode here in Paris and a gentleman from the British Embassy burned a dozen pages . . . he threw 'em into the fire in a rage.[33] Ulysses is a masterpiece and one day it will be ranked among the classics in English literature. Joyce is in Paris and I told him I would publish his book, after the publisher in New York[34] threw up the job in a fright.

Excuse such a long letter Marion, and write me one day soon wont you?!

> Much love from
> Sylvia

Sylvia Beach Papers, Manuscripts Division, Department of Rare Books and Special Collections, Princeton University Library (manuscript)

* * *

---

32. It was Ezra Pound, who served as a foreign editor for *The Little Review*, who first approached James Joyce about serializing *Ulysses* there. The editors referred to in this letter are Margaret Anderson (1886–1973) and Jane Heap (1883–1964). Like Beach, Anderson and Heap were influential American promoters of literary modernism. Their *Little Review* published pieces by authors including Ernest Hemingway, T. S. Eliot, Hart Crane, Ezra Pound, Amy Lowell, Gertrude Stein, and William Carlos Williams, as well as introducing works by French writers including André Breton and Jean Cocteau. After the trial of *Ulysses*, Heap took over the leadership of the magazine from Anderson.

33. Joyce's biographer Richard Ellmann relates that after various typists had given up on *Ulysses*, Beach and Joyce "found a Mrs. Harrison, whose husband had a post at the British Embassy. She made good progress until on April 8 her husband glanced at the manuscript, and, scandalized, threw it into the fire. She rushed to tell Joyce that she had hidden most of it, and surreptitiously managed to convey it to him a few days later. The missing pages had to be rewritten with the aid of a Photostat of an earlier draft" (*James Joyce* 508).

34. The New York publisher who declined the manuscript in the wake of *The Little Review* trial was B. W. Huebsch.

62. To Holly Beach   September 22, 1921

Dearest Holly,

I haven't written to you for so long and its an unworthy bloodsucking sister I am in every way for I'm going to ask you if you would be long-suffering enough to forgive me for asking you to lend me a thousand francs!!! My carpentry bill will be handed in any day now and mother who was going to lend me all the money for my moving expenses had to stop off in the midst, having had a great deal of expense getting Cyprian equipped as a rising star. She squeezed out enough for three weeks vacation I took down at Hyères[35] after which she drew in her horns. I kept my shop open with a nice Greek girl[36] to keep it and she took in money, but I had to pay her of course. My business is going well and I could tackle the carpenter bill if I didn't have to put every single centime aside to pay the printer of Ulysses five thousand francs on the 1st of December.[37] He requires it and naturally the cheques from subscribers will not arrive in time for that first payment. I am making an average of 100 [fr] a day in the shop but have to keep paying pounds to London publishers out of that, and my living expenses which I try to make as low as possible. If you could lend me a thousand I would start to pay you back each month after January all the fortune I owe you. I shall be sure to take in about 4000 [fr] a month this winter. My business has increased since I moved and it was a good move in every way.[38] But I've had to pay a good many of the moving expenses. Holly dear you must not hesitate to refuse if you cant afford to loan me anything. You have a right to turn with the "poorest sort of a worm" . . "Hell's Bells"! as Uncle Tom would exclaim.

You will soon meet Marie Draper and her husband Garvin Hodson I hope. They have just left for Italy and are going to spend the winter in Florence. She is an angel you will not fail to notice.

---

35. In the 1920s the town of Hyères in southern Provence was a resort attracting a glamorous clientele of celebrities, literary figures, and wealthy expatriates.

36. Two Greek women, Myrsine and Helene Moschos, worked as assistants at Shakespeare and Company. In 1932, Myrsine Moschos was hired by the Joyce family to care for Lucia Joyce, and according to Lucia Joyce's biographer Carol Loeb Shloss, she became Lucia Joyce's lover. For more details of this relationship, see Shloss, *Lucia Joyce: To Dance in the Wake*.

37. The French printer Maurice Darantière brought out *Ulysses* in collaboration with Shakespeare and Company (see also note 55).

38. Beach relocated her shop from rue Dupuytren to rue de l'Odéon in order to be closer to Adrienne Monnier's French-language bookstore, La Maison des Amis des Livres.

Holly what did you take in the way of a vacation? I got your postcard from Milan when you were looking up the Cathedral and I hope you found it.

What a splendid time I had at Hyères and bathing all day and sun-baked when I came back. Adrienne learned to swim and in fact wasn't able to sink owing to her splendid physique. We visited Marseilles and viewed the red light district where all the ladies were on their door steps in a state of nudity almost more than the law allowed I should think. They had on the thinnest shortest kind of chemises and high heeled slippers—no drawers no nothing and doing high kicks at that. Would you not like to see it!!?

Uncle Tom was so disappointed not to see you! We kept saying if only Holly were here. He was quite breathless to find that his nieces were doing such a lot of stunts. He is the nicest old thing and funny as ever. Douglas is coming up for a day soon. When are you making us another visit? How is your poor dumb-bear?

Lots & lots of love from
Sylvia

Sylvia Beach Papers, Manuscripts Division, Department of Rare Books and Special Collections, Princeton University Library (manuscript)

* * *

63. To Holly Beach   October 24, 1921

Dearest Holly,

You'll excuse me if I do this on the machine, won't you, but I have so many letters "all waiting in a row" to be answered and always someone interrupting me every instant that . . . .

You received, Holly, the enclosed post-card and I tried my best like Stella Kinnamon to read it but it was a hard struggle! The picture can be looked at from any angle.

Holly dear I shan't forget your sending me all that money and some day you are going to get an awful shock when you see me un-lending it again to its owner, ha ha! I hope you are coming to Paris in Nov. won't that be fun! Douglas[39] is in town and living at a pension and learning French,

---

39. Beach's cousin Douglas Orbison.

Holly. Cyprian did some film in the city the other day and there were crowds of star-gazers you may believe. There was a letter from Father tied up in the concierge's loge yesterday at Mother's house; you could see it through the glass door which was locked and she away somewhere. Finally Mother followed by the cat came down and dish-covered the keys under the sch . . . . . . mat and we released Father's words and read 'em.

Holly, they're coming in and I must stop.

> So, very much love from your loving
> Sylvia

---

*Sylvia Beach Papers, Manuscripts Division, Department of Rare Books
and Special Collections, Princeton University Library (typescript)*

* * *

64. To Alfred Kreymborg[40]   October 31, 1921

> B. Rue Dupuytren
> La Rue de L'Odeon
> Paris (VI)

Dear Mr. Kreymborg,

All the BROOMS you sent me are sold and please send me 6 more copies as soon as you receive this if you would be so kind. I do not know whether you sent a bill with the last set. I am afraid you did and that it has got mislaid, but if you will send me the bill for the 12 copies with the next ones you send me I will send a draft promptly.

> Yours with apologies and
> kindest regards,
> Sylvia Beach

---

*Broom Collection (Loeb), Manuscripts Division, Department of Rare Books
and Special Collections, Princeton University Library (typescript)*

---

40. Alfred Kreymborg, American writer and editor (1883–1966). He published the first Imagist poems of Pound in his journal *The Globe*. He came to Paris in 1921 to co-edit the short-lived review *Broom* with Harold Loeb. His autobiography, *Troubadour*, was published in New York in 1925.

* * *

65. To Waldo Frank[41] November 14, 1921

Dear Waldo Frank,

Thank you very very much for sending me The Dark Mother![42] and Adrienne Monnier was much pleased with her copy and the dédicace[43] which she declared très épatant[44] or words to that effect! I have just finished reading your book and it interests me tremendously. Nothing else in modern American or English literature has interested me half as much and I am glad that the author of The Dark Mother counts me among his friends and allies!

I am sending you the picture of Joyce & Co which has been waiting so long for you.

Yours very sincerely
Sylvia Beach

Waldo Frank Papers, Rare Book and Manuscript Library,
University of Pennsylvania (typescript)

* * *

66. To Harriet Weaver[45] June 6, 1922

12, Rue de l'Odéon
Paris (VIE)
June 6th 1922

Dear Miss Weaver,

It was so kind of you to send me a copy of the "Sunday Express" containing James Douglas' attack on "Ulysses" and all those mess writings.[46]

---

41. Waldo Frank (1889–1967), New Jersey–born novelist and social activist.
42. Frank's novel, published by Boni and Liveright in 1920.
43. Dedication.
44. "Very impressive."
45. Harriet Shaw Weaver (1876–1961), Joyce's major benefactor, editor of *The Egoist*, and an activist for causes including women's suffrage and communism.
46. James Douglas's negative review of *Ulysses* ("Beauty—and the Beast") appeared in the Dublin *Sunday Express* on May 28, 1922.

I took them at once to Mr. Joyce and read them to him as he is always impatient to hear of any articles. He gets very much depressed and bored lying in bed and Douglas' article quite made him forget the pain in his eyes for the moment but he seems to be somewhat too excited at present. I think it is good for him to have something to think of that takes him out of himself however. The doctor says that his eyes are better and that he is suffering mostly from his nerves now.

Mr. Joyce asked me to send you the letter and post card enclosed to ask you to be so kind as to send a copy of "Exiles" by registered post to the address on the post card (Mr. Claud W. Sykes[47]) and to reply to "Two Worlds" one or two words to the effect that he is unable to accept this proposition.[48] (It would be curious to see how they expect to bring out "Ulysses" in a number of their magazine!)

Also would it be too much trouble for you to send Mr. Joyce 2 extra copies of the Sunday Express of May 28th besides those you have already sent, and anything more that Mr. Douglas has to say about "Ulysses"?

I am sending you 3 copies of the edition at Fr 350 as you so kindly offered to dispose of them if you have enquiries. The other two editions are now sold out thanks to all the publicity given the book by Mr. Douglas and his confreres.

> Once more with many thanks and with kindest regards
> Yours sincerely
> Sylvia Beach

Harriet Weaver Shaw Papers, British Library (Manuscripts 57345–57352)

* * *

67. **To Harriet Weaver** June 8, 1922

12, Rue de l'Odéon
Paris (VIE)
June 8th 1922

Dear Miss Weaver,

Pardon me for not writing to you sooner. I have been so busy and so upset for the last week. "Ulysses" is sold out and Mr. Joyce is begin-

---

47. Claud W. Sykes (1883–?), American actor, translator, and friend of Joyce.
48. *Two Worlds* was a literary magazine published by Samuel Roth (1893–1974); it was later to reprint bowdlerized excerpts from *Ulysses* without Joyce's permission. In 1927 Beach issued an international protest against Roth.

ning to recover from his dreadful attack. Dr. Borsch's[49] treatment has obtained the best of results; the tension of the eye has been reduced to almost normal and Mr. Joyce has suffered very little during the last two days. After he is fully recovered from this attack we must see whether something cannot be done to prevent other attacks in the future. He wants to make a desperate effort to avoid the risks incurred by such a serious operation. Dr. Morax[50] has an enormous reputation as a surgeon here an he could scarcely wait until he could get his knife into his patient's eye, particularly as he believes this is the only cure for these cases. Dr. Borsch on the other hand seems to be very slow to adopt such drastic measures and has great faith in the results obtained by improving the general health of his patients. I think that possibly if Mr. Joyce had followed patiently the treatment Dr. Borsch had prescribed for him since last summer and had been able to adopt a more comfortable and wholesome mode of living this attack of iritis might have been avoided. He is such a terribly nervous, sensitive man that he and his family ought to live in a place where they have plenty of room to spread out and where Mr. Joyce could have perfect quiet for his work. All this past year when he was finishing "Ulysses" and quite over strung with the adventures attending the publishing of his book he was sharing a noisy hotel room with his wife and daughter and obliged to go out to restaurants for every one of his meals. I tried my best to find an apartment for the Joyces but as they required six rooms at least and as Mr. Joyce insisted on being in the Odéon quarter or very near it, there was nothing that could be done. There is never an apartment to be had in this quarter and excepting some impossible streets far from the center there is nothing on the entire Left Bank. Mr. Joyce wished to be in Paris as he would not absent himself for a minute while his book was coming out an also his family had begun to make friends here and dreaded the transplanting to a new place after having moved so many times already. Mr. Joyce himself has many friends in Paris. The French writers, contrary to their rather narrow traditions in regard to foreigners, have received him with open arms and have the greatest admiration for him. However something must be arranged to establish the Joyce family comfortably as soon as possible, perhaps in London

---

49. Dr. Louis Borsch, an American eye doctor working in Paris. Beach wrote that he "had been very kind when I once consulted him at the little clinic he ran on the Left Bank for students and working people. He listened very kindly . . . to the account I gave him of Joyce's woeful situation" (*Shakespeare and Company* 67). Joyce was pleased that Borsch agreed with him that his eye should not be operated on during an attack of iritis.
50. Dr. Victor Morax (1866–1935), French ophthalmologist who treated Joyce for iritis.

as Mr. Schiff spoke as if the pattern of lodgings there were not nearly as difficult as in Paris. I know it is not my business but in strict confidence I would like to tell you that I think Mr. Joyce's son George ought to begin at once to learn some profession or business so that he will not be a burden on his father all his life. He is seventeen and owing to the abnormal existence his family has led, has had no training of any kind to enable him to earn his living one day. George is a fine big fellow but he has nothing to do all the time but loaf. (He teaches Italian one hour a week.) Of course this is not my affair and I would not like Mr. Joyce to know that I have written to you about it. But it seems to me that if the problem of George were solved it would be a great relief to him. He is so absorbed by his work that he is quite unable to cope with any such situation. That's why I am consulting you, Mr. Joyce's best friend, about this matter.

Thank you for your letter enclosing Mr. Thompson's and telling about the specialists in London, also thank you for the copies of the New York Times Book Review,[51] one of which I gave to Mr. Joyce. He seems to be disappointed that the writers in England who understand his books and are qualified to review "Ulysses" adequately have not yet ventured their opinion on the subject.

> With apologies for this long letter
> And with kindest regards
> Yours very sincerely
> Sylvia Beach

Mr. Joyce asked me to tell you that it will be all right about his poems in Mr. Davie's anthology. Will you kindly arrange the matter. S.B.

Harriet Shaw Weaver Papers, British Library (Manuscripts 57345–57352)

* * *

---

51. "James Joyce's Amazing Chronicle" by Dr. Joseph Collins appeared in the *New York Times Book Review* on May 28, 1922.

68. To Harriet Weaver   June 11, 1922

12, Rue de l'Odéon
Paris (VIE)
June 11th 1922

Dear Miss Weaver,

Mr. Joyce has asked me to write and thank you for all the trouble you
have been taking for him and to tell you about what has been happening.
I sent wires to you and to Mr. Schiff[52] last night as by the time we got
Mr. Joyce home after the visit to the doctor it was very late.

When Mr. Joyce began to have this attack (three weeks ago tomorrow) he went to Dr. Morax. When Mr. Morax had seen him twice he
told him to remain at home and he sent his assistant to attend him
every day. Last week the assistant told Mr. Joyce that the iritis was disappearing rapidly and that the pain he was suffering from was caused
by a group of cilary nerves. On Thursday evening he told Mr. Joyce
that he was practically cured and could get up and go out the following
day. On Friday morning at eight o'clock Dr. Morax came and after an
examination of the eye he and the assistant announced that an iridectomy for glaucoma must be performed at once. It was a terrible shock
to Mr. Joyce; he was quite unprepared for it having been told by the
assistant only the night before that he was quite well again. He is unable to see to read or write with his right eye which was operated upon
in Zurich and he was in great despair to find suddenly that the left eye
was to operated upon, leaving him perhaps blind. Mr. Joyce managed to
arrange a postponement for the operation although Dr. Morax had declared at first that it must be performed immediately, and after receiving the wire from you and Mr. Schiff advising him to get the opinion of
other Paris specialists he arranged to consult Dr. Borsch yesterday. Dr.
Borsch, although rather noncommittal on the subject of an operation,
probably on account of professional reasons, at least told Mr. Joyce that
an operation was not urgently required the eye having reacted to the
electric [test] and to the drops he had put in. He said he must return on
Monday, prescribing meanwhile a treatment of ice-cold applications,
purges and a medicine to purify the blood. Mr. Joyce begun to follow

---

52. Probably Sydney Schiff (1868–1944), British author and translator who also published
under the pseudonym Stephen Hudson.

the treatment at once and thanks to a narcotic that Dr. Borsch gave him he was able to get some sleep although hitherto narcotics have had no effect on him. He seems to be suffering a little less today. I will let you know the result of the visit to Dr. Borsch tomorrow afternoon. It is to take place at four o'clock.

As regards Dr. Thompson[53] Mr. Joyce asked me to say to you that if Dr. Borsch is able to bring him through this attack without an operation having to be performed he would like to go afterward to London to consult the best specialist there. He wishes to do everything to find out whether there is not some remedy other than an operation that would cure him of his trouble. Of course the oculists claim that an iridectomy if performed in time saves the eyesight but it is not possible to know before operating what state Mr. Joyce's eye is in. Also as he says it stands to reason that this operation which consists of removing a piece of the iris must endanger the eyesight more or less. Dr. Morax has a great reputation as a surgeon and from his viewpoint the operation is inevitable with this disease and the longer it is delayed the more difficult the operation and the less favorable the result. Whereas I think Dr. Borsch believes in curing these cases by treatment and by eliminating the poison from the system.

This is a long letter dear Miss Weaver and with my ignorance of these technical things I do not succeed in making them very clear. But Mr. Joyce is so anxious for you to know all about the matter. He is deeply grateful for all you have done and regrets all the trouble he has been putting you to. He wishes to thank Mr. Schiff for his kindness also. These have been very anxious days and it terrible to see Mr. Joyce's despair at the thought that he is threatened with the loss of his eyesight and of how much depends the outcome of all this.

> With the kindest regards
> Yours very sincerely
> Sylvia Beach

At Mr. Joyce's request I am sending you the Mercure de France containing Ezra Pound's article on "Ulysses."[54]

Harriet Shaw Weaver Papers, British Library (Manuscripts 57345–57352)

53. Dr. Thompson: an unknown person, but possibly one of the physicians consulted.
54. Pound's essay "James Joyce et Pécuchet" appeared in the *Mercure de France* in June 1922.

* * *

69. To Harriet Weaver   **June 26, 1922**

12, Rue de l'Odéon
Paris (VIE)
June 26th 1922

Dear Miss Weaver,

Thank you so much for getting such a good price for the 3 copies of "Ulysses"! I have just received your letter enclosing a draft for Frs. 1128, 60. If I had not felt that it would be trespassing on your kindness I would have sent you more copies before the edition was sold out. It went off so suddenly that I scarcely realized how scarce it was getting. I did not hold back any copies for speculation for fear that the public might misinterpret it, but Adrienne Monnier ("Le Maison des Amis des Livres", 7, rue de l'Odéon) took over a number and is beginning to sell them at Fr 500 (edition at Fr 150) and will give the proceeds to Mr. Joyce. Perhaps you will give that address to people who inquire where they can obtain "Ulysses". I always tell them that Adrienne Monnier among other book-sellers subscribed for a good many copies and might have some left.

I think it was very dreadful of me to write to you about the Joyce family problems when you are too far away to do anything but worry about them. Please forgive me and don't think of them any more. As you say, you will have to see Mr. Joyce before doing anything and you will perhaps be able to make some good suggestions when he goes to London which he will no doubt do as soon as he is better. He tells me that he wired you last night about the relapse he is having. He is suffering very much again and the doctor does not seem to be able to give him anything to stop the pain. However he says there is no tension which means that an operation is not necessary for the present. I don't know of anything to be done except to have patience and wait for this attack to run its course. It is a great strain on him, five weeks of such suffering.

I am very glad to hear that you are beginning to plan the publishing of "Ulysses" and perhaps a private edition would be sagest. Persons like James Douglas might be able to make lots of trouble if an ordinary edition came out. Is a privately issued book never suppressed? I would suggest that you make all arrangements directly with Darantiere[55] my printer. He knows English very well himself if his printers do not and I think a correspondence between you in English would force him to be much less evasive and slippery. He is such a Jesuit that you will have to make him sign papers with official stamps promising to stick to his final estimate to a penny and to supply the exact number of copies you arrange to have printed—otherwise he will find subtle reasons for evavasions. He has kept the impressions for the entire volume—that is the "empreintes" but the lead type for a certain number of the first sheets was never made. The rest of the book all exists in lead type and can be printed from it as soon as the lead is "coulé" into the "empreintes" of the first sheets.

> With kindest regards
> And many thanks
> Yours very sincerely
> Sylvia Beach

Harriet Shaw Weaver Papers, British Library (Manuscripts 57345–57352)

✳ ✳ ✳

70. To Harriet Weaver   **July 9, 1922**

> 12, Rue de l'Odéon
> Paris (VIE)
> July 9th 1922

Dear Miss Weaver,

Thank you so much for the trouble you took to copy F. M. Hueffer's article in the Yale Review![56] Mr. Joyce has just received a copy of the review from the editor who says he will send more and I am writing to him to send one to you. Larbaud also enclosed the article in a letter which I received yesterday from Gensa. I don't know how he got it down

---

55. Maurice Darantière (1882–1962), Dijon-based publisher of *Ulysses*. Beach was attracted to hire Darantière because of his firm's publication of Joris-Karl Huysmans and other nineteenth-century French writers.
56. "A Haughty and Proud Generation" by Ford Madox Hueffer (Ford Madox Ford) appeared in the *Yale Review* in July 1922.

there. It was very kind of you to send copies of the New York Times Book Review and the Tribune. They came yesterday and I took them around to Mr. Joyce and read Padraic Colum's[57] article to him which he liked very much. He had already seen, or rather heard Ernest Boyd's.[58] These articles and your letters always liven up his dull existence in the dark room where he lies all day. His eye is clearing up gradually and the pain is not nearly so great now but he has not been able to go out yet except to the doctor's. Pound took a young doctor, a friend of his, to see Mr. Joyce yesterday. He thinks he can get at the cause of the trouble and eliminate the rheumatism from his system. He is very much interested in the case and when this attack passes off he is going to take Mr. Joyce in hand, have an X ray taken of his teeth to see whether there are abscesses and stimulate his thyroid glands or some such thing (he has a thyroid gland theory). I don't believe much in doctors except for setting broken bones and calming acute attacks of maladies. I think that plenty of sleep, food, work and out door exercise and perhaps to see one's family as little as possible is the only way to be healthy. But if this doctor can make Mr. Joyce well, so much the better.

You asked whether the "empreintes" were what English printers call plates. The "empreintes" are made by placing sheets of a sort of paper over the original type. A white powder is sprinkled over the sheets of paper which are hammered until they take the impress of the type when they are then removed and become hard as stone and can be preserved indefinitely. The type for reprinting a book is made by pouring melted lead into the "empreintes". The book is printed from the plates of lead type thus made. Darantiere has preserved the "empreintes" for the entire "Ulysses" and the lead type was made for all but the first part of the book and this can be done easily when the reprinting is begun. The reasons why the lead type for the beginning of "Ulysses" was never made are too subtle for any but the labyrinthine mind of a Darantiere to grasp.

Mr. Wyndham Lewis brought me 12 copies of Tyro No 2 I think.[59] Will you kindly let me know how much I owe you for them. As I have

57. Padraic Colum (1881–1972), Irish writer and friend of Joyce. His article "With James Joyce in Ireland" appeared in the *New York Times Book Review* on July 11, 1922.

58. Ernest Boyd (1887–1946), American literary critic and translator. His article "The Expressionism of James Joyce" appeared in the *New York Tribune* on May 28, 1922.

59. Wyndham Lewis (1882–1957), modernist painter and novelist. *The Tyro: A Review of the Arts of Painting, Sculpture and Design* was a short-lived periodical edited by Lewis; it lasted only two issues.

not sold "Explorations"[60] yet may I deduct 2–5–0 from the bill which you enclosed?

> With kindest regards
> Yours very sincerely
> Sylvia Beach

Harriet Shaw Weaver Papers, British Library (Manuscripts 57345–57352)

* * *

71. To Harriet Weaver   **July 15, 1922**

> 12, Rue de l'Odéon
> Paris (6E)
> July 15th 1922

Dear Miss Weaver,

Will you kindly send me through Hachette[61] "A Portrait of the Artist" and "Dubliners" a dozen of each.

Mr. Joyce is beginning to recover now I hope; he was feeling so much better yesterday when I called to see him and was talking very cheerfully and eating 2 mutton chops. Until now his improvement has been so gradual that it was almost imperceptible and after two months of pain he was getting discouraged.

> With kindest regards
> Yours very sincerely
> Sylvia Beach

Harriet Shaw Weaver Papers, British Library (Manuscripts 57345–57352)

* * *

---

60. *Explorations* was a book of poems by Robert McAlmon (1896–1956) published in 1921 by the Egoist Press.

61. Hachette Livre, a major French publishing house first established in 1853 as a chain of railway bookstores.

72. To Marion Peter   **August 7, 1922**

Dearest Marion,

I wouldn't dare to ask the following favour except from a very great friend such as you are. I'm in a grave predicament from which you only can extricate me. This is the situation—I got all the copies of "Ulysses" to the subscribers (in all states except New York) through the post without any trouble.[62] But the subscribers in New York are still waiting for their copies as I haven't dared to send them openly from Paris right into the jaws of the Summer S.P.V. monster. A friend in Canada[63] is smuggling in most of the copies for New York—those in the 150 franc edition; that leaves 10 of the more expensive ones which I am entrusting to you. Would you be an angel Marion dear and when they reach you by registered post stick labels over your address and send them on by <u>registered</u> <u>post</u> to New York? I know it is a great deal to ask of you and I do hope you will forgive me for giving you all this trouble! The trouble will be only in connection with the labels and posting the packages as sending them direct to you will prevent the authorities from knowing of their existence. You will receive 6 copies at 250 frs of which 1 is for Joseph Liepold, 318 West 20th Street, New York City and 5 for The Sunwise Turn, 51, East 44th Street New York; and 4 copies at 350 frs of which 1 is for Joseph Liepold and 3 for The Sunrise Turn

There will be no need to open the packages to find out which are which— the copies at 350 frs are more expensive because they are on Dutch hand-made paper and are signed by the author but they are <u>smaller</u> than the vergé d'arches at 250 frs. Therefore to Joseph Liepold, 318 West 20th Street
  1 larger package (so that there will be no mistake I will mark the smaller ones
    A. Monnier
  The large ones <u>Adrienne Monnier</u>
  1 smaller"
      To Sunrise Turn, 51, East 44th Street
          5 larger packages
          3 smaller ""

---

62. Because *Ulysses* had been banned in the United States, Beach had to smuggle in copies to the book's American subscribers.
63. The Canadian transporters of *Ulysses* were friends of Ernest Hemingway from Toronto.

I enclose the labels. All you have to do is stick them over the ones addressed to you (covering the Paris address on the paper) and mail them registered. Also, I enclose a cheque for the postage, $10 and you must be sure and let me know if its not enough. The book is 1–1 overweight here but they take it if the package is marked <u>Un Livre</u>[64]

I don't know whether that will be at home.

With apologies for my colossal nerve and very much love Marion dear

yours as ever Sylvia

Sylvia Beach Papers, Manuscripts Division, Department of Rare Books and Special Collections, Princeton University Library (manuscript)

* * *

73. **To Marion Peter**   **September 19, 1922**

Dearest Marion,

Your letter has just arrived and you say that the first 6 copies came through all right but that you will have to clear the 2 next ones at the Customs. O Marion I am distressed to think of so much trouble I am putting you to! With all you have to do at home taking care of babies and giving singing lessons besides—I know it is criminal of me to have asked it of you! Will you ever forgive me?! It ought to be forbidden by law to take such advantage of a friend; if you feel like prosecuting you must do so for I deserve it.

Mr Joseph Liepold's other copy will be sent to him from Canada; it is one in the ordinary 150 franc edition and those copies are being smuggled in by a friend who will then forward them to subscribers in New York State. I sent the de Luxe ones to you as I was afraid to entrust such valuable ones to the smuggler. Even the copies at 150 f are now selling for <u>1,000</u> francs here now and one of them brought £40 (<u>2,400</u> frs) in London the other day. The signed copies on Dutch paper will be worth a lot some day as there were only 100 of them made.

I haven't seen Blanche since I got back from Savoie where I spent three weeks, but I saw her several times just before leaving. She looked

---

64. "A Book."

very well and happy. When are you coming over, Marion? I would love to see you and the two little girls and to make your husband's acquaintance.

Thank you a thousand times for all the trouble you are taking for me!!! with very best love

Yours as ever

Sylvia

Sylvia Beach Papers, Manuscripts Division, Department of Rare Books and Special Collections, Princeton University Library (manuscript)

* * *

74. To Harold Loeb[65]   February 22, 1923

Dear Mr. Loeb,

I received your letter of the 14th and that of the 16th and no doubt if my copies were addressed to my former shop in the Rue Dupuytren the post office returned some and lost a great part of them. Since I saw you on Dec. 30 I have only received 2 copies of BROOM, the Jan. number. An invoice was sent me in January for 10 copies and this month an invoice for 10 copies so there are 18 copies missing besides those of the December number which you say you shipped me. Also on going over my books I see that the account which you made out in my shop shows great discrepancies. My assistant has noted on the enclosed sheet that whereas you state that I had received 175 copies in all, the total number which I received was 136, 70 of which are still on hand as you noted and 66 were sold. I paid you Frs.472 counting the sum I handed you in the shop and remittances I sent you in Rome, when I owed you Frs.297 only. Therefore, I now have to my credit Frs. 175,50. I should have given you a clear statement of all this instead of leaving you to struggle with the account alone and single-handed, but you will remember that there was so much going on in my shop at the time and I was so much occupied that I had to leave the matter of straightening up our account entirely to you. We have now gone over my books very carefully and the enclosed is

---

65. Harold Loeb (1891–1974), American; Alfred Kreymborg's co-editor of *Broom*. He was a model for the character Robert Cohn in Hemingway's *The Sun Also Rises*.

the exact record of copies received and those sold. I am sorry to give you this extra trouble and in future will be more careful.

        With kind regards,

        Yours sincerely,

            Sylvia Beach

Broom Collection (Loeb), Manuscripts Division, Department of Rare Books and Special Collections, Princeton University Library (manuscript)

❋ ❋ ❋

75. To Marion Peter   May 29, 1923

Dearest Marion,

Excuse me for typing this. I always try to write to my friends by hand but I see that the only way to get off a letter to you at once is to make such a noise with this machine that people will leave me alone to finish what they think must be some business correspondence. Marion, if you knew how I never get a minute until late in the evening when I am quite too "abrutie"[66] to think of anything! It was disgusting of me all the same not to write you a Christmas letter explaining about the present I was sending you. Mrs. Heyworth Campbell[67] whose husband is on Vogue was so kind as to offer to take home the garment and it was all arranged in a sudden rush—I had about one minute to get you something and to give it to her and I never heard from her afterwards, nor she from me, nor you from me nor her!!!!!!!!!!!!

I'm very glad you got the nightgown safely and hope it fits you and that you don't mind the color. What a pity you had the trouble of writing to Vogue about it. I am so sorry. Please forgive me, Marion dear. Yes, I see everything I mean one but you. Your father has often been in my shop and has told me all about your doings and was very patient when I made him describe over and over again just what little Sylvia looks like and behaves like. Also I saw not long ago your nice pianist friend who was on her way to Milan I think. Of course Blanche I used to see also when she

---

66. *Abrutie:* Moronic.

67. Heyworth Campbell was an art director for *Vogue, Vanity Fair*, and *House and Garden*. His wife was Jacquelin Campbell.

was in Paris. You will have to try to get over here soon. You must be very much tied down with the children, and perhaps your husband cant get away long enough to come to Europe.

Marion, you were such an angel to take all that trouble bootlegging for me! As for the two copies that were confiscated, it was a miracle they were not all taken. 500 copies of the 2nd edition which appeared in October were seized in the States and the same number were destroyed in England about two months ago by the enlightened (?) authorities. What a dark age we are living in and what a privilege to behold the spectacle of ignorant men solemnly deciding whether the work of some great writer is suitable for the public to read or not!

How is your voice? What has become of Charles Clark? I went with Joyce and his wife and son one night to hear John McCormack sing.[68] He and Joyce are old friends. He sang beautifully but it's a pity he doesn't keep away from the subject of that Old Rose of Summer. I went to the Ballet Suedois[69] and there was Ganna Walska in a box.[70] Oh la-oh-la oh la.

I am kept very busy with my little shop from 9 in the morning till about 8 at night but its an interesting life. The interesting people that come in make up for the raft of "vieux chameaux"[71] that make a business of pestering the life out of you.

Did you know that my father had resigned from his church?[72] The congregation has made him pastor emeritus so that he will have a little salary to live on and not be obliged to work any more. He was always such a hard worker; he even preached in the summer when he was supposed to be on his vacation. Mother is getting ready to move out of the

---

68. Irish tenor John McCormack (1884–1945) was the first singer to record the First World War hit "It's a Long Way to Tipperary," and he was well known for his versions of Thomas Moore's verse, including "The Harp That Once Through Tara's Halls" and "The Last Rose of Summer." A nationalist singer associated with the Irish Home Rule movement, McCormack first met Joyce in Ireland when Joyce was considering a singing career of his own.

69. The Ballets Suédois was Sweden's answer to the Ballets Russes. The company, formed by Rolf de Maré and led by Jean Börlin, combined classical dance with expressionist techniques. The company commissioned scores and sets from Parisian artists including Jean Cocteau and Fernand Léger. Perhaps Beach saw their 1923 work *Within the Quota*: conceived by Gerald and Sara Murphy and with a score by Cole Porter, *Within the Quota* tells the story of a Swedish immigrant's arrival in New York.

70. Opera singer Ganna Walska (1887–1984), born Hanna Puacz in Brest-Litovsk, Poland. For more details, see Walska's memoir *Always Room at the Top*. Lotusland, Walska's garden estate in Santa Barbara, is still open to the public.

71. "Old camels."

72. Sylvester Woodbridge Beach retired from his long-held position as pastor of the First Presbyterian Church in Princeton, New Jersey.

parsonage. She is going to sail for Italy on the 5th of June. Holly and Cyprian are running the shop in Pasadena and have done very well so far. Mother is coming to replenish the stock which has run low again.

Goodbye Marian dear and thank you again,

>With best love,
>Yours,
>>Sylvia

Sylvia Beach Papers, Manuscripts Division, Department of Rare Books and Special Collections, Princeton University Library (manuscript)

* * *

76. To Ernest Hemingway   August 8, 1923

>Chez Madame Josephine Gay
>Les Deserts. Savoie.

Dear Hemingways, How is the Book coming on? How is the group of Feather Cats standing the heat? Is it going to Anastasie's Stade this Saturday? We have a thatched cottage all to ourselves except for some cows in the next room. Our door opens into a field where we brush our teeth and everything. Adrienne sends her best love with mine

>Sylvia

Ernest Hemingway Papers, John F. Kennedy Presidential Library (manuscript)

* * *

77. To James Joyce   July 16, 1924

Dear Mr Joyce,

Adrienne and I thought that "gateau aux amants"[73] might do but Fargue[74] turned it down. He says its rather feeble. There is a cake called "puit

---

73. Lover's cake.
74. Léon-Paul Fargue (1876–1947), French poet and essayist.

d'amour"—round with custard in the middle—but Adrienne thinks it too messy for the purpose. She thinks "brioche" will have to do if you are willing. Fargue paid a nice visit to his friend the pastry cook's wife but he found nothing in her repertory corresponding to a seed cake.

Larbaud has written to Adrienne that Penelope (gide[75] calls her "hideura gemells sans accents") (see Corydon)[76] is to appear without accents and no remarks or explanations or apologies of any sort and he will take the entire responsibility for the translation.

I got a letter from Miss Weaver yesterday. She was very much pleased with Yeats' letter. I showed it to some of our friends here and they were impressed. May I send a copy to Larbaud?

The enterprising Jew who wrote to ask you to lecture for the League of Public Discussion in America has now come to Paris to fetch you. He wants to take you Back alive or dead with Shaw and George Moore for a whirlwind tour of the States. You would lose [letter ends here]

The Poetry Collection, University at Buffalo (SUNY) (manuscript)

* * *

78. **To Bryher**   **February 24, 1925**

Dear Bryher,

Please forgive me for letting so much time pass before acknowledging West.[77] Such bad behaviour is enough to disgust anyone. Your book is very interesting and the only real description of California that has been made. And the movie actress with her wedding ring and the breakfast good texts . . . how symbolic! You must sign my copy when you come to Paris. I think you ought to hurry up and see the handsome letter box you gave me for Christmas! I had such fun planning it with the carpenter. Did McAlmon[78] tell you about its being installed now and the little brass letters above the compartments and three large compartments, one for

75. André Gide (1869–1951), French novelist.
76. *Corydon*, a book of essays by Gide about homosexuality, published in 1924
77. Bryher's novel *West* was published by Jonathan Cape in 1925
78. Robert McAlmon (1896–1956), American writer and editor, and Bryher's husband.

you, one for McAlmon and one for Joyce and small ones for the others below. It is really fine!

Oh dear! What does Mr Douglas[79] take me for . . . ? a rich amateur no doubt.

Oh

dear oh dear oh dear! I haven't the slightest desire to have those de luxe copies made for Shakespeare and Company nor to pay forty pounds or anything although I like his book and D.H. Lawrence deserves to be held up as an example. Do you think I should write to Mr Douglas and encourage him to work with Messrs Bumpus or would you be so kind as to let him down easy for me? After all he never addressed himself to me directly on the subject.

Yours very affectionately

Sylvia

Bryher Papers, Yale University Library, Beinecke Rare Book
and Manuscript Library (manuscript)

✳   ✳   ✳

79. To Ernest Hemingway   November 5, 1925

12 rue de l'Odéon
Paris- VIe

Dear Hemingway,

Ernest Walsh[80] seems to be in an awful hurry to get your In Our Time.[81] The 12 copies have come and I can send him one if you haven't, and you ought to autograph it. Can you come around for a minute

---

79. Norman Douglas (1868–1952), Austrian-born novelist and travel writer who was involved with the Italian printing house Pino Orioli, which brought out D. H. Lawrence's *Lady Chatterley's Lover* in 1928, after the book had faced obscenity charges similar to those *Ulysses* had undergone. Beach had declined the offer to bring out *Lady Chatterley's Lover* under the imprint of Shakespeare and Company.

80. Walsh founded the review *This Quarter*, which published some of Hemingway's early works, including the story "The Undefeated." Walsh suffered from tuberculosis, which killed him in 1926

81. Hemingway's first collection of short stories, which introduced the character Nick Adams.

tomorrow He wants the Three Mountains edition too.[82] I'll show you his letter.

    Yours,

          Sylvia

Sylvia Beach Papers, Manuscripts Division, Department of Rare Books and Special Collections, Princeton University Library (manuscript)

* * *

80. To Bryher   **December 26, 1925**

Dear Byrher,

    I have been so busy with this cursed Christmas season that I have let a great many days pass before thanking you for your generous present to Adrienne and me. We were very happy over it but all the same we are going to scold you next we see you for being so extravagant!

    I hope you all had a good Christmas and got nice and light to put it elegantly.

    Tell H.D. a customer in my shop today put her finger on <u>Heliodora</u>[83] and said "<u>THATS</u> the poetry that beats everything else."

    And please tell McAlmon I am going to write to him soon to thank him for his letter.

    By the way his pudding hasn't come yet and we fear it was so good that it got eaten up on the way. O how sad! Adrienne has not given up hope yet though.

    Thank you again dear Bryher for everything. Lady Ellerman[84] sent another cheque for George Antheil[85] and you are very kind people.

          With best wishes for New Year
          and love
          Sylvia

---

82. In 1924, William Bird, the editor of Three Mountains Press, had released a shorter version of what would become the 1925 volume *In Our Time*. The Three Mountains edition was called *in our time* (with lowercase letters).

83. H.D.'s *Heliodora: and other poems* appeared in 1924.

84. Bryher's mother, Lady Ellermann, was a patron of the arts.

85. Beach's friend, the American composer (1900–1959), known for his *Ballet mécanique* of 1926.

Only 1 copy of the January Navire[86] is out so far—The rest will be ready next week—Monday no doubt.

Bryher Papers, Yale University Library, Beinecke Rare Book and Manuscript Library (manuscript)

* * *

81. To Marianne Moore[87]

July 12, 1926

Miss Marianne Moore
Editor, The Dial,[88]
152 West 13th Street,
New York.

Dear Miss Moore,

Mr Joyce is writing a new book, installments of which have appeared in some of the reviews.[89] He has just finished another section of it and has left it with me to dispose of as I have charge of such matters for him. It consists of four consecutive parts and there are from 30000 to 34000 words in all, 115 pages of typescript, commercial size. A certain review has made Mr Joyce an offer for it but I do not think it is a suitable place for his work nor the price offered sufficient for a thing that has taken him so long to write and is the finest piece of writing he has done. I should be very glad to give it to you for The Dial if The Dial would care to have it. Your review occupies the highest place among reviewers and is the most appropriate one to bring out Mr Joyce's work. What would you offer for the exclusive rights[90] in America and Europe to publish this section?

I hope that your work on The Dial leaves you time for your poetry of which I am a great admirer. Are you bringing out another volume soon?

Yours faithfully,
Sylvia Beach

---

86. Adrienne Monnier's literary review, *Le Navire d'Argent*.
87. Marianne Moore (1887–1972), American poet. Moore was editor of *The Dial* from 1925 to 1929.
88. *The Dial* was an American literary magazine which published many important modernist texts in the 1920s.
89. *Finnegans Wake* (published as a complete book in 1939).
90. Above the phrase "exclusive rights" Beach has penned "periodical."

P.S. There is nothing that the censor could object to in Mr Joyce's piece.[91]

S.B.

Dial/Thayer Papers, Yale University, Beinecke Rare Book and Manuscript Library (manuscript)

* * *

82. To *The Dial*[91]   July 21, 1926

The Dial,

152 West 13th Street,

New York,

Dear Sirs,

I am sending you under separate cover by registered post Mr James Joyce's manuscript. In case you do not accept it will you please return it at once to me by registered post.

Yours faithfully,

Sylvia Beach

P.S. If the manuscript is accepted will you kindly arrange for the payment to be made in dollars.

SB

Dial/Scofield Thayer Papers, Yale University Library, Beinecke Rare Book and Manuscript Library (manuscript)

* * *

---

91. *The Dial* telegrammed back to say "Two cents word but must see the manuscript before deciding." Joyce's work-in-progress was accepted by *The Dial* in a letter on August 31, 1926, from editor Gratia Sharp. Moore wrote to Beach on August 26, 1926, to say, "I also feel the benefit of your confidence in my own work and thank you for telling me of it."

83. To *The Dial*   July 21, 1926

Dear Madam,

I am sending you herewith a list of corrections that are to be made on Mr Joyce's MS. in case it is accepted by the Dial.

Yours faithfully,

Sylvia Beach

Dial/Scofield Thayer Papers, Yale University, Beinecke Rare Book and Manuscript Library (manuscript)

* * *

84. To Marianne Moore   September 16, 1926

Dear Miss Moore,

Thank you for your letter. I hope you had a good holiday in Maine. I am very glad to hear that Mr Joyce's work is going to appear in the 'Dial.'[92] It has no title yet and he says anything will do. The fragments that were published by the 'Criterion,' 'Le Navire d'Argent' etc., were called "From Work in Progress", "Extract from Work in Progress" so you may give it some such name. For the biographical notes Mr Joyce asks if you will kindly consult 'Who's Who' or Herbert Gorman's book. (James Joyce. His First Forty Years. Huebsch.)

Mr Joyce will correct the proofs himself. I sent three lists of corrections of the typescript at different times, and hope they did not give too much trouble.

With kind regards

sincerely yours

Sylvia Beach

Dial/Thayer Papers, Yale University, Beinecke Rare Book and Manuscript Library (manuscript)

* * *

---

92. Ultimately, Moore decided that they would need to reduce and cut sections of Joyce's work, and Beach withdrew the manuscript from consideration.

85. To Holly Beach   November 23, 1926

Dearest Holly,

I am sending you herewith cheque for $5 with lots of hugs and lots of love for Christmas. I got your letter and the reason I haven't written is that there's this awful pirating of <u>Ulysses</u> business that takes all my time. Douglas sent me a clipping of the Roth[93] interview in the N.Y. Evening Post and we had to take action at once. The enclosed will tell you all about it.

You must be working hard to make the shop so booming. Your friend Mary Minter (Miss Shelby) came to see me and is very nice.[94] She asked me if I knew of a French teacher for her so I sent her August Morel the translator of <u>Ulysses</u>. They arranged to begin the lessons but I have not seen either of them since they began. Perhaps it proved fatal. Morel is lucky to find such a fine pupil as Mary. She told me she had come to Paris to reduce her weight. She doesn't seem to be fat at all so what will she be after the cure? She spoke very affectionately of you.

Mother writes to me often. She has just gone back to Florence from Rome, and was received by her hotel Berchielli with bursts of joy. She says she is thinking of going to Algiers with a Mrs Fenner, a nice mother-bunny-of-mine.

George[95] had pneumonia. Now he and Böske are away for a change of air.

With much love Holly dear from your loving sister
        Sylvia

Sylvia Beach Papers, Manuscripts Division, Department of Rare Books
and Special Collections, Princeton University Library (manuscript)

✳   ✳   ✳

---

93. Samuel Roth (1893–1974), the American publisher who was prosecuted for the pirating of *Ulysses*.
94. Hollywood and stage star Mary Minter, known for her parts in *The Littlest Rebel* on Broadway and *Anne of Green Gables* in the Paramount film of 1919.
95. Antheil.

86. To Ernest Hemingway   **December 8, 1926**

Paris

Dear Hemingway,

Will you dine with me next Sunday at 8 o'clock? Mr. and Mrs. Joyce and
Paulham[96] and Larbaud and the MacLeishes[97] I hope are coming. I hope
you can. The Paulhams are on your track. They want your address.

Yours sincerely

Sylvia

Ernest Hemingway Papers, John F. Kennedy Presidential Library (manuscript)

* * *

87. To Bryher   **December 15, 1926**

Dear Bryher,

I have just received your letter and cheque for five pounds for Adrienne and me. We both thank you so much for thinking of us at Christmas. It is very kind of you indeed and we are going to blow ourselves
in to a regular treat in your honor! It is too bad that you are not going
to stop off in Paris on your way to Switzerland. You and H.D. must not
fail to make us a visit in the spring 'selon la bonne tradition.'[98] You didn't
answer my question about <u>Palimpsest</u>.[99]

I am sorry that McAlmon has not been able to settle down at last.
We always hoped that you would take a flat in Paris and spend part of
the year here, and that we would see you both very often. As long as he
goes in for 'night life' and surrounds himself with the bloodsuckers and
failures who are the only people who have time to share that life with
him he and his work must suffer. I pity him very much, and hope still he
will come out all right.

---

96. Jean Paulhan (1884–1968), French writer and editor of *Nouvelle Revue Française*.
97. Archibald MacLeish (1892–1982), American writer, and his wife Ada (1893–1984).
98. "In keeping with tradition."
99. H.D.'s *Palimpsest*, which was dedicated to Bryher, was published by Paris Contact Editions in 1926.

Will you and H.D., and Dorothy Richardson[100] if you happen to see her, be so kind as to sign the enclosed protest against the pirating of Ulysses? I am sorry to give you the trouble. I shall also ask Dr Havelock Ellis[101] to sign. The protest is being made by Mr Joyce's colleagues and is to appear in the papers here and in America.

With many thanks again for the Christmas present and much love to yourself and

H.D.

> Yours
> Sylvia

Bryher Papers, Yale University Library, Beinecke Rare Book and Manuscript Library (manuscript)

* * *

88. To Gertrude Stein   December 21, 1926

Dear Gertrude Stein,

Will you be so kind as to sign the protest of Mr Joyce's colleagues against the 'pirating' of Ulysses?[102]

> Yours very sincerely
> Sylvia Beach

Gertrude Stein and Alice B. Toklas Papers, Yale Collection of American Literature, Beinecke Rare Book and Manuscript Library, Yale University (manuscript)

* * *

---

100. The English experimental writer Dorothy Richardson (1873–1957) is sometimes credited with inventing the stream-of-consciousness technique. Beach admired her thirteen-volume work *Pilgrimage*.

101. Havelock Ellis (1859–1939), British doctor and sexologist. He co-authored *Sexual Inversion* (1897) with J. A. Symonds, as well as a host of other works on sexual behavior.

102. Beach's letter protesting the pirating of *Ulysses* is included in this volume as Appendix 2.

89. To Ernest Hemingway   **January 3, 1927**

Paris

Dear Hemingway,

Joyce suggested to the publishers of the German translation of Ulysses[103] that they publish you, which they are very anxious to do. Joyce finds them satisfactory as publishers. He doesn't want the suggestion of a different translator to come from him so please don't let on, but it would be well for you to insist on their getting someone who is thoroughly familiar with conversational English and sport terms so be sure and stipulate that.

I hope you and Pauline[104] are in good health & spirits and the sport good.

Happy N.Y.

Sylvia

Ernest Hemingway Papers, John F. Kennedy Presidential Library (manuscript)

✻ ✻ ✻

90. To Edward Titus   **March 4, 1927**

Mr. Edward Titus
4 rue Delambre,
Paris.

Dear Mr Titus,

To confirm our conversation in your shop yesterday, the 3rd inst., I examined the corrected proofs of the 1st edition of James Joyce's ULYSSES with the 'bon tirer' signed by James Joyce and myself, which you showed me and which you informed me that you had purchased.

I informed you that said proofs had been disposed of by the printer without the permission of James Joyce or myself. You assured me that

---

103. The firm Rhein-Verlag. Joyce was not satisfied with the German translation of his work by Georg Goyert.
104. Pauline Pfeiffer (1895–1951), Hemingway's second wife.

you would not dispose of them pending a settlement of the matter. You will hold said proofs available for any purposes demanded by the law.

> Yours sincerely,
> Sylvia Beach

Harry Ransom Humanities Research Center, The University of Texas at Austin (manuscript)

❊ ❊ ❊

91. To Ernest Hemingway — November 17, 1927

Paris
To Ernest Hemingway

Received following telegram will you be guest of honor as most distinguished American writer pen club dinner london april fifth club cannot pay your expenses obrien 28 cleveland square paddington london
Sylvia

Ernest Hemingway Papers, John F. Kennedy Presidential Library (manuscript)

❊ ❊ ❊

92. To George Antheil — December 22, 1927

Dearest George,

I don't want to let Xmas go by without sending you my best love. A long time has passed since I wrote to you last but you know how harassed a life I lead and you understand. I think of you always and Talk about you every day to visitors to the shop who gape admiringly at your photos and want to be notified whenever any of your music is played. I long to hear some, any or all of it myself and the musical landscape wherever you look seems quite dreary. We did have a good Stravinsky concert about a month ago and some of his things were very fine. Aside from that, Mme Du Bost's series of concerts that were announced as a unique musical season are just dreadful. Honnegger and the virtuosos star in them and the orchestra is so badly drilled and even A. so dead that even the Parisians don't like it.[105] We took an abonnement[106] but each time there are more empty seats, ours included, especially the Stravinsky night when the house was only half filled. Fouresteer is an awful conductor. The Stravinsky program was the only money's worth one so far. He played a Symphonie op. 1 (1ere ovation à Paris) that was very interesting. I like yours better. And the Etude 1ere and, Apollon and 2 suites pour petit orchestre which were a great success.

Joyce has been ill from worry over his eyes which are pretty bad. And Mrs Joyce has been in the hospital for an operation which was serious. She is better now. Adrienne has been laid up with the grip and myself with an awful neuralgia that drew my face all up on a side which I thought it was staying like that. T.S. Eliot[107] has become an Englishman and a Cathylic—an English catholic. Richard Aldington is in town and Aldous Huxley.[108] D.H. Lawrence's Lady Chatterley's Lover after being suppressed has now been pirated.[109]

What kind is the life in Berlin? Do you have fine music played by German orchestras? We heard *Spiel auf* or *aus* is it and thought it the worst piece we had ever heard. Charlotte and Sam I see often and they always ask after you. I gave them your address.

I hope you will stay away from Paris George. The climate is too harsh for you. Your fans can pilgrimage to see you. Lowenfels[110] went all the way to Berlin. But you risk your life in Paris. What news of your work? Was the Universsall satisfactory? I am glad you are off the Neo Classic. Where does it lead? Of what use is it to you who were such a good boy . . .

With very much love for yourself and for Bosky

    Sylvia

Estate of George Antheil (manuscript)

105. Arthur Honegger (1892–1955) was a Swiss composer who lived a large part of his life in Paris. He is best remembered for *Pacific 231*, an orchestral piece, as well as his musical setting of Jean Cocteau's *Antigone*.

106. Subscription.

107. Beach greatly admired the prose writing and poetry of T. S. Eliot (1888–1965), and as this letter reveals, she was amused by his personal idiosyncrasies.

108. Richard Aldington (1892–1962) and Aldous Huxley (1894–1963), British writers.

109. Lawrence had offered Beach the manuscript of *Lady Chatterley's Lover*, which she declined. The novel was printed privately in Italy in 1928, and subsequently in Paris. It did not appear in a British edition until 1960.

110. Probably the American poet Walter Lowenfels (1897–1976).

* * *

93. To Donald Friede[111] January 30, 1928

> Mr. Donald Friede,
> Boni & Liveright,
> 61 West 48th Street,
> New York.

Dear Mr. Friede,

Mr. Joyce requests me to enclose copy of a letter he has received from his lawyer.[112]

> Yours truly,
> Sylvia Beach

The Huntington Library (HM 41124), San Marino, California (manuscript)

* * *

94. To George Antheil March 25, 1928

Dearest George,

Thank you for your postcard. I hope you are taking good care of yourself and a deep breath before plunging into the Cyclop.[113] I am sending you a paper with a photo of a million volt spark.

Miss Harriet Weaver sent me 55 for you and I got a letter today from Florence Williams saying that Bill[114] was sending $100 to Meatham for you hooray! I enclose a list of contributors with their addresses but a good deal of the results are due to McAlmon's efforts.

Adrienne and I went with Böske and Ber to the Clurgot service. Gee what a bourgeois atmosphere! It was the best joke to hear your music

---

111. Donald Friede (1901–1965), American heir, was expelled from Harvard, Yale, and Princeton, but he went on to invest in Boni and Liverwright, and became its vice president.
112. A copy of the letter from Joyce's lawyer Benjamin H. Conner is also held at the Huntington Library. It is dated January 25, 1928.
113. Antheil's opera based on the "Cyclops" episode of *Ulysses*.
114. William Carlos Williams (1883–1963), American poet.

struck up in such a house. A very good thing for your social career. Mlle Clurgot and Madame Jacob played the first movement of your fine concerto, not badly at all. I thought it sounded very well and it is so interesting. I only wished they would play the whole concerto. It has such great things in it all through, as Sauguet[115] said to me. I wish you would stop making those melodies though, George. The more you put of them in your work the more it doesn't suit it, and they do give me slightly a bellyache. Excuse me for being so frank dearest George, its for your good!

Adrienne says you couldn't have anything better than that performance at Clurgots, and that [. . .] also was there, and others were duly impressed. There's no telling what might come of it. Only if you had been there they would have had a lot more of your music. Maxime Jacob[116] and Sauguet were continually off topic. What a bore! Sauguet's interminable songs. But [. . .] nicely about you afterwards, and asked me all about your health. And Jacob was a good fellow to play your concerto. Mlle Clurgot said she hoped you would have been satisfied with her playing of the Concerto and to tell you she was very anxious to do as well as possible. We saw your photo on the wall. She likes you very much as anyone can see.

Roy Sheldon[117] brought me your bust. The head is good and certain aspects of the front.

McAlmon is just back from his trip with the Birds found a letter and the $100 cheque from Bill Williams.

I am so tired I don't know what I'm writing, A lot of work and visitors interrupting all day long. I never see Boske, but she says she is coming to have a serious talk with me some time ? ? ?

> With very much love
> Sylvia

Estate of George Antheil (manuscript)

* * *

---

115. Henri Sauguet (1901–1989), French composer.
116. Maxime Jacob (1906–1977), composer.
117. Roy Sheldon, American sculptor.

95. To Crosby Gaige[118]   May 3, 1928

> Mr. Crosby Gaige,
> 229 West 42nd Street,
> New York City,
> U.S.A.

Dear Sir,

It may interest you to hear that a unique item for collectors of "Joyce-ana"—namely, the one surviving copy of the first edition of "Dubliners", the author's copy, signed by him and with a note about it in his handwriting, is now for sale in the States. Mr. Douglas Orbison, 133 East 73rd Street, New York, has charge of it.

> Yours faithfully,
> Sylvia Beach

Yale University, Beinecke Rare Book and Manuscript Library (manuscript)

* * *

96. To Sisley Huddleston   June 21, 1928

Dear Sisley,

I am getting the photo of Joyce and me and the others ready and you can pick out the ones you want whenever you drop in to see me. You will know best which are the most interesting and appropriate.

It is so long since we have seen you we were wondering what you were up to.

> With kindest regards
> yours sincerely
> Sylvia

I have received your fine little "kitbag" book on Normandy[119]

Harry Ransom Humanities Research Center, The University of Texas at Austin (manuscript)

---

118. Crosby Gaige (1882–1949), American theatrical producer and publisher.
119. *Normandy: Its Charm, Its Curiosities, Its Antiquities, Its History, Its Topography* was published in the Kitbag travel series in 1928.

* * *

97. To F. Scott Fitzgerald[120] June 23, 1928

Dear Scott Fitzgerald,

Don't forget that you and Mrs Fitzgerald are coming to dine with us next Wednesday at 8, (to meet Mr and Mrs Joyce) and we are counting on you. Adrienne and I live at 18 rue de l'Odéon on the 4th floor no lift.

Yours very sincerely
Sylvia Beach

F. Scott Fitzgerald Papers, Manuscripts Division, Department of Rare Books and Special Collections, Princeton University Library (manuscript)

* * *

98. To Sisley Huddleston November 2, 1928

Dear Sisley,

Bohemian Literary and Social Life in Paris has just arrived and we are awfully proud of being in it.[121] We expect to get murdered by a horde of envious persons now, so when you read in the paper about the mysterious crime in the rue de l'Odéon you will know it is your fault. But it is the first and only book of that kind (literary, I mean) about Paris and most entertaining to read. It should have a tremendous success. I expect to do a bustling hustling business with it.

Did you know that Joyce's "Anna Livia Plurabelle" has just appeared in New York? Crosby Gaige is bringing it out.[122] He publishes three or four little books a year (Stephens, Yeats, George Moore etc) in a very limited edition and makes about a thousand pounds apiece on them. But he is

---

120. F. Scott Fitzgerald (1896–1940), American author of *The Great Gatsby* and *Tender Is the Night*; he and his wife Zelda Sayre were synonymous with expatriate life in France in the 1920s.

121. Huddleston's *Bohemian Literary and Social Life in Paris: Salons, Cafes, Studios* was published by George G. Harrap in 1928.

122. Gaige's edition of *Anna Livia Plurabelle* appeared in 1928, with a preface by Padraic Colum.

so chary with the copies that Joyce was obliged to buy at $15 each the two copies that he gave to his children. As he sells them all off before the book appears he is not interested in its reception by the critics. At Joyce's request he promised to send press copies to The Times and Observer and they must be on the way now. But as you were the first English critic to write up Ulysses, I wonder if you would like to be the first to review Joyce's new work. I think he would be very pleased if it was you who once again were the one to begin.[123] In that case he would have to loan you his own copy of "Anna Livia Plurabelle" at once which he says he would be delighted to do, because it might be too late if you waited to receive the 'Observer' copy. I could send you immediately Joyce's copy. In case you would like to have a conversation with him he would be very glad if you could call on him or if you and Jeanne could dine with him some evening soon. Would it be convenient for you to call me up? I am here till 7 PM.

With most affectionate thanks and good wishes

yours sincerely
Sylvia

Harry Ransom Humanities Research Center, The University of Texas at Austin (manuscript)

* * *

99. To Sisley Huddleston   November 6, 1928

Dear Sisley,

Thank you for your letter. I have written as you suggested to Mrs Viola Garvin,[124] but I didn't say what I felt like saying—that there was no one but you who was capable of writing about ALP.[125]

Joyce wanted me to tell you that his wife is now in a "clinique" where she is to have an operation on Thursday.[126] The family is very anxious of

---

123. Sisley Huddleston's review of *Ulysses* appeared in the London *Observer* on March 5, 1922.
124. Viola Garvin, literary editor of the *Observer*.
125. The "Anna Livia Plurabelle" section of *Finnegans Wake*.
126. Nora Joyce had an exploratory operation to treat her cancer on November 8, 1928. See Richard Ellmann, *James Joyce*, 607.

course although they are assured she will be all right again. He is staying there at present. When Mrs Joyce is better he would like so much to see you, he says.

Yours affectionately

Sylvia

Harry Ransom Humanities Research Center, The University of Texas at Austin (manuscript)

* * *

100 . To Ernest Hemingway　　　　January 30, 1929

Dear Hemingway,

　　Your little sister-in-law said you said what the Hell and I don't wonder. She got the children's books herself and brought them to the shop, and I sent them off. Of course it is now entirely too late, but she said she thought it was better to send them anyhow. Hemingway dear please forgive me for not doing any of the things you asked me to do. Ever since your letter came I have had so much work and so many cares. I was laid up for two weeks with facial neuralgia that doesn't sound bad but hurts awfully. Then Myrsine and the little girl were ill and I had to do everything alone at the busiest time of the year. Adrienne had the grippe and two relapses and had to correct over and over again the proofs of the French translation of <u>Ulysses</u> that she is now bringing out.[127] The last and the worst is that Mrs Joyce was not well and had to be suddenly taken to a "Maison de Santé" for treatment (radium). Joyce was just getting over a breakdown brought on by worry over his diminished sight when he had this shock. After several treatments Mrs Joyce now has to undergo a serious operation.[128] They are very anxious about the outcome of it. She is really ill and had been for some time before it was found out. You will see that we have been very much upset and I hope you will forgive me for not writing. Now about <u>cinquante-milles dollars</u>.[129] Duplaix' wife got

---

127. The French edition of *Ulysses*, translated by Auguste Morel (with Stuart Gilbert), was brought out by Monnier in 1927.
128. Nora Barnacle had been diagnosed with a cancerous tumor and was operated on at a clinic just outside Paris, in the suburb of Neuilly.
129. Hemingway's short story, "Fifty Grand" (1927).

FIGURE 1 Sylvia Beach, aged 15

FIGURE 2 Sylvia and Holly Beach dancing a tarantella in traditional dress in Italy

FIGURE 3 Beach as agricultural worker, France,
during World War I, with unknown colleague

FIGURE 4 Cyprian Beach, silent film actress

FIGURE 5 Eleanor Orbison Beach by the Seine

FIGURE 6 Sylvester Woodbridge Beach, in Princeton gown
with tipped hat, pays last respects to Woodrow Wilson, February 6, 1924.

FIGURE 7 Looking down the rue de l'Odéon to the Odéon Theater

FIGURE 8 Beach attending to window at Shakespeare and Company

FIGURE 9 Beach spotting George Antheil as he climbs to his apartment

FIGURE 10 Bookplate with Shakespeare and Company logo

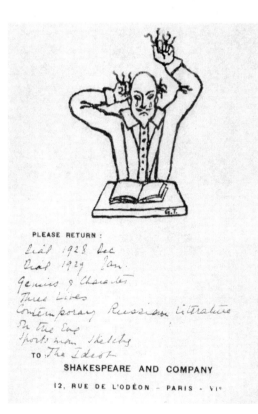

FIGURE 11 "Please return" card, Shakespeare and Company

FIGURE 12 Beach at her desk, Paris.

FIGURE 13 A definitive portrait of Beach

FIGURE 14 Sylvia Beach, Shakespeare and Company, rue de l'Odéon

FIGURE 15 Beach and her assistant Myrsine Moschos

FIGURE 16 Adrienne Monnier at her desk. Portrait of Sylvia Beach in the background by Paul-Émile Bécat (now owned by Princeton University Library).

FIGURE 17 Adrienne Monnier reading, Maison des Amis des Livres

FIGURE 18 Sylvia and Adrienne at Monnier family farm, Savoy

FIGURE 20
H.D. (Hilda Doolittle,
1886–1961)

FIGURE 19 Bryher
(Annie Winifred Ellerman, 1894–1983)

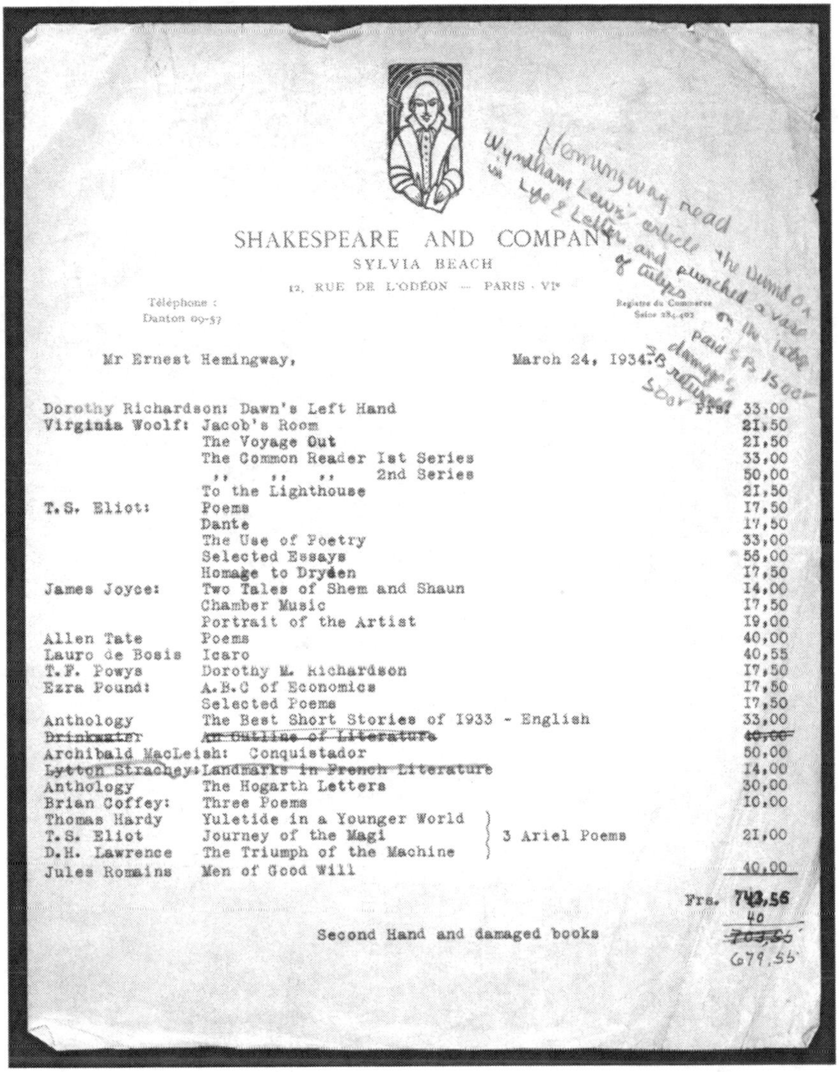

SHAKESPEARE AND COMPANY
SYLVIA BEACH
12, RUE DE L'ODÉON — PARIS - VI

Téléphone : Danton 09-57

Registre du Commerce Seine 284.402

Mr Ernest Hemingway, March 24, 1934.

Hemingway read Wyndham Lewis' article the Dumb Ox in Life & Letters and punched a vase of tulips on the table. Paid SB 1500 fr damages SB returned 500 fr

Dorothy Richardson:	Dawn's Left Hand		Frs. 33,00
Virginia Woolf:	Jacob's Room		21,50
	The Voyage Out		21,50
	The Common Reader Ist Series		33,00
	,, ,, ,, 2nd Series		50,00
	To the Lighthouse		21,50
T.S. Eliot:	Poems		I7,50
	Dante		17,50
	The Use of Poetry		33,00
	Selected Essays		56,00
	Homage to Dryden		I7,50
James Joyce:	Two Tales of Shem and Shaun		14,00
	Chamber Music		I7,50
	Portrait of the Artist		I9,00
Allen Tate	Poems		40,00
Lauro de Bosis	Icaro		40,55
T.F. Powys	Dorothy M. Richardson		I7,50
Ezra Pound:	A.B.C of Economics		I7,50
	Selected Poems		I7,50
Anthology	The Best Short Stories of I933 - English		33,00
~~Drinkwater~~	~~An Outline of Literature~~		~~40,00~~
Archibald MacLeish:	Conquistador		50,00
~~Lytton Strachey:~~	~~Landmarks in French Literature~~		14,00
Anthology	The Hogarth Letters		30,00
Brian Coffey:	Three Poems		I0,00
Thomas Hardy	Yuletide in a Younger World	3 Ariel Poems	21,00
T.S. Eliot	Journey of the Magi		
D.H. Lawrence	The Triumph of the Machine		
Jules Romains	Men of Good Will		40,00
			Frs. 743,56
			40
	Second Hand and damaged books		~~703,56~~
			679,55

FIGURE 21 Invoice showing Ernest Hemingway's borrowings (March 24, 1934). Beach's note reads: "Hemingway read Wyndham Lewis's article The Dumb Ox in Life and Letters and punched a vase of tulips on the table. Paid SB 1500 fr damages. SB returned 500 fr."

FIGURE 22 Beach and James Joyce at Shakespeare and Company

FIGURE 23 Beach at threshold of Shakespeare and Company holding
Collected Plays of Shakespeare

FIGURE 24 Beach after the Liberation of Paris,
displaying an American flag in her apartment's window

FIGURE 25 "Ernest Hemingway chez Sylvia Beach après la Libération"

FIGURE 26 "To Sylvia Beach, Sincerely Yours Richard Wright, June 7, 1946 Paris"

FIGURE 27 Maurice Saillet
(1914–1990), Monnier's assistant,
friend to Beach and Monnier

FIGURE 28 Jackson Mathews,
1907(?)–1978

FIGURE 29 Beach receiving her Honorary Doctorate at SUNY Buffalo

FIGURE 30 Beach in James Joyce's Tower at Sandycove, Dublin

lung trouble and they had to rush off to the Midi early in the fall. I have not heard a thing from them since. I asked the Paulhams several times you know Jean Paulham[130] and wife, to send me the copies that were to be sent out (service de presse etc) and that I would send them with a card stating that you were absent, but never a copy have I been able to get hold of. Prévost says they were all sent out by Duplaix. Duplaix promised to send me his address but never did. Of course his wife's sudden and very dangerous illness would account for his not doing anything much I suppose. Its very unfortunate 1° that you were not in Paris when your book came out (their attitude is that il s'en va—il s'en faut—nous aussi alors) Prévost[131] says only an author's presence assures the proper looking after of his new born book—2° that the translator's wife got consumption. I am very sorry that I could do nothing and Adrienne is rushed to death, struggling with the task of keeping the three translators of Ulysses from springing at each other's throats. As for the children's books, she doesn't handle them and I never could get a minute to go out and look for some. Miss Pfeiffer suddenly arrived for an hour or two on her way to Switzerland, and she got the book. It was very nice of her. I am returning your cheque herewith, and with my regrets. I was awfully glad to get your letter and to know that you and Pauline and fils Patrick were all right. Miss Pfeiffer told me what a fine young fella he was. I congratulate you both and send my best love. When is your next book to be ready?[132] That's what everybody is asking. O yes, I saw the son of your proprietor, Philippe Potier. We dined together at Mrs Pennant's. He said he had heard everyone in his entourage speak with enthusiasm of Cinquante Milles Dollars. When you return the best thing to do would be for you to present him and the real owner of the house with copies [dédicace]. They know you are away, and will wait till you come back.

  With much love to yourself and Pauline

    Sylvia

Ernest Hemingway Papers, John F. Kennedy Presidential Library (manuscript)

---

130. Jean Paulhan (1884–1968), French writer and editor of the *Nouvelle Revue Française* from 1925 to 1940 and again from 1946 to 1968 (it ceased publication during the Second World War). His relationship with Anne Desclos was the source for her erotic novel *The Story of O* (1954).

131. Jean Prévost (1901–1944), French critic who was killed while participating in Resistance activities during the Second World War.

132. Hemingway completed the revisions to *A Farewell to Arms* on January 22—it was published by Scribner's that year.

* * *

101. To Crosby Gaige   March 23, 1929

Dear Mrs Crosby,

Mr Joyce took the contract to his lawyer's office (Mr Benjamin Conner, Chadbourne Stanchfield & Levy) and Mr Conner who is in New
York was cabled to. He is expected to reply by Monday morning but if
his reply isn't here by that time it may mean a little delay in signing the
contract. It is only a formality however. As he is Mr Joyce's legal adviser
all such business has to be submitted to him. I will let you know on Monday morning if the signing of the contract has to be postponed.
   Yours sincerely

       Sylvia Beach

Yale University Library, Beinecke Rare Book and Manuscript Library (manuscript)

* * *

102. To James Joyce   May 15, 1929

Dear Mr Joyce,

Am I to send Miss Weaver the Preface? I forget. And the Revue Hebdomadaire and Europeéne?[133] SB

This is the proof of the ad in <u>Transition</u>[134]. What do you think of one in
the New Statesman as well Times Lit Supplement?

The printer told me it was too late to add an m to incamination in the
title on cover.[135] The plate has been engraved. It will be added to the title
page inside. SB

The Poetry Collection, University at Buffalo (SUNY) (manuscript)

---

133. *La revue hebdomadaire* was the journal for the French anti-parliamentarian group
Redressement français.
134. A literary journal co-founded by Eugène Jolas (1894–1952), his wife Maria McDonald,
and Elliot Paul.
135. *Our Exagmination Round His Factification for Incamination of Work in Progress*, a
book of critical essays on the work that would become *Finnegans Wake*, was published by
Shakespeare and Company in 1929.

* * *

103. To Ernest Hemingway October 8, 1929

Paris

Dear Hemingway,

Joyce would telephone to you if you had one. He asked me to ask you and Pauline to go to their house this evening at about nine. He hopes you will excuse the invitation coming at the last minute, but the party is quite impromptu. They only just now decided to have you. He hopes you are free.

> Yours hastily
> Sylvia
> (Please excuse scrawl)

Ernest Hemingway Papers, John F. Kennedy Presidential Library (manuscript)

* * *

104. To William Carlos Williams October 15, 1929

Dear Bill,

You have a right to feel awfully down on me for the way I have treated your MS. It is such a fine piece of your work, and I didn't deserve to have it entrusted to me. I should have written to tell you that I have received it and would arrange about its publication over here, and all this time you have been left without a work. It is quite unforgivable. Adrienne was ill at the time I got the MS., and since then we have had an unbroken series of what they would call "emmerdements" ranging from a felon on my thumb and a finger cut off in the door of the car to the dog nearly dying with typhus; and Adrienne after an abscess in her tooth is now being slowly cured of a "dilatation d'estomac" which we hope will wind up the series, but I know I should have attended to the MS. in spite of all that. You do everything under far greater difficulties, I am sure. I love your "Novelette", and am going to see what is the best arrangement for its publication after it appears in Transition.[136] Jolas was very much pleased

---

136. Possibly the novelette "January," written in 1929 and published in 1932.

to hear that Transition could bring it out and said it would appear in the one after this.[137] For the publication in book form, I will see the Crosbys of the Black Sun Press about it.[138] Unfortunately Harry Crosby seems to be going in for aviation mostly for the present, and a great deal of the funds that might be used for publishing must going in to flying now. I will see them and let you know. They would be the best ones, if they have the disponibilités.

I am sending you the last two copies of "The Great American Novel" that I have left.[139] Collectors in the United States are giving anything to get copies, I am told. The book is very rare and is likely to go up more and more. Will you please settle up with Bill Bird for them. He supplied them to me on sale.

Please scold me all I deserve. I am really very sorry to have been so remiss towards one I admire so much.

Give my love to Florence (if she will accept it now.)
　　　　　Yours very sincerely,
　　　　　Sylvia

Has M. Almon arrived safely?

William Carlos Williams Collection, University at Buffalo (SUNY) (manuscript)

137. Eugène Jolas (1894–1952).

138. Black Sun Press was a book publisher founded in 1927 as Éditions Narcisse by poet Harry Crosby and his wife Caresse, who at the time were expatriates living in Paris. The name was changed to Black Sun Press the following year.

139. Williams's work, first published in 1923.

IV

SHAKESPEARE AND COMPANY: 1930s

105. To Jacob Schwartz[1]   **January 13, 1930**

Dear Mr Schwartz,

Thank you very much for your offer of some copies of the Criterion for July 1925 containing a part of "Work in Progress" that afterwards appeared in the August No., 1927, of Transition. But it was not "Anna Livia", you know. That first appeared in Mademoiselle Monnier's review "Le Navire d'Argent" of which I am sending you a de luxe copy under separate cover, registered as it is very rare now. I thought you might like to have the real first appearance of "Anna Livia" to add to your collection. You will see a notice by Mademoiselle Monnier about its having been suppressed in England when about to appear in "The Calender", that having been the reason why it was published (in English) in an otherwise French review. The second version, as you know, came out in Transition No. 8, November 1927, and Mr Crosby Gaige brought out the third version in book form in 1928. If the Criterion is under the impression that A L P first appeared in it, you must put it right.

> Yours sincerely,
> Sylvia Beach

Yale University, Beinecke Rare Book and Manuscript Library
(manuscript)

---

1. Jacob Schwartz, American book dealer and owner of the Ulysses Bookshop in London.

* * *

106. To William Carlos Williams   April 10, 1930

Dear Bill,

In sorting out piles of books in my overcrowded storeroom I discovered to my horror all these copies of your book. After assuring you there were none left. I am awfully sorry, and hasten to send them to you now.

With affectionate greetings to all,

Yours,

Sylvia

William Carlos Williams Papers, University at Buffalo (SUNY) (manuscript)

* * *

107. To Helen Fleischman Joyce[2]   May 25, 1930

Dear Mrs Fleischman,

Thank you for taking the trouble to write me everything. I was so glad to get your letter, and will be waiting to hear the result of the examination at the eye hospital where I suppose Mr Joyce has now been moved. I hope another operation wont be necessary and that Mrs Joyce and Georgio's fears will turn out to be ungrounded. I'm glad he is cheerful. He must have been glad to hear you had brought your typewriter. He will be able to think up quite a lot of "little jobs" between the hours in the AM and P.M. he sees you. Tell him ALP doesn't seem to be out yet—those were only advance copies for the author.[3] The booksellers haven't got them yet. I will call up Mr Gilbert[4] tomorrow and see whether he has heard anything about his book.

I got a letter from the German publisher of Ulysses saying he had heard the operation was successful. He promises to send a little money

2. Helen Fleischman Joyce (1894–1963), wife of Joyce's son Giorgio.
3. The "Anna Livia Plurabelle" section from *Finnegans Wake*.
4. Stuart Gilbert (1883–1969), English translator of French authors including Antoine de Saint-Exupéry, Jean Cocteau, and Jean-Paul Sartre.

within the next few days.[5] The sales have slowed down for the moment he says.

Nino Frank[6] called up to enquire about Mr Joyce and sent his 'meilleurs voeux'[7] and lots of friends have called at the shop and phoned every day for news, tell Mr Joyce, not to speak of the Associated, Amalgamated, United and other Presses ending in 'ed'.

Thank you again for writing. Give my greetings to Mrs Joyce and Georgio and Mr Joyce

Yours sincerely
Sylvia Beach

Eugène and Maria Jolas Papers, Yale University, Beinecke Rare Book and Manuscript

Library (manuscript)

* * *

108. To Helen Fleischman Joyce   May 30, 1930

Dear Mrs Fleischman,

Thank you for your nice letter of the 28th. My shop was closed yesterday, Ascension Day, everything was closed, but I went to my shop to see if there were any news. I was sorry to hear about the iritis, but hope there will be no harm from it if it was stopped so quickly.

Today I did my best to attend to the Opera business. The Times Office seems to be closed on account of Ascension being extended by some over several days. So I couldn't get hold of Mr Daniels. No one answers the telephone there today at least I went myself to the Opera to see about the seats for tomorrow night. John Sullivan[8] is singing but the performance is a private one, they told me, and they said there was no way of getting any seats at all. He will be singing 'Tannhauser' next week and Volpi[9] is coming to sing Guillaume Tell. You'd better not mention this to Mr. Joyce—he would get feverish

---

5. Above this line, Beach notes "(RM.1200) (about Frs 7000)."
6. Nino Frank (1904–1988), French film critic and Joyce supporter.
7. Best wishes.
8. John Sullivan, Irish tenor promoted by Joyce in the 1930s.
9. Giacomo Lauri-Volpi (1892–1979), Italian tenor.

Tomorrow night its to be for the widows and orphans of the "fonc-tionnaires d'Etat"[10] as far as I could make out.

I will write to Dr. Brody.[11]

With best greetings to all the family
and thank you again for giving me news
Yours sincerely
Sylvia Beach

Eugène and Maria Jolas Papers, Yale University, Beinecke Rare Book
and Manuscript Library (manuscript)

* * *

109. To Allen Tate[12]   November 14, 1930

Dear Allen Tate,

I was having pneumonia when your letter of August 12th came, so I hope you will understand now why I have not answered it all this time, and why I didn't acknowledge the four copies of your beautiful "Three Poems".[13] The enclosed cheque for $4.00 just about covers them doesn't it? I am glad you sent them, and if you have anything else printed at any time, don't forget to send me some. It was a good idea to bring them out yourself. And these are very fine. I had to be away from my shop for three months and haven't been able to catch up with the work ever since. Meanwhile your stick seems to have disappeared. I seem to have seen it for some time in the jar by the door, but it is not there now. Oh dear dear dear, I do hope someone hasn't fancied it and walked off with it. You will be afraid to trust yourself in the place any more. I will see if it can be traced.

So you have seen Hemingway over there. He has never let me know anything about himself since he left here. He is finished with us, that's it. Tell him that I was showing those photos of him and Pierce at Key West,[14]

---

10. Civil servants.
11. Dr. Daniel Brody, Joyce's Swiss publisher.
12. Allen Tate (1899–1979), prolific American poet and critic. Along with Robert Penn Warren and John Crowe Ransom, Tate was part of the Fugitive Poets circle (later called the Southern Agrarians).
13. Tate's self-published volume *Three Poems* appeared in 1930.
14. Waldo Peirce (1884–1970), American painter, was one of Hemingway's friends in Key West. Beach is referring to pictures of Peirce and Hemingway marlin-fishing in scanty attire.

to a gentle young friend of Gide's the other day, and he blushed crimson. If I'd thought he was going to be so géné[15] poor dear, I would have been more careful. Anyhow he is going to write an article on Hemingway, and admires him deeply.

Mrs. Polly Boyden[16] must have left Paris. She hasn't been in the shop for some time. Some one told me you had bought a place somewhere in the country, and had F.M.F.[17] there. Do you like it? I would love to live in the country. I hope you and Hemingway are "shooting" lots of birds.

A number of my American friends have gone back home to live now. At one time there were such a lot of you in Paris, but it is very dull at present. I hope you will come riding in on a wave before very long, and not leave Paris to the French like that.

Meanwhile, with affectionate greetings to you both,

Yours sincerely,
Sylvia Beach

Allen Tate Papers, Manuscripts Division, Department of Rare Books and Special Collections, Princeton University Library (manuscript)

* * *

110. **To Alfred A. Knopf**[18]   **March 4, 1931**

Mr Alfred A Knopf
730 Fifth Avenue,
New York.

Dear Mr Knopf,

I understand from Mrs Colum[19] that you are interested in bringing out an anthology of Joyce's work. This anthology would be a fairly large

---

15. Embarrassed.
16. Polly Chase Boyden, author of *Toward Equilibrium* (1930) and *The Pink Egg* (1942).
17. Ford Madox Ford.
18. Alfred A. Knopf (1892–1984), influential American publisher.
19. Mary Colum (1884–1957) was a prominent poetry critic and literary reviewer. In 1930 she won a Guggenheim Fellowship for her criticism. Her husband was the Irish writer Padraic Colum (1881–1972).

book, very carefully arranged and edited, with representative selections from Joyce's work, and a portrait frontispiece. We think such a book might be sold for a good price—something beteen $3.50 to $5.00, but naturally you would be the best judge of that. If you have any offer to make on the subject, will you please make it to me, and then we can go on with the arrangements and send you a list of the extracts. I assume that an offer would include advance royalties.[20]

Yours sincerely,

SYLVIA BEACH

The Poetry Collection, University at Buffalo (SUNY) (typescript)

* * *

111. To Ernest Hemingway   April 21, 1931

Dear Hemingway,

Although I haven't written to you since your accident I think of you very often and hope you are getting well fast.[21] I was so sorry to hear you were laid up and to think that you were suffering. MacLeish gave me news of you when he was over here, and now writes that you are getting all right.[22] Tell Pauline I thank her for her letter at Christmas. What an anxious winter you must have had! I wonder if your son Patrick got the book I sent him for Christmas, addressed to Piggott. Perhaps he has forgotten his French by this time and become a cowboy. Is it true that you are coming over this spring?

A Berlin German bookseller was telling me the other day that you had by far the biggest place in Germany among all the American writers and that the sales of your books exceeded anything he had ever seen. Well I hope you get yourself paid the royalties.

Writers over here are all suffering from the 'crise des affairs' and 'le Krach americain,'[23] but Prévost has three children now. Ezra Pound is making us a visit and an Italian tried to stick a stiletto into him during

---

20. On April 3, 1932, Beach telegrammed Knopf: "Joyce declines offer."
21. In November 1930, Hemingway fractured his arm in a car crash in Billings, Montana.
22. Archibald MacLeish (1892–1982), American poet.
23. References to the stock market crash of 1929.

a soirée given in his honor at the Brasserie de l'Odéon. I think people should control themselves better.

    With love to yourself and Pauline

    Adrienne sends her love too

        Yours affectionately and with good wishes

        Sylvia

Ernest Hemingway Papers, John F. Kennedy Presidential Library (manuscript)

* * *

112. **To Ernest Hemingway**   June 8, 1931

Tel. Danton 09–57

Dear Hemingway,

    I am very anxious to ask you advice about a matter concerning Joyce—wasn't it stupid of me not to think of it when you were here! Would it be possible for you to find a minute in the short time you are in Paris to call me up or drop in again. Never mind if you can't manage it. I called up Hadley's apartment but she was out.

        Yours affectionately,

        Sylvia

Sylvia Beach Papers, Manuscripts Division, Department of Rare Books and Special Collections, Princeton University Library (manuscript)

* * *

113. To James B. Pinker[24]   July 4, 1931

> Messrs. James B. Pinker & Son
> Talbot House, Arundel Street,
> Strand,
> London, W.C.2.

Dear Sirs,

I have just come back from a holiday and found your letter informing me of Mr Claude Kendall's offer for the American and Canadian rights for the publication of Mr James Joyce's "Ulysses". I think the offer too small to interest Mr Joyce.

Will you kindly take note of the fact that I have a contract with Mr Joyce for "Ulysses", that I brought out the first edition in 1922 and have continued to publish it ever since. It is now in its eleventh large edition (28 thousandth). If an American edition appeared I should probably have to cease publication here. Any offers must therefore include the sum of twenty five thousand dollars to be paid to me on signing the contract. Considering that much time, expense and influence have been used in developing the sales during all these years, this is a modest estimate of the value that "Ulysses" represents for me.

> Yours faithfully,
> Sylvia Beach
> Shakespeare and Company

James Joyce Collection, Yale University, Beinecke Rare Book and Manuscript Library
(copy of original)

* * *

114. To James Joyce   November 10, 1931

Dear Mr Joyce,

I am returning you herewith Mr Pinker's letter of the 6th. [25] As regards "Pomes Penyeach",[26] I took out the American copyright of the book this

---

24. James Brand Pinker (1863–1922), Joyce's literary agent.
25. Eric Pinker, Joyce's literary agent after the death of his father James Brand Pinker in 1922.
26. *Pomes Penyeach*, Joyce's second collection of lyric poetry, was published by Shakespeare and Company on July 7, 1927.

summer and I do not consider its publication in a volume with Chamber Music at all opportune at the present moment. The five thousand copies of my 1927 edition being now exhausted, I am arranging about a second edition and would like to time it so as to coincide with the Oxford University Press edition. Has the date of this been fixed?

Yours very sincerely,

The Poetry Collection, University at Buffalo (SUNY) (manuscript)

* * *

115. To Sisley Huddleston   September 16, 1931

Dear Sisley,

I am going to take advantage of your kind heart of which I have many a proof, to ask a favour of you. Perhaps you remember our friend Jean Prévost who used to be on the staff of Adrienne's 'Navire d'Argent.' He taught in Cambridge for two years and now has come back and has been appointed 'chef d'information' on the 'Intran.'[27] Bailby[28] places his confidence in him to such an extent that all the time he was ill this summer, over three months, he had Prévost do the "Interim" in his place. Prévost has just written something called "Les Moeurs de l'Argent en France" which he thinks might interest the English public and which he would like to get into the 'Times.' I wonder, dear Sisley, if you would have the great kindness to give him your all-powerful 'apui'[29] for him. I know that a word from you would be the all-powerful 'open sesame', but I know too, that it is a good deal to ask of you. If it were possible to see you, Prévost would be very glad of the opportunity. Could you, do you think arrange a rendez-vous with him at any time convenient for you?

Thank you for so kindly mentioning me in "Back to Montparnasse."[30] Its such a delightful book and is having a great success. I hope Joyce who is in London has seen it. I like so much what you said about him. He is coming to Paris at the end of this week, I think.

---

27. Short for *L'Intransigeant*, a right-wing Paris newspaper.
28. Léon Bailby (1867–1954), French journalist and editor of *L'Intransigeant*.
29. *Appui*, meaning "Support."
30. Huddleston's *Back to Montparnasse: Glimpses of Broadway in Bohemia*, a sequel to his *Bohemian and Literary Life in Paris*, was published in 1931.

With affectionate greetings from Adrienne and me to yourself and Jeanne

Sylvia

Harry Ransom Humanities Research Center, The University of Texas at Austin (manuscript)

* * *

116. To Bernard d'Avout   **October 24, 1931**

Monsieur Bernard d'Avout
Imprimerie Darantiere
13 Rue Paul Cabet,
Dijon.

Dear Mr. d'Avout,

Excuse me for not having given you a response for "Pomes Penyeach" yet. I am very annoyed at the moment by the pirated edition of Ulysses which was made in the United States. I have been sent a copy, and they printed the book there as exactly as possible like my edition. It even says my company and "Darantiere, Dijon". It appears that they sold about twelve hundred copies in a few months. If you come to Paris one of these days, I will show you the specimen that I have here. Mr. Joyce and I, we are very alarmed. If this continues the sale of my edition will be seriously strained.

On the subject of your estimate for "Pomes Penyeach," I could not do an edition of this small book at such a high price. With the shilling at five francs and the payment of 50% to the English agent, Poetry Bookshop, and the royalties to the author, it is necessary that the book costs a frace at maximum. I believe that a decent edition can hardly be possible at this price? And at the same time, Mr. Joyce would like it to be pretty and to be sold for one shilling. This price, moreover, is required by the title of the volume.

Receive, Monsieur d'Avout, my best greetings.

Shakespeare and Company

The Poetry Collection, University at Buffalo (SUNY) (typescript)

117. **To Paul Léon**[31]   **February 4, 1932**

Monsieur Paul Léon
27 rue Casimir Perier,
Paris.

Dear Monsieur Léon,

In reply to your letter of the 3rd inst., I made a present to Mr Joyce last December of my rights to ULYSSES, as far as an edition published in America was concerned. Some time later, on the 25th of January, Mr Colum told me that Mr Joyce was not satisfied with the contract between us for ULYSSES "because neither party was free to act without the consent of the other". I replied that I supposed it resembled other contracts in that way, but, as I had already assured Mr Joyce in December, he might consider himself free from all obligation to me, and to dispose of ULYSSES to whomsoever and in whatever manner he pleased, without any question of an indemnity to me.

Of course I understand that Mr Joyce is anxious to have this assurance from me on paper, so I hereby agree to cancel the contract between us for ULYSSES, and to give up my claims to this work for future editions.

I do not think a new contract necessary.

With regard to Mr Rosenfeld's[32] letter, will you please tell Mr Joyce that in my conversation with that gentleman, as I informed Mr Joyce immediately after it took place, I merely said that he could not be expected to pay the lawyers any more money, for they had not put a stop to the pirating of ULYSSES, that he could not afford to, the pirating having robbed him of the profits from the sale of the book. Anything else that Mr Rosenfeld wrote to Mr Levy[33] was his own idea, and I shall ask him to write another letter saying that when I saw a copy of his letter I did not approve of what he had said. I quite understand that

---

31. Paul Léon, Joyce's close friend and adviser. They met in 1928.
32. Rosenfeld, lawyer hired by Shakespeare and Company to prosecute Japanese pirating of *Ulysses.*
33. Louis Levy (cf. *The James Joyce–Paul Léon Papers in the National Library of Ireland: A Catalogue,* compiled by Catherine Fahy [Dublin: National Library of Ireland, 1992], 160).

Mr Joyce was displeased at what he took to be an unauthorized step on my part.

Yours sincerely,

SYLVIA BEACH

The Poetry Collection, University at Buffalo (SUNY) (typescript)

* * *

118. To Paul Léon   August 18, 1932

Dear Monsieur Léon,

As the doctor said I must entirely forget my work during my vacation, Miss Henley[34] did not forward my mail and I only saw your letter of July 14th yesterday when I returned. The eleventh edition of UYLSSES is indeed nearly sold out, but, as I told Mr Joyce, I cannot risk reprinting it with an American edition pending. They would not have undertaken it over there if they had not had good reason to think it possible at present, and I hope for Mr Joyce's sake that all will go well. If, however, ULYSSES is suppressed in America, Mr Joyce may count on me to reprint it immediately here. We shall know this fall, I suppose. Meanwhile if ULYSSES is out of print for a while, everyone will quite understand the situation. A new edition would not take long to prepare and would go off all the better for having been unobtainable during the interval.

I am sorry to hear such a bad account of Mr Joyce's eyes, but hope Dr. Vogt[35] will be able to make them well again. I hope Lucia is better now.[36]

Yours sincerely,
Sylvia Beach

The Poetry Collection, University at Buffalo (SUNY) (typescript)

34. Jean Henley (1910–1994), Beach's assistant from 1932 to 1933.
35. Dr. Alfred Vogt (1879–1943), Swiss opthalmologist who treated Joyce for his eye problems. Beach says that Vogt was "considered one of the three great authorities in Europe" (*Shakespeare and Company* 68).
36. On April 17, 1932, Lucia Joyce suffered a nervous breakdown. She spent three months recovering at the l'Hay-les-Roses clinic outside Paris.

* * *

119. To Allen Tate   August 26, 1932

Dear Allen Tate,

I was sorry too to miss you. Hound & Horn for July is sold out
I'm sorry to say, and Brentano's has no more either. I shall be ordering some more but it will be too late for you, won't it. I'm sending
you Symposium. If there is anything in my library that would be of
any help for your article on recent poetry you could borrow it. How
"recent" must it be? Wouldn't it be a good idea to have a look at a
whole lot of your reviews (Comtempo, the Left, Pagany, Contact etc.)
and have you seen the Objectivist Anthology?—Unfortunately I haven't
kept back numbers of Poetry and I don't think they could be found
in Paris.

Yours sincerely,

Sylvia Beach

Allen Tate Papers, Manuscripts Division, Department of Rare Books and Special
Collections, Princeton University Library (manuscript)

* * *

120. To Paul Léon   August 30, 1932

Monsieur Paul Léon,
27 Rue Casimir Perier,
Paris.

Dear Monsieur Leon,

I enclose a letter that I have just received from the Japanese pirates of
"Ulysses." Will you please let Mr Joyce know and ask him what he would
like me to do about it. They sent a cheque for 200 yen, which at about 5
francs a yen makes the measly sum of a thousand francs. If Mr Joyce is
not able to attend to the matter just now there is no hurry.

Yours sincerely,

The Poetry Collection, University at Buffalo (SUNY) (typescript)

* * *

121. To Paul Léon   **August 31, 1932**

Mr Paul Léon
27 Rue Casimir Périer,
Paris—7.

Dear Mr Léon,

Your letter of the 30th has come. I would, indeed, feel it very deeply
if Mr Joyce thought it best to sever my connection with ULYSSES. But
in devoting myself to his work during the last ten years, combined with
the exertions of running my shop, I have sacrificed my health to such an
extent that my headaches, which the doctors agree are due to fatigue and
mental strain, have not yet yielded to any treatment, and it is obvious
that I must take care in the future if I am to continue to do any work at
all. If I were hurried into printing a new edition of ULYSSES just at the
present moment when the tourist season is over—and my books prove
that sales depend largely on American visitors in the summer—without knowing something definite of the plans of Mr Joyce's publishers
in America, there might be difficulties such as I have no longer, unfortunately, either the health or the courage to cope with. I am sure Mr
Joyce will understand that my decision in this matter has not been taken
lightly. To lose ULYSSES that I have always admired and loved above
everything would be so painful to me that I cannot bear to think of it, but
I must do what I think wisest, and Mr Joyce knows that he is quite free
to take any step that he considers best for his interests. There is nothing
to stand in his way.

I enclose a statement of sales up to date.

The Poetry Collection, University at Buffalo (SUNY) (typescript)

* * *

122. **To Paul Léon**   September 24, 1932

> Monsieur Paul Léon,
> 27 Rue Casimir Périer,
> Paris.

Dear Monsieur Léon,

I am returning to you herewith Mr Yeats' letter to Mr Joyce.[37] Of course Mr Joyce has his reasons for not accepting, but it seems to me it would have done no harm to accept, and that it might have been the first step towards lifting the ban on "Ulysses".

With regard to the copy of "Ulysses" that you saw marked "out of print" in a bookshop in the Rue de Castiglione, the booksellers are justified in saying that. I have announced to them that the edition is now exhausted except for a few copies (about 20) which I sell at the full price of 125 francs without discount to the trade. It may be some time before I can get rid of these copies at this price, and if Mr Joyce wishes to have the royalties on them paid without waiting, I will include them in the sum due to him for royalties up to date and send him a cheque at once. Adrienne Monnier tells me that it is quite customary for publishers to sell the last copies of an edition that is going out of print at full price only.

> Yours sincerely,
> Sylvia Beach

The Poetry Collection, University at Buffalo (SUNY) (typescript)

* * *

123. **To James Joyce**   September 26, 1932

> James Joyce, Esq.,
> Hotel Metropole,
> Nice.

Dear Mr Joyce,

I have sent you by telegram Frs.4,500 to-day. Mr Léon wrote that you would like to have the balance of your royalties for the eleventh edition

---

37. In September 1932, Yeats invited Joyce to become a founding member of the Academy of Irish Letters; Joyce refused the offer.

of "Ulysses". This sum is the balance. Within the next few days Mr Léon will receive a detailed account of all payments made to you and the copies of "Ulysses" sold every month since the eleventh edition appeared.

I am looking forward to seeing Lucia's book.[38] Mr Kahane[39] has not showed it to me yet and I did not know it was out. I will call him up about it.

Yours sincerely,
SYLVIA BEACH

James Joyce Collection, University at Buffalo (SUNY) (manuscript)

* * *

124. To Paul Léon   **September 28, 1932**

Monsieur Paul Léon,
27 Rue Casimir Périer,
Paris.

Dear Monsieur Léon,

I have sent Mr Joyce Frs.4.500 by wire. I got your letter this afternoon, too late to go to the bank, and as you said Mr Joyce was in a hurry to have the balance of his royalties for the 11th edition of ULYSSES I thought that by telegram would be the quickest. This sum of Frs.4.500 settles up the account between Mr Joyce and myself for the eleventh edition of ULYSSES. In a day or two, as soon as I have time to copy the items from my books, I will send you an account of the sums paid to Mr Joyce and the sales.

Yours sincerely,
SYLVIA BEACH

The Poetry Collection, University at Buffalo (SUNY) (typescript)

* * *

38. An illuminated edition of *Pomes Penyeach*, with initial letters designed by Joyce's daughter Lucia, was published by the Obelisk Press in 1932.
39. Jack Kahane (1887–1939), British publisher of the Obelisk Press.

125. To James Joyce   **October 4, 1932**

Dear Mr. Joyce,

Lloyde Banks in Nice will pay you the equivalent of francs on the Pinker and New Republic cheques that you sent me. The Pinker cheque for £12–10–2 at 88,50 comes to Frs.1.106,95, the New Republic, $25.00 at 25,50, Frs.637,50: total Frs.1744,45 less three francs for expenses. So you will get one thousand seven hundred and forty-one forty five.[40]

       Yours sincerely,

James Joyce Collection, University at Buffalo (SUNY)
(manuscript)

*   *   *

126. To James Joyce   **October 24, 1932**

Dear Mr Joyce,

I am sending you the complete Chaucer that you were looking for, a letter from Mr Okakura about that Japanese edition of ULYSSES and the articles that he sent, and a letter from Mr Daughtry asking for permission to quote from one of your poems in a book he is writing. As Mr Léon takes charge of all your affairs, perhaps you would be so kind as to ask him to reply to these gentlemen. Although I shall always continue to be devoted to your work, Mr Joyce, I am sorry that I shall no longer be able to serve you personally. My time and energy are entirely absorbed in the problem of keeping my shop going in these bad times. Since most of the English and Americans have gone away, the library terms have to be revised for the French who, I hope, will take their place. From morning till night I am busy cataloguing and arranging the books and attending to all the rest of the work that is always accumulating on account of my headaches so often laying me up.

I want to thank you again for the sacrifice of a part of your royalties that you make in the arrangement with the Albatross for their publication of

---

40. Beach noted on her copy: "Oct 4 SB got 2 cheques from JJ. Had sum sent to him by Lloyds."

"Ulysses". But I would have far preferred Mr Wegner's[41] first proposition to give me 1% on your royalties which you would have received in full, my part being paid by the publishers. If that saw fit to give me a little something on the sales I was naturally very glad, and Mr Wegner assured me that your royalties would not be affected by it. I regret that with the arrangement you make, it has to come our of your own pocket. As it is done now, I will accept it, as I told you, but now for an indefinite period. Only until they have paid me twenty thousand francs which I shall consider an indemnity for the plates that I had hoped to transfer to any publishers taking over "Ulysses" and which otherwise are a dead loss. After that sum I shall instruct the Albatross to turn over my part to you, in the future.

Yours very sincerely,

James Joyce Collection, University at Buffalo (SUNY) (manuscript)

* * *

127. To Paul Léon   November 6, 1932

Monsieur Paul Léon,
27 Rue Casimir Perrier,
Paris.

Dear Monsieur Léon,

In reply to your letter, "Pomes Penyeach" is nearly out of print. There are only fifty copies left, but they do not go off very fast at this time of the year. As they are the last ones and a first edition of James Joyce, I have raised the price to twenty francs. Mr Joyce need not feel that his contract with me for "Pomes" binds him in any way. He would be right in thinking that it is now time for it to be brought out by his publishers in England and America who would be only too glad to have it on their catalogues, and I am not well placed here to handle it properly. I haven't the money to advertise it as they would do.

With regard to Mr Joyce's kind arrangement with the Albatross for me, that I accepted unconditionally at first, in thinking about it I felt that, as no indemnity was given to me when "Ulysses" was trans-

---

41. M. C. Wegner, Paris representative for the German-based publishing house Albatross Press, which took over publication of *Ulysses* from Shakespeare and Company in 1932.

ferred to another publisher's, I could accept twenty thousand francs as an equivalent, at least, of the value of the plates, but considering that I am not going to be attending to Mr Joyce's affairs from now on, I would not care to take any more than that. Later, however, if he is as rich as he deserves to be, and has no particular need of the percentage of his Albatross royalties that he wanted me to have, I will then gladly accept it.

Yours sincerely,

The Poetry Collection, University at Buffalo (SUNY) (typescript)

*   *   *

128. To Robert McAlmon   November 9, 1932

Dear McAlmon,

I would have sent you the enclosed mss. as soon as your letter came, but Allanah Harper's 'Echanges' has crashed.[42] The princesses wouldnt give any more towards it and one or two even wanted their money back it seems. Madame Goldet took Steeple Jack and tried to place it but unsuccessfully and now she has returned it. They are only interested in crime stories and snappy things with plenty of action or sweet little sketches for families to read here now. How could they be interested in the very subtle psychology and the poetry in Steeple Jack. I gave Mme Goldet 'Contact' with <u>Its all very complicated</u> and she has proposed it to Ramon Fernandez[43] who seemed interested, she said today. I will let you know. That story is one of the best you've done or that anyone has done, I think. It is really a masterpiece. No one but McAlmon could have written that story.

So you have moved out of Mallorca. I should think it would get boresome with Montparnasse transferred there. But if you got an inspiration like in <u>Its all very complicated</u> from it I spose it was worth while. I'm

---

42. Alannah Harper (1904–1992), British editor of *Echanges*, a quarterly review that printed French translations of English writing and vice versa.
43. Ramon Fernandez (1894–1949), Mexican-born French literary critic for *La Nouvelle Revue Française*. He is also mentioned in Wallace Stevens' poem "The Idea of Order at Key West."

glad theres not so much chance to drink in Barcelona. No I dont think I ever met Miss Dahlberg. Is the Dahlberg who wrote <u>Bottom Dogs</u> her brother?[44] I know him.

Adrienne has been very busy with her catalogue which is just off the press. We went to the first night of Giono's[45] play at the Atelier last evening. It was awful. Gide was with us and we teased him about his Communism.[46]

Joyce is back in town, worried with Lucia's health, and left his ms. of Part II of Work in Progress in a taxi and hasn't been able to get it back.

goodbye
affectionately
Sylvia

Hiler[47] had an interesting exposition here but Louisa is making a scientist of him she tells me.

Yale University, Beinecke Rare Book and Manuscript Library (manuscript)

＊ ＊ ＊

129. To Paul Léon   **November 15, 1932**

Monsieur Paul Léon,
27 Rue Casimir Perrier,
Paris.

Dear Monsieur Leon,

Your letter of the 14th has come. As Mr Joyce insists so kindly on my accepting his arrangement with the Albatross, I will do so, and thank him very much indeed. Only I do think he has been too generous in this matter.

As for "Pomes Penyeach", of course I would like to have kept the remaining fifty copies to sell as Joyce firsts at twenty francs apeice. With

---

44. Edward Dahlberg (1900–1977), American novelist; *Bottom Dogs* was his first novel and was published in 1929.
45. Jean Giono (1895–1970), French playwright.
46. Like many writers of the thirties, Gide was interested in the Communist Party but was later disillusioned by a 1936 trip to Russia.
47. Hilaire Hiler (1896–1966), American painter.

this business depression[48] the thousand francs should not have come amiss. But as Mr Joyce does not wish it I will not insist. I am sending him twenty five copies and am keeping the other twenty five to give away to friends from time time.

Yours sincerely,

The Poetry Collection, University at Buffalo (SUNY) (typescript)

* * *

130. To Ernest Hemingway   November 25, 1932

Dear Hemingway,

Thank you for sending me Death in the Afternoon![49] I'm awfully proud of having a signed copy. Its such a great book and I don't mean the size. It is a very very fine achievement and places you right at the top. Theres no one but you that could have written that book and by golly what beautiful descriptions you have done of the fighting! gives you a true emotion and I don't think anyone could help being carried off their feet by your work. You have your readers "à la petite cuillière."[50] Such complete information about the fighting and the fighters and the bulls—you hang on breathless. And the funny talks with the old lady. And fifty cows for one bull. I have told Adrienne a lot of it and she is very pleased and interested in what you have done and thinks it was such a good idea and that you have a splendid "tempèrament d'écrivain."[51]

Well this time Shakespeare and Company was the first to get your new book in Paris. We had it October 10, long before Brentanos. And its the only Christmas present everybody seems to want this year.

I'm sending you an old print of a bull fight that we thought might amuse you, and an album that you probably have already or if not it

---

48. The economic effects of the Great Depression, precipitated by the 1929 U.S. stock market crash, began to be seriously felt in France in 1931–32.

49. *Death in the Afternoon* was published by Scribner in 1932 to good reviews but lower sales than Hemingway's previous successes, *The Sun Also Rises* (1926) and *A Farewell to Arms* (1929).

50. From the French expression "ramasser à la petite cuillère," which usually indicates someone so tired or hung over that he or she could be "picked up with a spoon." Here the expression is applied to the hypnotic effect of Hemingway's prose.

51. Writer's temperament.

might amuse Patrick.[52] I hope Pauline[53] is well and the two boys and yourself (your eyes better?) Tell her I wear the smart gloves she gave me but have to keep my thumb and little finger folded up against each other on account of her hand being smaller sized than mine.

With best wishes for Christmas and love to you both

Sylvia

Sylvia Beach Papers, Manuscripts Division, Department of Rare Books and Special Collections, Princeton University Library (manuscript)

* * *

131. To Paul Léon   **November 28, 1932**

Monsieur Paul Léon,
27 Rue Casimir Perrier,
Paris.

Dear Monsieur Léon,

In reply to your letter of the 24th which has just reached me, I would be very glad if you could take over Mr Joyce's affairs with his various publishers on the continent, and I will let them know at once that you are doing so. Also if you will be so kind as to come around to my shop some day I will hand over the papers to you.

It is interesting to hear about the limited edition of ULYSSES that is about to appear.

Yours sincerely,
Sylvia Beach

The Poetry Collection, University at Buffalo (SUNY) (typescript)

* * *

---

52. Hemingway's son Patrick was born on June 28, 1928, in Kansas City, Missouri. His mother was Pauline Pfeiffer (1895–1951).

53. Pauline Pfeiffer married Hemingway on May 10, 1927, shortly after his divorce from his first wife, Elizabeth Hadley Richardson (known as "Hadley"). Pauline was born in Iowa but had attended journalism school and was a *Vogue* editor living in Paris when she met Hemingway. The marriage ended in 1940.

132. To Paul Léon   March 20, 1933

> Monsieur Paul Léon,
> 27 Rue Casimir Perrier,
> Paris.

Dear Monsieur Léon,

Here is the two hundred yen cheque that you asked me to send you, and I am sending you under separate cover a copy of "Our Exagmination",[54] and to Mr Joyce the prospectuses for "The Joyce Book".[55] And will you please tell him that I will look up the books he mentions, but am wondering whether he hasn't got them put away somewhere himself.

> Yours sincerely,

The Poetry Collection, University at Buffalo (SUNY) (typescript)

* * *

133. To Paul Léon   March 31, 1933

> Monsieur Paul Léon,
> 27 Rue Casimir Périer,
> Paris.

Dear Monsieur Léon,

If it is not too much trouble will you kindly send me an acknowledgement that you received from me the Japanese two hundred yen cheque for Mr Joyce.

> Yours sincerely,

The Poetry Collection, University at Buffalo (SUNY) (typescript)

* * *

---

54. *Our Exagmination Round His Factification for Incamination of Work in Progress*, published by Shakespeare and Company in 1929, featured essays by critics in Joyce's Paris circle. Contributors included Samuel Beckett, Stuart Gilbert, Eugène Jolas, Robert McAlmon, and William Carlos Williams.

55. *The Joyce Book*, a volume of musical settings for Joyce's *Pomes Penyeach* collected by Herbert Hughes, was published by London's Sylvan Press in 1933.

134. **To Stanislaus Joyce**   **April 25, 1933**

> Stanislaus Joyce, Esq.,
> 6 Via Cesare Battista,
> Trieste.

Dear Mr Joyce,

Mr James Joyce tells me that you would like to purchase a copy of 'The Joyce Book'. I am sending you one to-day and enclose herewith the bill, payable in four instalments, which I hope will be convenient for you. There is a rather heavy duty on this book here, and that accounts for the price not being the exact equivalent of two guineas in francs. If it is too much trouble and too expensive to send a cheque on Paris each month perhaps you could send a fifty franc note in a registered letter for the first three payments at least. International postal money orders are a bother and only profitable to the Post Office. Or if you prefer to wait and pay the whole sum at once, in a month or two, that would be all right. Whichever is most convenient for you.

> With kind regards,
> Yours sincerely,
> Sylvia Beach

Division of Rare and Manuscript Collections, Cornell University Library (manuscript)

* * *

135. **To Paul Léon**   **May 8, 1933**

> Monsieur Paul Léon,
> 27 Rue Casimir Périer,
> Paris.

Dear Monsieur Leon,

A copy of Chaucer's poems in the Oxford edition containing the A.B.C. Hymn to the Virgin went off to Mr Reece[56] by express post this morning.

---

56. John Holdroyd-Reece, another Paris representative of the Albatross Press.

I think Mr Joyce's account now stands as follows—

Chaucer Frs.	14,00
postage	7
last bill, balance due	7,50

Frs.28,50

Please thank Mr Joyce for his cheque for Frs.70 of May 4 which Miss Weaver handed me.

Yours sincerely,

The Poetry Collection, University at Buffalo (SUNY) (typescript)

* * *

136. To Stanislaus Joyce   May 11, 1933

Dear Mr Joyce,

Thank you so much for your kind letter and the fifty franc note that you sent me on the 2nd for the first instalment of the 'Joyce Book.' It is a good idea to have it on view in the window of the best Trieste book shop. Even if the people there think in terms of "coffee beans, peanuts and ship's paint" as you say, it will advertise the book and do them no harm to see it. Such a tribute to a writer is rare, is it not? Europe is very much impressed, and I think your brother must have been quite touched. Is it as announced in the current Oxford Bulletin.

Is the bookshop you mention a good one, and do they have any French and English books I wonder.

yours sincerely
Sylvia Beach

Division of Rare and Manuscript Collections, Cornell University Library (manuscript)

* * *

137. **To Stanislaus Joyce**   June 21, 1933

Dear Mr. Joyce,

Thank you very much for your letter of the 16th enclosing a second instalment of fifty francs for the 'Joyce Book.' Its too bad no one in Trieste ordered a copy after you had it displayed in a bookshop window, but people are only interested in economics just now—debts, taxes, bread and lodging—that's what occupies their minds.

Your brother has just come back—I have not seen him yet but hope the news of his family is good.

> With cordial greetings
> yours sincerely
> Sylvia Beach

Division of Rare and Manuscript Collections, Cornell University Library (manuscript)

* * *

138. **To Robert McAlmon**   June 28, 1933

There isn't any very interesting in the way of reviews just now. Do you want any of the following:—

Contempo (March No all I have)

Hound & Horn April-June 1933

Windsor Quarterly No 1 (Vermont production)

1933 No 1 (Philadelphia)

Story

No New Masses left

Would you like to see the New English Weekly?

Pound wrote about you in it this winter.

Dear McAlmon,

I was glad to get your letter after not a word for so long. I thought you'd 'gone native.' Cleveland Chase[57] dropped in the day it came and I

---

57. Possibly Cleveland K. Chase, professor of Latin at Hamilton College.

gave him the last copy of Contact[58] I had. He promised to send it on to you when he had read your story. Moss & Kamin[59] never sent me the other numbers of Contact. I owe them for No 1 of course but was waiting till No 2 came—which it never did. Is Contact suspended for the present? Yes they certny are in a mess over there and its worse and worse here. You are wise to be way off down there on the map. Adrienne and I are nervous about our shops—specially mine. No one knows what'l become of it. Many nice little businesses are going under all around us. And living in Paris has not gone down. Everything is awfully dear.

Thats funny about your starting an American colony there. I didn't see that in the Tribune. But you always do seem to found a new settlement wherever you go. And bars soon spring up. Anyhow Paris has never been as much fun as when you were here.

Joyce is back from Zurich for a while but is returning there soon. Georgio & wife & baby are there already. Lucia is much better they say. I haven't seen her. Joyce's eye bulletin is not too good—a cataract in the right eye, very complicated and dangerous to operate. He might lose the sight in it and also in the other. And if an operation is not performed, glaucoma may start up in the left eye and spread to the right and affect what little sight is left in both eyes. So thats not very good, is it? Miss Weaver was here twice this spring and enquired about you. Since I have set down the load of Joyce responsibilities she has more and more the burden of them poor thing. But she is a saint, an authentic saint.

Adrienne got bitten by a dog we are keeping for a friend, above the eye, but is all right again now.

Katherine Anne Porter now married to Jean Pressley[60] is coming to dinner on Friday. He has a job at the Embassy and she is writing. I like her very much, dont you?

yours affectionately
Sylvia

Robert McAlmon Correspondence, Yale University, Beinecke Rare Book
and Manuscript Library (manuscript)

✳ ✳ ✳

---

58. *Contact* was McAlmon's magazine, co-founded with William Carlos Williams in 1920.
59. David Moss and Martin Kamin, New York booksellers who took over the Contact Publishing Company from McAlmon.
60. Katherine Anne Porter (1890–1980), American short story writer and novelist; she was married to American writer Eugene Pressley from 1933 to 1938.

139. To Paul Léon   July 1, 1933

> Monsieur Paul Léon,
> 27 Rue Casimir Périer,
> Paris—7

Dear Monsieur Leon,

I am sending you herewith a cheque for Mr Joyce for Frs.410,00, equivalent of $20 which the Whitman Publishing Co. has sent me for the right to include three of his poems in Miss Harriet Monroe's Anthology.[61]

Thank you very much for bringing me the book from Mr Joyce the other day. I forgot to ask him where to forward his letters in case any come here for him this summer, and you are perhaps going away. Will you please let me know?

> Yours very sincerely,

The Poetry Collection, University at Buffalo (SUNY) (typescript)

*   *   *

140. To Stanislaus Joyce   September 13, 1933

Dear Mr Joyce,

Your brother called me up to say that you were wondering whether I had ever received the last instalment of fifty francs that you sent me on the 9th of August for the Joyce Book. I did and I hope you will forgive me for not acknowledging it. I was away on my vacation at the time and only found your letter when I came back. By this time, I suppose you have heard from your brother. He has just returned to Paris too.

You have now paid three instalments on the Joyce Book: May 5 50 frs June 19 50 Frs August 9 50 frs Frs 150 in all. The price is Frs 213,40 including postage which leaves a balance of Frs 63,40 unpaid.

---

61. Monroe's 1933 anthology *Poems for Every Mood*.

I hope you had a good holiday this summer.

> With kindest regards
> yours sincerely
> Sylvia Beach

Division of Rare and Manuscript Collections, Cornell University
Library (manuscript)

* * *

141. To Marion Peter   October 5, 1933

Dearest Marion,

I was glad to get your card saying you and Pete[62] had got down there safely and were in school now and everything all right. Its too bad the rainy weather obliged you to cut your trip short, but it must be splendid and sunny in Cannes now. It is even in Paris for the last two days. You won't believe it, Marion, but I went to see you off at the Gare de Lyon, getting there at 8.30, as you said the train was at nine— and I inspected inside and out, every outgoing train capable of going to Nice and Cannes via Carcassonne Arles and Nimes which I remembered you intended to take in. I pulled people out of their couchettes to see if it was you and Sylvia, and peered and pryed into vagons-lits and disturbed the travelers in their privacy on every train in that station, till 9:30, when a lot of the better trains had steamed away, and the people in the ones left were beginning to resent somewhat the way I kept reappearing and looking them over and over for traces of you and Sylvia. It was quite annoying for everybody. Now I wonder if I misunderstood you when you said nine (p.m.) or did you go by water, perhaps, or air, or on donkeys. Quite mysterious. Anyhow I was very much disappointed not to see you once more before you left. And Marion I do hope you will change your mind about coming back here before you sail. That would be so nice! I didnt half realize you were in Paris before you had gone. And thank you again ever so much for the fine dinner we had together which I enjoyed immensely. Let me know if I

---

62. The nickname of Marion Peter's daughter Phyllis.

can do anything for Pete—be a 2nd mother to her or anything else that might occur.

give her my love

and ever so much for yourself

from Sylvia

＊　＊　＊

142. To Stanislaus Joyce   January 12, 1934

Dear Mr Joyce,

Thank you so much for your letter of the 2nd, enclosing cheque for sixty-three francs, the balance for the 'Joyce Book.' I meant to acknowledge it at once, but, as usual, am very much behind hand in my correspondence, so please excuse me! I hope you will be able, finally, to get hold of someone to play the songs for you. I imagined all your family could play and sing.

I hope you had a happy Christmas and New Year. Everyone here is in a great state of excitement over the Stavisky scandal.[63] Yesterday they had out all the police of Paris, besides troops, and there was quite a row in the neighbourhood of the Chamber of Deputies. All the "grilles" where the trees are planted were torn up and several trees uprooted, as we noticed last evening in going up the Boulevard Saint Germain. I don't know why they took it out on the poor trees.

Also, people are spending all their spare cash on newspapers now, that recount all these exciting events and 'hot news' so there is nothing left to buy books. And there are no Englishmen nor Americans in Paris any more. They have all gone home on account of the exchange and the depression. I wonder how things are in Italy. They are making a great effort to get visitors there, cheap railway fare and hotels, polite reception etc, a special number of the 'Chicago Tribune' with Mussolini's picture and warm message to America and even an article by Ezra Pound endorsing the fascist regime. It is all very tempting.

---

63. Alexandre Stavisky (1886–1934), French financier and embezzler.

With thanks again, yours very sincerely Sylvia Beach

Division of Rare and Manuscript Collections, Cornell University Library (manuscript)

* * *

143. To Edward J. O'Brien   January 22, 1934

Mr. Edward J. O'Brien,
Editor, New Stories,
118 Banbury Road,
Oxford.

Dear Mr. O'Brien,

It is very interesting to hear of your 'New Stories' and I am sure it will be a success. Unfortunately there are so few English and Americans in Paris these days that it still will be no use sending me more than two or three copies at most. After the second number we will be able to judge how many will be needed each time, but remember, the first copies of new reviews always go off very fast and the sales decrease afterwards. Perhaps it will not be the case with your 'New Stories', which ought to be a big seller, specially in England, but here nothing sells at present. I might be able to get rid of six of No. 1, but please send only three of the others. May I return the covers? It is very expensive when the whole magazine has to be returned and I would have to deduct the postage from your bill. Already I have to pay a heavy duty on reviews as well as books coming into France, and this is dead loss when copies are unsold.

With regard to subscriptions, it is less expensive for me when people subscribe directly to the magazine. 10% doesn't even cover my expenses. I will encourage everyone I know to subsc but directly.

With best wishes for the success of 'New Stories'.

Yours sincerely,

Sylvia Beach

---

*Sylvia Beach Papers, Manuscripts Division, Department of Rare Books and Special
Collections, Princeton University Library (manuscript)*

* * *

144. To Elkin Matthews Limited[64]   **June 7, 1935**

Messrs. Elkin Matthews Limited,
78 Grosvenor Street,
London, W.I.

Dear Sirs,

In reply to your letter of the 5th., we regret that, in the circumstances, we are unable to send the 'Corrected Proofs of Ulysses' on approval. You may have seen in the papers the account of the experience we had when we were trying to arrange to sell the collection at Sotheby's; we had to call it off because the Joyce things would have been confiscated. The only way we could get them into England would be through friends in the diplomatic service, and we could not resort to this unless the 'Proofs' were actually sold. And an attempt to pass through the customs a parcel weighing about nine pounds, without its being noticed would be useless. So if your client is unable to come over to Paris to see the 'Proofs' at our premises, and you cannot send someone yourselves to see them, we can only refer you to the reproduction in the catalogue, which is a fair example. There are 190 sheets of 86 page proofs, besides a dozen or more loose pages; and there are 69 odd sheets of specimen pages (or signatures) of 8 pages each; each page of proof and every specimen page contains, some of them few, many of them very numerous author's corrections and additions. We are sending you an extra, uncorrected proof that we have, to give you an idea of the format.

We realise that a sale in such unusual circumstances is more or less inconvenient for you, and we would give you a discount of 15% instead of 10% off the price in the catalogue.

Yours faithfully,
Sylvia Beach
Shakespeare and Company

James Joyce Collection, Yale University, Beinecke Rare Book and
Manuscript Library (manuscript)

* * *

64. Elkin Matthews Ltd., founded in 1885 by Charles Elkin Matthews (1851–1921), published Joyce's *Chamber Music*. Beach's memoir recalls "the little bookshop of the publisher and bookseller Elkin Matthews" where she stocked up on Yeats, Joyce, and Pound titles before opening Shakespeare and Company. "He was sitting in a sort of gallery, with books surging around and creeping up almost to his feet" (*Shakespeare and Company* 19). It was from Matthews that Beach bought her Blake drawings.

145. To Bryher   **September 21, 1935**

Dear Bryher

I hope Adrienne has given you all my messages and explained why I haven't written to congratulate you yet for the coming-out of your fine 'Life and Letters To-Day'.[65] My assistant is away on her vacation and there is a good deal to do, and also my letterwriting is somewhat hampered by headaches, although they are better. The mountains helped them a lot.

'Life and Letters To-Day' in its handsome cover—the colours and lettering are beautiful—the bestlooking of any existing reviews, I think—was the first thing I saw when I got back. It must have made a sensation in England; there is nothing like it there or in America either, and now I shall have it to show to people here who ask me what 'interesting' review we have at present. I hardly knew what to reply before. The first number is 'swell', with Gide's paper; and Havelock Ellis; H.D's beautiful poem; Petre's story which is very good; and Mary Butt's are always good; and I liked Macpherson's 'Out of Air' and John Pudney's story about the swan's eggs. The Editorial—bravo for It! and I loved the News Reel. Its a good idea too to have a cinema section, and it looks very interesting, but I'm sorry to say I haven't got as far as that, or the reviews of music theatre and books; I intend to read it from cover to cover—and by the way who designed the cover? Adrienne and I admire it so much.

The only disappointment is that there is nothing of yours in this number. I was hoping to see some of your new work. That's a pity. But there will be something in the next No., won't there?

Adrienne is busily planning the famous reception to be held in honour of the Editors of 'Life and Letters To-Day', which, although everyone isn't back in town early in October, as a rule, promises to be an event. I think it is very important for you all to be present, on account of the friendly relations with French writers. And you know it won't be at all formal, never is in our house, and people don't dress up here. I never wear an evening gown no matter what they invite me to—haint got none.

I was amused and interested to see in your letter to Adrienne that you would have liked to see what women were being invited, if any. All have wives and will be accompanied by same, and very fine wives they are, mostly. But aside from the two brilliant exceptions of Colette and Adrienne Monnier, I can't mention a single woman writer in France today who is any good. That's the plain truth. There are some few writing

---

65. From 1935 to 1950 Bryher financed and operated the literary journal *Life and Letters Today*.

about love and the latest fashions in the papers, and French women are so clever, but their talents at present don't run to writing. There is nothing to compare with the English and American women writers. Strange, isn't it.

Thank you so much, dear Bryher, for your kindness to us this summer! You rescued me just in time and I shall never forget it. With many good wishes to <u>Life and Letters To-Day</u>

Yours affectionately,
Sylvia

Bryher Papers, Yale University Library, Beinecke Rare Book and Manuscript Library (manuscript)

* * *

146. To Bryher   **No date**

Dear dear Bryher!

What a kind thing you have done for me! I can't tell you how deeply grateful I feel, and how much touched I was at your letter saying I was to keep the Blake for you in my shop as long as Shakespeare & Co existed! It belongs to you but it makes me very happy, dear Bryher, to see it still here, and it will always remind me, although there is no danger of forgetting it, of your great kindness. It was so thoughtful of you, too, to send your cheque for three thousand five hundred francs by air so that I could rush and change it into pounds, which I did at once. And now I feel safe if anything happens to the franc. My situation was very precarious. I've been owing all the English publishers money since the end of March and the longer I waited for some to come in, the riskier it was. I was really very much alarmed to think of what I might eventually have to pay for pounds. And my business is practically at a standstill.

Please forgive me going into all this. I only wanted you to know how timely your cheque was.

With many many thanks,
and much love,
Sylvia

Bryher Papers, Yale University Library, Beinecke Rare Book and Manuscript Library (manuscript)

* * *

147. To Bryher   October 10, 1935

Dear dear Bryher!

I am still dazed after opening your letter a minute ago, and don't know what to say to thank you for your immense kindness. But I want to acknowledge it by return post so am only sending you a few words to say that I am deeply grateful and feel undeserving and unworthy of such a friend. It is more like a fairy tale than something that is happening just one Thursday morning in real life! Your cheque for four thousand francs will be a great lubricator for Shakespeare & Co's creaking works. Already the Blake gift did so much for us last spring! But dear Bryher it is your kind encouragement that is so wonderful to me when I was feeling like giving up the whole "racket"!

           With many thanks and much gratitude and love
             Sylvia

We enjoyed the 'Life and Letters Today" reunion immensely and our French friends were delighted. But what a journey you had in the floods!

I hope the articles of Romains[66] in The Oeuvre reached you quickly—I posted them right off Monday morning

---

Bryher Papers, Yale University Library, Beinecke Rare Book
and Manuscript Library (manuscript)

* * *

148. To Bryher   November 30, 1935

Dear Bryher,

Many thanks (all my letters to you start that way) for your cheque for one thousand francs for Paul Valéry![67] He will be awfully glad to get it, I know, because, between you and me, he has a really hard time making

---

66. Jules Romains (1885–1972), French poet.
67. Paul Valéry (1871–1945), French author.

a living out of what he writes under present circumstances. In spite of continually working with wretched health it is difficult to support his family and he has a boy still in his teens to educate, François who is to be a teacher when he is grown up. Valéry kindly said I should take anything coming from the translation—rights and all, but Adrienne and I couldn't let him do that, especially as he has offered to give readings at the 'séances' that they are organizing for my benefit. My darling Bryher you have been a wonderful fairy godmother to me and I shall never never never forget it! Thank you so very much! And my beautiful Blake drawing—yours to be truthful—is a continual reminder of your kindness.

The Freud book too that you sent me and for which I am grateful arrived, and I intend to read it attentively.[68] I know he is one of the greatest men of our time. And some time when more pressing things than headaches are all straightened out I will seriously take up the question of consulting Dr. Löwenstein.[69] For the present, your great kindness and the pleasant feeling of encouragement have done more for me than anything else could have done. It is so grand to know one is not abandoned in hard times! The headaches are not as bad as they were and its only once in a while a bad attack comes on. Dr Thérèse Fontaine[70] is still, or rather, has begun again the auto-vaccine injections with Calcium Sandoz and they really seem to do me good.

We are waiting and looking forward so eagerly to seeing you soon, so please don't fail to turn up. With much love your most grateful

Sylvia

I am so pleased that you all think well of my translation.[71] I did take a good deal of trouble with it but Valéry is difficult to render, sometimes almost impossible.

Bryher Papers, Yale University Library, Beinecke Rare Book
and Manuscript Library (manuscript)

---

68. Possibly Freud's *An Autobiographical Study*, published in 1935 by the Hogarth Press in James Strachey's English translation.
69. Rudolph Löwenstein, Polish-born psychoanalyst and founder of ego psychology.
70. Beach's doctor, Thérèse Bertrand-Fontaine, was one of the first members of the lending library at Shakespeare and Company and to Beach's amazement, "found time to read all the new American books" (*Shakespeare and Company* 22).
71. Beach translated Valéry's essay "Littérature" for a French edition of *Life and Letters Today*, a British little magazine edited by Desmond MacCarthy and Hamish Miles, and taken over by Bryher in 1935.

* * *

149. To Marion Peter   May 1, 1936

My dearest Marion,

Your kind letter of the 20th of April enclosing a cheque for five hundred francs has come—your very generous donation to Shakespeare & Co—and you say I'm not to feel grateful—! Well I'm afraid that's not possible Marion dear—I do feel awfully grateful and so much touched to think that you want to help me in the struggle to hold out this year and next, and that your big contribution is certainly more than you can afford at this moment when you are feeling the hard times. It is a proof of the truest friendship which I shall never forget. And the letter you wrote me was so kind and encouraging, I cant begin to tell you how I felt when I read it! You must ask me anything in the world except not to feel grateful! There is nothing else I wouldn't do for you.

The readings have been a great success—I wish you could have attended the three that have taken place this year—Gide led off in January, Valéry followed in February and Schlumberger in March. Last month T.S. Eliot was to read but he was not able to get here and his reading has been postponed till the 6th of June. Jean Paulhan, editor of the "Nouvelle Revue Française" is giving one a week from today, and perhaps Eliot's will be the last before the autumn when I hope Duhamel[72] and Maurois[73] will read something. It is very interesting at these readings, about sixty-five people, the members of the group that are in Paris— unfortunately some of the best friends like yourself are far away—and families of the writers, all seat themselves around the shop which somehow manages to accommodate them comfortably, and the writer sits at a little table at the left of the fireplace (if you remember how the land lies) and it is so wonderful to hear a great poet like Valéry, the Milton of France to-day, as Adrienne Monnier says, reading aloud from some unpublished manuscript. And everyone listens so attentively, but the atmosphere is not at all formal. It is like a party of a few intimate friends. I do hope you will be here just at the time a reading takes place, Marion dear! I would be so glad. A number of interesting people are always present, Joyce, for instance, much to the excitement

---

72. Georges Duhamel (1884–1966), French poet.
73. André Maurois (1885–1967), French novelist.

of everybody curious to see him, and the New York Times has asked if they can take a photograph of the Eliot reading. This Shakespeare & Co group is considered a very significant friendly meeting of the French and American book lovers.

I'm glad those scamps Sylvia and Phyllis[74] had a good time in Florence. When are you coming over to fetch them home? They must be learning lots of Italian and will be very remarkable linguists when they finish this schooling—like you and Blanche. And wont you be glad to see them again! And Marion the 2nd to laugh at Sylvia's jokes. Well her own are not bad either. She made me laugh till my sides were sore, when she was over here this winter, and I felt all of a sudden too sober when she left me. Does she remember all the French she picked up and used to such purpose? and shall I send her something French to read? About the political situation in France perhaps? Tell her the elections went rather red[75], and the worst is yet to come...next Saturday when they are to vote again.

With ever so much gratitude dearest Marion for your kind generosity to me, and your friendship, and ever so much love

Sylvia

Sylvia Beach Papers, Manuscripts Division, Department of Rare Books and Special Collections, Princeton University Library (manuscript)

* * *

150. To Marion Peter   August 6, 1936

Peacock Inn
Twenty Bayard Lane
Princeton, N.J.

Yes sir dear Marion, here I is!

I decided suddenly to come over and see my father this summer—he is about 84—and he seemed anxious to see me and insisted on helping

---

74. Marion Peter's daughters, now teenagers.
75. The French legislative elections of May 1936 marked a major victory for the left-wing Popular Front.

me with the expenses of the trip, et voilà! I got in via 'Normandie' on Monday and am staying all this month. My sisters are expecting me in California and I was planning to stop off to see you on the way out and give you a big fat Kiss, but father is feeling the effects of his sweltering day in New York when he met my boat—the hottest day of this hot summer, and I am going to take him right out to California next Monday the 10th, where he can rest and get away from the numerous demands on him in Princeton. But I shall be coming back at the end of the month to sail, and must make connections with you in passing through Chicago—if you are there. You may be in Europe bringing the girls home, but we must meet somehow.

I hope you and all the family are well—I am longing to see you!

With much love
Sylvia

My address is California will be

To Rev Sylvester Beach

Crown Hotel, Pasadena

---

*Sylvia Beach Papers, Manuscripts Division, Department of Rare Books
and Special Collections, Princeton University Library (manuscript)*

* * *

151. To Marion Peter   **August 15, 1936**

To Rev Sylvester Beach
The Crown Hotel
Pasadena
August 15th—36

Dearest Marion,

I'm so sorry we were up at Mt Wilson[76] yesterday when the girls were arriving at Los Angeles and your telegram reached me too late. We didn't get home till midnight. I would have liked ever so much to

---

76. In the San Gabriel Mountains of California.

have seen them, and had set my heart on seeing you on the way out. Father and I never dreamed that the plane would not be stopping at Chicago and it was only at the last moment it turned out to be not even flying anywhere near Chicago. It was a great disappointment not to be able to catch at least that little glimpse of you. And if I had seen Sylvia and Phyllis what fun it would have been! You must give them a big hug from their old auntie and tell them how sorry I was to miss them. So that babe Sylvia is about to make her début—well her aunt Sylvia predicts that she will be the most popular debutante this season—and wont she have a good time! It doesnt look like I was going to be able to count much on her assistance at Shakespeare and Co just at present.

I hope she and Phyllis enjoyed their experience as nuns in a Roman convent and that they're not converted to fascism.

I'm staying with Cyprian and her friend in Altadena and spend a good deal of time with my father who had a fall in Princeton and wasnt very well but is much better now. Holly is at Santa Monica but came up with her nice little boy to see me. We are going down there to spend the day on Monday.

You know I decided quite suddenly to come over on account of my father who hadn't been able to get over there to see me for seven years. He is 84 and I didn't want to wait any longer for a visit to him. I proposed to spend August with him in Princeton and not try to do California and my sisters this time, but our plans were changed by father's little accident and the best thing was to get out here as quickly as possible so we came by plane. It was not fatiguing like the several days journey by rail, and saved time for me. I have to sail on September 2nd and shall leave here towards the 24th of this month for New York where I expect to stay a few days with my friend Marian Willard and try to see some people in the hopes of interesting a collector in some of the Joyceana I've brought over. I'm going back by plane but perhaps could arrange to go through Chicago and get a sight of my dear Marion—I'll let you know when my plans are all settled, but I must see you! I have to stop at Princeton too, to pick up my trunk on the way to New York.

Its been such fun to see Holly and Cyprian again and California is so fine, never sweltering as it was in New York when I landed.

Well au revoir and ever so much love darling Marion

Sylvia

Its too bad I shall not be on this side the ocean for Sylvia's début!

Sylvia Beach Papers, Manuscripts Division, Department of Rare Books
and Special Collections, Princeton University Library (manuscript)

* * *

152. To Adrienne Monnier   **August 22, 1936**

2885 Santa Anita Ave
Altadena, California
22 (!) August 36

My very dear Adrienne,

I hope that all goes well over there and that you are rested after the holiday. Paris is unfortunately very boring this time of year. New York is overwhelming and since I was not able to get in touch with Dr. Rosenbach until I got here and that everyone is gone during the month of August I made the decision to stay here where it is nice and where I see my dear papa and my sisters until the end of the month. And I will remit my departure for France to Sept. 14. I think there is a departure that day. In any case I will let you know as soon as that is final.

I saw Toni yesterday in Los Angeles. She asked for news about you. This return to my country has done me good and it's so interesting to be back again with Cyprian who is a unique girl to the world. She is so beautiful and extremely nice for my father—looks after his clothes like a mother. Helen also is downright charming and I get along well with them. I am wrong in the American atmosphere as much as it's possible—the evangelical Aimee MacPhearson and all that . . .

I wrote to Marian Willard that I will leave for New York until the beginning of Sept.

I hope that nice Margaret is starting to get along well and that the readers are finding what they need. With a big kiss. Sylvia

---

Harry Ransom Humanities Research Center, The University of Texas
at Austin (manuscript)

* * *

153. To Adrienne Monnier   **August 28, 1936**

(Cyprian says hello)

> 10 Mira Cyprian Beach
> 2885 Santa Anita
> Altadena, Calif.
> 28 August 36

My very dear Adrienne,

I changed my trip to 16 Sept. and will not return to New York more than one week in advance. Marian Willard asked me to stay in her house in Long Island these few days and I will try to see Dr. Rosenbach. I wrote to him, but without reply and I think the hope of interesting him in my Joyceana is a tiny bit illusionary. But I am very happy to be in contact again with the United States and my family and that was the actual goal of this trip.

My father is happy to see me again and Cyprian too and if I ever had a good idea it was that of revisiting my country. It's very interesting and I only regret that you did not see it with me. Holly and Fred are in the process of settling down in their new house with their precious little Freddie who is a clearly successful child—so handsome and very well-mannered. Fred is pro-Landon and the rest of us—especially papa—for Roosevelt, a truly grand president in the best democratic tradition. Everything promises his reelection, I hope. Things are in the process of resuming all over the country, except 11 million unemployed. But the number diminishes just the same and the public projects destined to resolve this problem is getting more resources. Roosevelt is working to reduce the vast specialized and impoverished fields for the farmer and to create kitchen gardens, small like in France, that would make families seen, and encourage specialized manual labor.

If you see announced a film with the Dionne "quins" go watch it. You will see Helen Jerome Eddy[77] who plays a small role in it. And she just got engaged after it. She's a very remarkable girl. Between films she works as a real estate agent and she gets on like a man with all the details of architecture and house construction. You would love the houses here with the perfect comfort for which Americans have a true instinct.

---

77. Helen Jerome Eddy (1897–1990), Cyprian Beach's partner. She was a film actress best known for her role as the title character's aunt in *Rebecca of Sunnybrook Farm* (1916).

Everyone has a car—they are dirt cheap—and when you stop at a gas station the nice staff bustles about around your car, does everything necessary without tip, brings you something to drink or eat in your car, or cigarettes, all at a minimum expense. Gas costs almost nothing and cars, which seldom need repairs, don't require more than small maintenance costs. I've noticed that not even one worker is deprived of a car. And the crisis had an effect of rapprochement and cooperation between all the citizens who failed to be cast away. Each time something is about money spending you talk in a low voice like during an illness. Besides Americans have always been caring amongst themselves, and very nice.

I must have more bad punctuation even than usual in writing this letter. It's because my little curse that hasn't stopped since I've been here, has forced me to stay layed out. It's extremely annoying and is stopping me from seeing the country and Hollywood and visiting the beach where it would be a pleasure to dive in. Nevertheless I was with Holly once, and Helen and Cyprian made me climb Mount Wilson one evening to see the stars through the biggest telescope in the world. Besides that I stay stretched on the porch and try to wait it out. Helen and Cyprian take care of me and spoil me with peach ice cream, hot cakes and waffles, iced tea, and beautiful fruits, and it all will end in the long run, I hope.

Our friend toni is in Los Angeles and I saw him twice. She seems a bit discouraged, poor girl, and thinks of Paris and the rue de l'Odéon with nostalgia. But she is still a nice girl and laughs heartedly. She told me that George Antheil and Bosky are en route to California where he hopes to find a job as a musical director in some Hollywood studios. What I hear of his work ethic in his music is not very reassuring.

I hope Margaret begins to get along in the affairs of my shop and that she will not need to bother you all the time—rested in vacation and reposed as you must be right now.

You will hug your parents for me and I embrace you tightly.

Side Notes: My good recollections to Mlle. Therenet and to Bianche.

If you see Valery or Gide or someone else who I love you will give them a good kiss on my behalf.

Sylvia Beach Papers, Manuscripts Division, Department of Rare Books
and Special Collections, Princeton University Library (manuscript)

* * *

154. To Marion Peter   **No date, September 1936**

2885 Santa Anita Ave
Altadena, California

Dearest Marion,

You have got my wire by this time congratulating Sylvia dear about her debut and regretting that I can't be there for the great event. I am so terribly disappointed not to see you for at least a few hours, but my plans have been at a complete standstill on account of my being knocked out by headaches and my father knocked down in Pasadena by a car and in the hospital ever since. Fortunately he was not seriously injured and will be out next Monday, but he is 84 years old and my sisters and I were pretty badly scared. I have had to postpone my departure till the last possible moment and shall not be leaving till Wednesday night. Isn't it annoying to think that my plane will be stopping (for only ten minutes) at Chicago on Thursday the 10th the very day of Sylvia's coming-out, and that owing to my being so pressed for time I cant spare even a few hours to see you on my way to New York?! I must go first to Princeton and then to New York to see about some business before I sail on the 'Normandie' on the 16th.

I would have loved so much to go to Lake Forest for a little look at you all but those cursed headaches first, then Father's accident kept me tied down here. I was obliged to transfer my passage from the 2nd to the 16th and the extra time it gave me was not even able to be of any use to me in seeing you and other friends. It was you darling Marian, above all, that I wanted to see, but you must come over to Paris soon.

If you have a minute to write to me before I sail, my address will be to Miss Marian Willard, Locust Valley, Long Island.

You must be in a whirl of preparations at this moment. I do hope everything will be fine and jolly and wish I could see how lovely Sylvia looks, admired by millions! thanks for her picture in the paper.

With ever so much love, and please tell your husband that I would have liked to have at last made his acquaintance

Your loving
Sylvia

Sylvia Beach Papers, Manuscripts Division, Department of Rare Books and Special Collections, Princeton University Library (manuscript)

❋ ❋ ❋

155. **To Adrienne Monnier**   September 24, 1936

To Miss Marian Willard
Meudon, Locust Valley
Long Island
September 24 1936

My good dear Adrienne,

I had protracted my departure to the 30th after a series of events; however now I see that I will miss the departure again set on the 30th and will only be able to leave by a ship that will follow "Normandie" a few days later. I will warn you as soon as I know which ship to take. All this is because of my poor health that has not stopped giving me problems since my departure from Paris, and even before my trip to Jersey. Actually, I have not been feeling well this whole year. Finally, once at Marian Willard's it was going well at all and the doctor who takes care of her family sent me to the hospital where they gave me a scraping. (A sort of scraping on the inner walls of the uterus) and where I stayed for four days to get over it—I am finally leaving today. Afterwards, I will be forced to obtain x-rays an hour everyday for six days so that I would be in condition to travel, which, as you see, will make me miss "Normandie" again. The doctor discovered, during this little operation, a good amount of bad things. What a bustling trip I had, in the name of God. First, my sick father and his fall in Princeton. Afterwards, my bad health in California; Then my father knocked over by an automobile and transported to the hospital; and me at the clinic to finish. All that we can say to be seen on the good side is that all this could have been worse, a lot worse. My dear dad has escaped death, a miracle, and I could have had the crane fractured or a leg amputated. And I had a lot of chance from Marian's side who was of extraordinary kindness for me and I even think that she will buy a Joyce of my items. She's a unique person, and so tactful and so relaxing. She has a lot of courage to defend her ideas in her surroundings which is of the most frightening bourgeois rich New Yorkers. She does not care about anything that seems important to them.

At last I missed the occasion to see some people here and all of New England that Marian would have made me visit by car and the entertaining things to see in New York—like in California, besides where Helen and Cyprian had projects to walk me all the way to San Francisco and to the Arizona Desert etc. finally it's like that. And provided that you have enjoyed yourself and rested this summer and that Gisela is better and that my poor little shop abandoned by its owner is well kept by Margaret!

Marian's "bulldog" Rococo is very good and you will like him very much. Suddenly, he is really "gray" as Burgine would say.

Hug all my friends for me and most of all your parents and your sister.

And to one of these days in the beginning of October.
I hug you strongly,
Sylvia

Harry Ransom Humanities Research Center, The University of Texas
at Austin (manuscript)

* * *

156. To Böske Antheil   November 3, 1936

Dearest Boske:

I was glad to get your nice letter of Oct. 14 and had been intending to write to you long ago to thank you for the apartment (which, alas I was never able to make use of) and to let you know why I didn't go up there. But you know now the reason, and you understand that I was too ill to write any letters at all. When I finally sent up to New York a few days before sailing, and looked in at your flat, that nice Mrs Evans told me it had been rented, and that she had given me up after a month. No wonder. It was kind of you, Boske to write and tell her to look out for me, and she told me she stayed around out of hours to receive me early in September. She suggested getting a room in the hotel next door—the something-or-other which I did and found it very comfortable and not too dear. And my old friend and abonné Elliot Carter called me and invited me to tea in your-his rooms. He played me some of his ballet on Pocahontas that he is doing for the American ballet at the Metropolitan, and I was very glad to see him again. And I saw Miss Soharrer a minute— in bed wore out from the White Horse Inn. But you can imagine how miserable I was feeling in New York just escaped from hospital. Anyhow I'm glad I had all that done in the U.S. as I believe they are a little more careful, and I haven't forgotten how George was nearly railroaded into a sanatorium by that Dr. Moinson here, and that it was Bill Bullit[78] who

---

78. William Bullit, American ambassador in Paris during the 1920s.

had him re-diagnosed by a man in the Avenue des Ternes. The doctor on Long Island said if I didn't have this operation done the malady I had would have my work licked, as he expressed it. But it was a terrible shock for my purse, and I can say that I have had severe financial losses or reverses this summer. It'll take me six months to get over the operation and it'll be years before my finances will be anything like re-covered. So you see what comes of wanting to see the world.

I'm glad to hear you and George have found a good place to live in and that he is prospering in Hollywood.[79] That's splendid. I don't see any use of not getting some of their money away from them. whenever possible.

Yes, I think you and Cyprian would get along nicely together. She is quite a wonderful person when you know her, and Helen Eddy is too fine and interesting for words. When you have time you must see them.

Paris is rather sombre and although Americans are supposed to be all coming back now with the dollar rising, the only American that has reached here so far is Mr Tom Gibbons, a friend of Toni's. Still it is Paris and I don't know what there is about it that makes it IT of cities. I had the same old feeling when I got in. And it was fine to see that next to my carpenter's in the rue Grégoire de Tour 'Ida'and 'Marcelle' look as prosperous and homelike as ever. And I dont think Rockerfeller Center (or City) can compare to the rue de l'Odéon in conception.

By the way, if George should run across one of those Hollywood collectors with which Dr Rosenbach says it bristles, would he mind asking him to buy while he has this unique chance that wonderful collection of world-famous signatures appended to the Ulysses protest.[80] I have marked it in the catalogue of which I am sending you a copy, with a red cross.

Please thank George for inviting me to use the apartment, and yourself for all the trouble you took to write and everything.

> With very much love
> Sylvia

Estate of George Antheil (manuscript)

* * *

---

79. Antheil composed the scores for several films, including *Once in a Blue Moon* (1935) and *The Plainsman* (1936).

80. This famous 1927 protest, publicized by the *New York Times* (February 27) and elsewhere, was signed by, inter alia, D. H. Lawrence, W. Somerset Maugham, H. G. Wells, and W. B. Yeats. It is included in this volume as Appendix 2.

157. To Marion Peter   **November 3, 1936**

Dearest Marion,

Your letter of the 21st enclosing cheque for five hundred francs has come and it is very very kind indeed of you, my dearest Marion, to help me so generously! I can't tell you how grateful I feel, too, for the interest you take in Shakespeare & Co. Your contribution is most opportune at this moment when my business has reached a new low and is weaker than it has been since the beginnings of it. All business over here has been affected by the present political stir-up and war scares, but mine, of course particularly. And the critical time is now until the Group begins in January to contribute the second year support—provided the French are not too impoverished by that time to continue.

What would I have given to see Sylvia's début! She must have been 'a wow' (is that what you call it) and I'm sure she is the most popular girl in Chicago sassiety. But they must nearly kill her with parties. I loved the newspaper picture of her you sent me, and also Phyllis who seems to be as good as out herself too. Oh my, Marion, what a winter you have let yourself in for with those giddy girls! And what of little Marion? I hope you are holding her back on reserve. I'll bet she is all dated up too though and is trying to make up her mind already, who not to marry. I do wish I could have stopped on the way from California to New York to see you all, but was rushing to catch a boat which I never boarded after all, nor made the next two sailings. I was laid up at my friend Marian Willard's on Long Island, finally had to go to the hospital and have operations and x rays and only managed to sail on the 14th of October, getting back here just two weeks ago. You see I was ill all summer and until I was examined by the doctor at Locust Valley, didn't know what was the matter with me. But now they say I'm all fixed up and will be as good as new in another six months. And it's a good thing this was done when I was on Long Island with an excellent hospital and doctors to take care of me. Marian Willard, too, was very kind, keeping me at her beautiful place in Locust Valley while I was convalescing, and looking after the doctors' bills which I've no idea how I could have paid at this inopportune moment. So I was very lucky. In fact everybody has been terribly kind—the French line that gave me special rates on 'Normandie', and a friend who paid half the passage, and my father blew me in to the flight to California and the only day or two I spent in New York friends were so cordial and reporters interviewed me and a publisher offered to publish my memoirs if I'd write 'em. . . .

But it was a funny kind of a visit to my country after 21 years, don't you think so! I liked it so much, though too sick to do anything or see people that I counted on seeing—yourself, for example, Marion dear.

Paris is quite a contrast to America where things seemed to look lively and hopeful—here still dull and depressed and everyone anxious over the European situation—il y a de quoi![81] By the time you get this the fight in Spain may be finished—temporarily—and you will have elected somebody as President over there—Right now you're doing it.

Day after tomorrow I'm going to a dinner at the Pen Club where Jules Romain, back from America where he lectured at Mills College in California is to preside. The guest of honour is to be Pio Baroja.

With loving gratitude dearest Marion for your gift, and much love to yourself and the gels.

from
            Sylvia

Sylvia Beach Papers, Manuscripts Division, Department of Rare Books and Special Collections, Princeton University Library (manuscript)

* * *

158. To Marcelle Sibon[82]   March 10, 1937

Dear Marcelle,

Excuse me for not answering your letter all this time. As usual, I have been swamped with work. I handed over your translation of Dal Stivens'[83] to Louis Guilloux[84] who is a great friend of Chamson's, asking him to try to get it into 'Vendredi'.[85] Also I thought Guilloux and his crowd ought to be interested in Dal Stivens; and when Mr Church comes back I will see if we can't interest him in the stories. If anything comes of this I will let you know and perhaps other stories could get published. Don't

---

81. With good reason!
82. Marcelle Sibon, translator best known for French versions of Graham Greene's novels.
83. Dal Stivens (1911–1997), Australian novelist. His first book, *The Tramp and Other Stories*, was published in 1936. Sibon's translation is unpublished.
84. Louis Guilloux (1899–1980), French novelist and anti-fascist activist.
85. André Chamson (1900–1983), French critic, novelist, and co-editor of *Vendredi*, an independent leftist weekly journal.

you think the first one—about the boxing match, is good? I like the book, all except about the sheep which is too terrible to bear, isn't it?

How are you and what have you been doing besides working? Did you know that Katharine Anne Porter has got a prize of two thousand five hundred dollars?[86] It is a yearly one awarded to the best but little known by the ordinary public book. Excuse this funny sentence but someone is trying to keep up a conversation with me while I write. I hope you will not mind. I am sending you Elizabeth Bowen's 'House in Paris' this time.[87] She is one of the best novelists in England at present. This book seems to have been somewhat influenced by Henry James—perhaps—but that's no crime, is it?, and Bowen is not the only one to have read him. Its funny but I wonder if every generation of writers lately hasn't either an American or an Irishman as a master: after Henry James—T.S. Eliot, and now all the younger writers take after Hemingway.

I saw Hemingway yesterday. He is on his way to Spain.[88] And Spender was here also a few weeks ago, likewise on his way to Spain to do the broadcasting for the Government at Valencia.[89] He said he would write to you. He is returning some time in the spring. His new little wife was charming.

> With affectionate greetings,
> Sylvia

Mairie de Paris, Bibliothèque Marguerite Durand (Paris) (manuscript)

* * *

159. To The Friendship Press   March 17, 1937

> The Friendship Press,
> 150 Fifth Avenue,
> New York.

Dear Sirs,

The French Negro students in Paris rely on my lending library to keep them in touch, as much as possible, with American Negro literature. I have

---

86. Katherine Anne Porter (1890–1980), American novelist and journalist.

87. Elizabeth Bowen (1899–1973), Anglo-Irish novelist. *The House in Paris*, her fifth novel, was published in 1935.

88. The Spanish Civil War broke out in July 1936, and many left-leaning writers and artists traveled there to fight on the side of the anti-fascist Republican resistance. Hemingway reported on the war for the North American Newspaper Alliance.

89. Stephen Spender (1909–1995), English poet and critic.

a number of very interesting books by the poets and novelists, and studies on the subject of the problems of the American Negro, but not as many as I should like and would purchase if I had the funds for it. Unfortunately my little shop is going through a crisis just now, and would have gone under if it had not been for the help of friends. Pardon me for telling you this, but it is to explain why I have to make a very careful selection of only the most essential books, and to ask you to help me by suggesting a few representative ones that my library should possess; also what is the best Negro paper or review to which I could subscribe? Meanwhile, will you please send m e, with your bill, the following: Ina Corinne Brown: <u>The Story of the American Negro</u>: Charles Johnson: <u>A Preface to Racial Understanding</u>:

Edwin Embrie: <u>Brown America</u>: Mary Feness (or Jeness?) <u>Twelve Negro Americans</u> and the current number of THE CRISIS and OPPORTUNITY.

Sylvia Beach Papers, Manuscripts Division, Department of Rare Books and Special Collections, Princeton University Library (manuscript)

* * *

160. **To Alfred A. Knopf**   **March 17, 1937**

Mr. Alfred A. Knopf,
730 Fifth Avenue,
New York.

Dear Sir,

Will you kindly send me the pamphlet:

<u>Willa Cather: A Biographical Sketch</u> issued by hour house in 1927: and a copy of <u>One of Ours</u> and <u>O Pioneers</u>. And could you please suggest a good critical study of Willa Cather that would help a French student who is writing a paper on the subject. If it is not asking too much of you, I would be glad to obtain a copy of Dorothy Canfield Fisher's article: <u>Daughter of the Frontier</u> which appeared in the Herald Tribune on May 28, 1933.

Will you be so kind as to send off the books (without waiting for the information) by the first fast boat.

Also please send me a few copies of Jules Romains' letter to his American critics.

Yours truly,
Shakespeare and Company

Sylvia Beach Papers, Manuscripts Division, Department of Rare Books and Special Collections, Princeton University Library (manuscript)

* * *

161. To Marion Peter   May 25, 1937

Dearest Marion,

You must be thinking you were never going to get an acknowledgment of your very swell letter and very generous offering for Shakespeare and Company. And now it looks as if 'Normandie' that was to take this to you so rapidly would be held up by strikes and not sailing tomorrow unless someone gives in. I was quite overwhelmed by your large 500 franc cheque, Marion dear, and how can I thank you for your thoughtful friendship that touches me more than I can say. It is too kind of you. If I can look out a bit for my namesake I shall be only too glad, and, in my next letter I will send you the information you want about where she might stay here and the Sorbonne programs for her studies. As for her help once a week in my shop, why that means a crowd of fresh customers coming to buy their books at Shakespeare and Company's only for the pleasure of seeing the fascinating Sylvia-Jeune.[90] But lets hope there won't be too many nasty suicides for love un-requited messing up the street in front of the shop. I'm afraid though, that she wont find it very amusing work. We dont often have a Hemingway-Spender reading like the one last week, and its not particularly lively handing out books all day to some of the types who have to have something sweet that ends happily, or a copy of Omar that has the exact measurements required. For a lively young, and pretty person its not apt to be so funny, even when she's got lots of brains as I know Sylvia has. So at least I have warned her.

I was sorry to hear of the streptococuss germs' descent on your nice family, and Phyllis with the mumps. You must have had a big time and lots of worries in spite of your wonderful disposition. I hope you have got the family all fixed up again now and will keep them so. I'm surprized that anyone as sassy as Marion the second let a mere bug get ahold of her. But cheer up—you still have two more coming-outs to work ahead on. I dont think you spanked 'em up enough, your gals; just wait til Sylvia gets over here with her auntie and see if she doesn't improve with much beating. You wont recognize her after a bit. You can send the others later.

---

90. Young Sylvia.

I've been horribly busy for the last two months, with a Maurois reading followed close at hand by Hemingway and Spender which Sylvia would have loved. They had just arrived from Spain where Hemingway was doing some articles, and insisted on having a double reading. Spender is a gentle boy with nice manners and Freddy Bartholomew English; Hemingway is, as everyone knows, a Tough Guy, and several times while he was reading one or two of the older un-married ladies almost got up and left, but stayed hoping for worse, which they got. Joyce did leave, but not for the same reasons. I think it was more, as Adrienne said, the sight of all the beer and whiskey displayed on the table in front of the boys, of which they were partaking freely, that made him too thirsty to stand it any longer.

As for André Maurois, there's nothing to tell, that's why I'm not telling you; he just read a number of stories for the sophisticated mostly about adultry, so its just as well Sylvia wasn't here.

Then I spent what our English cousins call 'Whitsuntide' with a friend who has a little house called 'Rien du Tout' down near Dieppe. And this weekend I'm going to spend in Switzerland at my friend Bryher's viller by Lake Geneva. She's paying my fare, that explains it. I'm also arranging to exhibit her review 'Life and Letters To-Day' at the Exposition. Perhaps some of the nit-wits who pass through there will have their attention called to my little shop. Anyhow that's what Bryher is hoping. And then I've been in bed with a very bad headache which lays me down hard every week or so, in a way that would disgust anyone. That's why the cables from two firms who seem to be expecting my memoirs never get an answer, and never will probably unless Sylvia hurries up and comes over to the rescue.

Thankyou once more, my dearest Marion, for your very kind gift, with ever so much love to yourself and all the family,

        from

          Sylvia

Sylvia Beach Papers, Manuscripts Division, Department of Rare Books and Special Collections, Princeton University Library (manuscript)

* * *

162. To Raphael King   January 29, 1938

Mr. Raphael King,
28 Museum Street,
London, W.C.I.

Dear Mr King,

You may assure your client in America that the MSS. of 'Pomes Pen-yeach' which you purchased from my catalogue in 1936 are authentic Joyce MSS., I guarantee it. Mr Joyce himself gave them to me at the time I was publishing the little volume of 'Pomes Penyeach' and anyone famil-iar with his handwriting could not doubt their authenticity.

I am sending you, as you request, a copy of my catalogue in which this manuscript is listed.

Yours sincerely,
Sylvia Beach

The Huntington Library (HM 41123), San Marino, California (manuscript)

* * *

163. To Marcelle Sibon   October 27, 1938

Dear Marcelle,

Thank you so much for your letter. I don't believe I ever received the letter and card you mention—something must have happened to them during August and September when I was up in the mountains. But my friends all know by this time that, on account of the continual headaches from which I suffer, their letters usually remain unanswered and they take my gratitude for granted. And we have been going through a rather trying period, haven't we? I hope you are well and that you will drop in to see me next time you come to Paris and we shall renew our old friendship.

I enclose a prospectus of the library in case you care to renew it too. I work in my room above the shop while a temporary assistant takes care of the shop, and am trying in spite of one headache after another to finish a history of Shakespeare & Co that the publishers asked me to do.[91]

---

91. Beach's memoir *Shakespeare and Company* would finally be published in 1959.

They have been waiting over two years and are beginning to wonder whether they are ever going to get a look at them. If I could only work it into some sort of a shape and the history interested these publishers they might pay me something that would help me out during the hard times.

However, if I am not in my library when you come my assistant will call me and I will rush down to see you.

Yours affectionately,
Sylvia Beach

Mairie de Paris, Bibliothèque Marguerite Durand (Paris) (manuscript)

* * *

164. To Marion Peter October 28, 1938

Dearest Marion,

Now you are going to say: 'Ha-ha! I told her so in my letter last summer—she only writes when she gets a cheque—it's a sure way to hear from her!" And the cheque has come and you're never going to believe that I was really about to write you at last—a nice long letter.

In the first place, please accept my most loving gratitude for your gift of five hundred francs. It is very very very kind of you to remember my needs and to help me as you do so generously. You are indeed a good friend, Marion dear! And these unearned cheques are a windfall and awfully cheering things to get! Our Sylvia will tell you that we can work days on end in the bookshop without being able to pull down any such sums in spite of all the pressures we can bring to bear on our reluctant 'bunnies'.

Your letter and Sylvia's that were forwarded to me in Savoie gave me a lot of pleasure and I was glad to hear what the Peter family was doing and how. I intended to write to my former assistant and namesake after she left and to thank her for her help in my library and getting hold of a new aid—Priscilla Curtis—which it was very nice of her to think of—but, with my other friends, you have long ago lost any illusions about me as a correspondent. My headaches, as you know, are mostly responsible for this sad state of affairs—and then the sad state of my affairs themselves, which does not permit me to have a secretary to take off all the business scribblings that have to be done every day—routine stuff while my friends are kept waiting for news. As for the holidays, they were spent entirely on the history of Shakespeare and Co that the publishers

asked me to send them over two years ago and which I have been trying to finish in spite of the many difficulties and interruptions, making
it almost an impossible enterprize for me. Eleanor Oldenburger's presence in the shop enables me to go ahead with the tale, though headaches
have knocked me out several times since I came back. It was only in
the mountains that I was free from them. I rushed here when war was
about to hit us and found Paris darkened and Parisians fled. As for our
compatriots, the Embassy has advised them to leave as quickly as possible—and they did. It seems a pity, particularly for the groups of students
that had arrived for the winter and had to hurry right home—likity-split.
They may never have the opportunity again to do a year in Paris.

Priscilla went over to London to her aunt and grandmother but came
back when things settled down. She is a dear and works hard every day
with Eleanor who has been with me nearly a year now and runs the shop
marvellously. Her husband came over in the summer and wanted to take
her back to Chicago where he is now professor at the University. But he
consented to her staying on with me till December so that I could finish
the memoirs. When she leaves Priscilla and I will carry on together, that
is, if her mother lets her stay a while longer. She, Priscilla, is very intel-
ligent and a great help, but of course she lacks the experiences Eleanor
has had and is much younger. But she is learning and I expect to lean on
her a lot after Eleanor leaves.

To go back to war—everyone was relieved when it didn't come off,
and, with the exception of some people at the Quai d'Orsay and others
who talk about 'la déhonneur',[92] think it was right to give up everything
and anything for the sake of peace. I am sure the German and Italian
people were as glad as the English and French that, at least for the present, they were not to be engaged in stupid warfare. Things don't look
so cheerful even now but we are hoping all the same we can keep the
peace. France was not prepared to fight and there was not a single gas
mask ready for the civilian population, I am told—can't spare sons for
the battlefield—hasn't a sou either to finance a war, and had the courage
and good sense to get out in time—England likewise. Don't you think so?

You must have been jolly with all your girls at home. I miss my Sylvia
and tell her I am wearing the beautiful scarf she gave me last Christmas
and always think of her. I only wish I had beaten her with a broom-
stick to make her stick around at Shakespeare & Co but I felt that she
was too young and attractive—and attractive is a mild term to apply to

---

92. Dishonor.

Sylvia—to bury herself in my dusty little old bookshop, though she made herself very useful when she was there, that I didn't like to bring pressure to bear on her life that was nobody else's business. A bookshop is mostly tiresome details all day long and you have to have a passion for it as Eleanor seems to, to grub and grub in it. I have always loved books and their authors, and for the sake of them swallowed the rest of it, but you can't expect everyone to do the same. However, as a recognition of my so-called services, the French last summer—you may have heard of it—bestowed the Legion of Honour on me.

Well don't let the girls get the better of you – hold out to the last ditch, and send me back my Sylvia before some rascal gets hold of and marries her. I told her she would make a lovely ambassadress so look up a diplomat for her – one with a big future

With once more my big thanks dearest Marion, and ever so much love to yourself and Sylvia

from Sylvia

Sylvia Beach Papers, Manuscripts Division, Department of Rare Books and Special Collections, Princeton University Library (manuscript)

* * *

165. To Norman Douglas

February 3, 1939

Dear Uncle Norman,

Excuse me for not answering your letter at once. I've been suffering terribly with my head again.

I have enquired about 'South Wind' and it has not appeared in French nor has a translation been announced.[93] They would surely let you know first, wouldn't they? Last summer in June, I think, I asked the critic René Lalore to come to see me—he has something to do with the publishers Stock who do a collection of translations from English writers and are said to be very satisfactory people to deal with—and Lalore seemed quite interested in the idea of introducing you to the French—a great honour for him. I told him I thought it a disgrace that one of our great-

---

93. Douglas (1868–1952) was the Austrian-born author of the 1917 novel *South Wind*.

est writers was still unknown in France. I lent him 'South Wind' and he hurried away to read it and then the War came in the summer and upset everything. But he is coming to see me tomorrow and will tell me what the prospects are at present for bringing out 'South Wind'. If Stock is not ready to do something about it at once I will approach another publisher. I have already given many a hint to the Nouvelle Revue Francaise but they are hopelessly slow and beknighted or benighted whatever you call it and their present reader knows even less about our literature than the former one who took no interest whatever in anything good that competent people proposed to him. In fact all the publishers here are looking for is another Mary Webb[94] or Rosamund Lehmann[95] who have 'gone over Big' with the French public—either the 'gaffer and gammer school'[96] as Edith Sitwell calls it or the vaguely vicious 'jeune fille anglaise'[97] so that's the situation. But I shall persevere and let you know any developments.

With affectionate greetings

Sylvia

How and when and for how long did you go to Russia? Bryher thinks you were about seven when you went to England.

I forwarded a letter from a young Hungarian lady who is writing a thesis on you and would be very grateful if you would supply her with some biographical details – were you born in the Vorarlberg and where? And where did you go to school?

General Manuscripts, Yale University, Beinecke Rare Book

and Manuscript Library (manuscript)

---

94. Mary Webb (1881–1927), English novelist who wrote about rural life in the style of Thomas Hardy. Her books became bestsellers after her death.
95. Rosamond Lehmann (1901–1990), English novelist who wrote of women's lives, educations, and loves. Her novel about of college life, *Dusty Answer*, was a bestseller of 1927.
96. *Gaffer* was British slang for "grandfather" and gammer for "grandmother."
97. Young English girl.

V

POSTWAR

166. To Adrienne Monnier   **No date (c. 1940)**

Dear Adrienne,

You do me the honor of asking me to say a word about which English writers I like. Is this a struggle? First, it's no longer a secret that my favorites are my associate "Bill" Shakespeare, William Blake and James Joyce. And I like De Quincey and Melville.[1] I know very well that the professors of The Gazette des Amis des Livres[2] have never heard of the question of our literature,[3] but if my preferences interest less of the world, cross the rue de l'Odeon and enter into my library of the moment where I make suggestions to one or another of my subscribers, whom we refer to affectionately as 'the Bunnies'. The majority of my 'Bunnies', I draw to your attention, know our literature perfectly . . . I don't hesitate to say, that it's they who have given me precious advice on the subject. Often, a client requesting a book will reveal it to me for the first time. I'm by no means an academic, and during the years of the existence of my bookstore, I have been taught while teaching the students. I am, in sum, my most faithful 'Bunny'.

---

1. Writing to Carlotta Welles Briggs in 1948, Beach noted "how oldfashioned my tastes are—mostly running to Jane Austen—am reading the autobiography of Trollope—The Castle of Indolence—La Princesse de Clèves – Burrrns – Beowulf etc. and of course always Joyce who is the greatest English classic" (SBP, box 58, folder 16, manuscripts).
2. *La Gazette des Amis des Livres* was the journal Monnier published from her bookstore.
3. By "our literature," Beach is referring to specifically to American literature and its still-fledgling status in France.

Unfortunate prejudices would have prevented me from knowing books that a sanctimonious atmosphere surrounded if certain of my friends hadn't insisted that I read them. It's thus that Mrs Norledge[4] made me read one of the most beautiful works in the world, 'The Story of my Heart' by Richard Jeffries.[5] Another book that I have changed my opinion on, by dint of having seen so much coming and going, without doubt, is 'The Good Earth'.[6] Happily that you, Adrienne, made me read it.

Well—listen to our quarter of an hour's interview—

—Oh Miss Beach, what do you suggest I take today?

—Well, you've already read all of Virginia Woolf, Joyce, Mansfield, Lawrence,

D.H. and the Colonel,[7] Huxley, Hemingway, Faulkner—and even Dos Passos. But wait—have you truly read *all* of these authors? Do you know, for example, "Classic American Literature" by D.H. Lawrence, with its curious study of Melville and American Puritanism?—that would interest you, Adrienne; and you're a lover of Joyce, but the lovely piece "Exiles" do you know it? (During this time you become impatient because the choice of the "Bunny" is left to fall without resistance on one of these titles and we're in the process of searching the rack but the book isn't in its place, naturally. So it goes.)

A translator approaches: What do you suggest that I translate by Dorothy Richardson, Yeats and Norman Douglas, whose names are unknown by the French public. Even so, these are the writers who have so high a place in our literature. Yeats, Irish poet and the greatest poet in the English language of our time. His daughter, Miss Ann Yeats, was shocked last year, when she asked for the works of her father translated into French and they told her that they don't exist except in magazines.[8]

---

4. Louise Norledge, a British expatriate, longtime Shakespeare and Company subscriber, and friend of Beach's.

5. Jefferies's autobiography of 1883, detailing his passionate experiences in nature.

6. Pearl S. Buck's story of a Chinese family, *The Good Earth* (1931), was awarded the Pulitzer Prize, and in 1938 she won the Nobel Prize in Literature.

7. The Colonel is T. E. Lawrence, whose autobiographical *Seven Pillars of Wisdom* appeared in 1926.

8. A French edition of Yeats would not appear until Madeleine L. Cazamian's volume of 1954.

For Norman Douglas, Madame Dorothy Bussy, the sister of Lytton Strachey, asked me when they would translate "South Wind" which has been one of our classics for a long time.

As for Dorothy Richardson, the difficulties presented by the eleven volumes of "Pilgrimage" explain a little why she's not more known in France. At the moment Monsieur Gabriel Marcel[9] is working on a large study of Dorothy Richardson and I have high hopes that she'll be launched one day. While waiting, he lives by translating good detective novels—one of Dorothy Sayers, for example, called 'Nine Tailors'. There you will ask about the job of the bell-ringers in the great English cathedrals and the complicated way of 'sonner les changes' 'ringing the changes' an art transmitted from father to son.

But here's Madame de M.—what are you going to give me for Francoise? That's easy. I also have my favorite subscribers: those who like poetry.—I recall that Francoise worships Gerard Manley Hopkins but told me that she'd never read 'Piers Ploughman' ('Piers Laboureur') by William Langland which was often spoken of by Hopkins. All our poets talk to each other.

—Miss Beach, Miss Beach, you gave me such good suggestions last time (sometimes it's the opposite and they reproach me) is there another book for me today?

Without hesitation I bring out 'Euphranor' by the author, or rather the translator, of Omar Khayham, which is an exquisite little book, and one which the author of Ulysses recommended to me. The life of Fitzgerald is so strange and you can read it after 'Euphranor'.

To another subscriber I recommend without reservation, 'Recollections of the Lake Poets" by De Quincey: this book full of gossip and I must say spitefulness about Wordsworth and his lake colleagues—which 'debunks' them and they were not as happy as all that, it appears.

Want something new?—fresh arrival—the 'Nonsense' poems of T.S. Eliot and his 'Practical Cats'. All these cats have a name by which they're known, a name that they only know, but they never confess, this name.

There's also 'The Idea of a Christian Society' by T.S. Eliot which is to be published. Why, oh why not translate absolutely all the prose of

---

9. Marcel (1889–1973) was a playwright and philosopher, sometimes credited with coining the term *existentialism*.

T.S. Eliot? He's the most fascinating and interesting personality at the present moment from across the Channel.

> It's late . . . a beautiful American novel that needs translating is 'The Yearling' by Marjory Rawlings. It was a huge success there last year and it's beautiful. And 'Grapes of Wrath' by John Steinbeck, a great book about the unfortunate farmers forced to migrate from their land to California to look for work.—-but it's Late—

Au revoir

Sylvia

Sylvia Beach Papers, Manuscripts Division, Department of Rare Books and Special Collections, Princeton University Library (manuscript)

* * *

167. To Carlotta Welles Briggs   August 14, 1941

Dear Carlotta,

Your other friends have been lucky enough to get letters from you lately and I hope it will be my turn soon. The main thing is that you are all well and enjoying the riding & swimming, and you are playing your violin in concerts—what a triumph! Carlotta dear, weren't you scared at first? 'While Rome burns' and everything else, I think you can't do better than play the fiddle. Meanwhile I am a war profiteer, that's plain enough, what with all my holidays in your beautiful place.[10] And Baptiste has kept me supplied with vegetables which with your jam have fattened me way beyond what Cyprian would allow. I am now having a holiday—business is closed. It is cool and windy and sometimes rainy here but the flowers in the border are as gay as can be and you know how the fountain and the green lawn and the trees are swell at this time of the year—and at all times. I'm afraid I'm not getting on very fast with the catalogue I'm mak-

---

10. Beach was staying at the Briggs's home in Bourré, which they had abandoned at the outset of the war, leaving "enough goods to provide a possible refuge for Sylvia," who had decided to remain in France (Fitch, *Sylvia Beach and the Lost Generation*, 396). Beach's cheerful tone belies the grim nature of life in the French countryside in 1941.

ing of your library. Mrs de gallais[11] seemed to think it was a good plan but perhaps you don't particularly want one. Anyhow it's a big amusement for me and can't do any harm I think. The de gallaises are coming soon after the 15th when I shall be going back to town. When they told me they were going to look after your affairs I was so glad. Something of the sort is indispensable in the circumstances. Maria has done nobly and is looking forward to another coal-less winter with great courage but the de gallaises can do things to alleviate, I imagine. Fuel is of course our biggest problem. I am simply having a nice couple of gas radiators put in my library for next winter. You are allowed to have one turned on for 3 hours a day, then you turn on the second one—total: 6 hours and I only open in the afternoon.

Carlotta dear, thank you very very much indeed for your kindness in sending me three thousand francs which came the 6th of May. I couldn't even acknowledge it but you understood and knew how grateful I felt to get such a present all the same. I send you a right hug and much love to yourself and Jim and the two athletes. And heres hoping this business will soon be over and the Briggses back again, though I hope you will introduce your sons as otherwise I shall never recognize my old pals.

Please kiss Cyprian for me and tell her she had better make the most of her holiday from letter writing. She'll have a hard time catching up afterward. I hope she is well and managing the problem of living.

I have tried to get messages through to Holly from time to time but never hear a squeak from her.

Your friend Mme Basseglian died in May 194[?]. Her son is a prisoner. The

neighbours told me all about them. An operation on her eyes was unsuccessful.

Raffy came to see me—very scared—but I think she has nothing to fear.

Miss Watson is staying on and I am often invited to lunch at the Foyer.
With much love as ever from Sylvia

PS Your guests have gone—others may come. Jim's piano has always been treated carefully, and after looking around with Juliette I have been relieved to note a minimum of destruction. Juliette is bringing up a pig in the next-door cave. She is clean and odorless—the pig.

There's a magpie in the village who is going to be someone's dinner if she doesn't stop flying into rooms and stealing anything it can lay its

---

11. The De Gallaises were family friends whom Carlotta Welles Briggs had appointed to oversee their affairs.

hands on. Trinkets or a whole cheese, the coiffeuse says, disappear in the magpie's secret cache.

Mlle Arbel has moved into a small house Jacqueline says, as the big one was 'en viager' (?).[12] Jacqueline is here—thin, but fine morale. Like the white queen, all her yelling was beforehand.

Corn is just beginning. There are no lima beans this year.

A great big hug from Sylvia

Please thank Jim hope Jim wont mind my using his bike very carefully a godsend to all his friends me and de gallaises I took yours to Madeleine de Cuy who has a field a long way off. She was writing to ask if she could borrow it. I took the liberty.

Sylvia Beach Papers, Manuscripts Division, Department of Rare Books and Special Collections, Princeton University Library (manuscript)

* * *

168. To Adrienne Monnier   **August 25, 1941**

La Salle du Roc
Bourré
(Loir-et-Cher)

08/25/41

Dear Adrienne,

I am staying here longer than we thought, eh, but I will return without a doubt at the end of the week and Juliette has pretty much promised me a bunny. Can little Saillet come look for us, me and bunny—at the train station this Saturday night to the train that is arriving in Paris around 8?

The victuals are completely lacking in this country—not one chicken or eggs or butter or cheese or rabbits. It's undreamed of to want to separate yourself from this treasure and it's possible that at the last moment it will slip out of my hands. If only I could rip the ribs out of the hog that she is raising, the "pig" that she calls it gently. But I went to bow down to all the contacts here to have a chicken. Yet we see some peck around the houses.

---

12. "In life annuity."

They will give me a few eggs to be crushed on this trip towards Paris with the crowd that I am hoping to find in the trains in this end of month.

I hope that you took a vacation and that you have rested just like me. You needed one after so many months of fatigue and deprivation and to bear another winter of the same kind that is awaiting us.

I am reading the Father Huc's trip to Tibet that you love so much—how beautiful it is! One of the greatest books.

Miss. De Vigan was really happy to have the books that this angel of Saillet sent her. Soon I will be able to thank "viva voce" for this clutch that he made. Until Saturday night at 8.

And a hug,

Sylvia

Harry Ransom Humanities Research Center, The University of Texas at Austin (manuscript)

* * *

169. To Adrienne Monnier   August 7, 1943

12 rue de l'odéon,
Paris VI
7 August 43

My little Adrienne,

What joy to receive your letter yesterday afternoon! And 7 days since it was sent! Anyway you are over there with my dear Fine and my dear gay and you drink good milk and breathe the air of Les Désert. It seems to me a bit hazardous to go down to Aix. I would have preferred to pass the day in Chambery and climb, maybe late, with the car. But you wanted to have that experience and there you did it. I was horrified by your trip—pulling around your baggage like that! Poor Adrienne! It's Rinette who will be happy to read all that, and your mother also. I was not able to go to HiM street yesterday evening and might not be able to go before tomorrow. It's that lo and behold many nights in a row I dine at the Foyer to bring myself up to date with the events that palpitate at this time. During the day other things occupy me. Our friend J.B.M.[13] finally sent a nice letter and it was necessary that I pay him some visits. And now I've done all that I could

---

13. Jacques Benoist-Méchin, a patron of Shakespeare and Company who used his connections to organize Beach's release from internment at Vittel.

do for Mabel too and I wait. But that poor little Françoise—that which
one fears for her has finally happened. She left a week ago. One has in any
event hope that she will drag herself out of it. It will be immediately or
otherwise never. That made us so worried. Me I could not do it anymore
naturally. I stayed in the apartment while Argentina handled you there,
and I climbed up there from time to time to check on mites and mice—
but I didn't see any. Mme Fournier is going to lend me one of her two cats
that do the service at the Foyer to make a tour at your house later when
the mice would have digested the product. It seems that it is necessary
to leave them alone fifteen days so they infect each other in biting themselves after that you are rid of them. This cat does not give satisfaction to
his mistresses. He sucks his penis all night and Lucienne, saying that it
was a worm that he had at the tip, cut him that tip with a pair of scissors.
He continues to suck himself and although he eats like three persons does
not "profit". With that he has legs set in an arc. It was decided that I would
bring him to the negro veterinarian's office for a consultation, and if this
one said that he would never be very strong would not render the services asked of him vis-à-vis with the rats in the Foyer, that I will get him
injected. I brought him there then. The negro advised to keep him, cut
him then and there, and I brought him his ladies that would have just as
soon have liked never to see him again. But that poor Bijou. One should
not have cut the tip from his penis. From whence comes that superstition
of a worm? Your concierge at 7 thinks so too. She says that all cats have a
worm at the tip of the penis and that their Mickey does not stop to shake
his because of it. The negro said that was false.

I was happy to have all those details on the Plateau and on Fine and gay.
Next you will write me about your visit below to Germaine and her girls.

As to the utilization of certain things of mine—it's normal and I do
not grudge my [. . .] to my little Odette. I hope that they rendered her
service, comfortable as they were. But my leather shoes from Williams I
would love to find as soon as possible. If not I no longer think of it. Nor
the rest. It's the war.

You went through all the trouble of writing me that long letter soon
after your arrival up there. I hope that you will rest well and will walk in
the forest and on the heights and will pick raspberries and mushrooms.
And stay there also as long as possible.

I received a note from Paulham on the subject of [. . .] and half of his
letter was for you. Him and Germaine embrace us and he rues the way of
the dictator of going away "like a simple Chautemps."[14] I responded that

---

14. Camille Chautemps (1885–1963), mayor of Tours who resigned as the result of a scandal.

you were in Savoie—and to make a niche I said that I had spent the night in a tree close to the train station to get a place on the train. Well done for the [word(s) not clear], you find me not?

Also there is Gordon Craig[15] who invites both of us to dine "after the 15 when his favorite restaurant will be reopened". I replied to him as well.

My migraine did not leave until Friday. After that, it's ok. This dinner on the 15 for which you've already made the menu with Fine will be magnificent. But the alcohol will be missing, alas. If you miss meat, do you want me to send you a box of Bully Beef? Without eggs, without butter, what are you going to do to feed yourself?

M. Allier did not have a place for [Chalon?] either—yet he had been at the train station at 5 before 10. And nobody in your compartment! I comprehend nothing about it.

I went to go see your father last Sunday and brought him his wine. He was in very good health and said that he had all that he needed. I stayed a good time chatting with him and relating to him your departure to Savoie. Rinette went to see him without a doubt Thursday the day before yesterday, and her mother another day I do not recall which one. In returning to Hay-les-Rosen I passed by her house and she kept me for soup. She told me how her week would be filled with, besides her parents, P.E's[16] mother one day for dinner.

I saw little Clark the other day. He has gotten along well.

We have rain every day and it is less hot.

I embrace you strongly. Embrace Toni and gay for me. Tell them they were very nice to take up the affaires of the cabin—without them they would have surely taken it all from me. You will ask Germaine to pay the taxes as she has the habit. As to the insurance you need to only send a money order. I am so happy that the new toilets pleased you. Have you tried them?

Big kiss.

Sylvia

Harry Ransom Humanities Research Center, The University of Texas at Austin (manuscript)

---

15. The son of the actress Ellen Terry, Gordon Craig (1872–1966) was a multitalented and influential figure in London theater.
16. Rinette was Adrienne Monnier's sister. Paul-Emile Bécat, her husband, was a painter and illustrator.

* * *

170. To Katherine Dudley[17]   July 17, 1944

Katherine dear, Have regular conferences your concierge. She takes good care of everything. Paid gas, elec, tel etc amounting to 742 fr 10. I paid balance after sum you left was spent. Better to keep up with those things, specially telephone not to get cut off. Knew you wd. want. Cleaners Halles will keep your things—4 articles 147 frs but told them keep till you come—didn't pay. Bougnet corner Guenegaud. Mazarine says not a single speck of coal to be had till the end of war, his wholesale merchant no right to deliver him any. Am keeping eye on your place and things. Concierge having chimney studio swept as chimneys in your house now being done. Room where your stove only—that right dear K? Everybody sends love and regrets your enternment. Bloody bore tis! think of your being my ex-neighbor's successor! Those cardboard fires. I suggest your drawing out a lot of books from the library like she did. Will send them some more to replace. She was a great reader too—loved Robt Burns poems. 'Browning—'Smoke' by Turgenev, 'Psychanalyse du Feu' 'Fire away-and-Long-ago' the 'Burning Bush' by Sigrid Undset, all very good & entertaining titles. Adrienne been very ill, now better but not up yet. Sarah & Marcelle coming to see her this p.m. Monique also in bed—has temperature, hope better soon. D700 busy planting, hoeing watering & whenever theres anything, picking, to come to town except once for a day a while ago. Her health the same but no time for treatment. Very glad Mabel doing beautiful watercolors. Soon back home
    Much love
        Sylvia

Maurice Saillet Collection, Harry Ransom Humanities Research Center,
The University of Texas at Austin (manuscript)

* * *

17. Katherine Dudley, the American friend with whom Beach had been interned at Vittel. Dudley was still incarcerated when Beach wrote this letter (Beach was looking after Dudley's affairs in Paris).

171. **To Alice B. Toklas**   **July 28, 1946**

> 12 rue de l'Odéon
> Paris-VI
> July 28 1946

Dear Alice,

I am very sad to hear about Gertrude leaving us[18], and send you my deepest sympathy

I know it must be terribly hard for you.

> With much love
> Sylvia

Gertrude Stein and Alice B. Toklas Papers, Yale University,
Beinecke Rare Book and Manuscript Library (manuscript)

* * *

172. **To Richard Wright**[19]   **May 26, 1947**

Dear Dick,

Thankyou for your fine letter of the 3rd which I got on the 12th and hoped to answer right away. But this is the nearest I could get to 'right away'. I was so very glad to hear from you, how you and Ellen and Julia[20] were, what you did about your house, how you found things over there when you got back, etc. I have your photos before me, and think of you often. I knew you were terribly busy and that was why you didn't write— besides, I am the last person to reproach anyone with not writing letters. But I am sorry to hear you have not had time for your next books. All that business about the house and the crook lawyer must have been disgusting. It is too bad you were not able to hold onto your house, though owning property, they say, has its drawbacks too.[21]

---

18. Gertrude Stein (1874–1946) died July 27.
19. Richard Wright (1908–1960), American author of *Native Son* (1940) and *Black Boy* (1945). He moved to Paris in 1946.
20. Ellen Wright, Wright's second wife, and Julia Wright, their daughter.
21. Wright had put his Charles Street home in Greenwich Village up for sale in April 1947.

I am sorry to hear what a disgrace our people are, smashing all our hopes in a new world—a rotten business. Makes me sick to think of it. And from what you say, not even interested—just bogged. Well, over here, I wouldn't say anything was settled yet—its fairly seething, at least underneath. Two great extremes are waiting the first opportunity to meet in a clash and the middle had better skedaddle if it doesn't want to get pressed flat. Backers: Right: U.S.A., Left: URSS,[22] as you know. Meanwhile bread has gone down to 250 gr. a day, there is no meat ever, nor coal, nor sugar nor nuthin. It doesn't sound possible to have less than nothing, yet we are told to expect less next winter. There is always the B.M. for people with money.[23] But 7.000 frs is the minimum set for workers. And by the way, your radio friend, Benjamin Le Blévennec, is very pleased because he has a job in a government-owned television factory and is now earning from 12.000 to 13.000 a month. His wife and little girl Julia's age have arrived from Austria. And I wonder, dear Dick, if you mind if I use your radio occasionally. Benjamin says it is better to use them, keeps them fit, but perhaps you think it awfully cheeky of me. Dont hesitate to tell me what you think of me. My set broke down, and it was Benjamin who advised installing yours in its place, in the kitchen where, as you know, I spend a great deal of my time. He will set it up as soon as you come back wherever you are living. Where are you going to stay? I hope in Paris, and that an apartment will be found for you. The situation for lodgings is worse and worse. There are the hotels, and certainly they are cheaper than in America or in London. I have been the round of them lately for information for a friend who has a travel bureau in London and I think they are not dear.

Thankyou for your kindness in mentioning my memoirs to your publishers.[24] I have had offers from quite a number of publishers, but would rather be at your Harpers than anywhere. In fact I would be very lucky if they were interested. Will you please tell them to hold on till I can send a piece over for them to look at. I will do my best to have it there before you leave, but unless I can send it by air I wonder if I can make it now. I would so much like to have you hand it to them. The trouble is I am getting a translation of Michaux' 'Barbare en Asie' ready for Laughlin[25]

22. Beach uses the French acronym (Union des républiques socialistes soviétiques) for what in America and England was called the USSR (Union of Soviet Socialist Republics).
23. The black market.
24. Wright's books were published by Harper and Row in the United States.
25. Beach befriended Michaux in the mid-1930s while working on the review *Mesures*, dedicated to publishing French translations of British and American work.

who wants it immediately, so my book has got swept aside. He wants my book too, but if it is sellable Harpers would be much better. Now MRS BRADLEY.[26] She wrote me the same day your letter came to say Harpers would be interested in the memoirs and she said to come and see her about it. What is the use of her coming into this? She replied, when I said you were attending to the matter for me, that she represented Harpers over here, arranged all these matters for them. But I really don't see the necessity, and told her so. Said I must get all I could out of my one book, and with your help could do without an agent. She then said she quite understood, but would write to Harpers and everything could go through her hands as usual 'without any expense to me' Why did Harpers communicate with her, I wonder. In this case her services are not needed, are they? With such a friend as you on the spot, and I am very grateful dear Dick!

I hope Sartre has been sending 'Les Temps Modernes' with 'Black Boy' which has interested French readers tremendously.[27] They are waiting impatiently for 'Native Son' now. It is to come out any minute I hear. You may be sure Saillet[28] will be doing a big business with it as soon as he can hold of it. You will see for yourself when next you drop in at the Rue de l'Odéon. And I think it is a very good thing for 'Black Boy' to appear in Sartre's review. Everybody reads it. But as these things are very expensive, the real impact with the public will only come when your beautiful 'Black Boy' appears in book form. I suppose you have arranged with a press-cutting agency here to collect the ones about your work. I will set aside anything important on the subject I see, for your files when you get here. I shall be in Paris around the middle of July but not long after. The Briggses (you remember Jim Briggs) are to arrive towards the 10th, but after a day or two in Paris they will go on down to their house in Touraine. Then I will retire to my mountain in Savoie. Am going to Switzerland on the 12th of August to visit a friend. Where have you decided to go? Italy perhaps? Switzerland? By the way, Adrienne Monnier will be closing her library on the 20th of July till the end of August.

With best love to Ellen and Julia and yourself, with thanks again

from Sylvia

---

26. Jenny Bradley (1886–1983), French literary agent who represented Wright.

27. The French translation of Wright's novel was serialized in Jean-Paul Sartre's review *Les temps modernes*, the leading intellectual organ of postwar France.

28. Maurice Saillet (1914–1990), an employee of Adrienne Monnier's at La Maison des Amis de Livres and one of Beach's closest friends in her later years.

PS I haven't heard any strange rumors about Gertrude, except that Virgil Thompson is producing another opera in collaboration with her (ghost).[29] As for Alice, she is now running the whole show and seems to be thriving. Talks just as though she were the original Stein.

S

Richard Wright Papers, Yale University, Beinecke Rare Book
and Manuscript Library (manuscript)

* * *

173. **To Carlotta Welles Briggs** December 17, 1947

12 rue de l'Odéon
Paris–VI

Dearest Carlotta

Merry Christmas and love to you all! Owing to the strikes your parcel is not going to reach you this Christmas—but next—think of that! But this is to bring you my love and greetings. Jimmy will be home from college and the family all together again. I wish I could hear him tell his experiences as a Yale student. I hope he is enjoying everything. Maria mentioned his being rather fatigué—I hope he is all right now, and Tommy doing a big job with his maths. You know I don't hear from you scarcely any, but I know that you and Jim have plenty to do and if you write a letter, holding the pen in the right hand, you have to stir something for supper with the left, all the while. To be truthful, its I who owe you a letter—of thanks again—for the lovely honey, the delicious Bourré walnuts, and the dress all of which fine presents were sent to me by Maria as I couldn't go down there when you so kindly invited me. I had to get my translation off to New Directions and after that was expecting a visit from Laughlin of "New Directions" who never turned up after all till this week—whether it was due to the strikes—he says so—or skiing in Switzerland where he and his wife are with their two children—I can't quite make out.

Phew! What a relief to have the translation translated and re-re-re-vised and re-re-re-typed!

Now I can get down to my own works if any. Am working on my headaches and think have got somewhere at last. A friend took me to

29. Stein's opera libretto *The Mother of Us All* was posthumously set to music by the composer Virgil Thomson, Stein's friend and frequent collaborator.

a doc who does massage and has you do exercises and its not Chinese nor Swedish nor Hindoo but his own invention. I've had osteopathy, and napropathy, and electro therapy, and pressure on the nerve centres, and all the injections that have been discovered, and this is the first time any-one ever seemed to get anywhere near my headaches. Will let you know what happens, then Jim might like to try this Dr. Only he will have to hurry as the Dr is 81 yrs of age. But I hope Jim is feeling better this winter.

Did you have anything to do with that great fire we heard about? wasn't it in your neighborhood or something?

We have just come through a sort of a crisis over here—which you may have been following in the papers. Every morning you rushed first thing to turn on the water to see if there was any. Lots of people had none, and likewise no gas nor electricity. Adrienne got hold of some sweet potatoes for me and then the gas was so low it took all day to cook them. The streets were piled with great drifts of garbage that got sweeter and sweeter smelling as the days went by. Finally, so as to leave a path on the pavement the stuff got moved out into the street and cars had to pick their way. No trains, no mail and at times no telephone. But breadlines again. But everything is running again now.

There is great excitement over the Friendship Train.[30] A real Ameri-can peoples warmhearted thing to do. All the evening papers (except of course you know which ones) have big headlines, I noticed, as I came home from lunch at Reid Hall, "The American Santa Claus" etc. When all those presents are distributed among the working people—politics or not—its going to be a joy for them—that's sure. I bet nobody will turn them down even if told to do so. The majority of workers were opposed to the strikes and now bear a resentment against the leaders. Yet they would be glad to earn more money. You know the cost of living here and how far 6.000 frs would go in a worker's family. From 6 to 8 thousand is what a lot of them get. So next time unless something can be done it may be worse trouble for everybody. But what? And why these problems at Christmas I wonder. All I want is to send you a big hug, much love to yourself and Jim and boys with heartiest Christmas wishes

Ever your very grateful
Sylvia

Sylvia Beach Papers, Manuscripts Division, Department of Rare Books
and Special Collections, Princeton University Library (manuscript)

30. An American initiative for helping France rebuild after the Second World War, the Friendship Train traveled through the country delivering food and supplies.

* * *

174. To Richard Wright   January 11, 1948

Dear Dick

I'm very sorry to have missed you yesterday—hardly ever go out since I got this bronchitis business, but had just run up to see Adrienne a minute.

I've been wondering how you all were after Brussels—did you enjoy the trip?

Keep warm etc.? How's the next Richard Wright book going?

I'm looking for the 2nd installment of a piece I like that you published in Aug 44—have only got the 1st unfortunately.[31]

Would like a visit from you whenever you can spare the time to try again.

> Love to all
> Sylvia[32]

I heard a little bookseller wanted to ask you to sign your books in her shop one day—best writers never consent here—stupid of her!

Richard Wright Papers, Yale University, Beinecke Rare Book and Manuscript Library (manuscript)

* * *

175. To Richard Wright   June 14, 1948

Dear Dick (you let me call you that?)

I hope you'll be able to drop in on your way across town. A French friend of Saillet's will be here towards noon and he admires you so much

---

31. Most likely "I Tried to Be A Communist," published originally in *The Atlantic Monthly* and later in the anthology *The God That Failed* and in Wright's autobiography *American Hunger*.

32. In a January 11, 1948, letter to Carlotta Welles Briggs, Beach writes: "On Christmas Day I was able to have dinner at the Richard Wrights and enjoyed it very much, though it was the last time I was anywhere for several weeks. He came for Katherine Dudley and her niece Anne and me in his car as he lives in Neuilly—couldn't find a place anywhere else. Little Judy is a most interesting child. Five years old now, and goes to the American school in the Bd. Raspail. Her father wants her to be mindful that she is American. As for Dick Wright, we may well be proud of such a citizen. Such good sense and such responsibility for others are pretty rare" (SBP, box 58, folder 16).

I gave him a little hope that he might meet you if he hung around towards that hour. A big event it would be for him.

Adrienne Monnier would be happy if you could come to supper—maybe a meatless one—Sunday at 8. She lives up the street at No 18

Just ourselves and Saillet and Soupault—you know him perhaps.[33] I hope you can come

Please dont have another date

Yours affectionately

Sylvia

Richard Wright Papers, Yale University, Beinecke Rare Book

and Manuscript Library (manuscript)

* * *

176. To Richard Wright   September 18, 1948

Dear Dick

Good gracious! I was almost knocked down when I saw your huge bunch of roses! So beautiful and red—am enjoying them all the time—but it was wrong of you dear Dick—specially as I'm an extortionist—overcharged you a hundred frs the other day—the concierge, after consultation, thought it was another parcel—not the 'Twice a Year' one, he paid 100 franc for while I was away—there was a flock of them that came, and now he's sure he made a mistake about yours being dutyable.

So a hundred is coming back to you—otherwise I shall have a feeling of guilt all my life.

Was going to join the throngs who crash your gate, to thank you and say hello to Ellen, but was prevented yesterday all day.

A bientot

wonderful, my roses!

Love

Sylvia

Richard Wright Papers, Yale University, Beinecke Rare Book

and Manuscript Library (manuscript)

33. Philippe Soupault (1897–1990), French Surrealist writer and longtime friend of Beach.

* * *

177. To Richard Wright   No date, c. 1948

Dear Dick

Have got your parcels of 'Twice a Year' from the Central P.O. in case you are beginning to need them.[34] Arguing was no use—customs is customs—Fraid you'll be mad—come, and I'll tell you all about it.
Love
From
Sylvia

Richard Wright Papers, Yale University, Beinecke Rare Book
and Manuscript Library (manuscript)

* * *

178. To Richard Wright   No date, c. 1948

Dear Richard,

The friend who was fixing my radio says the man wants 10.000 frs for the record player—'pick-up' they call it.—all complete—sounds terribly expensive doesn't it?—you might pick up one cheaper yourself with your good luck in finding things, but Benjamin[35] says that's the best he can do for you—they're so hard to find here. He's coming to finish up the job on my radio on Thursday after lunch if you could spare time to see him a minute. If you dont drop in or leave word or anything I'll understand that you prefer to wait and look around and that will be O.K.
Yours truly
Sylvia

Richard Wright Papers, Yale University, Beinecke Rare Book
and Manuscript Library (manuscript)

34. *Twice a Year* was an American journal of the arts that Wright co-edited with photographer Dorothy Norman.
35. Benjamin Le Blévennec.

* * *

179. **To H.D.**   **March 3, 1949**

Dear H.D.

How splendid that Ezra got the award![36] Unfortunately when the press got hold of the information here I was laid up with a headache and didn't see a paper for a week. A friend told me she had seen it, but couldn't remember in what paper—nor the date. The only thing I've found so far is 'Carrefour' of this week with a cartoon about the event. But there was something I think in 'Combat' or perhaps the 'Figaro Litteraire', vague rumours is all I hear, and I'm trying to track them down. Also hope to get the 'Mercure' to print the news and perhaps a piece of Ezra translated. The trouble is—who is to do the translating without murdering his poetry? Anyhow as soon as possible I will send whatever turns up to Dorothy Pound.

How exciting about your book 'By Avon River', a beautiful title! How can I wait till May? Dear Hilda what an event!

With much love

Sylvia

Am wearing at this very minute one of your blue sweaters so warm and so pretty! Have been enjoying everything in your great parcels—living in them—never chilly.

S

Pound Manuscripts, Lilly Library, Indiana University, Bloomington

* * *

180. **To Mary Reynolds**[37]   **April 4, 1949**

Dear Mary,

Excuse me for not telephoning—I'm not very good at it, but maybe when I get one of my own again I'll be always ringing you up. About

---

36. Pound was awarded the Bollingen Prize for the *Pisan Cantos* in 1948.
37. Mary Reynolds (1891–1950), American bookbinder and patron of Marcel Duchamp.

McAlmon's books, I couldn't find anything but <u>North America</u> 14 copies which if he wants me to I'll send him. There's a copy of each of the Contact books in my library, same as there's always been—<u>Ashe of Rings</u> only my own copy, and perhaps somewhere put away (I'll make another search) a copy or two of the de Luxe editions of <u>Quaint Stories</u>, and <u>Portrait of a Generation</u>. But I gave back all his Contacts to McAlmon before the war except one or two. I think the business was practically wound up as far as Shakespeare & Co as concerned.

Its very kind of you, Mary, to reply for me. I owe him a letter—he wrote a long one after the Liberation and told me about everything. Said he'd like to hear from me—he will some day. Meanwhile he will hear from you, which he'drather anyone.

It was fine to run into you around at the Wrights.[38] I'm always complaining to them that I never see Mary Reynolds. Please move into this immediate neighborhood.

With thanks for helping me with McAlmon

Yours affectionately
Sylvia

Yale University, Beinecke Rare Book and Manuscript Library (manuscript)

* * *

181. **To Dorothy Pound**   **April 15, 1949**

Dear Dorothy Pound,

Your letter enclosing cheque for $4 came yesterday and I passed on your order for 5 copies of Cocteau's 'Poemes' to Adrienne Monnier as I am not in business any more. She will get any books you need in future.

(Adrienne Monnier, 7 rue de l'Odéon, Paris-VI)

They could only get one copy of "Poèmes" today, and I sent it to Hilda at once. The other four are promised for next Friday the 22nd and they will be sent right off to the other four addresses you gave me.—Olga Rudge, W.C. Williams, Ezra Pound, G.B. Vicari.[39] I put a slip of paper in Hilda's copy to say it was from you.

---

38. Richard Wright and his family.
39. Giambattista Vicari, Italian literary journalist and editor.

The four dollars just about covers the cost of the books and postage if unregistered. I don't think its necessary to register them.

5 *Poèmes* at	Frs. 220	Frs. I.Ioo
Postage, 15—		75
	———	———
		Frs. I.I75

By cheque £4
(about 300 frs) I.200
I.I75

———

Balance to your credit: Frs 25

Shakespeare and Company has gone, but I still live at No. 12, was interned during the Occupation, was lucky enough to save my library, but bookshop went under.

Have made a few notes on Ezra for the "Mercure"[40] and will send it when they appear—probably not before June.

Yours sincerely,
Sylvia Beach

Pound Manuscripts, Lilly Library, Indiana University, Bloomington

✳   ✳   ✳

182. To Jim Briggs   **April 25, 1949**

12, rue de l'Odéon
Paris-VI
April 25, 1949

Dear Jim,

Thank you for your letter. I could hardly believe it was you writing me, as it happens so seldom. And thankyou for letting me know about my pitcher in the paper. Have just received the clipping from Justin O'Brien whose mug as he pointed out, as also in that issue of the Times. Well, as long as they show me as I was in those days, though goodlooking I never was, and don't use some they took last year, its all right.

---

40. *La Mercure de France*, French literary journal.

I'm glad you like Gide's Journals. You must read his "Lafcadio's Adventures" if you haven't already done so. Its first title in the translation was "The Vatican Scandal," but it was changed—something about the Catholic Church suppressing it, I remember. Gide is delighted over his success in America, and chuckling to see his "Corydon" with its bellyband "PRIX NOBEL" in large letters.[41] His American royalties are in the shape of large comfortable car in which he visits the rue de l'Odéon etc., he has a house near Rambouillet, three little grandchildren crowding him out of it, and for a man of about 80 with heart attacks one of which nearly carried him off last month, he is doing very well.

The "Barbarian in Asia" ought to be out soon. You must tell me if you don't think it interesting and funny, and how bad my translation really is. Never again. If Jimmy is going in for pomes now, and would like to have a go at Michaux's I will send him some. But he's a strange poet.

Ever since I got Carlotta's letter telling me the good news that Jimmy was back at Yale I've been intending to write to her. It was such wonderful news I was awfully happy over it. And to hear the Briggses were sailing on the 21st of June. Splendid. Thankyou for wanting me to go down to Bourré. I must try to have a weekend with you before I leave for Savoie first of all. And as little buzzing around as possible for yourself. And by the way, you didn't say how you were feeling these days. As soon as I find a magnetizer who cures my headaches I'll have to take you to him (or her) I was "helped" for quite a while, then relapsed, but am not discouraged.

Now with regard to the beautiful sweater your sister knitted for you, I'm sorry I couldn't recall at first who it was distributed to. At last, it all comes back to me, and it was to one of our boys who had been shot down and was hiding with three others in one small room on the top floor of that house in a street off the rue Claude Bernard—I forgot its name, where a woman in the resistance lived. She hid a lot of our aviators, fed them, washed their clothes and communicated with them by gestures as she couldn't speak a word of English—and none of the ones I saw could speak any French. They used to ask me to "tell her" this and that. And to ask her why they hadn't been sent home yet—they got very tired of waiting—and of being stuck up there with nothing to do but play cards. But they were all very fond of her, and told me how she bought butter in the black market, and bread also. But they wouldn't have had

---

41. Gide won the Nobel Prize in 1947.

enought to eat, at that, if Drue Tartière hadn't brought them cakes and pies she baked for them. I only wish I knew the name of the boy who got your sister's sweater. I did put down all their names, but you had to be so careful, maybe I burnt them up.

With much love to Carlotta and yourself & Tommy

Sylvia

P.S. Yes I do work every once in a while on my memoirs

Would be delighted to see Jimmy's poet friend but will I be in Paris when he comes I wonder—?

Sylvia Beach Papers, Manuscripts Division, Department of Rare Books and Special Collections, Princeton University Library (manuscript)

* * *

183. To Richard Wright   May 22, 1949

To Miss Weaver[42]
4 Rawlinson Road
Oxford
May 22nd, 1949

Dear Dick

Hello! I hope all are fine. Am here till about June 1st. Have ordered a Heidegger—'Existence & Being'[43] from Parker & Son[44] here—it is about to appear, it seems and they are to send it directly to you as soon as it does—is all settled up postage included to your address but of course they may charge duty on delivery according to the way the wind blows that day. They had Heidegger in German but I turned that down.

If you know anything about a person named Edwin R. Armstrong, theatrical producer in New York (he is making an adaptation of Joyce's Finnegan's Wake set to music, Irish voices etc) would you be so kind as to let me know here if its not too much trouble? Only I'd like to know if you

---

42. Beach's return address for this letter.
43. Martin Heidegger (1889–1976), German philosopher. *Existence and Being*, a translation of Heidegger's *Being and Time*, was published by the Henry Regnery Company of Chicago in 1949.
44. John W. Parker and Son, London distributor of Heidegger.

ever heard of him and what opinion they have of him in New York theatrical circles. It seems Padraic Colum recommends him. This, of course, strictly confidential. Negotiations are now going on, but I said I'd enquire among writer friends. If you re like me and never heard of him perhaps you can find out something later and in that case will tell me when I get back to Paris.

Hope all your Little Women are well

Much love to Ellen and to your self, dear Dick from

Sylvia

Richard Wright Papers, Yale University, Beinecke Rare Book and Manuscript Library (manuscript)

* * *

184. To H.D.   July 14, 1949

Thankyou, my dear H.D. for your beautiful "By Avon River"![45] I can only say I love it. You have cast such a spell over me—am in a dream. Lucky readers! invited by H.D., Shakespeare present. I have rows and rows of books on Shakespeare in my library—what for? "By Avon River" is going to replace them all—only one fit to be in his company, by a poet. . . .ah..!

But what about this piece of paste-board "with the compliments of the author"? Am taking the liberty of sending you my copy with request—if I may have the honour—of your signature, my dear H.D. and perhaps Bryher will be so kind as to bring it back to me next time she comes to Paris.

Meanwhile, I am ordering some copies for friends here—friends who will be delighted to join me "By Avon River"—it would be selfish of me not to share such a pleasure, and such an initiation.

And again many thanks! And loving greetings to the Book & Author

from

Sylvia

---

45. "By Avon River," H.D.'s lyrical essay on Shakespeare, was published by Macmillan in 1949.

Thank you for your card of July 1st—such a pretty card & stamps. Had a letter from Ezra—he seemed pleased so I'm glad.

H.D. Papers, Yale University, Beinecke Rare Book and Manuscript Library (manuscript)

* * *

185. To Maria Jolas   September 8, 1949

Dear Maria

I heard from Miss Weaver this summer that your two little girls had gone and got married[46]—then your announcement this morning—I was still trying to realize they were grown-up and this is a double shock—must have been a little bewildering for their mother too. That's what comes of having such attractive daughters!—if they'd been plain you would have been able to hold onto them longer.

Whenever you have time, come and see me and tell me how all your plans are progressing. Miss Weaver will be here at the end of the month, as no doubt she told you, but I hope to see you meanwhile.

With congratulations and all good wishes for your newly-weds

Yours affectionately
Sylvia

Eugène and Maria Jolas Papers, Yale University, Beinecke Rare Book and Manuscript Library (manuscript)

* * *

186. To Richard Wright   December 9, 1949

Dear Dick

Help help . . . ! If you could get the enclosed printed in some paper or other (the

Sat. Rev. for example) as soon as possible I would be so grateful. You see, as Ellen has very kindly explained to you, someone has got hold of my

---

46. Jolas's daughters Marie-Christine and Betsy were both married in 1949.

letter from Shaw and is supposed to be using it in a book she has done on Joyce—which I understand is about to appear in England.[47] I would like to get there first if that is possible—if its not too much to ask of you at this moment, dear Dick—would be ever so grateful!

With much love,

Sylvia

Sylvia Beach Papers, Manuscripts Division, Department of Rare Books and Special Collections, Princeton University Library (manuscript)

---

47. Beach was eager to be the first to publish the memorable letter she had received from George Bernard Shaw explaining why he would not subscribe to *Ulysses*.

VI

OLD FRIENDS AND TRUE

187. To George Macy   **March 18, 1950**

Mr. George Macy,
Chairman,
The Denyse Clairouin Memorial Award,
c/o The George Macy Companies,
595 Madison Avenue,
New York 22.

Dear Mr. Macy,

Many thanks for your kind letter of March 9th announcing that this year's DENYSE CLAIROUIN prize has been awarded to me for my translation of UN BARBARE EN ASIE by Henry Michaux.

It was such a surprise that I have hardly realized yet that it is true and I am extremely touched by the honor you have conferred on me in the name of Denyse Clairouin.

Also I thank you for considering me worthy of a prize that has been won by Professor O'Brien and Mrs Louise Varese.[1] Though I took a good deal of pains to preserve as far as possible the charm and subtlety of one of the masterpieces of French literature, I am well aware of the short-comings of my translation.

---

1. Justin O'Brien won the prize for his translation of *The Journals of André Gide*, and Louise Varese for the poems of Baudelaire.

The copy of the notice issued to the Press that you enclosed in your letter was very kind indeed. I would have acknowledged the letter immediately, but you mentioned in it that I might expect a visit from James Laughlin and I have been waiting ever since for news of him. Now he writes that his business in Switzerland will prevent him from being present at the ceremony of the Award in Paris, so I am writing to you without further delay. I hope you will excuse what must have seemed discourteous on my part. With regard to the generous Prize money offered me, perhaps you would be so kind as to deposit it in dollars in my account at the Princeton Bank & Trust Co., Princeton, N.J.

With deepest gratitude to the Members of the Jury and the Governing Committee for honoring me with the <u>Denyse Clairouin Award</u>.

Yours Sincerely,
Sylvia Beach

---

*Sylvia Beach Papers, Manuscripts Division, Department of Rare Books
and Special Collections, Princeton University Library (manuscript)*

* * *

188. To Ezra Pound   May 24, 1950

Dear Ezra,

Nice to get your "gentle" letter. Do tell me what the "factual error" was in my piece. Not the color of your shirt, I hope. I could swear it was blue. But I know how inaccurate I am. Adrienne is in despair over it.

I was ashamed enough over the "Exile" error—no excuse as I had it right before my eyes.

You may enjoy F.M. Ford[2]'s works, but I have put them all away, and don't intend to get them out for ever so long.

Young friends in Oxford etc tell me they are doing in a great deal for Pound these days.

Yours affectionately,
Sylvia

Pound Manuscripts, Lilly Library, Indiana University, Bloomington (manuscript)

---

2. Ford Madox Ford.

* * *

189. **To John Slocum**   **No date, circa 1950**

John J. Slocum,
Tuxedo Park,
New York.

Dear John,

Thank you for your kind letter of May 30th. I'm sorry you and Eileen won't be able to come over this summer.[3] We shall have to put off the pleasure of seeing you till next summer—then we must all go out to 'Léopold's' in the Vallée de Chevreuse where the "Déjeuner Ulysse" took place, given by Adrienne in honor of the French edition.

Its just as well you didn't come—unless you'd brought your bathing-suits—there's been a flood in my 'flet', pouring down from my upstairs neighbors, spoiling a hundred and thirty-two thousand frs worth of books (don't gasp! there were no Joyces among them) and you should see the mess. It was very annoying as this is the fifth flood those people have sent me—the child leaves the faucet open, or the old uncle takes a foot-bath or something. Anyhow its not supportable and this time I sent for the 'huissier'—whatever he is called at home, and had him come and look. He is to give me an official 'contestation' which I'm to pass on to the agent representing the proprietress and eventually the thing will go before the Justice of the Peace—in about three years time, the agent thinks. Meanwhile everything is to be left exactly as it is so as the expert can expertise it. I don't believe I will ever be coming into the matter again, nor the people upstairs who caused the accident. It was due to their negligence so the insurance is out of the question; they are insolvent so unable to pay a penny of damages, so the agent tells me. No doubt they will even claim an indemnity from me for disturbing them in the middle of the morning when the downpour came. The last one was when Miss Weaver was visiting me; I went out to do an errand and coming back, found her with a bucket and mops, water splashing on her from the ceiling.

Yes, lets let the N.Y. Times print the Shaw letter—and the sooner the better.[4] Never mind about paying me for it; but please could you

---

3. Eileen Slocum (1915–2008), Slocum's wife and future "grande dame" of Newport, Rhode Island, society.

4. Beach is referring to a famous letter written to her in 1922 by George Bernard Shaw (1856–1950), refusing to subscribe to *Ulysses*. For a full account, see Fitch, *Sylvia Beach and the Lost Generation*, 104–105.

explain that I authorized you to tell them they could use it, and that I have Mr Shaw's permission to publish it in my memoirs of which a piece including the letter recently appeared in the 'Mercure de France'—would you be so kind?

I'm afraid you are going to come to a dead end in that 'Dubliners' mystery story. If Georgio Joyce knows nothing about, then certainly no one else can tell us what happened to it. This is the conclusion I have come to after your investigations and particularly the discovery of Joyce's letter to Miss Weaver. Failing to get his price for the copy, he must have got it back—and destroyed it in despair—or disgust over the haggling. Ireland, at any rate, is the last place to look for it. As for my cousin, I'm sure that Joyce would have claimed his book from him in a very short time if Douglas Orbison hadn't found a purchaser for it.[5] I never heard a mention of it again. And it was so long ago, no wonder he doesn't remember how and when it left his hands. As for the book cover you saw, Joyce probably handed it to me with a bunch of papers, and he had by that time burnt up the rest of the book. At least it never fell into my hands.

I would have liked to see the Joyce Exhibition in London, and all the interesting things they must have got together in England and Ireland. Gheerbrant left a note to-day saying he was off tomorrow to London and could he do anything for me.[6] I have lent them some proofs of Ulysses with Joyce's corrections etc., but took some of the things that I thought more suitable for Paris, or already available over there. I know Maria Jolas will be delighted to have the items you have sent from your collection. She told me what an admirable collection you had and how beautifully arranged it was in your house. You must really show it to me some day. And thank you for inviting me so kindly. Maybe you will see Adrienne too, turning up one day, if I can persuade her to have a look at my country with me. Her loyalty to us has already converted her to trying Coca Cola— think of that. As soon as our favourite drink was attacked by some wicked politicians here, she answered the calumny by taking to Coca Cola.

> Affectionate greetings to you
> from
> > Sylvia

Yale University, Beinecke Rare Book and Manuscript Library

---

5. Beach's cousin.
6. Bernard Gheerbrant (1918–), friend of Beach and founder of La Hune gallery in Paris, which published his catalogue *James Joyce, Sa Vie, Son Oeuvre, Son Rayonnement* in 1949.

* * *

190. Carlotta Welles Briggs   **November 29, 1950**

12 Rue de l'Odéon
Paris—VI

My dearest Carlotta,

I was very glad to get your letter which to my surprise was post-marked "Altadena". I hadn't heard from Cyprian since last spring, but its not her fault this time—for once I owed her a letter. But it was a great satisfaction to hear all about her from you, and reassuring to know that all was well with the household and the pets and the two household-ers after the couple of fires they had. Of course you didn't say whether Cyprian looked well or not, and probably it was because she didn't—she never tells me, though if she eats plenty of the scientifically worked out dog and cat food she hands out to the crowd it might do her good too. Anyhow I'm glad to hear you were spending an evening with Cyprian and Jerry. And that all is well.

I am very sorry to hear the news about Paul. That must have been very sad for you, even if it was better for him not to go on suffering indefinitely.

It was a good plan for you to fly out there and see Nanna and go on a cruise with Robert and see Anita's new baby. Good for you to have a ride in the clouds—I shall never forget the one I had with my father and the sight of our grand country from New Jersey to Los Angeles and the clouds and all. It must have done you lots of good, Carlotta dear. Jim ought to take a little jaunt next—tell him to come over and see us. But this is no time for lighthearted frolics, is it? Alas. This awful Korea news. And France gloomy with their colonial troubles. You ask about Adrienne's plans—well, everything is pretty much at a standstill here and buyers not plentyful. The only buyer has been herself—she had a chance to buy her shop at a very low price and her friends advise her to take advantage of it. So she is now proprietress of the shop at No 7, her own premises. She can wait til she gets a good offer and meanwhile is adapting everything for the hopefully-awaited purchaser of her busi-ness. She will probably arrange for a "gérant" to take over as a great many businesses do now-a-days, but anyhow she is not able to carry it on her-self any more. Saillet, unfortunately is not interested in bookselling—wants to go on with his writing and support himself with journalism. He has plenty of openings—like my sheets when they come back from the blanchisseuse—and in fact always does combine the work he does at Adrienne's library with regular articles for Combat and the Mercure de France. We haven't given up the idea of Adrienne moving in with me in my spacious, rather antique quarters. She has had an electric radiator installed in the large room she is to occupy—an instrument that used to be in her shop and accumulates heat in a remarkable way. And she has also put in some new kind of lighting called Phillips Fluorescent or something quite hideous, it seems to me. In my part of the house I'm holding on to my balls (sounds obscene) suspended from the ceiling like in the cafés of the more or less popular sort. Sheds a soft light (preferable on account of the dust and the awful devastations caused by the floods from the upstairs neighbors' open sluices) and after trying one heating system after another I have finally got a gas radiator answering to the name of "Auer" set up and throwing out plenty of heat—at least as far as I can tell in this mild weather. We had a very cold spell but nothing compared to your terrific blizzards that we have been reading about. I hope it wasn't too bad at Wilson Point, and that you have all escaped from colds and things and the boys well and happy at Yale. If you have any snapshots don't forget to send me some of your two Yale students. I have to say that over several times to myself to realise Jimmy and Tommy are now college boys. Think of it Carlotta and Jim. And I hope you keep on with the fiddle. A friend of ours named Renée de Saussine has written a book on Paganini—just coming out—which I am going to send you for Christmas. I am late this year with Christmas posting on account of so many interruptions—floods, a visit from Miss Harriet Weaver Joyce's literary executrice who asked me if she could stay with me for a few days and was here a month and a half. I had to make her porridge every morning, a satisfying tea and an ample supper. Thank goodness we lunch outside. Then there were the Joyceans to meet while she was here, and now Stuart Gilbert who is editing the Joyce Letters comes to discuss some of the questions with me. Haven't even had time to see a doctor at the American Hospital about the Anti-Hystamine injections after Jim took all that trouble to bring me the stuff. And by the way, I see all the American doctors have resigned as a protest against the invasion of the French out there in Neuilly—another war oh dear. And the American Library is opening 9 branches in other parts of France. I hope Miss Leet isn't opening many branches of the Rue de Chevreuse for the present.

Well, it sure was funny to see your handwriting on an envelope with the postmark "Altadena". I wish you wuz in Bourré. And did I ever thank you for the big basket of fruit you had them send me? Lovely large pears and apples and a lot of walnuts and I had them all set out on a bookcase where callers could admire the display as soon as they entered—till one by one they (the fruit not the callers) were devoured by meself. I enjoyed them immensely, and thank you for such a gift. Also the honey you gave me last summer was a big treat for me.

A lady from Greenwich just sent me 45 Union Suits of her late husband to bestow as a tribute on the French. Mens Underwear it simply said on the label. Flannel coming down to the ankles, you know, but coming from the best houses like Sulka, Altman and Brooks Bros. Some were light weight too. I was about to take them all to the Quakers to distribute, when my French men friends spied them and made off with all they could lay their hands on—were in raptures over them. There was a run on my stock. Now if you hear of any pants and coats that could be worn over the Union Suits my friends could come out and show themselves ANYWHERE. They wouldn't be so conspicuous. I'm asking them meanwhile to have themselves photographed for me to send the lady.

Joking aside, I believe our poor boys in Korea are glad enough to have that kind of underwear—my French friends are really glad.

> With much love to you dear Carlotta
> and to Jim as well,
> from
>   Sylvia

Sylvia Beach Papers, Manuscripts Division, Department of Rare Books and Special Collections, Princeton University Library (manuscript)

* * *

191. **To Ezra Pound**   **January 8, 1951**

Dear Ezra,

Thanks—very much overdue—for your kind congratulations for the Prize they gave me for my translation of "Un Barbare en Asie".

This is to wish you happiness in the new year, and to say that our friend Jean Aubier[7] is presenting you with a copy of a little book he has just published in which you are mentioned. (page 12 of the preface). The booklet is Flaubert's "Dictionnaire des Idées Reçues".[8] A footnote refers

---

7. Jean Aubier, French publisher and editor.
8. Gustave Flaubert's satirical *Dictionary of Received Ideas* would be released in a New Directions translation by Jacques Barzun in 1954.

to your article on Joyce. And by the way, I have looked up the two dates you mention in yours of last May 26th—am afraid V. Larbaud beat you to it—his article appeared in the N.R.F.[9] of 1er avril 1922: Ezra Pound's in the Mercure 1er juin same year.

> Affectionate wishes
> from
> Sylvia
> wish J. Laughlin[10] would supply me with your 'Cantos'!
> S.

Pound Manuscripts, Lilly Library, Indiana University, Bloomington (manuscript)

* * *

192. To John Slocum   **February 2, 1951**

February 2nd (Joyce Day)[11] 1951

Thank you for the delicious food parcel you sent me for Christmas, which arrived not long ago, owing to delays in shipping in December. That's why I haven't acknowledged it sooner. It was very kind of you indeed to remember me. I wonder whether food parcels can still be shipped from the U.S.A. to Britain; someone mentioned that it wasn't going to be permitted any more—but maybe it didn't mean from our country. That would be dreadful for the British. I hope Miss Weaver is getting enough to eat. They've practically no meat, eggs, butter, bacon, sweets, judging from the tales of those who have managed to escape for a few days.

I hope your address at the Joyce exhibition at Yale was heard by lots of Joyceans—I regret that I couldn't be among those present. If a copy of it has been printed or typed or anything, do send it to me!

I know by this time you must have given up hope of a reply to your letter of September 7 1950. But you would forgive me if you knew how bad my headaches have been all winter. Whenever they let up for a day I had to hurry in some work on my memoirs. My friends are getting so

---

9. *Nouvelle Revue Française.*
10. James Laughlin, New Directions publisher.
11. Joyce was born on February 2, 1882.

used to not hearing from me that it they do happen to get a letter, they don't know what to make of it.

Of course you have settled the questions you put to me some way or another long ago without my help—but with regard to the <u>Cyclops Episode (Item No. 3)</u> I think I've held on to that: <u>typescript pages of ULYSSES</u> (item no. 3) No idea how many, nor can recollect to whom they went—Joycean friends mostly—for example: Jacques Mercanton in Lausanne.[12]

As for the POMES PENYEACH MSS. of ten of the poems Joyce had given me, I might be able to find a record of the sale, but would even you succeed in tracing their present whereabouts?

I've no idea how Robert Barry or Stonehill & Co got hold of the Penelope Episode typescript—not from me in any case.[13]

Finally—when I make a complete list of the Joyce items I possess you will have it at once. If I make up my mind to sell any more Joyceana, it will be for the same reason as then—so they'd go to the highest bidder, wouldn't they?

I hope Mrs Slocum and your children are well—bearing up under the present events. You must try to fly over to see us soon and not wait till the summer when we might be gone to our mountain.

Miss Weaver was staying with me for over a month in the fall. As usual, during her visits, there was quite a round-up of Joyceans. Unfortunately Mrs Joyce was not able to get here this time as it is getting more and more difficult for her to travel with her arthritis.

With so many thanks to you, dear John, for the parcel,

> and affectionate greetings from your friends in the rue de l'Odéon,
> specially,
> Sylvia

Yale University Library, Beinecke Rare Book and Manuscript Library (manuscript)

* * *

---

12. Jacques Mercanton (1910–1996), Swiss writer and friend of Joyce. Beach notes in the margin "he purchased a page or two."
13. Robert J. Barry, Sr., president of New Haven publishing house C. A. Stonehill and Co.

193. To Maria Jolas   **April 4, 1951**

Dear Maria,

I am very sorry to hear from Katherine Dudley such sad news of Nora Joyce,[14] and would like to know how she is now—I hear from what Katherine tells me, that she hasn't had much chance of recovery. It was only yesterday that I learned all this as K. didn't succeed in finding me at home when she came several times to give me your message.

It seems also that you have been getting Lucia settled in England[15] and that you took her there yourself—a very wise step, it seems to me—and another act of your extraordinary kindness.

I hope to see you, either at your house or mine—am calling at yours just on a chance.

Affectionately yours
Sylvia

Eugène and Maria Jolas Papers, Yale University, Beinecke Rare Book
and Manuscript Library (manuscript)

* * *

194. To Ian Forbes Fraser[16]   **April 23, 1951**

Dr. Frazer,

You mentioned a little story you were sending to the Herald-Tribune to acknowledge my gift of books to the American library. In case you wanted one or two facts (I'm afraid Ive kept Who's Who in America waiting a long time for the answers to their questionnaire):—

I am the daughter of the late Rev. Sylvester Woodbridge Beach who was pastor of the First Presbyterian Church in Princeton, New Jersey:

Opened an American bookshop-lending library on the Left Bank, Paris in 1919—called Shakespeare and Company: which was rather

---

14. Nora Joyce died of uremic poisoning in Zurich on April 10, 1951.
15. After her mother's death, Lucia Joyce was transferred from Zurich to St. Andrews' Hospital in Northampton, England, where she lived the remaining thirty years of her life.
16. Fraser came to Paris after the Second World War with a staff of two American librarians to take over the directorship of the American Library in Paris. After Shakespeare and Company closed, Beach donated much of her inventory to this library.

famous as a resort of writers. Some of those who were connected with it from the beginning and as you might say—grew up with it, were Robert McAlmon, Ernest Hemingway, Thornton Wilder, Scott Fitzgerald, Archibald MacLeish, Kay Boyle—to name only a few: their elders were Sherwood Anderson, Gertrude Stein, T.S. Eliot, James Joyce, Ezra Pound:

Shakespeare and Company brought out James Joyce's Ulysses in 1922, which had been suppressed in the United States, Ireland and England. Also published Pomes Penyeach by Joyce, and a collection of essays by 12 different writers on Joyce's Finegans Wake: Our Exagmination. These three titles are all that Shakespeare and Company ever published: William Bird's Three Mountains Press and Robert McAlmon's Contact Editions were closely connected with it: almost like members of the family, and later Eugene and Maria Jolas's Transition, which published Joyce's Finegans Wake.

A few years before the war, a Group of Friends of Shakespeare and Company was formed with the names of the greatest French writers on the Committee, all the most faithful old friends: Paul Valéry: André Gide: Jean Schlumberger: Jules Romains: André Maurois. All these writers: also T.S. Eliot: Ernest Hemingway: the principal ally of Shakespeare and Company was La Maison des Livres on the opposite side of the Rue de l'Odéon, where Adrienne Monnier's famous bookshop is.

I was interned in the German Camp at Vittel with my friends of the American colony who had remained in France:

To my regret, as I had lost my premises, and for reasons of health, I was unable to re-open Shakespeare and Company after the war: but my library had been hidden during the Occupation, so was not dispersed: its home was in Paris: as an American I am glad to feel that the place for my books now is the American Library of Paris.

SYLVIA BEACH[17]

Sylvia Beach Papers, Manuscripts Division, Department of Rare Books
and Special Collections, Princeton University Library (manuscript)

* * *

---

17. Preserved with Beach's letter is a clipping from the *New York Herald Tribune*, April 25, 1951 (SBP, box 182, folder 11).

195. To Janet Flanner[18]   November 7, 1952

My dear Janet

What a lot of lovely flowers poured in yesterday! For Adrienne and me too—I came in for such fine red carnations! Like them so much! It was very kind of you indeed, dear Janet—

How funny and consoivatire [?] they are about Sartre! Adrienne had rounded up a good many things on the subject. Tant pis.

> Love to Janet
> from Sylvia
> Beach

Janet Flanner/Natalia Danesi Murray Papers, Library of Congress (manuscript)

✳ ✳ ✳

196. Adrienne Monnier   February 3, 1953

> The Beverly
> One Twenty-Five East Fiftieth Street
> New York
> > (one is not obligated to write out
> > the address simply '125' E. 50th St
> > March 2, 1953

My dear Adrienne and Janotte,[19]

You can write to me to the address above—it's Camilla's, and mine when I come to New York. I will be there often, for the rest, but Holly will come tomorrow and after lunch she will bring me to her house at Greenwhich to give her a little visit. My very dear Adrienne, I hope that you were not too tired after having accompanied me to the train station Saturday evening, and that your health is ameliorating under the current diet that you follow so courageously.

The plane left on time and, as Saillet had predicted, I had 3 places instead of one. But one could not lie across because of those two arms

---

18. Janet Flanner (1892–1978), *New Yorker* columnist who wrote letters from Paris under the name Genêt.
19. Janotte was a stuffed rabbit that Beach gave to Monnier.

of the seats, unless you cut your legs in three pieces and placed them as such on the chairs. You prefer to recline, and one saw all the travelers sleep with their knees drawn up under the chin. Besides that, I was very very good—I am only happy in an airplane and the trip seemed very short to me! I had very little time to do anything other than to eat the numerous meals that they would bring you on a platter—such good things all the time! Barely taken from the earth—a diner composed of a delicious plate of veal with English apples with peas and with tomatoes, (truly a good food) a salad with asparagus, endives, lettuce, etc with mayonnaise, a good little bread, butter, a peach purée, an orange juice, cakes, coffee—and before they offered you a cocktail (cherry). Afterwards we stopped in Ireland, at Shannon, that which was very ordinary like all the airport stops. All the countries after the same, you sleep with your knees brought up under the chin—then the hostess brings you, at 2 in the morning, another meal and at 4 in the morning breakfast where you have:—two fat hot soft-boiled eggs— (all very hot) on toast, little bread buns with butter, a coffee, cream, cornflakes, and even more cream, a grapefruit juice, a fat orange, salt pepper sugar at will, jam, etc. And a fat orange that I forgot to mention with dinner. Then between Boston, where we descended to fill ourselves up with gas, and New York, a final little snack of: tea or coffee, little breads—butter—fruit etc. It was truly a lot of food for a single night in the air, but I ate everything and enjoyed it. In the morning, I stayed a while in the bathroom to fascinate myself with the numerous comforts that were installed there—beautiful electric razors and all that—and the poop deck in the lavatory where one does not flush—because that is immediately absorbed by the septic tank, like they make you take note, when the hostess came to ask me politely if I thought of staying there much longer "it's that it's that of the men you're in", she told me. "That explains all those electric razors, I told her". We arrived at Idlewild airport (New York) an hour late—at 7:20 instead of 6:20. Camilla was waiting for me at the exit and a bus brought all of us to New York. Besides a little bit of migraine, I was not tired at all. Camilla thanks you for your letter—she embraces you and she will write to you soon. Holly came yesterday and we were very happy to see each other after so many years. She is so very gay and nice! I will write to you again soon. I embrace tightly tightly tightly embrace you and also Janotte. And Rinette and Saillet.

Harry Ransom Humanities Research Center, The University of Texas at Austin (manuscript)

* * *

197. To H.D.　　　　　　　　February 12, 1953

Love and best wishes to our dear H.D. and hoping she is well again, and running up and down those hilly streets

I wish I could get some flowers for you at the florists near your hotel—at least Cézanne supplies a vase along with his bouquet so you won't have that problem 'en moins'.[20]

Your grand CARE parcels are so valuable and so well-planned! Adrienne is very pleased with hers and particularly the sugar—she has a sweet-tooth, you know, and its one of the food items she can eat, and those wonderful prunes—! She sticks them in some water and eats them uncooked. But the bacon—she looks sorrowful and gives it to her sister. Poor Adrienne's diet doesn't include any fats.

　　Again all good wishes and with love from Sylvia

H.D. Papers, Yale University, Beinecke Rare Books and Manuscript Library (manuscript)

* * *

198. To Adrienne Monier　　　　　March 5, 1953

> 10 Mrs. F. J. Dennis
> Martindale
> Greenwich, Conn.
> March 5th 1953

My very dear Adrienne, Janotte,

I received the letter from the 2 of you yesterday, so so happy to have your news! You have received my cable and now, without a doubt you received the letter with the news of my trip—with, that which you call "every single detail"—maybe too much. Anyway, it went by in the best of conditions, with almost no fatigue and the minimum of migraine—and the air in New York does the same effect on me as that

---

20. Beach was writing on a postcard featuring a reproduction of Cézanne's painting "The Blue Vase."

of Les Déserts—here it's the same—that raises your astonishment. It is colder than in Paris, also, and a lot of wind at this time. Camilla took a hotel room for me, waiting to find something else. The something else was found the next day, a small two-room apartment with a bathroom, kitchenette, in a hotel, that which costs half as much as being in a hotel and it's what is done if one stays a month or even a week. Service, heating, etc is all included and a "au poil"[21] facility as Saillet says. On Tuesday Holly invited us to lunch at her Harvard Club and she brought me afterwards to Greenwich (pronounced "GRENICH") where we were much awaited by Bubbles who had a heart bursting with joy and affection to receive us at her house. That dog, he barks before the fridge where the lettuce is stored and he is seized by the sight of the lovely salad that one takes out for him and that he eats quantities of leaves—he throws himself above—I will not come back to that. It's like Kleenex tissues—those papers—he eats those too—Holly tells me that one cannot give him a greater delicacy than a leaf of Kleenex.

Holly's house is white like all the other houses of Greenwich, with beautiful trees all around, elms, maples, pines, etc. Two levels ½-basement, garage, heater (oil and combustible), ground level: a living room with many windows, dining room, kitchen where one takes their meals, a little office where Holly works; stairs—H's room and Freddy's room and a two-bed room for visitors (me for instance. Each room has a bathroom—even on the lower level there's one—higher up there is an attic with another bedroom. This house is very nice and Greenwich is charming.

I am happy to see how Holly is comfortable and happy with a perfect son and a life that suits her so well. We are both very happy to meet with each other again after so many years, and what we tell each other! I had a sore throat yesterday evening, each bound to give her accounts. Holly made me meals according to my diet, potatoes, salad (when Bubbles lets us) eggs so freshly lain as one brings from the farm, exquisite milk, bread as made at her place, grapefruits, enormous red apples, oranges and orangeade, lemonade still under pressure, good butter, oatmeal porridge and coffee, tea and all. Holly hardly eats any meat—there's only Bubbles who, himself, has horse and meat from a packet called "dog rations". In the morning he eats a poached egg on toast—like Holly, for breakfast.

We wait for Carlotta for lunch—I called her since my arrival in Greenwich. She wants to bring me to her house in South Norwalk that is maybe an hour from here, to stay for a while, but I explained to her that people and

---

21. "Spot on."

things would keep me in New York for the moment. It's true that, except in my sister's case, I have no intention of moving. Write to me then to the address that I gave you in my last letter, and above all—write me often! I am happy to know that you're doing your "Menotti" and you should do your "Baudelaire" next. I will impatiently wait to read them. And I would have loved to hear Nadaud and Saillet interviewed on the radio. I hope that Saillet doesn't have to much concerns with those authors etc., and that the Lettres Nouvelles has really good momentum at this time.

I need to stop—Carlotta will arrive—and I embrace you strongly strongly strongly. My little Adrienne very very dear. I hope you're eating enough food to give you energy (a letter that I received from Bryher tells me that she wonders if your meatless diet is what you need). Holly gets along very very well without eating meat—has an extraordinary energy.

I embrace Rinette waiting for her to send a letter soon. I embrace Saillet and thank him again for coming to the train station for my departure.

> And I re-embrace Janotte.
> Your Sylvia
> Holly sends her love.

Harry Ransom Humanities Research Center, The University of Texas at Austin (manuscript)

* * *

199. To Adrienne Monnier   **March 10, 1953**

> The Beverly
> 125 East 50th Street
> New York
> March 10, 1953

My very very dear Adrienne & Janotte,

I was very happy to have a letter from you, and happy and reassured to learn that you are not getting along too badly, despite your sweet little diet, so vegetarian or more so vegetable garden with jam. I wonder if the "Beaf-Wine & Iron" that Holly takes a spoonful every day, wouldn't perk you up. I will try to bring you some. In the meantime, you could try Roberts if you go shopping in that quarter one day. Holly hardly eats any meat, but seems to be full of energy and jumps higher than Janotte. (What a lovely signature, Janotte's!)

I am getting along well and without migraines since I've been here—
for the time being, at least. The climate, for instance, strikes me as
extremely hard—so cold, so penetrating. But careful! Do not wear wools
if you do not want to start sweating in the stores and homes! It's tropical.
In the streets a heavy coat—and again—the people here don't seem to
dress very outdoors. It's true that they don't walk—always in a car these
people. Or in a train. With that, the air is very dry and one is all chapped,
the lips cracked as for a fever. And not only the air is dry, but the water
too—that is to say, calcareous. Above all, one is very uplifted by that air
that blows around Manhattan, and by the lively and clear colors of persons, buildings, restaurants, children, taxis, sky and sidewalks. Even the
foods are of a lively color. In the stores, sometimes you see windows full
of gay garments, sometimes pharmaceutical articles just as gay—at each
step snack bars with posters affixed on the windows that compel you to
take the specials that are always the same and the adjectives too. I intend
to make a list of those dishes and some adjectives that accompany them,
as soon as the surprises of this trip become a little less vivid—(if ever). In
any case, everything in New York interests me. As a city, "c'est au poil"
as Saillet would say. I hope that Saillet has recovered from his fever, and
that there are not too many concerns as editor-in-chief of L.N. I talked
about him with Norman Pearson who is highly ranked at Yale as you
know—I don't have anything besides my sample No. I, and Camilla has
the one that you gave me for her, but you would be so kind – in telling
me numbers and carriage costs—to send me a few so that I could show
them to our friends here. I have still not started my "contacts", except,
naturally Holly, and seen Carlotta twice. The day before yesterday she
invited Holly and me with Mrs. Baldwin's daughter (Elizabeth like the
Queen), to the York Club for lunch. Elizabeth walks on crutches, you
remember that she had been in a boat to cross the English Channel during the other war, and she jumped. Wounded, drowned, *trépanée*, Elizabeth is getting along well and is very nice, young and gay. Her mother is
in Florida and she is, according to the girl, absolutely doing well.

I received a letter—and her nice contribution for my trip—from Bryher: a welcome letter from Norman Pearson and to invite me to make
chit-chat by the Elizabethan Club at Yale—paid—a very amiable letter:
one letter from Michaux on the subject of some rectifications to make
to my translation of "Movements" that he just received, but since I'm in
New York these days, I need to wait until next week when I return to
Greenwich, to worry about the Michaux affair. My first visit will be for
Madame Varèse. And I just received such a nice letter from our Rinette
to wish me the Nanni. She will have some of my news soon. Saillet too.

I hope that your "Menotti" is finished, and that it did not tire you much. You will send me the number of the releases—I will be so impatient to see it. I have not done any project nor made any dates as of yet, but if I accept the invitation to the Elizabethan Club who is for me that is for the month of April, that could postpone my return. It seems that the only females who had such a privilege are Katherine Ann Porter, Edith Sitwell and Mlle Bitch. And I see that at that 'Poetry Center' that invited Michaux there will be a performance by Edith & Osbert Sitwell. I will, perhaps try to see that. But I cannot concentrate that high—and even the base literature before that sort of permanent spectacle that to me seems New York. It is also cold. Fortunately the weather is finally mellowing. Today it's raining, fortunately. More winter sports in town. But don't forget that you're on the border of the sea here. You go down by bus just to Battery, and there is the Statue of Libbetty and the big transatlantics, in an extraordinary New York décor—bondzeu! What colors sea and sky and what aweful wind that tears away your "berry" as Marian Willard says.

So, I embrace you over and over again my dear very dear Adrienne. Thank you for your letters of 2 and 7. your Sylvia.

Camilla says "Kiss Adrienne" and that she will write you a letter – after her sister to whom she has yet to write, the first will be for you. She is very busy.

Janotte has no American competition—there are enormous amounts of bunnies (for Easter) but of a far inferior class. She can around her have ornament rabbits when she would like.

Camilla is taking us, Holly and me, to "Porgy and Bess" next week. There is one of those queues at Ziegfeld theater! That show just returned to N.Y. It's the biggest theatrical success of the moment.

Harry Ransom Humanities Research Center, The University of Texas at Austin (manuscript)

※　※　※

200. **To H.D.**   **January 18, 1954**

Dear H.D.,

We are now in the midst of getting your two wonderful CARE parcels, Adrienne and I, and I fear we just go on enjoying them and leaving you, meanwhile, utterly un-thanked for your kindness. Yet we bless you every day for your bounty. We don't, however, approve of your spending all that on us—one of those giant parcels would have "served two" as they say at home on their packages. But we are comfortable for a long time, thanks to Hilda. Did I tell you that my concièrge thinks the word "CARE" is on account of their being SQUARE—"un colis carré," she says I've received.[22]

I hope you are feeling stronger and stronger in Zurich which seems to suit you so well. And I hope too that you will find a pleasant place to install yourself and your books etc. in. I was only a few hours in Zurich but got the impression it was more zippitty than Lausanne. And one is not obliged to follow Jung—be a Junger.[23] Like those Bollingen people I saw in N.Y.

I hope "Les Successeurs" as we always call those who have succeeded Adrienne at her library have sent you by this time the Sixteenth Century Poets that you wanted to give a friend there. Bryher too mentioned it, and I placed the order with them immediately, but when you haven't had any experience in bookselling it doesn't always go smooth at first.

Perdita[24] wrote me a delightful letter, about the French studies of Valentine, and the little Nicholas crawling so fast all over the house. And how the last time we met was at the Coronation.[25] I'm so sorry you weren't able to come. Such a spectacle, yet the young Queen and her People made it so real and so moving. I was mighty glad to see it—gladder still to see Bryher. We don't often get the chance.

I wonder if you ever did manage to come across those "Laies de Marie de France"[26] that you wanted so long ago. I am still looking, and the other day a copy just slipped out of my hands, though when I heard of it I galloped around to Flammarion's[27] flourishing the letter about it. Alas! it was already gone, so said the odious young man who was supposed to be getting it for me. It was no fair. I was disgusted. Je ne serai jamais plus sa cliente.[28]

---

22. "Square parcel."
23. Carl Gustav Jung (1875–1961), Swiss psychoanalyst. He founded the C. G. Jung Institute in Zurich in 1948.
24. The daughter of H.D. and painter Cecil Gray.
25. Queen Elizabeth II's coronation took place in London on June 2, 1953.
26. *Les Lais de Marie de France*, a series of poems by a twelfth-century French poet.
27. French bookstore and publishing house.
28. "I will never patronize them again."

Adrienne and I saw Antony and Cleopatra performed by the Stratford Memorial Theatre here. It was a great success, crowded, all sold out at once. Peggy Ashcroft[29] was lovely, though anything but sinful looking I thought. The show was very well done and Shakespeare was pressed to the French bosoms—as usual. As for me, I wish I could hear him oftener, rolled on the British tongue.

With much love to our dear H.D., and many thanks and good wishes from us both—

Sylvia (Bryher in London for the present..?)

PS Adrienne is to broadcast to Belgium, Germany this week, and to lecture at the American University Women's Club next week . . . and so on.

Yale University Library, Beinecke Rare Book and Manuscript Library (manuscrip)

* * *

201. To Ernest Hemingway   January 29, 1954

January 29th—54

Dear Hemingway

The news of your crash was so dreadful![30] I was weeping over you and Adrienne was too. We were happy when the next news came—very very glad that you and Mary escaped with some bumps.

I am sending up a few French papers in case you haven't seen what a fuss it made here. They were almost getting the Panthéon ready for you.

Much love and congratulations!

from Sylvia

(and I thought now I didn't tell him how I admired his beautiful "Old Man and the Sea"! A great poem, the greatest I think our country "in our time" has given us—so there!)

Ernest Hemingway Papers, John F. Kennedy Presidential Library (manuscript)

---

29. Peggy Ashcroft (1907–1991), English actress.
30. A chartered airplane carrying Hemingway and his wife Mary crashed in Uganda on January 23, 1954.

* * *

202. To H.D.   **July 5, 1954**

V.VII.54 (5 July 1954)

My dear H.D., I was glad to hear you were settling in a some rooms of your own and having such fun with the unpacking and all. Sounds wonderful.

The book you want to have sent to Dr Heydt-Leibowitz: "Shönberg et son école"[31] is out of print so they haven't been able to supply it at A's old bookshop. They will keep on searching for it and hope a copy will turn up. Unfortunately this may delay things—if Dr Heydt doesn't mind waiting a little while. I don't think it's hopeless.

If Bryher drops in please tell her I know I owe her a letter..and meanwhile send my love.

> With much love to yourself
> Sylvia

H.D. Papers, Yale University, Beinecke Rare Books and Manuscript Library (manuscript)

* * *

203. To Harriet Weaver   **February 2, 1955**[32]

12 Rue de l'Odéon
Paris VI
February 2, 1955

Dearest Josephine,[33]

Thankyou for your letter of December 27th (!) which gave me news of all your family and particularly of Robin and his interesting job in the school at Clifton.[34] I was sorry to hear of the little boys catching the

---

31. *Schönberg and his School.*

32. James Joyce's birthday.

33. Weaver's nickname was "Comrade Josephine," due to her involvements with feminism and her association with the Communist Party.

34. Weaver's nephew Robin Hone. His father Campbell Hone was the Bishop of Wakefield. Weaver's biographer reports that it was he who looked up Beach in Paris after the Second World War, had tea with her, and wrote to assure Weaver that she had survived the war and her internment (Lidderdale, *Dear Miss Weaver*, 402).

measles and I hope they have completely recovered by this time and that their father managed to escape. But you never never say how you yourself are—which is very reticent of you dear Josephine. Next time you write you must tell me whether you had bad colds lately and those horrid chillblains. No flu nor nothing I hope. Your family and friends in Oxford must have been very much pleased at having you in Oxford this Christmas.

I went to see the Gilberts[35] the other day (crossing the bridges over such a swollen Seine!). Moune who has now left for the South was looking tired and I'm afraid she has had another rather bad winter. But she said all she had to do was to move down south to get rid of her bronchitis immediately. Stuart can't get away as he is plunged in the "Letters" and was expecting Mrs. Graecen any minute to come to the rescue.[36] He thought it very fortunate she could come and sort the letters for him. I called him up this morning to tell him that I had chosen 3 or 4 letters from my files for his volume—he had said he would like some of mine to be included. I picked out some that seemed particularly amusing or touching and with the minimum of 'business' in then, but I have hardly one that is entirely free of it. I was going to cross off everything of the sort but Adrienne tells me that I'm as bad as those relatives of Rimbaud who wanted whole passages suppressed in his letters and whom everybody criticizes for the attitude they take. Well, I wonder.

Adrienne is not getting well very fast. The last two specialists have nearly killed her with their violent medecines and maybe they were really making a desperate effort to cure her but they have only succeeded in increasing her sufferings instead of alleviating them. They don't seem to know what to do for this 'maladie de Ménière'[37] and poor Adrienne goes on with those noises in her head and the pain in it, the deafness, the giddiness and sleeplessness. She eats so little she has got quite thin. She is taking a week or so of holidays from doctors and their remedies but soon we shall be trying another doctor as she must find someone who can help her.

I am trying to finish my memoirs and have done a certain amount of work on them this winter. My headaches are better which is somepin.

---

35. Stuart Gilbert (1883–1969), English translator and friend of Joyce, and his wife Moune (1919–1985).
36. Patricia Greacen (later Hutchins), American literary critic and author of *James Joyce's World* (1957).
37. Ménière's disease, a hearing disorder named after the French doctor Prosper Ménière.

How is Richard Ellmann getting on with his book on Joyce, I wonder.[38] And what is Professor Prescott[39] doing now on the subject. I met
Ellmann during the war when he was in the navy, a young fellow in a
sailor suit and very much interested in poetry. He translated a great deal
of Michaux's[40] and did a very good job of it I think. He suddenly appeared at night at the door of our little chalet in Savoie summer before
last, and told us he was doing a biography of Joyce. I fear I wasn't helpful
at all—shooed him away as soon as possible from our mountain retreat.
And what about Herbert Gorman?[41] Is he ever heard from these days? Is
his biography of Joyce out of print?

I'm glad you like "Major Thompson".[42] He has had an enormous success here. Do you have a little time to read and would you like me to send
you a French book from time to time dear Josephine? You know you
mustn't drop the French.

I went up the Seine as far as Villeneuve-St-Georges and saw people
rowing boats in the streets and leaving their houses by boat and it was
terrible. All over France it was the same. Luckily all the rivers except the
Garonne have subsided now—it is rising again.

Gilbert says he is going to publish about 600 "Letters" out of 1000 he
has in hand. Moune seemed to think that they would be ready in about
a month.

With very much love to you,
From Sylvia

Please give my greetings to Misses Saunders.[43]

P.S. The enclosed proofs belonging to you of course turned up among my
papers and should have been restored to their owner long ago. S.

Harriet Shaw Weaver Papers, British Library (Manuscripts 57345–57352)

---

38. Richard Ellmann (1918–1987), American literary critic and biographer. The first edition
of his classic biography *James Joyce* was published in 1959.

39. Joseph Prescott, Joyce scholar and author of *Exploring James Joyce* (1964).

40. Ellmann's translations of *The Selected Writings of Henri Michaux* were published by New
Directions in 1951, two years after Beach's translation of Michaux's *A Barbarian in Asia*.

41. Unbeknownst to Beach, Herbert S. Gorman (1893–1954), American journalist and writer,
had recently died. His biography *James Joyce* was published in 1948.

42. Les Carnets du Major Thompson was a novel by the French humorist Pierre Daninos
(1913–2005). A film adaptation by Preston Sturges was released in the U.S. as *The French,
They Are a Funny Race* in 1955.

43. Earlier in her life Weaver had established a friendship with Helen Saunders (1885–1963),
English painter associated with the Vorticist art movement. The reference here might be
to her, but is more likely to refer to the women of the Saunders family with whom Weaver
lived in Oxford as a paying tenant for fifteen years (see Lidderdale, *Dear Miss Weaver*, 386).

* * *

204. To Harriet Weaver July 1, 1955

> 12, Rue de l'Odéon
> Paris (VIE)
> July 1st 1955

My dear Josephine

I have very sad news to give you—Adrienne died on the 19th of June[44] – but you have perhaps heard of it from the Gilberts. She suffered so much that I'm glad its over, but you can imagine how I feel without her. It is strange not to be able to run up and see Adrienne any more. And I do wish she had been spared all that suffering. For some time she hadn't been seeing her friends on account of the disturbing noises in her head and almost total deafness—she couldn't sleep nor read nor of course write—spent most of her time in bed and was terribly thin though her sister tried her best to put a little flesh on her bones. Rinette came to stay with her and nursed her which made her last days as comfortable as possible but nothing really relieved poor Adrienne.

She didn't want any fuss so nobody knew till after the funeral which only her sister and Maurice Saillet and I attended. My sister too as she was staying with me at the time. She spent the month of June here as her son was in the Arctic regions on his service in the coast guards.

Adrienne's illness and my sister's visit prevented me from answering your last letter in which you so kindly said you hoped I could go over to make you a little visit in Oxford. But I couldn't leave Adrienne as since last September when she was so ill in Savoie she had been getting worse and worse—with the help of several doctors. But there is not much one can do probably for someone with Ménière's Disease.

Stuart Gilbert has returned from Switzerland but I haven't felt able to see anyone yet. He wants me to give him a photo from my collection for the Letters which I must do as soon as I can concentrate my mind on the subject. It seems the volume is to appear before long.

---

44. Adrienne Monnier, after suffering for many years from Ménière's disease, committed suicide by taking an overdose of sleeping pills.

I hope you are well and getting away by the sea or somewhere for a holiday. I am going to a high place in the Engadine[45] with Adrienne's sister on the 14th. We both need a change.

>   With very much love dear Josephine
>   Sylvia

Harriet Shaw Weaver Papers, British Library (Manuscripts 57345–57352)

* * *

205. To H.D.   September 1, 1955

Dear H D: As I said on our postcard to-day in a funny hand-writing I'm sure you couldn't read—it would have been perfect at Orbe if only you had been with us! This is in case the writing was too obscure and Bryher forgot to give you my love—here it is dear H.D.! Bryher says you have been rather tired but are better now. And she is going to see you in a day or two. And Perdita, it seems, is coming over in October.

Adrienne's sister and I have been in cool, windy, high Sils-Maria where there are so many marmots, they say, but they never crossed my path as I was promised they would do, and I have an unsatisfied feeling about marmots. We spent 10 days in lovely Evolène: we had rooms in a little chalet back of the hotel and a sunny or rainy balcony you could breakfast on and hang out your wash. On the path behind our chalet, groups from the village going up the hill: someone leading a mule and a goat following or a black cow.

It was raining this morning but the afternoon was perfect and there's a moon tonight.

Its wonderful seeing Bryher again and hearing about her experiences since I saw her last.

The Italian maid smiles every time she appears before us. Is it her nature or are we funny looking?—no doubt its that.

We had so much trouble writing postcards with Bryher's ball-pen I'm giving her another kind I got in Yverdon as a surprise for her birthday tomorrow—probably worse than the other.

---

45. The Engadine is an alpine valley in Switzerland.

Thankyou dear H D for the letter that was a poem you wrote me so kindly and forgive me for the delayed thanks!

> With love
> Sylvia

H.D. Papers, Yale University, Beinecke Rare Books and Manuscript Library (manuscript)

* * *

206. To Ernest Hemingway   November 6, 1955

Dear Hemingway

As you have perhaps heard, I have lost Adrienne—it's very sad here without her. If you are ever in Paris and could find time for the rue de l'Odéon I would love to see you—or if we could meet somewhere in the U.S.—I must ask whether you approve of the way I have 'handled' you in my memoirs—and whether you authorize my quoting from letters: and perhaps may I use one or two photos from my valuable collection of Hemingways? These yere memoirs are coming out maybe one of these days at Harcourt Brace & Co. I might be going over there this winter and if you were anywhere to be seen—I was trembling for you and "Miss Mary" in that African journey!—and it wouldn't disturb you in the midst of your next work—we could look at these things together.

I have written to you at times, for instance to tell you how beautiful and great I thought "The Old Man and the Sea" but it must have been the wrong address—don't know your whereabouts now, old friends and true though we be.

Maurice Saillet says he has written to ask you to contribute something to the special No the Mercure is publishing in honor of Adrienne an éxtract or a page or something from what you are working on? Would that be 'faisable'? Its not coming out till January.

> With love from
> Sylvia

Ernest Hemingway Papers, John F. Kennedy Presidential Library (manuscript)

* * *

207. **To H.D.** December 5, 1955

My dear Hilda,

What a surprize and pleasure to get a letter from you, and how kind of you to think of me! I had just sent a 'pneu' to Françoise Hartmann asking her to come and see me and what was the news and all. She has a way of disappearing suddenly, now is off to London, next time its Florence. She has to work on her Italian of course as its one of her curricular languages or whatever you call it. But she does seem to do what she has to do and that's something I might learn from her. But of course she is the grandchild of the late Recteur de la Sorbonne and was born brilliant. I imagine members of the family greeting each other in the morning by asking: "and how's your Aggrégation this morning"? "fine—and how's your license these days?"—and to the one in the cradle: "did ye get your Bachot?" and everyone rushing off in the middle of breakfast to get to the "Oral" or the "Ecrit" or to defend their thesis or something. For me who never went to school at all its quite hard to follow.

Think of Bryher in America again: As soon as she lands there she gets a blizzard and she must do it on purpose I think. She gets on very well with blizzards. When I was over there last time rain was in torrents and a high wind blew everybody's umbrella inside out—the gutters were full of such umbrellas.

Its a good idea to get down to Lugano—Zurich must have a rather trying climate at least in the winter, though, from what Bryher told me, you are very comfortably installed in your apartment there. But she spoke of a plan to stay more or less in the Lugano region which you both liked. I have heard it's a paradise there.

You are wise not to attempt the journey to Rome if it tires you. Yet you felt so well last time you went there, didn't you?

It was too kind of you, dear Hilda, to think up another parcel for me, and Bryher bothering about it in New York. You know I still have so many of the clothing and equipment items you sent me from Lausanne in such huge exciting parcels. I use the bag with a strap for your shoulder every day and to this day, and the pajamas and the underwear are as fine as ever too. That handsome weekend bag has just had its handles mended by an excellent 'sellerie' in the Rue Saint Jacques—Adrienne and I always took turns using it. You know how we shared everything.

Isn't Perdita a wonderful little mother—and now this little gal coming. I hope the boys won't get tough with her. Three men against two women it would be. The whole family must come over next summer and let us have a look at it.

With much love and many good wishes to you

Sylvia

H.D. Papers, Yale University, Beinecke Rare Books and Manuscript Library (manuscript)

* * *

208. To Harriet Weaver   **December 15, 1955**

12 Rue de l'Odéon
Paris VI
December 15th, 1955

My dear Josephine,

Thankyou for your kind, interesting letter, and for "The Philosophy of Time" by Dora Marsden,[46] which did interest me, in spite of your being so sure it wouldn't. Though very ignorant in those learned matters, and not able to grasp more than a tiny percentage, I always hope to learn something.

It was just like you, dear Josephine, to hurry up and prevent me from sending you a little book, but of course if you have to think of moving your belongings somewhere else when the Misses Saunders give up the house in Rawlinson, the fewer the better. It's a pity you have to look for rooms elsewhere and adapt yourself to other arrangements. It must be difficult too to find anything in Oxford. Your many friends will be helping you in the search, I'm sure. Meanwhile, Mrs. Saunders is flourishing—she is wonderful. But when are you making us another visit? You would find Paris much quieter since the tooting of horns is forbidden. But an increased number of cars and motorbikes has increased the perils of the pedestrian terribly. The idea must be to discourage walking once for all and oblige everyone to buy a car and encourage business.

I haven't seen the Gilbert lately; I believe Stuart is in Switzerland on his artbook job again,[47] from what Moune told me on the telephone. She

---

46. Dora Marsden (1882–1960), English feminist editor and philosopher. Her pamphlet *The Philosophy of Time* was published in 1955.
47. Stuart Gilbert worked as a translator for the French art book publisher Albert Skira (1904–1973), based in Geneva.

said she was not well at all. The climate here certainly doesn't agree with her. Now that I have a telephone, that is the way I 'see' my friends instead of running around town and to the postoffice.

Next time you visit me, you shan't pick ockum, do you remember, dear Josephine? All those dusty strings. As for the mending you did for me, my sheets, thanks to you, lasted much longer than their normal span of life.

The newspapers here don't know what to write about now that the business of "Margaret et Toonsend" is settled.[48] Of course they have more politics than ever.

Maurice Saillet is editing a special number of the Mercure de France – a tribute to Adrienne by some of her writer friends. It is to come out the 1st of January—I will send you a copy. Saillet wrote several times urging Mr. Eliot to contribute something but he has refused. Yet nobody is obliged to write about Adrienne; they may send any small piece of anything they can find, a direct or indirect tribute. Saillet is disappointed over Mr. T.S.E.'s refusal, particularly as Adrienne was the first to publish his verses in a French translation.[49] He did write a letter, a sort of evasive account of seeing Adrienne after the war, and said it might be used as his contribution. But it wasn't worthy of Adrienne nor Eliot.

It must have been very interesting seeing Georgio and his wife.[50] I believe she is a doctor, isn't she? A good thing for him to have got married so happily.

Carola Giedeon[51] was in Paris in October, but I was in Touraine at the time, where a friend lets me use a little house—ni eau, ni gaz, ni électricité[52] nor running water, something similar to the one you used to go to in the mountains, but on the banks of the Cher and lovely surroundings. I like it better than Paris now, since Adrienne has gone.

48. The romance between Princess Margaret (1930–2002) and Group Captain Peter Townsend (1914–1995), which was terminated at the behest of the British Royal Family, was a major news story in England and apparently also in France.
49. Monnier and Beach's French translation of "The Love Song of J. Alfred Prufrock" was published in the review Le Navire d'Argent in June 1925.
50. Giorgio Joyce (1905–1976), James Joyce's eldest son, married his second wife Asta Jahnke-Osterwalder (1917–1993) in 1955.
51. Carola Giedion-Welcker (1893–1979), Swiss art critic and friend of the Joyce family.
52. "no water, no gas, no electricity"

Carola left a scribbled note—she is doing a book on Joyce??? and wanted I don't know what. I must write and ask her.

The other day I happened to be in Gheerbrandt's bookshop when in came Maria Jolas,[53] beaming and exuberant as ever. She has just bought an apartment big enough for her daughter Betsy and her husband and two babies (I think its two) and also herself to share with them. The other child Tina has at least two children now and I think Maria is kept busy as a baby-sitter.

Have you heard from our friend Joseph Prescott? I recommended him for the Guggenheim Fellowship which they can hardly refuse him with or without any recommendation, and I suppose in the spring he will be found most any day sitting at one of those big tables in my dusty room, with all the Joyce material spread out, and Joseph burying himself in it. If however, I happen to be in the United States where I expect to go on business with my publishers, his will have to wait. Then there is Dick (Ellman) who is threatening to look us up soon. I hope you will keep them busy in England.

As for our holiday in Engadine, Adrienne's sister and I were in a beautiful place, Sils o the two lakes Sils and Silvaplaner, two thousand metres altitude and walks taking you higher and higher to frozen lakes and glaciers. You had St Moritz at one end, half an hour's bus ride and Maloija at the other, same distance, the place where Thomas Huxley[54] used to stay. In spite of all these attractions, and the murmeltier or marmots playing among the rocks and whistling, and Nietsche writing his "Thus Spake" at twenty minutes from our hotel,[55] Sils was not the place for me. As soon as I got there I fell and broke my ankle, and wore a plaster cast for the rest of the summer. The altitude gave me the mountain [sickness,] dizzyness and nausea. Luckily the doctor had had much experience with patients falling and breaking their bones, and also with those suffering fro the altitude, so I was in the best hands. Luckily a woman writer who had lived in Sils left her library to the town and I could hobble and get all sorts o interesting books there including Gottfried Keller[56] in German on which I practised German but made little progress, and Joyce Hemingway and Cocteau.

53. Maria Jolas (1893–1987), American editor and translator.
54. Thomas Henry Huxley (1825–1895), English biologist.
55. Friedrich Nietzsche conceived the idea for his *Thus Spake Zarathustra* (1885) while vacationing in the Upper Engadine.
56. Gottfried Keller (1819–1890), Swiss writer of German literature.

On the way home we stayed in Bryher's for a few days. Hílda's daughter Perdita[57] now has 2 boys and is expecting a girl next time. Bryher writes historical novels and goes in for archeology. Edith Sitwell is converted to the Catholic religion.[58]

> With much love Josephine and many Christmas
> greetings—Sylvia

Harriet Shaw Weaver Papers, British Library (Manuscripts 57345–57352)

* * *

209. To Françoise Hartmann   April 10, 1956

Dear Françoise:

It is very distressing to hear from Mrs Bryher that, although she did finally receive the part of your work that was missing, she is not at all satisfied with your translation.[59] She now seems quite disheartened and I fear is greatly disappointed over the outcome of her plans. From what she says, the translation would have to be completely revised before it is acceptable for publication.

What, I wonder, do you propose to do about it? I am leaving for the United States within the next fortnight so hope to hear from you soon.

> Yours very sincerely,

Bryher Papers, Yale University Library, Beinecke Rare Book
and Manuscript Library (manuscript)

* * *

---

57. Perdita Macpherson Schaffner (1919–2001), daughter of the poet H.D.
58. Edith Sitwell (1887–1964), English modernist poet, converted to Catholicism in 1955.
59. Hartmann had translated H.D.'s historical novel about the Pre-Raphaelites, *White Rose and the Red*.

210. **To H.D.**   **June 23, 1956**

(c/o Mrs Frederic Dennis
Martindale
Greenwich, Connecticut)

Dear H.D.:

Bryher has given me your new address and my first letter to you there is about your nice new granddaughter. I went up to see Perdita to-day. She was looking very well, got up and showed me the view of the Hudson from the sittingroom at the end of her corridor, showed me THE BABY through a glass door—the nurse wheeled her up for us to gaze at—she is lovely, not red and puckered like most people of her age, and she has lots of pretty hair, like her mother. She opened her eyes, took one look at me, you could see she preferred Perdita. She didn't 'mew' once and I bet is going to be easy-going. Bryher will see what a Queen she's got as a namesake when she comes over and you with her for the christening.

Perdita's room was full of flowers, a big red-white-and-blue bunch— I never saw such corn-flowers! and lovely roses with long stems, pink ones: a yellow chrysanthemum in a pot, more longstemmed roses coming while I was there—the nurse said they should all be kept "in the deep freeze" or perhaps "airconditioned" but that would be too bad, wouldn't it? Not even enjoy them. Poor Perdita! Then another long box of roses was brought, opened, and Perdita read a note saying "so glad its a boy" which turned out to be for a Mrs Somebody-or-Other who was probably being congratulated about her "little girl" at that very moment.

The two boys will be quite surprized to hear of their sister—thought it was to be a brother but baby took so long—they gave it up after a couple of days waiting.

She will be having lots of visitors tomorrow Sunday so I won't go back till Monday. She is coming home next Thursday it seems.

I am very glad to be around town for this event—have been lucky, everything turning out so far favorably, as far as my publishers are concerned.

I hope your proofs are all corrected and the book on Freud is now in the press. I would like to see Mr Norman Pearson but hesitate to disturb him at a time when University professors are busy closing down for the summer.

What a delightful address youve got, dear H.D.! Bryher, from whom I just had a letter (she was with you) said you liked this place you have found, and hope to spend the summer there. It must be pleasant if it is near the lake. And you will have a place to put your books and all.

And Bryher off to the Shetlands this time!

> With much love to you,
> Sylvia

H.D. Papers, Yale University Library, Beinecke Rare Book
and Manuscript Library (manuscript)

* * *

211. **To Ernest Hemingway** **September 8, 1956**

Dear Ernest:

It was wonderful to hear your voice and to know you were so fine and hearty as ever.

You will be just getting the extract from my memoirs ("Shakespeare and Company")—the part concerning yourself, which Harcourt Brace and Company sent you yesterday. The book isn't set up yet so they haven't been able to send you the proofs, only the typescript, but the thing is "en chantier" and will be out before long.

After they had gone off, I realized, too late to make any changes, that perhaps some should be made, and I think you will agree with me about this. A certain number of references to your domestic life in the days when I first knew you could easily be spared and should be deleted. I left these un-touched they were written some years ago—when you said the other day to "go ahead", but I do feel that in the present circumstances they have no particular interest. I know you will understand, and the others too.

I wrote to Maurice Saillet that you were going to see him and give him something about Adrienne. He will be holding his breath and crossing his fingers. But he won't have got back yet perhaps from his farm in Haute Savoie: Burdignan, près Boege, The Savoie. His telephone in Paris: Danton 32–39. He lives in the little apartment on the 'entresol' at No. 12, I used to have.

Ever my love to you,

> Sylvia

Ernest Hemingway Papers, John F. Kennedy Presidential Library (manuscript)

* * *

212. To Harriet Weaver   **No date, circa 1956**

[c/o Mrs. Frederic Dennis,
Martindale,
Greenwich, Connecticut.]

My dear Josephine,

I am over here this summer as you see, to arrange about those old memoirs of mine that are at last coming out, I hope, and going to leave me in peace. You know that long ago, too long for anyone to remember, I signed a contract with Harcourt, Brace & Co and they have been very kind and patient with me ever since. At this stage it was necessary for us to meet and discuss some of the details of publication. It is a great help to have established a contact with them, and my country, and I expect to stay through August to attend to matters over here before disappearing again over the Atlantic.

I wonder, dear Josephine, whether you are away, staying with your family this summer, or perhaps at the seaside. And are you still in Rawlinson Road? If you have moved, have you found a nice place to live in? do let me know as soon as you can find time to write me. I would like so much to know how you have solved your problem of a new home.

I imagine that Mr. Ben Huebsch,[60] like everybody here just now is away on his vacation. Otherwise I would try to see him and find out something about the Joyce "Letters". I have heard nothing since I came, to announce the forthcoming publication, but no doubt if I had seen Mr. Huebsch he would have told me the latest news on the subject. I have been so sunk in these here memoirs that I couldn't see anybody except the publishers and of course my sister Holly. Would you have any objection to our using your portrait by Man Ray as an illustration in my book?[61] Of course we would get his permission and he would be paid the usual fee. But I would like to have you in my book, and particularly that photo of you.

My nephew Fred is to finish his four years in the Boast Guards[62] a year from now. He can hardly wait to board a freighter for a voyage to Europe the minute he is free.

---

60. Benjamin Huebsch (1876–1964), American owner of Viking Press.
61. Man Ray (1890–1976), American photographer who took portraits of many important modernists. Her book was her forthcoming memoir, *Shakespeare and Company*.
62. Fred Dennis, Holly's son, was in the Coast Guard.

And our friend Dr. Joe Prescott is going over to spend next winter in Paris. He has already found a place to live there and a school for Eleanor. You will have many a visit from them too.

> With much love to you, dear Josephine, and hoping to hear from you soon,
> Very affectionately yours,
> Sylvia

Harriet Shaw Weaver Papers, British Library (Manuscripts 57345–57352)

* * *

213. **To Harriet Weaver**   October 9, 1956

> Beekman Tower Hotel
> 1st Avenue at 49th Street
> 3 Mitchell Place
> New York 17.
> October 9th, 1956

My dear Josephine,

You will be surprised to hear I am still over here. My memoirs' business obliged me to stay on and on as it is the crucial moment now. But I shall be going back to Paris towards the end of this month and my flight ticket allows me to stop over in England on the way. This must be the wrong time for you to see anybody, when you may be moving any minute, or perhaps have already done so. Otherwise I would have run down to spend a day in Oxford with you. I want to see you so much, and also to ask you one or two questions on the subject of my memoirs. But I can write to you—though it would have been a pleasure, dear Josephine, to see you again. I was very glad to hear from you and to know that you have found a place to go when you are obliged to leave Oxford. You will miss it, won't you? But you will be with your family and in a place with such a fascinating name—Saffron Walden.[63] You will let me know where to address you there, or is that the name of your sister-in-law's place? I wonder if you could come up to London for a day or to spend the night. It must have been very jolly seeing your Canadian cousins and going

---

63. A town in the county of Essex in England.

with them to a play at Stratford-on-Avon. The weather, I fear, was horrible at the time. Adrienne's sister says that it rained all summer in France and wherever she went on her holidays. Now it has got suddenly balmy it seems and its no use to anyone. Our friend "Joe" Prescott and his family have now arrived in Paris, as you have heard, no doubt, and he expects to get to work on my Joyce material as soon as I return.

He understands that I have been detained over here and says he can wait. But they took a trip to Belgium and Holland before settling down. They are looking now for a place to live in he says. I saw Mr. Huebsch the other day. He was back from his summer tour of Europe—even took in Prague, and looks remarkably young and skittish. He said the Joyce Letters are coming out in the spring of 57—that is, next spring.—at last. He seemed very much interested in them. He has retired from his publishing business but still goes to his office daily and follows everything personally. He had not seen the notice in the New York Times about the Joyce play adapted from the story "The Boarding House" that is to be produced in New York this season. He had heard of it but said these theatrical things don't always come off. When I came over at the end of April they were doing an adaptation of the story on television and it had a great success—was repeated by request. Mr. Huebsch spoke with regret of not having secured Ulysses for the Viking Press though he had an opportunity to do so. It was too difficult and too expensive an undertaking he told me.

I am staying a few days at this hotel which is a few steps from the East River which I am very fond of.[64] It is a big, rough, rushing workingman of a river with tugboats busy with their jobs and barges and freighters interesting to watch. It is next door to the United Nations, but I prefer the tugs. I find it more convenient to stay in town when I have appointments and things. Bryher came with H. D. to attend an exhibition of H. D.'s—that is in commoration of her seventy years. Also to see her third grandchild, [Perdita's] little girl. They are going back to Switzerland in a few days.

With much love to you dear Josephine
Sylvia

Please greet the Misses Saunders for me. They must have an anxious moment with their mother's accident.

Harriet Shaw Weaver Papers, British Library (Manuscripts 57345–57352)

---

64. The Beekman Tower Hotel in New York City.

* * *

214. To Harriet Weaver   **October 19, 1956**

Beekman Tower Hotel
1st Avenue at 49th Street
3 Mitchell Place
New York 17
October 19 1956

Dearest Josephine your letter came yesterday—I am so glad you can arrange to see me and I hope the date I have now set to fly over—next <u>Saturday week the 27th</u> will be convenient for you. If not just let me know! I couldn't get off earlier in the month.

Thank you very much for offering to put me up at your Nursing club place—I would be so glad to stay there if they can give me one of their little rooms—I get in Sunday morning – and I plan to stay till the 30th and go on to Paris then—but please say if that suits you, won't you? The Prestons will be awaiting me in Paris—November 1st—otherwise I would like to stay longer in London. I am very happy to be looking forward to seeing you again dear Josephine! And isn't it wonderful that dear Mrs. Saunders keeps well! She has lots of vitality and the doctors here tell me people live on twice as long as they use to.

With much love and thanks—
Sylvia

It would be better if you wrote to me at the Beekman Hotel from now on as I shall be in New York a good deal. S.

Harriet Shaw Weaver Papers, British Library (Manuscripts 57345–57352)

* * *

215. To H.D.   **November 13, 1956**

Dear H.D.,

I was so sorry to hear of your accident—what a horrid thing to happen after you got back from your exciting trip to America and before you had time to sit down again and preen your feathers ruffled by the flight. You must have suffered when they pinned up your poor bone, but I hope you are feeling it less now. From what Bryher tells me, you were in Küssnacht when it happened where I know they are looking after you very carefully, your friends there. Switzerland seems to have the best doctors for broken bones on account of all those Alpinists. You can simply put your accident down to winter sports, though a bit early in the season. Poor dear H.D.: I am sorry you went in for them.

It was delightful getting those glimpses of you in the U.S.A. and how thrilling I found your exhibition at Yale. These are the only real events in our funny little life.

I stopped in London on my way back to see Miss Weaver. She was very much interested in the news of your having three grandchildren.

Paris hadn't changed at all except that there were a few more cars and no place to park them and no essence to run them till they can raise the Egyptian "triremes and quadriremes" from the bottom of the Suez canal. I am busy all day with my proofs and stuff and all those fine Swiss pencils you gave me with your blessing on my job.

I wish I could send you something to help pass the time while you are laid up, though no poet is ever bored by leisure. But perhaps you could think of some French book or other you would like and that it would be a joy for me to send you. Anything except 'du Sagan'.[65] The Troubadours seem to have dried up for the moment—or lying low.

> With love and many good wishes for your recovery as
> quickly as possible,
> Sylvia

H.D. Papers, Yale University, Beinecke Rare Books and Manuscript Library (manuscript)

* * *

216. **To Harriet Weaver**   **December 13, 1956**

> 12 Rue de l'Odéon
> Paris–VI
> December 13 1956

My dear Josephine,

---

65. Françoise Sagan (1935–2004), popular bestselling French novelist and playwright.

I have just received your letter with the sad news that Miss Saunders and her sister have had the sorrow of losing their mother and you a dear friend. If I haven't written to you for a time it was not because I was not thinking of you all, but because I was hesitating to intrude at a moment when I feared dear Mrs. Saunders might be going from you. From what you had told me about her increasing weakness and her age I was prepared for bad news. I am very very sorry dear Josephine. It was a privilege for me to have known her even for so few hours. She impressed me as a person of much charm and livelyness. You are going to miss her a great deal I know.

And now the household where you have lived together so long—how many years is it?—is to be scattered, the Misses Saunders will be just next door to where they lived which is a wonderful piece of luck for them. But what about you my dear Josephine going away so far from where you were so much at home?—"dans vos meubles" as they say here—you will write to me often, won't you please, to tell me how you are getting along in that place with such a romantic name Saffron Walden, and all about the family you are taking up with. The packing of all those books and things that seem to accumulate in places one has lived a while in must be rather fatiguing—but you have time to do it without hurry, I hope.

I have been hurrying a bit myself these last weeks, slicking up my memoirs and cataloguing or at least trying to, some of my library which might have to be moved across the Atlantic one of these days. This is a job I would have preferred to do after, not during, the one on my book, but owing to circumstances I had no choice. Luckily that little piece snipped off from the hunk coming out supposedly in the fall of -57 is to be printed towards Christmas and you are to get one whether you will or no. The publishers do this at Christmas, usually with a better book, to a few of their friends, but I can't for the life of me see why.

"Joe" Prescott is hard at work and though he lets himself in with the keys—your keys you once had to carry about—and lights his gas bottle radiator and settles down for hours in his front room workroom, we usually run into each other some time during the day. No one could be more thoughtful of others nor more courteous than he. I work on my job in the kitchen, but once in a while there's a tap on the door and there's Joe showing me something on Joyce he wants me to see, or giving me some information he has looked up for me. He is really a good fellow. As for his wife and daughter, I am going to invite them to tea soon but they understood that I was very busy just at this moment. They haven't tried to see me except once when they kindly invited me to have Thanksgiving Dinner with them at a kind of American student centre in the Boulevard. Raspail, Myrtle, Eleanor Joe and I had a good evening together, ate lots of turkey and cranberry sauce, sweet potatoes and pumpkin pie in true yankee traditional manner. Myrtle attends a course on Civilization française at the Sorbonne and is taken around with her fellow students to the churches and museums and is kept quite busy she says. Eleanor is a bubbling child, 10 the 9th of this month, and two years ahead in size of the French little girl. Her parents speak of her as their "little girl"—but she's not as little as all that! She bravely goes to the hardest school in Paris—"l'École Al-Sacienne" where Gide once was a pupil. Eleanor has a hard time keeping up with her class but in spite of the handicap—she knew very little French when they came—she manages to get along with the help of private lessons three times a week. She misses her friends at home and the life, but her parents do everything they can to make her happy there. They have such family affection and such a kind way with everybody—they are wonderful. I think, from what Eleanor said, she found the French girls at her school much less warm and hospitable than at her English school. That, unfortunately is the French way at first. As soon as they do decide to be friendly they are extremely so, I always found. Foreigners find it very difficult to know the French when they come to stay with them.

Anyhow, I asked a friend of mine who has four children, about the age Eleanor to invite her to their house, which she did. I wish I had time myself to have them all meet here, but its impossible for the present.

How are you making out for heat this winter? I hope you keep warm. Coal is not available here. I have some wood left . . . after that . . . ?

Will write to Miss Saunders. Meanwhile, please say I send my warmest sympathy.

Your picture does remind me of Adrienne—though her costume was more nun-like—but there is something of her about it. I've a queer feeling about Adrienne—that not only is she gone but I've gone away myself somewhere—I dunno where. Thank you for card and letters.

    With much love to you my dear Josephine.

      Sylvia

Look back with so much pleasure to the pleasant time spent with you at the Nursing Club, going to the book league with you and all those ducks we saw in the park and the comfortable atmosphere of the little dining-room and all—specially being with you again. Think of your books in a cupboard all by themselves! We must see them some time—make them a visit!

Harriet Shaw Weaver Papers, British Library (Manuscripts 57345–57352)

* * *

217. **To Harriet Weaver**   **December 27, 1956**

Sylvia Beach
12 Rue de l'Deon
December 27th 1956

My dear dear Josephine: I am so sorry to hear of your illness, and to think that you had to take the trouble to write me such a nice long letter to thank me for such a tiny book. I think this must have come from having so much to do these least few months, added to the great amount of work you always had to do. And it distresses me to think that coming to London to look after me just at this time may have contributed to your fatigue: it was very fatiguing I am sure.

Now do take a little care of yourself, and stay in bed till you have completely recovered. I envy those who are near enough to you to be able to run in and see you every day and do things for you. But it must be a bore to take it easy when you are accustomed to dash here and there and be so active. Please don't answer this letter but dear Josephine you will write me a little line every once in a while to let me know how you are, won't you? I did love your letter that I didn't deserve in reply to the small book, and the rhyme about the Zodiac which is new to me is most amusing. What's not at all amusing is to hear you are not well. You must follow carefully your doctor's orders now and please get well soon. I shall be thinking of you—but that I always do.

Yesterday I went to the Gilberts', showed them the slight extract from my book a copy of which was sent me for Christmas by my publishers. I know they are sending you a copy as I gave them your name and address as the very first to receive it. They get out a sort of traveller's sample of something they are to publish and this is that, or else that is this. Gilbert said the "Letters" are coming out in May he imagines. I told him about my meeting Mr. Huebsch and hearing the news that the "Letters" were to appear in the spring. Gilbert said that so much material had come in that he could fill volumes of letters. Yours, he told me, made up half the book and were by far the most interesting.

The Joseph Prescotts seem to have been spending the Christmas holidays with colds and a little sightseeing. I saw them the day before Christmas at least Joseph and his daughter, but Myrtle was in bed suffering with a cold. He told me he was not expecting to do any work for a while as he planned to travel about to places near Paris.

Now dear Josephine, if you only knew my admiration and affection for you and how I wish you wouldn't go and get under the weather.

With much love
From
Sylvia

Harriet Shaw Weaver Papers, British Library (Manuscripts 57345–57352)

* * *

218. To Harriet Weaver   January 23, 1957

12 Rue de l'Odéon
Paris VI
January 23rd, 1957

My dear Josephine,

I was so glad to hear you were better and able to walk about for a while out of doors. You must be very careful now, dear Josephine and not lift any pianos etc. it was very kind of you to take the trouble to write to me about the erroneous account I gave of those "sheets" which you bound up but didn't print from: it was the sheets themselves that constituted your edition of "A Portrait of the Artist". It has at last penetrated through my thick numskull: and how grateful I am to you for calling my attention to this in time to save such an error from going into my book: at least that will be avoided. Imagine how Mr. Huebsch would have cracked down on me when that caught his eye. Thankyou so much, and please forgive me. If you are familiar with Molière's "Etourdi"[66] he reminds me terribly of myself. I am given to dwell endlessly on something of no importance, then rattle along in an airy way when I should be paying attention. For example, M. André Spire tells me that the whole story of the party at his house where I first met Joyce is an invention of mine.[67] He says the food, the house, the dog are not at all as I described

---

66. *L'Etourdi* (*The Blunderer*), a play by Molière.
67. André Spire (1868–1966), French writer and political activist at whose home Beach first met James Joyce. She narrates the encounter in *Shakespeare and Company*.

them. He even denies having any wine: says it was tea. I accepted all his objections quite humbly, except the wine: I am positive there was wine, and about Mr. Pound's prank. Maybe there was no cheese, and nothing nice to eat which he asserts, and the dog wasn't his nor was it little: all right, but I told M. Spire I would stick to the wine and it certainly wasn't tea. I should never have written memoirs without a memory. I should have Joseph write them for me. He is a walking filing cabinet, everything neatly in its place.

Joseph has been working on the micro-film of some "Ulysses" MSS. which the Lockwood Library at Buffalo is allowing him to use. The American University Center has one of those machines like the one you showed me in Oxford and he has spent several days working there. The micro-films were sent over from Buffalo. It shows what confidence they have in Joseph. Everyone has, I'm sure.

The Prescotts have invited me to a performance of Paul Valéry's "Mon Faust" his charming little play that he read for the first time at Adrienne's house.[68] Joseph knows I am fond of Valéry and thought it would give me pleasure which it will. He lent me J. Byrne's book (Cranly) "Silent Years" with sub-title: "Memoires of James Joyce."[69] Have you seen it? It was published in 1953, tells nothing very interesting about Joyce and makes himself out as something of a wonder: he invented a cypher that couldn't be broken the State Department in Washington turned it down and will regret it some day. A queer chap.

> With much love to you, and may your health be better
> Yours affectionately
> Sylvia alias l'Etourdi

Harriet Shaw Weaver Papers, British Library

(Manuscripts 57345–57352)

* * *

---

68. *Mon Faust* by Paul Valéry was published in 1946.
69. J. F. Byrne (1880–1960), friend of Joyce and model for Cranly in *A Portrait of the Artist as a Young Man*. His *Silent Years: An Autobiography with Memoirs of James Joyce* was published in 1953.

219. To Harriet Weaver   **April 8, 1957**

                                              to Miss Harriet Weaver
                                              4, Rawlinson Road,
12, rue de l'Odeon   Oxford
Paris–VI

                                              April 8, 1957

My dear Josephine,

    I am addressing this to Rawlinson Road as perhaps you haven't moved yet and if you have already done so it will be forwarded. I have been thinking of you and wondering if your ordeal of moving was now over and whether your health was improving. I do hope so dear Josephine. I have been very anxious about you.

    Besides the work on my memoirs I have been busy making a minute catalogue of my library. I have been given some hope that an American Foundation will be interested in acquiring my Joyce collection in order to donate it to one of the University libraries in America. I understand that the Foundation's interest in the collection would be considerably less if any of the material had been published. Please don't give anyone including Mr. Joseph Prescott your permission to publish anything in my Joyce collection. Perhaps your solicitors too should know this and that you would be so kind as to let them know, any time of course you happen to be writing to them.

    I hope the Miss Saunders had a satisfactory offer for their house and have been able to settle down comfortably in the neighborhood. I am afraid you will miss Oxford, at least at first, then you will begin to feel at home in your new quarters.

    The Joyce "Letters" are coming out the 1st of May—so I was told, but Mrs. Gilbert thought the other day that the date of publication might not be exactly the 1st. Anyhow Mr Gilbert has sent back the last proofs some time ago.

    My sister sent me the enclosed account of the performances of "Exiles" in New York. You have probably received the press cuttings yourself. She said she was going to see the play and would tell me all about it. Mrs. Steloff of the Gotham Book Mart said she thought the production was very good. If the other newspaper articles were as bright and hearty as this specimen "Exiles" must have been a "Broadway Hit".

With much love and very good wishes
to you
from

Sylvia

Harriet Shaw Weaver Papers, British Library (Manuscripts 57345–57352)

* * *

220. To Harriet Weaver   **April 9, 1957**

To Miss Harriet Weaver
12, rue do l'Odeon
Castle End,
Paris–VI
Saffron Walden, April 9th, 1957
Essex

My dear Josephine,

    I hope your health has improved since your last letter and that your ordeal of moving to your new quarters at Saffron Walden is over. I have been very anxious to hear how you are, and whether you were comfortably settled there. But of course you have been too busy to write letters.

    I too have had a good deal to do lately, with the end of my memoirs: and also have been obliged to make an itemised catalogue of my library including the Joyce collection. There is some hope that an American Foundation may acquire this in order to donate it to one of the University libraries in America. The Foundation's interest in it would, I believe, be considerably less if any part of the collection were published before its acquisition.

I have been much disappointed in Mr. Joseph Prescott. He has worked four months on my Joyce collection, and at the same time on the microfilms of the Ulysses manuscripts lent him by the Buffalo library. He has persisted in his efforts to retain access to my material regardless of the inconvenience to me at this time. Last summer I explained the situation and said it would not be convenient for me to allow him to work here this winter. He replied that it was too late for him to change his plans;

so considering his interests rather than mine, I reluctantly consented to interrupt my business in America and return to Paris so that he might be able to work on my collection of Joyce manuscripts. I warned him however that I couldn't say how long I could stay in Paris: it depended on my work.

Early in March I was obliged to tell him that he could no longer continue to work on my collection. My plans required my remaining free at present to go and come, and perhaps to dispose of my library.

Mr. Prescott, on learning my decision, spoke very unpleasantly of what he called my "dishonorable" behavior. He seemed to think I should not refuse him access to the collection as long as it suited him to work on it. Yet I had warned him before he came that he could not count on my presence for any specified time. According to Mr. Prescott, I would now be to blame for "ruining his whole academic career". He has been exceedingly aggressive and indiscrete, trying to force someone by whose courtesy he has been given the privilege of studying a private collection in her own home, to sacrifice her convenience to his ambitious schemes: that's what he demands. But his plans, which I now see were to "scoop" my Joyce collection before it is transferred to some University library, henceforth becoming accessible to others, do not interest me. I do not think it necessary to make any sacrifice on my part to further them.

Pardon me dear Josephine, for burdening you with this matter, but in case of any future demands of Mr. Joseph Prescott, I would like you to know my intention to have nothing more to do with him.

With ever much love Sylvia

Harriet Shaw Weaver Papers, British Library (Manuscripts 57345–57352)

* * *

221. To Harriet Weaver   **No date, circa April 1957**

Dear Josephine,

I have your letter. Indeed you are right to take my troubles so lightly and to support Mr. Prescott's claims which you have no doubt deemed just.

I will say only that I see. And we won't waste any more time.

Yours sincerely,
Sylvia

Harriet Shaw Weaver Papers, British Library (Manuscripts 57345–57352)

* * *

222. **To Harriet Weaver**   **No date, circa April 1957**

Dear Josephine,

I have your letter, and am surprised to hear of Mr. Joseph Prescott's demand. He himself assured me that in disposing of the material to one of the universities I had in mind, it would certainly expect to reserve for itself, with of course your authorization, the privilege of using it. Since Mr. Prescott told me this, I have been informed of it by others. They have warned me that in case of its acquisition by an institution, prior claims to the use of it would be a serious objection to the acceptance of the material.

Mr. Prescott was aware of my hopes to see the Shakespeare and Company manuscripts of James Joyce in a suitable library in the United States. He is determined to let nothing stand in the way of gaining his ends.

This only confirms my impression of Mr. Joseph Prescott's methods, which seem to be more those of a go-getting business man than of a scholar.

Yours sincerely,
Sylvia

Harriet Shaw Weaver Papers, British Library (Manuscripts 57345–57352)

* * *

223. **To Jackson Mathews**[70]   **April 24, 1957**

White Hall Hotel
Montague Street
London, W.C.1.
April 24
Gate B
Air terminal
West End.

Dear Muscle Man:

Member this? Unless it was the hotel with the same name in Montague Peace? But this reminds me of you and our hurried visit to London—this visit is rather hurried too with a good deal to do about my book at Faber's etc—its coming out at the end of May so will not interfere with Margaret's wedding.

The Faber & Faber cocktail party was very delightful and Mrs. T.S. Eliot is lovely. They spoke of you and your great work on Valéry—said D. Cooper[71] had a wicked tongue and many prejudices but was a very good critic. I couldn't find that good bar you took me to. Went to a play by Graham Greene—unfortunately heard everything.

With ever gratefulness for out last visit and everything and love to you both—

I mean much love,

Sylvia

This didn't get off to you in London—gate B opened too soon.

Jackson Mathews Collection of Sylvia Beach, Manuscripts Division, Department of
Rare Books and Special Collections, Princeton University Library (manuscript)

* * *

---

70. French literature scholar and Foreign Service Officer Jackson Mathews (1907?–1978) and his wife Martheil rented Adrienne Monnier's apartment after her death.
71. Possibly Lady Diana Cooper (1893–1986).

224. To Harriet Weaver   **April 30, 1957**

12, rue de l'Odeon,

Paris–VI

April 30th 1957

Dear Josephine,

I am sorry to hear in your letter of April 28th., that you have been convinced by Mr. Joseph Prescott that you should grant him the priority in making use of the material in my James Joyce collection. Yet he himself assured me that any of the universities I had in mind would expect to reserve for themselves the privilege of using the material acquired: it would be taken for granted, and add to the interest of the acquisition.

This, of course, would be with your consent.

Mr Prescott knew this all along. He went quietly ahead scheming to get hold of all my material before my disposal of it to one of the University libraries in the east of the United States, which was my intention as he knew. Regardless of any interests or the convenience of any but himself, he tried to force me to let him have his way. I told Mr. Prescott that I would not be able to allow him to continue his work in my library, was going to be too busy with my memoirs, and my plans to stay in Paris were too uncertain, and dependent this year on the publication of my book.

As my friends know, I am not in a position to hold myself and my library at the disposal of a professor who is determined to build up his whole career on the things I have earned myself by many years of hard work.

On hearing that he would not be able to work here any longer, he expressed his anger in such a way that he appeared in a new light to me: my only regret was having done anything at all for a man so totally lacking in consideration for others. I was disgusted.

Affectionately yours,

Sylvia

Harriet Shaw Weaver Papers, British Library

(Manuscripts 57345–57352)

*   *   *

225. **To H.D.**   September 7, 1957

My dear H.D.:

Anything I could say about things as beautiful as your "Selected Poems" would be much much too little, so deep is my admiration for them, and my love. But its Heaven we should thank for inspiring these poets: and I do thank gods for H.D.! She has the gift of perception and the mastery that's a joy to H.D. lovers.

How lucky those dear brats, Valentine, Nicholas and Elizabeth Bryher!

Bryher I imagine will be with you on your birthday—and all good wishes and love and admiration to H.D.

from

Sylvia

H.D. Papers, Yale University, Beinecke Rare Books and Manuscript Library (manuscript)

* * *

226. **To Harriet Weaver**   December 9, 1957

Dear Josephine:

Rather than say disagreeable things to an old friend, particularly at Christmas, I would have preferred not to write at all. But your kind letter, full of good wishes and friendliness only serves to remind me of an act that you saw "no harm in", but that was, on the contrary, harmful to me, and it makes me quite sad to think of it in connection with you.

It was your privilege to grant priority rights to edit two manuscripts in my collection when finally deposited in some library. You knew, however, that the right to reserve the editing of the material for the professors on its staff, would be an inducement to one of the universities to acquire it for their library. I thought the most suitable place, and the one where I think Joyce would have wished it to be, was one of the two leading universities in the United States.

I hoped too that these manuscripts, the gift of James Joyce and the acknowledgement of my services to him, in view of their present value and if disposed to the best advantage, might be of some help to me financially.

But these are questions that you feel are unimportant, as your hasty act of handing over priority rights for two of the manuscripts proves.

It might have been [more friendly] kinder, perhaps, to have hesitated before taking such a step.

from

Sylvia

Harriet Shaw Weaver Papers, British Library (Manuscripts 57345–57352)

* * *

227. **To Maria Jolas**   **December 26, 1957**

Dear Maria: Thank you so much for your card from Chérence![72] I know that view so well from the days I spent at Chantemele—I forget the spelling—

I knew you would be out there for Christmas and busy with your jolly children—otherwise would have sent you greetings and all sorts of good wishes—and taken Clairette a book I had for her—I do hope she hasn't got it already—

I hope too your translation[73] has progressed in spite of my interruptions and all that business turning up in the midst of it!

Tell your son-in-law De Bouchet[74] I think his translation of "Finnegans Wake" piece extremely good—poetically and linguistically to use such awful expressions for his beautiful translation. Its not often you have one you can enjoy as much as the original—in fact never hardly—

Please congratulate De Bouchet for me

With love to you dear Maria

and lots of good wishes

Sylvia

Eugène and Maria Jolas Papers, Yale University, Beinecke Rare Book
and Manuscript Library (manuscript)

* * *

---

72. Village in the Ile-de-France to which Jolas retired following the death of her husband.

73. During these years Jolas translated all of the novels of her friend, the nouveau roman author Nathalie Sarraute, as well as the philosopher Gaston Bachelard's *La Poétique de l'espace* (*The Poetics of Space*).

74. André du Bouchet (1924–2001), French poet, translator, and husband of Marie-Christine (Tina) Jolas. His partial translation of *Finnegans Wake* was published by Gallimard in 1962.

228. To H.D. January 8, 1958

Dear H.D. not to have thanked you[75] long ago, for the "small check" you were so very kind as to send me on December 24th, to find myself "some little gift": is that what you call "a small check"? dear H.D.! it was much too generous of you and I should give you a big scolding indeed, I must think up how to punish you for playing Santa Claus for me. Just let me get a hold of you!

Bryher tells me you are gradually improving—how long and boring it has been for you! It will be such a joy to hear you can at last chuck out those crutches and kick a football around the field again! Won't we celebrate that, dear H.D.! Luckily you have good bone-menders in Switzerland to look after you.

I am enjoying Selected Poems of H.D. always beside me: but not yet inscribed—will send it to you when you are able to run to post-offices again, as you must be sure and return it.

I got a nice 'greetings' from John and Perdita Valentine, Nicholas and Elizabeth Bryher: they are fine people and I am going to drop in and look them over again soon. Elizabeth Bryher must be about 1½ now, and walking and talking.

> With a little frown for what you done,
> and many thanks
> and much love
> and prayers for your complete recovery
> affectionately
> Sylvia

H.D. Papers, Yale University, Beinecke Rare Books and Manuscript Library (manuscript)

* * *

229. To Jackson Mathews April 22, 1958

April 22nd,1958

My dear Muscle Man:

I hope you will be able to drop everything you are doing pack up your diskuses and take the fastest train to Detroit Michigan: then you creep up

---

75. In the upper margin, Beach added "yes, and I'm ashamed."

on you know who: and I don't want to know the details: just GET HIM. I have just been talking things over with Mr. Gordan[76]: he came yesterday and spent the afternoon and I completely forgot to mention Prescott[77] and his priority game. So I called him up and asked him to drop in this afternoon. I did what had to be done: told him about the claims and Miss W. and asked him what he would do in case of his acquisition of the Coll. He told me that the lawyers held different opinions on the subject of right to edit or publish something: he is in the middle of some such case himself: some unpublished manuscripts they possess at New York Public Library, which, I believe, the estate doesn't want them to publish. He says how this comes out will maybe establish the rule one for all. However, the executor (Miss W.) can authorize the publication etc of any material: that if I have allowed anyone to work on material in my collection and Miss Weaver has given the priority to have access to it or edit it the Library could go to law if they didn't agree to any such arrangement: but wouldn't do so on account of the expenses: and I couldn't for the same reasons no doubt. He thought what Prescott has got is gone: and nobody knows how much of the material he has gone over: this would certainly affect the value of the material for a possible acquisition. Mr. Gordan asked me if anyone has seen the Letters: I said [no one], nor the First Draft of a Portrait of the Artist:[78] Miss W. has granted priority rights on that to Megalaner,[79] but he has never even seen it and Mr. Gordan thinks I might be able to prevent it from being grabbed. But he spoke plainly about the effect on the possible purchase if a certain amount of the material is not "fresh". [Anyhow], I feel very much relieved now that I have seen Mr. Gordan and talked it all over with him. He has gone into the question himself you see, and it seems it's a fairly new problem: nobody used to bother about it: and there are various opinions but no one really knows. That is about authorizing the publishing of unpublished material. But there is no doubt at all that what has happened is not going to boost my sale. And of course I shall have to go into it with any of the others who may be interested. He said you mentioned to him that there might be others in the field and he understood perfectly looking around before deciding anything. As for his Library, he went over carefully the whole collection, noted the prices set by Rota,

---

76. John Dozier Gordan (1907–1968), literary scholar and curator of the New York Public Library's Henry W. and Albert A. Berg Collection of English and American Literature.

77. Joseph Prescott, Joyce scholar and author of *Exploring James Joyce* (1964), as well as the first doctoral dissertation written on Joyce in 1944.

78. Eventually published, in part, as *Stephen Hero*.

79. Marvin Magalaner (1920–), Joyce scholar and editor of *A James Joyce Miscellany* (Carbondale: Southern Illinois University Press, 1959).

and the price of the whole collection as I ant to have it intact. But I said I wanted to keep back the Letters, at least for a time. And that I would like fifty thousand: without the Letters.

Mr. Gordan noted all this, told me it was a committee that had to be consulted before making any purchase, and if the committee didn't think the entire sum at their disposal should go to one subject but be sprinkled here and there then there would be no question of the Joyce Collection. I wonder myself if he hasn't a good deal to say in these matters: and how much Joyce matters to him. No sparks seem to fly: but I may be mistaken. And another thing. It would all be engulfed in the Berg Collection, he did say that. Which a little disappointed me.

Anyhow this Gordan is a nice man and quite a distinguished person isn't he?

Your letter of April 18th came the very day I was to see Gordan. I felt very much encouraged by what you said. I don't know about Professor Oscar Shinwell Department of English at Buffalo[80]: it was the Lockwood Library at Buffalo that bought all the items in the Joyce exhibition at La Hune. They didn't haggle over the price and Slocum (Cahoon)[81] did, so the buffalo hauled it off. So I believe, from Mrs. Jolas's story. Slocum wrote to me that he was very grieved. And I did write to Mr Jackson at Harvard, at Mr. McCallum's suggestion (Harcourt).[82] He was travelling in Europe at the time and I was travelling in America, but he wrote he would like to hear more about my Joyces. In deed if you would be so very kind as to sound any of these brothers on the subject I wouldn't be any gratefuller as that is impossible, I am already bursting with gratitude, but I would be very glad to get some idea of their appetite for Joyce. I have no doubt at all that Cahoon would like the collection for Yale, specially if he could get it on the bargain counter. My friend whom I saw in Switzerland at Easter seemed to think Mr Norman Pearson at Yale,[83] since it has been valued, has lost interest. But there's no telling. If he and Cahoon really want it, and they hear it is actually going somewhere they may do something about it. All this, c'est la bouteille a l'encre[84] for me.

---

80. Oscar A. Silverman, Joyce scholar and then chairman of the English Department at Buffalo University.

81. John Slocum and Herbert Cahoon, Joyce collectors and compilers of *A Bibliography of James Joyce, 1882–1941* (1953).

82. John McCallum, senior editor at Harcourt Brace.

83. Norman Holmes Pearson, professor at Yale and close friend of H.D. and Bryher.

84. An allusion to the expression "It's clear like a bottle of ink;" used to describe an insoluble problem or complex situation.

I hope Marthiel[85] is having lots of fun and not too much hard work fixing up your place in the country. You will be happy to have it now the spring has cooooome. But I miss you dreadfully. You'll end by drawing me over there.

I met Michaux in the market, rue de Seine, the other day. He walked slowly with a stick, sort of holding his broken arm, the hand still discoloured, in front of him. But he said he could now use it, could write with it: said he was better, but I thought he was a good deal changed after his terrible mescaline adventure. I have hopes of a translation of "L'Infini Turbulent" coming out over there. A young feller is working on it, friend of Bryher's. he thinks he can get it published, which has sort of cheered up poor Michaux. Dieu veuille.' He's difficult to publish.

I've not met the Lattimores[86] yet. She is always marketing and he lecturing I suppose. And now we have Oppenheimer, and the French government has lent him a car and are almost as nice to him as they were to Charlie Chaplin.[87]

How is your book on Valery progressing?[88]

Thankyou for all your kindness to me dear Jack,

I'm not worried at all about the sale of my collection: if I don't get so much, instead of the Rolls Royce, I'll simply order one of those Eggs: Isetta[89]: the best people go around in them to this day.

And I would hate to give you any more trouble: you have done so much for me

With much love to you both
Sylvia
Many many thanks!

Jackson Mathews Collection of Sylvia Beach, Manuscripts Division, Department of Rare Books and Special Collections, Princeton University Library (manuscript)

---

85. Marthiel Mathews, Mathews' wife and frequent cotranslator.

86. Richmond Lattimore (1906–1984), American poet and translator of Homer.

87. Robert Oppenheimer (1904–1967) was a visiting professor at the University of France in 1958.

88. The Bollingen Foundation was about to publish Mathews' translation of Paul Valéry's *The Art of Poetry*, the seventh volume of his projected 15-volume translation of Valéry's collected works.

89. The Isetta was a brand of microcar popular in Europe after World War II, sometimes nicknamed "Egg" because of its compact rounded design.

* * *

230. To Jackson Mathews   June 7, 1958

June 7th, 1958

My dear Jack:

Thankyou for your letter which I have just received as I was away when it came. I am very sorry to hear of your mother's accident and hope her bone is mending all right in spite of her age. You must be quite anxious about her.

I love hearing from you and am glad we have this Joycean business: otherwise you would certny never write to me at all. you and Marthiel have left a big gap here. I haven't met the Lattimores yet and maybe never will meet them as they are not staying much longer. A very pleasant letter came from another professor at Johns Hopkins: Rinette[90] showed it to me: about perhaps taking the apartment. Unfortunately she counted on Miss Ferguson taking it and didn't keep the letter nor note the address of the sender as Miss Ferguson has decided it was too expensive for her and perhaps the others might have come: Rinette replied that someone else was taking it. the Lattimores said they knew this professor, at least who he was, but not personally I believe. All they knew was that they were expecting a baby and they didn't seem to think this was in their favor. Rinette has now left for her holidays in Switzerland, to a place you reach by donkey. It doesn't look easy for her to be carrying on a correspondence about her apartment by donkey, does it?

I was much interested in hearing of the celebration of the Saint John Perse publication at the Bollingen.[91]

I think I reported the result of Mr John D. Gordan's visit. He seemed quite interested in the items but replied that the committee that decides these things preferred not to spend such a sum on one subject. He had in fact warned me that they liked to spend in several directions rather than on one point. I quite understand it, particularly as from what he told me, I think the Berg Collection goes in more for Dickens and Mark Twain with Conrad for dessert than the Joyce sort of thing. But I was sorry as Mr Gordan seems a very fine man. It might not be very interesting however to see this Joyce

---

90. Adrienne Monnier's sister Marie was nicknamed "Rinette," from "Marienette."
91. St.-John Perse (1887–1975), French poet. The Bollingen Foundation published his *Sea-marks* (an English translation of *Amers*) in 1958.

collection absorbed under the Berg heading and, so he said, be henceforth simply a part of those Bergers. Do you not agree with me? Whereas, in one of those libraries where they lose their identity and get mixed up with Mark Twain and Dickens—huh? Anyhow, you have been immensely kind to take all the trouble and I feel very guilty to have bothered you with my problems, when you are so busy and have Valéry and your own book and they must come first. I will be over there towards the end of the summer I hope, and we can ponder over my Joyces together then. Or wait till the end of the Recession and the next Presidential election etc.

And Margaret Marshall[92] tells me that my book is not coming out till Christmas 1959: that is: à la Saint Glin-Glin.[93] I was too slow writing it.

With much love to yourself and to Marthiel

Sylvia

Jackson Mathews Collection of Sylvia Beach, Manuscripts Division, Department of Rare Books and Special Collections, Princeton University Library (manuscript)

* * *

231. To Harriet Weaver   June 25, 1958

June 25th, 1958

Dear Josephine:

Since a first letter from Lucia dated the 21st May and postmarked "Saffron Waldron" I have received another, now, from the place where she is spending the holidays in North Wales. You will know best what I should reply to her questions about her father. Mrs. Jolas tells me that Lucia was informed of his death, but she is asking me how he is.[94] I want to write to her, but first would like to hear from you, if you would be so kind as to tell me, whether she is able to hear the truth, about her father, and also her mother about whom she is inquiring. You, who are always closely in touch with Lucia will know what to advise me in

---

92. Beach's editor at Harcourt Brace.

93. "À la Saint Glinglin (on Saint Glinglin's Day)" is a French expression meaning "some day in the indefinite future, or quite likely never."

94. For more information on Lucia Joyce's later years, see Carol Loeb Schloss's *Lucia Joyce: To Dance in the Wake*.

this matter. If I should evade her questions would it make her suspect something?

Hoping you are well, and comfortably settled in your present home,

Yours sincerely,
Sylvia

Harriet Shaw Weaver Papers, British Library (Manuscripts 57345–57352)

* * *

232. To Jackson Mathews   **July 9, 1958**

July 9th, 1958

My dear jack:

I am very happy with the <u>Paul Valery the Art of Poetry</u> that Bollingen Series and yourself were so kind as to send me: I haven't had time to more than skim over the translation: T. S. Eliot's preface is as usual fascinating.[95] Thank you for your kindness and your many other kindnesses, dear Jack!

I hope you are not working too much and resting sometimes in your country retreat.

Marie Monnier has just come back from a month on a mountain top in Switzerland. Miss Fergusson didn't rent the apartment after all but Marie is going to find someone else by seeing the people at the Embassy in August when the Lattimores are gone—she destroyed, unfortunately the letter the other professor in Baltimore wrote enquiring about the apartment: she was sure at the time Miss Fergusson would take it.

I am busy with an expo about the american writers and their French friends in Paris in the Twenties—or the "Twunnys" as they would say in Philadelphia. The embassy asked me to do this and seem to need me and my archives and have agreed to pay me a good price for my soivices & documents: so I'm hard at work on it: so is the photographer the designer and organizer, and all the big, medium and small tables are covered with this rue de l'Odeon material—Adrienne's is of course in it

---

95. Eliot wrote the introduction for Mathews' translation.

too. Clouds of dust. I had to get out a lot of it for my Shakespeare and Company Bouquin which of course is a help. And its interesting work I must say—quite fun.

Thankyou so much once more for Valery and ever so affectionately yours

Sylvia

Jackson Mathews Collection of Sylvia Beach, Manuscripts Division, Department of Rare Books and Special Collections, Princeton University Library (manuscript)

* * *

233. To Jackson Mathews   October 30, 1958

October 30th 1958

Dear Jack:

Your letter has just come and I am very much concerned over all the trouble you are taking for me, and never a word of reproach nor a mention of the huge load of work you have to do with your writing and Valéry. How can I thank you dear Jack! It is quite exciting to hear about the interest these nice Buffalo friends take in my collection: I think I would be very lucky to be adopted with the entire Shakespeare Joyce & Company library by people who seem to really love them and not grudging spending their funds on something that I must say would be worth having—the trouble is this exhibition: I'm in the midst of what has turned out to be sort of vast—about 500 items to be catalogued and several people from the embassy sweating with me every day to get the things into groups and arrange how they are to be displayed etc. and in a few days those huge sheets of cardboard on which the items are stuck— a lot of little photos they took are pasted on these sheets: or else they write what isn't photographed and every single item has been measured: well I wish you'd see my expo! But you must explain to Mr Silverman that its quite impossible to show these things to him at present—not till February when the exhibition is to open. I have them all put away and the catalogue must be typed ready for the printer—we are working on it now and I will try to get off to the US as soon as I finish this job, leaving the designer to do the planning.

I intended to leave by the beginning of October has a flying ticket for them—still good for a flight but when Mr Jodnovich, President of

Harcourt[96] came to see me and said my booklet wouldn't be out till nearly a year from now and Margaret Marshall wrote that if I went over in December that would be soon enough for them to see me—I can understand that!—I decided to stay and finish up my expo before rushing off—and everybody seems to think it a wise decision.

But I'm afraid if Mr Silverman and his friends must spend their funds before the end of the year I'll have to but regretfully let what was a wonderful chance slip away—I can't even get this collection appraised till Mr Jadonovich—"Bill" he wants me to call him—I must get it done as the Embassy has to ensure it—but though your friend Carter[97] is crazy to come along—writes to me regularly—these dealers only want to get the things into their hands—there's no such thing as a detached view of rare books. I asked them at Harcourt to help me with this problem and they are going to try to do it. But I'm beginning to know the dealers and Joyce–rag pickers and don't want to bother with them. And if the people who are interested can't wait till after the exhibition and till I have time to get my breath—tant pis!

You, dear jack are wonderfully kind—never saw such a man! I say Hell too: well why don't you come over here? That would be fun.

Thankyou for sending your M. Teste[98] and a daguerreotype (!!) of yourself—you mean of your granpaw in the .20s you were a little boy—and hurry up please—the designer is in a hurry. (I'm never) And tell Mr Silverman if he comes in November I'll be on the other side by that time and trying to "reach" him on the phone.

By the way, I sent you a cable which wasn't delivered—then I insisted it was not a hotel but a private address—then they send it off again and I have heard no more from them nor it. What a bother you have had with your apartments—poor Marthiel—she must have a time—and off she tuck with the dog, leaving such a nice husband at several addresses! And always changing zones.

With ever so many thanks and love
Sylvia

96. William Jovanovich (1920–2001), president of Harcourt Brace Jovanovich.

97. Most likely John Carter (1905–1975), book collector and co-author (with Nicholas Barker) of *ABC for Book Collectors* (1952).

98. Mathews' translation of Valéry's novel *Monsieur Teste* was originally published by Knopf in 1948.

Before you report again to Silverman wait for my next letter and till I can think up some way to arrange with them—say—turn over the Joyces for the price they were valued at: provided I'm allowed to keep the items for the present as I need them—they can pay immediately (very pleasant!) and get rid of quite a sum burdening their wallets—and when I can get the other things valued which I must for my expo, they can take . . .

Jackson Mathews Collection of Sylvia Beach, Manuscripts Division, Department of Rare Books and Special Collections, Princeton University Library (manuscript)

* * *

234. To Jackson Mathews   December 4, 1958

12, Rue de l'Odéon

Paris

December 4th, 1958

Dear Jack:

Mr. Silveryman and his two younger Buffalos announced that they were coming whether I would or no, and here they are between two Sundays, and very pleasant people you have rounded up for me: they came to see me and I showed them the exposition workshops and went to the bank and brought back the Joyce items and they looked at them. They intended to make the deal at once, and probably I couldn't do better than to let Buffalo have Joyce to add to their Joyce as they want it so much and are ready to pay the price according to the valuation of Rota. They seem to want particularly the Shakespeare and Company collection: at least that's what they say. That, however, has not yet been appraised, but Harcourt, Brace and Company is very kindly finding someone who will try to set a value on the items on the exhibition in order to have them insured by the Embassy, but they have to have a list first and I hope to send them one in a few days. Meanwhile these Buffalos want to settle about the Joyce collection at one: Silverman is peremptory or whatever you call it. They have come by jetplane to fetch the things, at least on paper, and they say they are in a hurry to spend the money before the end of the fiscal year. . . . I think the truth is that the professor has some characteristics in common with our former friend Joe P.: plus his friends with the funds. He too, maybe, is building up his career upon Joyce: he seems to be terribly eager to have the Sketch of a Portrait, says he must edit it himself. As he mentioned seeing "Joe Prescott", who I know is always prowling around Buffalo on account of the Joyce items they got at the time of the La Hune exhibition in Paris. I thought I would have to tell him about my disagreement with J.P. and of course the priority he had cooked up with Miss Weaver. I might be wrong: is Silverman playing into the hands of the other scholar-businessman? I think not: he wants the Sketch himself and has found the funds so will consider it his property—do you agree with me? He quite reassured me on the subject of the priority business: swept it right away as something that was of no importance. So as he knows all about Prescott beforehand and will certainly never let Megalaner have the Sketch in spite of any paper Miss Weaver may have given him, that worry would be removed at once if Buffalo buys us.

When I think how kind you have been to look after me, dear jack, and all your trouble you have taken to get hold of buyers, I am more grateful and touched than I can tell you. I intend to take my revenge on you somehow and you will not even be consulted when the time comes.

I haven't settled anything yet nor will do so before hearing from you, and also my friend Bryher to whom I have written: it was she, you remember who had the collection appraised. And something has to be done about the rest of the collection. I could sell the Eliots etc separately after all, and give the English literature library to the Bibliothèque Ste. Geneviève: it is valuable for studies but I couldn't get a good price for the books here: at home they have them all in the libraries.

I was very very happy to get your "Monsieur Teste" for my exhibition, and you will see it prominently displayed when you come over in February or early March: which you must do, you and Marthiel. I will take good care of this precious copy with your own marks in it, and only regret that you never attended to my getting a copy o my own when the book came out. The photo of yourself is charming and I am particularly glad to have it. Forgive me for not acknowledging these long ago. I have been all tied up with this expo: its more octopus than even Joyce. I hope Margaret Marshall will excuse me for not arriving over there long ago. She has written that they would like to see me. She very kindly suggested getting an agent for my business: but why? I have better than an agent: a friend.

I hope to see Madame Valéry as soon as I can get off from my job, and to see François and remind him of his promise, now that the elections are over and lid replaced on the boiled-over French dish. I want to tell them about the exhibition and the Valéry section in it.

> With love to yourself and Marthiel,
> very gratefully
> Sylvia

Jackson Mathews Collection of Sylvia Beach, Manuscripts Division, Department of Rare Books and Special Collections, Princeton University Library (manuscript)

* * *

235. To William Bird   December 15, 1958

Dear Bill Bird,

Thank you for your help with this exhibition of my old friends of the Twenties! At least it has put me in touch with one of them I haven't seen for ages but you know I think of you so often. Fortunately Cody hasn't lost sight of you and when he told me he was going to ask you to lend us some items and to write an introduction for the catalogue I was very very glad. The Three Mountains Press and Contact editions are chief stars in this show—what else would it be about?—and I have managed to keep together a certain number of your publications—hid them away during the occupation. You will see in the catalogue a photo signed "Bill Bird": "French Wines" "avec dédicace" and there's Pound's "Indiscretions," Ford's "Women and Men" and a copy of <u>16 Cantos</u> which may even belong to you and in that case you must step up and claim it.

Thank you for sending us those <u>Cantos</u> unbound sheets: they will make a sensation—and I have a little sort of invitation to see them displayed at Shakespeare and Company that you printed. Also I have:

The items you mention in your letter of the 12th to Cody

> <u>The Criterion</u> vol 1 No 1 containing <u>The Waste Land</u>
> <u>The Transatlantic No 4</u> with the 1st instalment of Joyce's <u>Work in Progress</u>

The Hemingway story <u>Indian Camp</u>
and <u>The Making of Americans</u> 1st installment

items I'll be very glad to have when they come:—

<u>In Our Time</u> Ernest Hemingway
<u>The Making of Americans</u> etc

I think it was your daughter who kindly sent Joyce's Storiella, a splendid addition to the Joyce exhibits. I don't own this work—nor the <u>Pastimes of James Joyce</u>.

am returning to Cody:—items I have: some of yours perhaps

Man Ray <u>Photographs 1920–1934</u>
Marsden Hartley <u>Twenty-five Poems</u>
Ezra Pound: <u>Quia Pauper Amavi</u>
Robert McAlmon: <u>Post Adolescence</u>
W.C. Williams: <u>The Great American Novel</u>
Lincoln Steffins: <u>Moses in Red</u>

Magazines <u>Mercure de France</u> with Pound's article on Joyce
<u>The Little Review</u> Spring 1923 Exiles No.
<u>transition</u> Paris summer 1928 American No, No 13
<u>The Criterion</u> April 1924

I received to-day your Introduction to the Exhibition like it immensely! And specially about Bob McAlmon. I met this Roger Dévigne you say you caught the publishing fever from—saw him a few years ago at the Musée de la Parole where he had a job in the recording department: he made a copy of my Joyce Ulysses record for me.

Will you come to 12 rue de l'Odéon (upstairs now) next time you are in Paris? I hope so. And of course to the Exhibition where you will see us all again: "Here Comes Everybody!"

With love to Bill Bird
Sylvia

My typewriter is on strike so I have to write by hand (this big black pen!)

William Bird Papers, Lilly Library, Indiana University, Bloomington (manuscript)

* * *

236. To Maria Jolas   December 24, 1958

My dear Maria

Thank you for all your trouble bringing the items for the exhibition[99] at a moment when you were so busy busy—but when are you not busy, dear dear Maria?!

And Thank you for the lovely little bouquet of Christmas roses! We were disappointed, all of us working, that you couldn't come up to see us, but the first day you have a minute to spare please do come up!

With love and Christmas wishes for yourself and all your goodlooking merry family of youngsters

> from
> > Sylvia

I enclose a letter from Lucia

> *Eugène and Maria Jolas Papers, Yale University, Beinecke Rare Book*
> *and Manuscript Library (manuscript)*

* * *

237. To Morrill Cody   February 10, 1959

> Mr. Morrill Cody   (Sylvia Beach)
> Cultural Councellor
> c/o Mrs. Fred Dennis
> The American Embassy
> Martindale
> Paris
> Greenwich, Conn.

My dear Morrill Cody:

After attending to a few last details—illustrations etc for my memoirs[100]—you yourself, a friend of the Twenties, are in the book,

---

99. *Les Années Vingt: Les Écrivains Américains à Paris et Leurs Amis, 1920–1930* (*The Twenties: American Writers and Their Friends in Paris*), a public exhibition of artifacts from Shakespeare and Company's archives, which ran for ten weeks at the United States Embassy in Paris, from March 11, 1959.
100. Sylvia Beach, *Shakespeare and Company* (New York: Harcourt Brace, 1959).

you know, I will take a jet plane back to Paris and our exciting Exhibition.

You were kind to me long ago, and continue your kindness right up to to-day. I am very grateful indeed! But is it too much to ask of you one or two more favors now? Its about one or two of my old pals who were also McAlmon's or/and Hemingway's and Joyce's whom, I think should be included in our catalogue and in the exhibits: there is Thornton Wilder[101]—he is to give me a photo of the 20s.—he was too shy in those days—and Archie MacLeish,[102] who was very important to us at Shakespeare and Company—and helped Joyce and me in the matter of the pirating of Ulysses (1926): then please one of McAlmon's favorites and miss Marianne Moore[103] (she is acknowledged one of our best poets)—would that be too much to ask of you, dear friend?

I am not asking this lightly, but as something I feel is important in a literary sense, not only for Sylvia Beach, but for the prestige of our Embassy and yourself. I know you feel as I do on the subject of writing and writers, and that no considerations other than the literary values are to come into it.

With again all my thanks

and my very affectionate greetings
Sylvia

Miscellaneous Manuscripts Collection, Amherst College Archives
and Special Collections, Amherst College Library (manuscript)

* * *

238. To Morrill Cody   April 17, 1959

Mr. Morrill Cody,
Cultural Counselor, American Embassy,
Paris.

Dear Bill:

Thankyou very much for your kind letter of the 8th, and copy of the letter from the French Foreign Office concerning the possible undertak-

---

101. Thornton Wilder (1897–1975), American playwright. He first met Beach in 1921, when he was twenty-four years old.
102. Archibald MacLeish (1892–1982), American poet and habitué of Shakespeare and Company.
103. Marianne Moore (1887–1972) and Beach had corresponded with each other since the late twenties, though they didn't meet in person until 1936.

ing of the transfer of the Exhibition of the Twenties to the French Centre in New York.

I needn't say how delighted, of course, I would be if the French plan could be carried out: I know too that you would be very happy to receive this appreciation of your efforts in behalf of Franco-American cultural relations.

As for my forthcoming book, "Shakespeare and Company", it would indeed be a fine thing for it if the Exhibition of The Twenties were to coincide with its publication in New York next October.

In case you wish to talk about this matter with me, please let me know what day and hour would be most convenient for you.

With my apologies for the delay in replying to your letter: (it is due to the success of our Exhibition which has involved me in so much publicity I have difficulty in keeping up with it) and with my thanks for your many kindnesses,

> Yours very gratefully,
> Sylvia
> SYLVIA BEACH

Miscellaneous Manuscripts Collection, Amherst College Archives and Special Collections, Amherst College Library (manuscript)

* * *

239. To Jackson Mathews   May 12, 1959

> 12, Rue de L'Odeon
> Paris Vie
> May 12th, 1959

Dear My Muscle Man:

and dear Marthiel

and the dear Dog who's been waiting so long for a French Bone!

I don't know how to face you all: don't expect any of you to speak to me again

Et ce sera bien fait.[104]

---

104. "And that will be a good thing."

You are my best friends and I am your worst. Its this exhibition they got me into: my job at Shakespeare and Company was restful compared to what's piled up on me now—well I hope it'll all work out somehow. And that you will understand why you didn't hear from me. This bustle of talks and interviews and appointments—I never used to make any of them— and receptions and chats and conducting guided tours around the exhibition and that terrible Dragon center! One day a tawk, another a causerie followed by a conference or a lecture or something—all this so strange, wasn't it? I didn't even have time to acknowledge the letter from the Buffalo chancellor inviting me to have an honorary degree there till the other day. They seem to be expecting us and are providing me with a gown etc (but nothing to wear under it as we all feared). Miss Leet, you know, of the American University Womens Club[105] here who has had a quantity of these hon. Degrees offered to lend me her outfit which she thought would be much too big for me but I could hold it around me and try not to fall over it when getting up on the platform or whatever you do. But now Buffalo wants my exact measurements and "I dare say" as Miss Weaver always says, the thing will fit. And you and Marthiel don't forget are coming to Buffalo on June 7th. Are you all right? not overworked? How is the book on Perse? Have you taken off time for the country?

I saw Agathe Valery,[106] first at the opening of the show, then at my causerie-party and she seemed to enjoy everything—and Gide's daughter Catherine and her mother Elizabeth Herbart[107] came too and she and Agathe were photographed in front of their papaase.

The French like this exhibition—I'm so glad—and thanks to our friend O'Brien[108] who mentioned it to the cultural people over there they have asked Cody[109] to let them take it to New York in October—But there is the problem of the expense—it cost our Embassy here such an amount they are cleaned up and haven't a penny left for further activities all the rest of this year. But what could be more interesting than our show after all? But I am very anxious to have it moved over there in the fall. It has been a good thing for Margaret Marshall's book[110]—its more hers than mine she's kneeded it up and smoothed it down—I spose publishers have to do that with young inexperienced writers – but I only recognize

105. Dorothy F. Leet (1895–1994), American cultural diplomat.
106. Paul Valéry's widow.
107. Catherine Gide (1923–), daughter of André Gide and Elisabeth van Rysselberghe. In 1931 Van Rysselberghe married the writer Pierre Herbart (1903–1974), thus explaining her appellation here.
108. Translator Justin O'Brien.
109. Morrill Cody (1901–1987), American diplomat, writer, and friend of Beach.
110. Beach's editor at Harcourt Brace.

a word here and there in it as mine. At least it will have the Harcourt stamp of perfect distinction. And Margaret tells me it will be out August 19th—before the Dogwood in New England.

Oscar says its understood about the Joyce collection: he doesn't know whether more funds can be found for the Shakespeareanny. I'm thinking it over, I wonder if I shouldn't dispose of them, perhaps the Eliots etc, to any pop-up customers—after all, Buffalo is more interested in Joyce than the rest and I think it would be nice to conclude that, and just be contented with our lot.

By the way, Carter has written again about this collection—so has the Princeton Library. I will have to break it to them soon, perhaps?

Saillet is down with lumnbago: he suffers horribly.

At my suggestion, that Rochefoucauld woman has sent you her little book on Fargus[111] which I like very much – and thought you might be interested in as you are one of the deux or trios personnes over there who knows about Fargue—and Larbaud[112] and the rue de l'Odeon come into it. So you see my exhibition is enabling me to get into the upper classes.

With much love to you and Marthiel, from their worst friend Sylvia.

> a dog I met here had a French
> but couldn't tell me where
> she got it.

Jackson Mathews Collection of Sylvia Beach, Manuscripts Division, Department of Rare Books and Special Collections, Princeton University Library (manuscript)

* * *

240. To Morrill Cody   May 23, 1959

Dear Bill:

Before leaving for America today, I want to thank you again for your kind invitation for June 4th and to say that I regret so much missing the opportunity of seeing you. I would like too to have been able to see

---

111. Léon-Paul Fargue (1876–1946), French poet. The critical book Beach is referring to, simply entitled *Léon-Paul Fargue*, was written by French literary critic Edmée de la Rochefoucauld (1895–1991) and published in 1959.

112. Valéry Larbaud (1881–1957), French writer and translator and friend of Beach.

Mr Weld before his departure to take up his new post. Please convey my regrets and good wishes to him.

And please let me thank you again for all the wonderful things you did for me and to make our Exhibition of the Twenties such an event.

gratefully and affectionately
yours
Sylvia

Miscellaneous Manuscripts Collection, Amherst College Archives and Special Collections, Amherst College Library (manuscript)

* * *

241. To Jackson Mathews   June 25, 1959

12, Rue de L'Odeon
Paris VIe
June 25 1959

My dear Muscle Man:

I hope you had a little rest in the country and are going away this weekend again. The more I see you working so hard the worse I feel about all this trouble you have taken for me.

Justin O'Brien writes that he has managed to flee at last and I'm glad he is safe among his vegetables. Though working on some Valéry for you too. He seems to have been appealed to by Cody but doesn't know a single millionaire he says to move the Twenties over to New York. When you happen to communicate with him please assure him that this exhibition in New York doesn't interest me at all—ca m'est complètement egal! In fact the prospect of another of those things quite frightens me. Do tell Oscar so, next time you might.

Your friend Mrs Tretiakoff is away, her concierge told me—she says "they" so that must be Mr Tretiakoff I saw last time I went there. The concierge seems nice and said to leave the little parcel—she would give it to her as soon as she comes back. She showed me some mail she was keeping for her. I have been enquiring about sending medicine through the post or by air mail and they say: don't! its apparently only hearing aid supplies that come through! They want to encourage hearing no doubt. I have not even got started on my catalogue what with this theft of my door keys—stolen right off a hook in the concierge's 'loge'—and business with the Embassy insurance—perhaps we'd better not mention it to Oscar but beside the breakage of Anna Livia Plurabelle record 1st Version (only existing copy) the fire or what they extinguished it with at the Expo stained the binding of my copy of 'Ulysses'—but the Embassy is trying to get the insurance money. Of course I will inform Oscar but not on an empty stomach—his naturally.

Camilla and I talked about the taxes and she quite likes the idea of the Morris Ernst office but thinks capital gains should bring us down to much less than Ader mentioned—(7,000 bucks) or $40, 000)—she thinks the plan of cutting off 10 000 as Buffalo's payment of my services keeping up the collection for them wonderful. I'm sure the taxes will get all they need and the Morris Ernsteses enough to live on, only you and I will not be able to clear anything—

> With best love
> to you dear Jack
> Sylvia

Jackson Mathews Collection of Sylvia Beach, Manuscripts Division, Department
of Rare Books and Special Collections, Princeton University Library (manuscript)

❇   ❇   ❇

242. To Jackson Mathews   **June 29, 1959**

Grand Central
June 20th, 59

My dear Muscle Man:

Our Mr Ader[113] called me up to say he had seen Morris Ernst[114] and told him about our business. He will call you up when you come back from the country. He wants to get us together in New York with

---

113. Richard Ader.
114. Morris Ernst (1888–1976), founder of the American Civil Liberties Union. He successfully defended *Ulysses* against obscenity charges in 1933.

Silverman—without me of course as I'm leaving, but you and Silverman and himself, to discuss ways & means. I told him Dr S was away on his vacation just now, so his secretary informed me—he thinks (Ader) the matter can soon be settled up, but Buffalo would have to arrange the part about the $10,000 to be deducted from the total price of the coll. they must make a statement that the sum of the odd $10000 is to be under the head of my services in the upkeep of the Joyce Coll. Then the remaining 40 000 would be taxed %25 and cost me 7–8 thousand taxes—he has given up the other plan of getting it set down to Joyce salary to me.

That's why he wants Buffalo to collaborate with us.

I asked if it might be better to keep it entirely my business—he says no: Buffalo must work on it. I couldn't find out what his legal services would cost—he said—as you said—it depends on what has to be done.

I hope this tiresome work for me won't take your time too too long and that you had a little rest in Maryland.

> Dear Jack
> much love to you
> and to Marthiel
> Sylvia

Jackson Mathews Collection of Sylvia Beach, Manuscripts Division, Department of Rare Books and Special Collections, Princeton University Library (manuscript)

* * *

243. To Jackson Mathews

July 2, 1959

> Sylvia Beach
> 12, Rue de L'Odeon
> Paris, VI
> July 2nd, 1959

My dear dear Muscleman:

You are so tired of hearing from me but this is just to let you know strictly in confidence as they asked me to keep it so, that the University of Texas has cabled and telephoned and written about wanting my whole collection of what they call "Memorabilia" including letters, photographers, manuscripts in fact the whole business and would pay my price "within reason". I told them the Joyce items were just about arranged for but the other stuff might perhaps be available. They would wait till I sent them an idea of what there would be, and I will try to give them an idea of the items in the Shakespeare and Company Library before I leave for the mountains. The doctor says I should get up and away there now as I am really tired, but don't you think if these people offer me a good price it might influence our part of plans concerning the extra things? I know you and Dr. Silverman must be waiting to hear what they amount to, but I haven't had a single minute since I got back to get out of these books and etceteras and make a list of them, not to speak of valuing them. Once at Les Deserts[115] everything but the cows will have to be dropped: correspondence is quite delayed, specially cables, wires, special deliveries and other urgent matters: the postoffice you know is a long way off down a steep mountain and there's no telephone in the Chalet de Sylvia. Only Les Vaches. Now Dr. Silverman spoke of coming over in September: would that be better: give us time to work out the tax problem and have our vacation, make all the lists: and by the way, dear Jack, if I may ask you to be so kind has Mr. Ader had the one I gave him copied? If I could have it back—have lost the only copy I had left with vacation.

But instead of giving you the trouble of calling Ader, why don't I write to him and ask for the list? Will do so.

There has come up an additional bother: these performances of "Ulysses in Nighttown" they are to give at the Theatre des Nations on the 7th of July.[116] I am going away before then [that is I thought so, but am now staying here till end of July while having a tooth treated—will let Dr Stafford know I'll be here instead of in Savoie all through July][117] but have had visits and telephoning and photoresearch concerning the play, and the publicity is what they are counting on me to help them with: I don't like to refuse these friends I met at the Gotham Book Mart, and Zero Mostel[118] is a splendid Mr Bloom and all that, but the man who has wormed his way into the affair is someone to avoid: I'll tell you why when I see you: and when are you coming? Don't think you are going to escape from me: I'm a clingstone-beach.

---

115. Les Déserts, a small group of hamlets in Normandy where Beach and Monnier vacationed.

116. *Ulysses in Nighttown*, a stage adaptation of the fifteenth chapter of Joyce's novel, was originally produced for the Peacock Stage at Dublin's Abbey Theatre in 1958. The Théâtre des Nations production took place shortly afterwards.

117. The text in square brackets was added later.

118. Zero Mostel (1915–1977), American actor and comedian. He starred as Bloom in the New York production of *Ulysses in Nighttown*.

With ever my gratitude
and much love
Sylvia

If you happen to talk with Buffalo you could mention that I have had offers for the OTHER ITEMS. Might be a load off the minds of our friends.
But until I know whether they (the offerers) want the Joyceless part of
the collection all the same, its vague. Indeed it is.

---

* * *

244. To Ezra Pound   July 13, 1959

Dear Ezra:

Thank you for your picture—looking fine! The Pound exhibits delighted your fans at the Exhibition—Bill Bird contributed items—had a
lot myself.

Hope your work is progressing—

Yours affectionately
Sylvia

---

* * *

245. To H.D.   January 4, 1959

Villa Kenwin
Chemin du Vallon
Burier-la-Tour
Vaud

January 4th 1959

My dear dear H.D.:

Thank you for taking the trouble to write me such a lovely letter—a
delight that greeted me on my arrival here—but it only made me miss

the writer of it all the more. Oh if H.D. were here! I complained of this to "The Management" but what could they (Bryher) do!

Otherwise they are showing me such a good time: weather dried up and sunrise over the Lake and mountains, moon too overhead. It's a real holiday, this is!

And Bryher has done me the honor to let me read her book, at least the first part of it about her childhood, and travels as a child, and school days.[119] I am carried away by this book that's going to make a huge mark: it's going to be like Bryher, and as fine and original and deep as this Bryher people are now to meet. I am very interested in all she tells me and her way of seeing and doing whatever hoes on in her life and world. Now for the continuation as soon as she has done this important job of hers! It is hard to wait. It will be the one autobiography of our time.

I hope you're having some outings in the sun: Bryher says you get around quite "briskly" as Adrienne used to say. What a relief to have Christmas behind us and all over safe and sound, isn't it? Two flutes etc . . . ! Holy Night Peaceful Night!

Kenwin is really quiet in spite of the warning about dogs that's so frightening on the gate. Only this tortoiseshell tabby cat of Elsie's and she hardly meows at all.

> With many, very affectionate wishes to H.D.
> for a complete recovery in 1960
> and love from Sylvia

H.D. Papers, Yale University, Beinecke Rare Books
and Manuscript Library (manuscript)

---

119. *The Heart to Artemis: A Writer's Memoir*, first published by Harcourt, Brace and World in 1962.

VII

LEGACIES

246. To Morrill Cody   **January 1, 1960**

Dear Bill:

Before leaving Paris for a week, I want to thank you for sending me your article on <u>Shakespeare and Company</u> in the <u>Foreign Service Journal</u>.[1] I was very pleased with it, had already been sent a copy by someone and liked it so much. I am very grateful for your encouragement and many efforts to help the spread of my book. I hear from people everywhere that they received it from you and were delighted. It was awfully kind of you to think of getting it into the hands of friends who might not have been able to get hold of it at all over here but are really interested in Shakespearean history—and by the way, Katherine Dudley says she knew you as a little boy—near Chicago—

There is an article in the Times Book Review of December 14[2] and there have been some recent things which I will show you and also Alice B. Toklas' as soon as I return to Paris. I am among those the New Yorker wishes a Happy New Year to on Dec 26 in a poem.[3]

---

1. Morrill Cody, review of *Shakespeare and Company* in *Foreign Service Journal* 36.12 (December 1959): 38.

2. Possibly referring to a review of *Shakespeare and Company* by Charles Poore in the *New York Times*, September 17, 1959, 37.

3. Frank Sullivan, "Greetings, Friends!," *The New Yorker* (December 26, 1959), 22. This comic poem contains the lines: "Merry Christmas to Margaret Leech, / Diana Wynyard, Sylvia Beach." Other cultural figures addressed by Sullivan include Khrushchev, Lionel Trilling, Brigitte Bardot, Eleanor Roosevelt, Truman Capote, Stephen Spender, and Jack Paar.

With very affectionate New Year's wishes,

Sylvia

Miscellaneous Manuscripts Collection, Amherst College Archives
and Special Collections, Amherst College Library (manuscript)

* * *

247. To Elsie Volkart   January 15, 1960

12, rue de l'Odéon
Paris. VI
January 15th 1960

Dear Elsie: This is exactly the way it looks at present in Paris:[4] very snowy and so cold! I hope you are able to keep warm at Kenwin and haven't had too much neuralgia in your head. I do hope you will soon be better . . .

I enjoyed my visit and thank you for all the trouble you took to give me such nice meals and so comfortable a room. I felt quite rested and braced up after that pleasant week in your Swiss surroundings, and wonderful hills.

There is a great deal of snow underfoot in Paris. I went in a snowfall to dinner at

the house of André Gide's daughter Catherine who lives in the Boulevard St Germain near the rue du Bac. She is now married to a doctor and has four children: two of them were away for a month at the Ecole de Ski where all the French children are sent in the winter.

Rinette wanted to hear all about my visit to Kenwin. She is very busy nursing her husband. The doctor thinks he will not get well.

I will soon return the book Bryher lent me—Have you read Three Guineas now?

With much love from
Sylvia

Bryher Papers, Yale University Library, Beinecke Rare Book
and Manuscript Library (manuscript)

4. Volkart was Bryher's housekeeper. Beach wrote on a postcard depicting A. Marquet's *Paris: Pont Neuf sous la neige* (1938).

* * *

248. To Jackson Mathews   February 9, 1960

12, Rue de l'Odéon
Paris, VIe
February 9th 1960

Dear Jack:

I have been enjoying the Singletons and was very sad to see them go.

Thank you so much for the two copies of 'Kenyon Review' you sent me: I think our conversation in it is very good, don't you? Quite "informative" as the journalists would say. Marthiel's remark about not deserting "an old friend just because he's the devil" is one of the best things in it—wish we have got more from her. But the whole talk was fun. I wonder if this man Laurence D. Stewart of something, do you know him (or it), called Verve Records Inc, Beverly Hills, California, wasn't influenced by the "Conversation" when writing to ask me to let him record a reading from S & Co for his series called "The Recoided Word". Don't know what they would pay me, but if Harcourt knew they would scoop up all the proceeds—or nearly all. I gave Michaux one of the copies of the Kenyon Review, though what I said about him might make him sore: very likely it did, as not a sound has come from the rue Séguier ever since. He had brought me a copy, printed from the 'Lettres Nouvelles', of his Psilocybin.[5] Singleton will show you the review: this latest experience would have 'depersonalized' anybody but Michaux.

I think we misjudged Princeton: there is now a movement on foot to entwine Gide with Joyce—see le 'Mercure' de févriér.

I hope you are not working too hard on Valéry but taking time off for your on works. I hear you are now a vice president of the Bollingen Foundation— Singleton told me and I congratulate the Bollingen Foundation for their good luck.

I spent a week in Switzerland visiting Bryher: she showed me a part of her memoirs now in progress, which I thought very interesting and its publication something to await in a year or two, she says, it will be ready. Very exciting!

Marie Monnier was charmed with Eula and Charles. They will tell you the news about her husband's death. Her sister's books have just appeared Saillet is – sending you Rue de l'Odéon I believe.

---

5. A psychedelic drug.

With much love to you dear Jack and Marthiel and many many thanks for Kenyon Review!

From Sylvia

Jackson Mathews Collection of Sylvia Beach, Manuscripts Division, Department of Rare Books and Special Collections, Princeton University Library (manuscript)

* * *

249. To Jackson Mathews   March 25, 1960

12, Rue de l'Odéon
Paris
March 25th, 1960

My dear dear Jack:

I'm afraid if I settled down in Maryland you wouldn't write to me any more, and I couldn't do without your letters: no!

Thank you for the one of Feb. 28 with so many interesting things in it. And thank you for this beautiful <u>Paul Valéry Degad-Manet-Marisot</u> your Bollingen office sent me, and which I got on the 21st of this month. Rinette also showed me her copy the other day and told me she has read the essay on her embroideries and thought the translation very good: you know she has taken up English with her usual vigor and after an interruption these last months she has gone back to it now and in the valise she took to Les Déserts yesterday was her persoot of "Mr. Smith" in his daily doings in London. I think he is a rather dull character but Rinette seems to like him. So she is going to have him come along with her to Savoie. She expects to stay at Les Déserts, at Zoé's, for about three weeks and it is just what she needs now.

How hard you must have worked on your Valéry! The result is perfection: the translation by David Paul of these essays is so good, Valéry himself is present in it as you read along unaware that it's a translation: what an effort it must have cost Mr. David Paul and of course the Editor. This is indeed a very great achievement, dear Jack. I hope it hasn't tired you too dreadfully. Are you taking off a while for a rest and holiday before the next volume? I hope so. When is Marthiel's book to come out? What are your plans from now on? Your tripticktticket to here and on to Greece you know is deposited in your names and awaiting your mot d'ordre. Holly backed out of her visit: you and Marthiel wouldn't do that to me!

I met François[6] at the vernissage of a photograph of New York show at the Dragon (American cultural) yesterday. He spoke with admiration of the volume 12 of his father's works he had just received: we agreed on the wonders of your labors. We are planning to meet soon again.

Except for Shakes & Co coming out, or supposed to be coming out, at Faber and Faber on the 27th May, progress of this book and my business with Harcourt Margaret & Co is sluggish. The Figaro Littéraire was the only pleasure I've got out of my French world so far: they seem to feel that Adrienne's books cover sufficiently the rue de l'Odéon history. The volume "Rue de l'Odéon" and her very sad "Agendas" have attracted a great deal of attention and I only regret that Adrienne herself isn't here to enjoy her success. Her sister is quite happy over it.

As for Harcourt, as Pogo says: "Who owes who? Who owes what? Always a argumint." But the Mathews-Buffalos that recently yielded the balance has been so satisfactory, and my Mathews pardner's part of it so very very kind, I can't express anything like the gratitude I feel towards him. I hope the Singletons will pardon me for delaying so the reply to their letter. I have been waiting to see about any decisions for my future whereabouts till those for the present can be made. But I am writing to Eula now: her proposal delighted me and only one or two things might stand in the way of going right ahead with this happy ending by the lake among the Singletons and Mathewses.

I gave a copy of The Kenyon Review to Michaux who has been speechless from that day: pleased or angry I don't know which: he is busy with his paintings—very successful as a painter, I hear.

> With ever gratefully and loving thoughtses
> Sylvia

Jackson Mathews Collection of Sylvia Beach, Manuscripts Division, Department of Rare Books and Special Collections, Princeton University Library (manuscript)

❋   ❋   ❋

250. To Maria Jolas   April 6, 1960

Dear Maria:

I know you said you were going away for a while: perhaps you could let me know when you come back and I could see you about OUR

---

6. Valéry's son.

EXAGMINATION. I have discussed the German edition with Stuart Gilbert[7]: he said I should insist on demanding that the Authors be paid what they proposed to pay the Authors. My two letters have remained unanswered: now I have received a letter from a Mr. Eugene Power, who is president of University Microfilms, Ann Arbor, Michigan,[8] asking for permission to make a microfilm of OUR EXAGMINATION. He applied first to New Directions, who published this book in the United States, but like the Faber & Faber edition, I never had anything to do with it. New Directions informed Mr. Power that he must ask me for permission to microfilm the book. I see in his prospectus that he reproduces an out-of-print work, and supplies copies on demand: but there is no mention whatsoever of anything paid to the authors for issuing their work. I wonder if the request of Mr. Power might be connected with the proposal of the German publisher: it may be only my imagination: but having received no reply to my letters, has he perhaps heard of this much cheaper way to obtain Our Exagmination, though his idea was of course to bring out a German translation.

When you return to Paris I must show you the letter and prospectus from University Microfilms, Inc., and see what you think of it. This is of course a book that should be in University libraries but the Universities are always printing works of criticism and why don't they re-print Our Exagmination and pay the authors for their essays? I don't see why they should give them away, do you? I'm sure, if he had been able to discover a copy of the book he would have gone right ahead and supplied it as a microfilm. He says: "a copy will be produced as each request is received."

I will take up this question with Stuart Gilbert, and also with Samuel Beckett and Robert Sage,[9] and also with those in England.

Mr. Power asks me to send him a copy to reproduce by microfilm: he will return it to me carefully. I would be very glad if it were reprinted by some publishing house, but unfortunately, neither Faber & Faber nor New Directions seem to have any idea of re-issuing it. Meanwhile,

---

7. Stuart Gilbert (1883–1969), close friend of James Joyce and contributor to Our Exagmination.

8. Eugene Barnum Power (1905–1993), founder of University Microfilms (now ProQuest LLC).

9. Samuel Beckett (1906–1989) and Robert Sage (1899–1962) were two of the other contributors to Our Exagmination.

Joyce students are very anxious to get hold of it. But we must talk it over together.

Yours very affectionately
Sylvia

Eugène and Maria Jolas Papers, Yale University, Beinecke Rare Book and Manuscript Library (manuscript)

* * *

251. To H.D.   **April 7, 1960**

Am bothering you with a request to inscribe my *Bid Me to Live*[10]— returning it to you and please forgive expense sending it back

My dear H.D.

I have just received <u>Bid Me to Live</u>: it far surpasses anything the blurb on the jacket says in its perfection and beauty—it is so lovely, dear H.D.! so living it breathes: its moving . . . but I can't express what it is—not being a writer only a reader, an amazed, a 'shook-up' reader of a poet's book—a genius's. Yes, dear dear H.D. you've done it! I opened the parcel, saw <u>Bid Me to Live</u> by H.D, sat down and immediately read the hundred and eighty-four pages of this unique story you have told me—or rather sung to me—but what can I say to give you any idea of my delight?!

thank you for "H.D. 1917"! Why oh why didn't the publishers use this interesting photograph? It should have been the frontispiece of the book but I know nothing about the mysteries of book making—

It is a very good idea to fly over there in May—you can't let them down. You know, your friends & reader-friends—they won't forgive you if you don't take advantage of these jets that carry babies and poets back & forth. And you'll stop off in Paris, of course, or Sylvia wouldn't like it.

With love and admiration for <u>Bid Me to Live</u> and the
author H D.
And again thank you
Sylvia

---

10. H.D.'s novel, *Bid Me to Live: A Madrigal*, was published by Dial Press in 1960.

P.S. No, I didn't go back to the Beekman Tower so well situated on dear East River and for you so conveniently near Perdita-Timothy.[11] $10.50 they wanted for a night. I got a room at the little Collingwood Hotel for $4.50 34th Street near 5th Ave. But I stay at my sister's in Greenwich, Connecticut.

I expect to be in Paris through May—am going to London on April 21 my publishers have invited me to a cocktail party

---

H.D. Papers, Yale University, Beinecke Rare Books and Manuscript Library (manuscript)

* * *

252. **To Maria Jolas** **April 10, 1960**

Dear Maria:

I have to own up to a stupid mistake I made about Mr. Eugene Power of Ann Arbor, Michigan, who has written to ask permission to make a microfilm of "Our Exagmination": he is offering a royalty of 10% as I discovered on a contract slipped in with the other papers he sent me. I should have looked at his papers more carefully: have been so busy I could hardly even open any letters. So dear Maria, please forgive me and tear up my first letter. I have told Stuart Gilbert all about the "Our Exagmination" business, including my injustice toward Mr. Power who seems a very good man. But of course I will wait to take any steps until I have seen you and the other Authors. I took all the papers, those of the German publisher and the University Microfilm Inc. to Stuart Gilbert and as soon as you come back to Paris we must examine the whole question together.

> Love from
> Sylvia

Eugène and Maria Jolas Papers, Yale University, Beinecke Rare Book and Manuscript Library (manuscript)

* * *

---

11. Perdita's son Timothy was born in 1960.

253. To Marthiel Mathews   April 16, 1960

12, Rue de l'Odéon
Paris
April 16th 1960

My dear Marthiel:

Thank you for your letter o the 12th – it must have crossed mine to Jack: it doesn't make any difference whether you decide to 'do' Greece this year or next: what I enclosed was earmarked and there's no use returning it: 'adresse inconnue' it would just be whacked back to you. We will all go to Greece whenever you feel like Greece and it will be fun for me to do Greece with the Mathewses, if they can stand me.

I will send you the Martin Du Gard soon—have it here, it so happens.

Good news about your novel! You will have no trouble finding a publisher—I am eager to read it ever since you let me see a mysterious pile of typewritten sheets in your room—I do think you might have let me read a piece of it! Dear Marthiel, I bet it's most exciting! Don't allow anything to interrupt your winding up of it this summer.

I am going to London next Tuesday the 19th (isn't it?) am coming back the following Sunday after we have met, Messrs Faber & Faber, & Messrs Shakespeare and Company. Already we are friends by post and they have a very pleasant way of keeping me informed, step by step. The date of publication has been delayed till early June, but I don't think Margaret's marriage is to blame for that.

The usual Easter invasion of the British in Paris while the Parisians are all out getting killed or maimed on the roads.

I must run over soon to have a look at our Maryland heaven. The thought of it makes me long to be there NOW.

How disgraceful, that review in the Sunday NY Times of the Valéry Degas volume! Makes me furious—I've been reading the Sunday Times (English) reviews by Cyril Connolly if our scholars' works—he lays them out—he's tough and so funny. But he would certainly admire Jack's Valéry—but I forgot he doesn't know the French writers.

I shall be thinking of Pomme's motherhood on the 20th hope it will be easy for dear Pomme.

Very much love to my Marthiel and Jack
Sylvia

I met François V. at the Dragon (American gallery) and he seemed more interested in meeting Alice B. Toklas than anything—I promised to take him though when you think of Gertrude's "the French have no Alps" you'd be surprised his wanting to see Alice. Not that she isn't quite interesting and remarkable herself.

Please give my love to Eula and Charles.

Very curious press cutting you sent me: its not Klein but Kain: and did Oscar relinquish A Portrait 1st Draft? He was supposed to hold onto it— edit it himself. He never let on to me about the outcome of the struggle.

Jackson Mathews Collection of Sylvia Beach, Manuscripts Division, Department of Rare Books and Special Collections, Princeton University Library (manuscript)

* * *

254. To Jackson Mathews   May 1, 1960

12, Rue de l'Odéon

Paris

"May Day 1960"

Dear Jack:

Thank you for your lovely cable and letter and photo dear little Pomme now a Mummy of EIGHT! My! You didn't say whether Sex M or Sex F like in passports. Was there a sprinkling of various sexes? They must be beauties if they look like Mrs. Pomme.

How absurd of you to make all that fuss over the paltry amount you mistook for something to do with your services! It would have to be a great deal more, and even so, could never be estimated as they are priceless. No, this as only what we agreed would be my share of the Odyssey the three of us were to undertake some time. As you can't make it this year: you have stuffed cottonwool in your ears: I don't have to: when the Sirens sing out, then just let us say that it's for Pomme to do anything she likes with. An Academy Award for what she done. And that settles that.

I have been back from London since last Sunday: stayed at our Whitehall Hotel, my favorite hotel now. I like everything about it, the beds are so comfortable, the meals very nice, the personnel nearly always having tea or lunch or supper when you need them, the dowagers in the lift and the groups of men and all. I attended the Faber cocktail party in the old-fashioned house they occupy in Russell Square: everybody in the firm was charming and particularly Miss Faber who is the head of the business I think. Mr. Monteith invited me to lunch with her and young Ms. Bodley at the White Tower restaurant: as usual a "Gugusse" as Adrienne

called me, I went to the wrong Greek restaurant and kept them all waiting for quarter of an hour at the right one before my mistake as revealed
to me by the proprietor of the Acropolis where I was sitting. Mr. Monteith, Miss Faber and Mr. Bodley were very nice and forgiving and we have
a good time together.

---

*Jackson Mathews Collection of Sylvia Beach, Manuscripts Division, Department
of Rare Books and Special Collections, Princeton University Library (manuscript)*

* * *

255. To Jackson and Marthiel Mathews   June 18, 1960

White Hall Hotel
Montague Street
London, W.C.1.
June 18 1960

Dear dear dear Marthiel and Jack

Thank you both for your very dear letters and photos of the little
Pommes—I wish they could hop on a plane and come over to my show
but they are too young. It is opening day after tomorrow, and everything including The Shakespeare and Company Store—a real godin—is
in place. Oscar has kindly set over some items from his collection of
Joyce "materials" and Miss Harriet Weaver is lending some of hers that
are in the library of the Nat. Book League. She herself is attending—she
invited me to supper day before yesterday but we neither of us mentioned our mutual Jo. I dunno who all is coming to the show: the only
visitor we can be sure of so far is Miss Weaver. Bryher is on a fishing
boat in the roughest seas she could find. Mr. T.S.E. is not coming he
informed our cultural representatives here: Edith Sitwell sends love,
accepts kind invitation but Bryher says she has leg trouble and can't
walk: and I hope to be there. And by the way: I didn't like your returning my token. Catherine Gide and her husband are arriving tonight—to
see the London parks and [illegible word] Exhibition. I booked a room
for them here.

Much love from your loving Sylvia

---

*Jackson Mathews Collection of Sylvia Beach, Manuscripts Division, Department of Rare
Books and Special Collections, Princeton University Library (manuscript)*

* * *

256. **To Jackson and Marthiel Mathews**   July 13, 1960

Sandy Cove
Dublin, Ireland
July 13 1960

Dear Marthiel & Jack: am just back from them Aran Islands—umm! On my way back via Dublin, London to Paris supposed to be home by Saturday. They had this story spread around Dublin that I was tight and fell downstairs in the Martello Tower—if you hear it deny it!

I hope you are enjoying the lovely landscape you are in and mine some day. Dublin is thick with Joyceans who know even more than Ellman about JJ. I spoke on Radio Eireann and was written up as a purveyor of obscenity.

My love to my dear Marthiel and Jack and Pomme and her children.

Jackson Mathews Collection of Sylvia Beach, Manuscripts Division, Department of Rare Books and Special Collections, Princeton University Library (manuscript)

* * *

257. **To H.D.**   **No date, circa 1960**

To my dear H.D.
Joyeux Noël
Heureuse Année

and a terrible scolding for sending me that huge cheque in such a lovely Christmas letter! There must be some mistake, I thought, on finding this too large gift enclosed with Winslow Homer's "Winter Scene", but I know what I'm going to spend it on "right now" as they say in our country, but at the beginning, not the end of nearly every sentence. You may consider the Livre d'Heures of the Duc Louis de Savoie, reproduced from the MS in the Bibliothèque Nationale by an Annecy bookseller-publisher, your Christmas present to me. You have chosen exactly what I was longing to possess. And how can I ever thank you thank you for so much, dear H.D.? You can imagine how I'm engrossed in all the pages of wonderful pictures in this great book.

You know they are celebrating the hundredth anniversary of the join-ing-up of Savoie to France, and all sorts of commemorations are to be around Chambéry etc, and a tall tree from their pine forests was sent to Paris by the savoyards and stands all lighted up, in the place de l'Hotel de Ville with its feet wrapped all around with the Savoy flag. Think how proud I feel of my savoy nationality!

You will be with Bryher through Christmas and New Year's Day. I shall be seeing her soon myself and am looking forward to it with joy. Meanwhile, to you both my most loving wishes for this New Year and very much love.

Sylvia

H.D. Papers, Yale University, Beinecke Rare Books and Manuscript Library (manuscript)

* * *

258. To Maria Jolas   July 14, 1961

Dear Maria,

Thank you for your kind letter of the 13th: indeed I was delighted to have some of the Authors of "O.E"[12] present at the rue de l'Odéon the other day. I didn't hear your generous plan of dividing any profits the book may bring in between Lucia and myself. Of course I will not accept it: you may make a present to Lucia of your royalties if that is what you wish, but I think you should claim them, no matter how tiny, once divided among so many of you, the share of each may be. And I have made it plain, in writing to Faber and Faber, that there is no question of claims on my part, only the rights of the authors are to be respected.

Also I mentioned Joyce's wish to see "Our Exagmination" in the cata-logue of the publishers of "Finnegans Wake".[13]

I enclose a copy of the reply from Faber and Faber.

I will write, as Mr. du Sautoy[14] suggests, to James Laughlin and ask him what the situation of the book is at New Directions.

---

12. *Our Exagmination.*

13. *Finnegans Wake* was published by Faber and Faber in the United Kingdom and by Viking in the United States.

14. Peter du Sautoy (1912–1995), chairman of Faber and Faber and trustee of the Joyce estate.

I will take up the mention of the articles as having been published first in "Transition" as soon as we arrive at that stage in our negotiations.

> With love to you, dear Maria,
> From
> Sylvia

Eugène and Maria Jolas Papers, Yale University, Beinecke Rare Book and Manuscript Library (manuscript)

* * *

259. **To Maria Jolas**   July 17, 1961

Dear Maria,

Thank you for letting me know about the Joyce program on the radio. I would have liked so much to hear it but was away in Touraine at the time and didn't get your card till afterwards. If they only had a paper like the English "Listener"[15] in French you could read the whole emission printed in it. I'm sure the Joyce was very interesting.

I hope you are feeling all right again and are enjoying the country: and not having the atrocious weather rainy and windy we are 'stuck with' up here in the mountains.

I am going back to Paris at the end of July to meet the friends who turn up in the middle of the summer. Have managed to write my little forward for Our Exag and sent it in hope it will do.

> With love to you dear Maria
> Sylvia

Eugène and Maria Jolas Papers, Yale University, Beinecke Rare Book and Manuscript Library (manuscript)

* * *

---

15. *The Listener* was a weekly BBC periodical that reproduced the content of radio broadcasts.

260. To Marthiel Mathews   February 2, 1962

12, Rue de L'Odeon
Paris VIe
February 2nd 1962

My dear Marthiel,

Thank you for your letter of Jan. 28th, and several others, also for Jack's darling invitation to occupy your future house somewhere together. I think you are such wonderful friends, and many hugses and thanks[16] enclosed herewith. I owe you several letters but its because of all this apartment business that's been going on for the last two or three months, which I hope is now about terminated: this is the final round: I hope that instead of moving out on the pavement I shall be up here for at least a while, still a European as that seems to be where I belong, visiting my friends over there but not staying with them—never inflicting that on them even on my very best such as yourselves. So please don't go in for a big house and in debt for a European friend like me—and look me up in Greece!

You did mention getting the knives – forks Holly calls them—several times—it happened to be a moment of dreadful trouble for the poor man who made them, as Mr Tucker told you, I think—he had an operation at the Quinze-Vingt eye hospital, one eye removed, and was retiring, rather suddenly I imagine, from his business immediately after Christmas. I went twice to see him about your order, as on account of my deafness, he hadn't been able to get me on the telephone, his bill had to be attended to before he closed his shop, and the knives collected before they too disappeared behind closed shutters. But as I assured Mr Tucker, there was no hurry—he needn't refund the new francs before he left—but he insisted on doing so.

I am using your Baby Magic—have plenty ahead am saving those lovely slippers for my wedding trip—Biggest Love

Sylvia

---

* * *

---

16. Beach drew a heart on the paper.

261. To Maria Jolas   March 13, 1962

Dear Maria:

I hope you are well—you looked flourishing the other day when I saw you! This is about this pote Lloyd Frankenberg who would like to show you his opera on <u>Finnegans Wake</u>[17]—may I give him your telephone No. rue Malebranche? I didn't like to till you gave your consent

He is lecturing here and in outlying districts—Fulbright lecturer etc he says he tried to see you but you were ill at the time.

With love from Sylvia

Eugène and Maria Jolas Papers, Yale University, Beinecke Rare Book
and Manuscript Library (manuscript)

* * *

262. To Morrill Cody   June 6, 1962

Mr. Morrill Cody
Director United States International Services
Washington D.C.

Dear Bill:

You were so kind to say that your Offices would give their support to my SHAKESPEARE AND COMPANY whenever it appeared in the French translation. That moment has now come: the book is appearing before the middle of this month at the MERCURE DE FRANCE, 26, rue de Condé, Paris-VI.[18] Any encouragement you can give my publishers and French readers would be ever so much appreciated by us.

The book has come out in Germany, at Paul List Verlag in Munich,[19] and in Italy at Rizzoli Editore, Milan[20] and everybody seems very pleased over it.

---

17. Lloyd Frankenberg (1907–1975), American writer and editor.
18. The Mercure de France imprint, associated with the Symbolist movement of the 1890s, was bought in 1958 by Éditions Gallimard. They issued the French translation of *Shakespeare and Company* in 1962.
19. *Shakespeare and Company: Ein Buchladen in Paris* was published in 1961.
20. The Italian translation of *Shakespeare and Company* was published in 1962.

I am off to Dublin next week to attend the ceremonies at JAMES JOYCE'S TOWER on the 16th of June: Bloomsday.[21] They have invited me to open them. I only wish you were going to be beside me as at our Exhibition of the Writers in the Twenties in Paris.

I miss you very much and don't like Paris without you at all; I hope Jane[22] is well and that you will both come back soon.

With ever my best love to you and to Jane

from

Sylvia

Miscellaneous Manuscripts Collection, Amherst College Archives and Special Collections,

Amherst College Library (typescript)

✳ ✳ ✳

263. To Morrill Cody　　　　　　　　　　**No date, circa 1962**

La Féclaz

Les Déserts

Savoie

Dear Bill:

Thank you for your letters of June 14th and 29th and for so kindly calling attention to the French edition of "Shakespeare and Company" at the Embassies over here and the German and Italian editions too. At the Mercure they told me someone from the Paris Embassy had called. I appreciate so much your help in the past and present.

I regretted being away in Dublin when the Mercure suddenly brought out the book and they had to put slips in it saying 'auteur de Paris' but it couldn't be helped.—and now its the holidays so I came up here—will be back at the end of August—and how happy I will be to see you and Jane in September!

Please don't let all your other friends monopolize you!

Love and ever gratefully

Sylvia

Miscellaneous Manuscripts Collection, Amherst College Archives and Special Collections,

Amherst College Library (manuscript)

21. On June 16, 1962, Beach was present for the formal dedication of the Martello Tower at Sandycove as a center for Joyce studies. This was her last public appearance.
22. Cody's wife, Jane.

* * *

264. **To Morrill Cody** July 18, 1962

Dear Bill,

Thank you for your letter of the 9th, enclosing the clipping from the 'Washington Post':[23] the article, which appeared first in the "Guardian" got people quite excited over my apartment troubles: I think they saw me dumped in the street on top of a pile of books. When you come to Paris I will tell you the whole story—meanwhile, the situation is briefly: a year ago the house at No 12 was bought by a man who was determined to sell all the apartments in it: I was unable to pay the price he demanded for mine: he threatened to put me out: could have done so, the lawyers I consulted thought, as it was insufficnt occupation—4 rooms for 1 person and much cubic space. Finally, after discussing it back and forth, we came to an agreement which was expensive for me, but allowed me to stay in the apartment, and if, in two years I want to buy it, a rather large sum that I put down will be deducted from the price: otherwise that sum will be a total loss. I can only recouperate it by purchasing the apartment, which, if I wish to sell, is, with present value of the rue de l'Odéon, a good investment, they say. Meanwhile, I continue to pay rent, and whether I purchase or not, may remain in the place till the day I am ready to move out of it. So, you see, there's no immediate need to make a decision. But when you come over, we will go into it further.

I would indeed love to think of you and Jane at No 12 when I depart from it! Are you coming back to live in Paris eventually? Looking forward to the joy of seeing you.

Ever affectionately yours

Sylvia

Miscellaneous Manuscripts Collection, Amherst College Archives and Special Collections,
Amherst College Library (manuscript)

* * *

---

23. Peter Lennon, "Farewell to Shakespeare and Company," *Washington Post, Times Herald,* July 6, 1962, D2.

265. To Jackson Mathews   September 3, 1962

> La Féclaz
> Les Déserts
> Savoie
>
> September 3rd, -62

Jack Darling,

Thank you for your letter of August 25th that was so interesting and delightful, and a real event for me up here with my chopped-off wrist and waiting for it to stick on again.[24] I heard through Holly about your lunch at the Zoo and that you had found a house in Bucks County of which I once knew the "Boss" in Bristol Pa. I will certainly accept as soon as possible your invitation to ring the Greek goat I mean donkey bell at your gate. Am dying to see the house and my Mathewses.

Most exciting is your program on WBAI for the Valery series,[25] but very trying for me to hear about it and never never to listen in to it myself! The one most beautiful broadcast ever to be heard! You might have mentioned the date of each one, but I have asked Holly to look it up in her papers. They must certainly be preserved on tape recordings that you will let me hear some day, and the whole series of course preserved in typescripts and a copy for me, naturally. Dear dear Jack I am so excited over your Valérys, and shall be looking forward to vol 10 in the fall! No wonder you have been too busy all summer to take a holiday! Marthiel will simply have to carry you off to some country and take Yves Bonnefoy[26] with us, the first minute you can stop to draw breath. I see he is expected over there in January: he didn't mention it in a letter I had from him about his translation of "Hamlet"[27] which he was going to bring me. Perhaps I would have had a visit from him by this time if I hadn't been pinned down in the Alps by this breakage. They are hoping to take off the plaster cast this week so that nothing will prevent my breaking it again. Then as soon as travelling is no problem I will return to the rue de l'Odeon and my concierge's 'famille nombreuse'.

---

24. Beach had broken her arm while chopping wood.
25. WBAI, New York noncommercial radio station, then owned by Russian-born philanthropist Louis Schweitzer.
26. Yves Bonnefoy (1923–), French poet and translator of Shakespeare.
27. Bonnefoy's translation of *Hamlet* was first published in 1952.

Saillet came to spend a day with us from his old homestead in Hte Savoie: he has sent you no doubt his "Riverdy" and Adrienne's "Poésies" that he has just brought out.[28] Michaux's "Vents et Poussiéres" appeared just before I left Paris: a Michaux de haute [classe]: he has outdone himself this time.[29]

Rinette was pleased with your messages and sends you and Marthiel her love.

With a great deal of love to you both

dear Jack & Marthiel

Sylvia

Jackson Mathews Collection of Sylvia Beach, Manuscripts Division, Department of Rare Books and Special Collections, Princeton University Library (manuscript)

---

28. In 1962 Saillet published an homage to French poet Pierre Reverdy (1889–1960) and a volume of Adrienne Monnier's poetry.

29. Michaux's *Vents et Poussières* was published by Flinker in 1962.

Appendix I

MORRILL CODY'S ARTICLE
ON SHAKESPEARE AND COMPANY

MORRILL CODY: "SHAKESPEARE AND COMPANY—PARIS: SUCCESSFULLY SELLING ENGLISH BOOKS ON A FRENCH SIDE STREET." *PUBLISHERS WEEKLY* 12 (APRIL 12, 1924): 1261–63

* * *

Tucked away in a little narrow street leading up to the Odéon in Paris, hangs a sign on which is painted the head of one Shakespeare, poet and dramatist. Behind the sign is a small American bookshop whose influence on the book-loving people of the Latin quarter and on the English and American writers of Paris, is yearly becoming greater.

"Shakespeare and Company" is the intriguing name that Miss Silvia Beach has given to her library, for she claims there is more real "Shakespeare" in Paris today than there has been in Stratford-on-Avon in a hundred years. Overlooking the bookshelves of her shop hangs a large engraving of Shakespeare looking down with kindly interest on the rich and the humble who pore over the volumes of what is termed "the best literature."

Miss Beach's bookshop is essentially a "character" store, the brown burlaped walls, the grotesque Chinese goldfish, the pair of brass scales (just as tho books were sold by the pound as they were in the olden days), and the feeling of old wood, homeliness, comfort, always clean without being shiny. But Silvia Beach is the principal character. Here is a rendezvous for the writers of today and tomorrow, each an inspiration to the other. There is an air of seriousness and witty intelligence about the shop that attracts those lovers of literature who consider books in the light of living characters rather than plots that turn out happily or unhappily.

The writers have brought their friends and admirers. Shakespeare has made them welcome; all can sit by the hour reading any book they fancy; they pick the books off the shelves just as they would pick them off the shelves of their own library. Miss Beach rarely urges anyone to buy a book that is unknown to him. Read it first, she suggests, then if you like it, buy it. If the author is in Paris, perhaps she will introduce you to him. Miss Beach is always sympathetic, kindly, witty, and has a thoro knowledge of the books she sells, can discuss them with the highly read and with the slightly read.

The author who is best known in connection with this shop, is James Joyce, the author of *Ulysses*. Miss Beach arranged for the publication of this book after it was banned in America. The shop is full of associations of Joyce, many photographs, the stick which was his inseparable companion for years. Mr. Joyce with his strikingly good-looking face, has indeed attracted many people to the shop.

The Lending Library

Three of the four large bookcases in the shop contain books for the lending library, which is the main feature of Shakespeare and Company. Miss Beach points out with scorn that in a public library the borrower of a book cannot purchase the books he likes, but must return them on a set date and wait perhaps weeks, before taking them out again. Miss Beach has no system for lending—a system would spoil the intimacy of the library. When a new subscriber joins, a card is filled in with the person's name and address. This is kept on file, while another card is given to the subscriber showing the date of expiration of his subscription. When the subscriber takes out a book, the name and date are entered on the first card only. When he returns the book and takes out a new one, the new title and date are marked. On the inside of the front cover of each book is an ex libris with the name of the shop and a drawing of Shakespeare. There are no other formalities, no numbers, no cards for the subscriber to worry about, no references required. No more books are lost by this method than in the more complicated systems—less, if anything. The lack of formality appeals strongly to all American patrons.

The deposit required is less than a dollar, except on old and rare editions. The fee of fifty cents per month entitles the subscriber to one book at a time and as many different books as he desires. By subscribing for a year the fee is reduced to a little over four dollars. Miss Beach has about one hundred subscribers whose fees are enough to cover her expenses, and what profit she makes is on the sale of new books.

Patrons Largely from Humble Classes

The shop has all kinds of patrons, the youngest subscriber is four and a half years old, and she picks out such books as the Jungle Book to have her nurse read to her. Another subscriber is nine years old and comes in for a new book practically every day. Every time he comes Miss Beach thinks that she has exhausted the supply of books that will interest him, but he always finds a new one. The only requirement is that the book be "right to the point." Another subscriber is so old that he must be carried in on a wheel chair.

Miss Beach has not located her shop in a particularly convenient neighborhood, but rather selected the place because of the interesting character of the district, it being in the oldest part of Paris, full of quaint narrow streets, beautiful arched doorways, and moss-covered stone courts. Miss Beach is convinced that only the people really interested in books, buy them and those people will come from any part of the city, no matter how far it may be.

In fact Miss Beach has all the theories that so many booksellers would like to believe, but nearly always sacrifice because of "financial interest." In Shakespeare and Company these theories are put in practice, and they work! It does not follow, however, that they would work anywhere else.

About half of the people who come to the shop are French who prefer to read English literature in the original. Many of these people are themselves writers and bring to the patrons of the shop a thoro knowledge of the best in French literature.

The patrons of Shakespeare and Company are largely of the humble classes, the students and the artists. Miss Beach does not believe that a bookshop in the more fashionable districts would be a success. To illustrate her belief she tells of a fashionable lady who drove up to the shop in her car, accompanied by her daughter, age fourteen. The daughter asked for a copy of Alan Seegar's poems.

"Mamma, may I have this book," said the daughter pointing to a recently published diary.
"No! I told you you could have only one book, and now you have it."
"But, mother, I want it very much." They argued as they went out the door.

"May I have it instead of the manicure set?" This suggestion brought horrified exclamations from the mother. Eventually the book was bought.

"But," says Miss Beach, "how many prefer the manicure set! And even if they do prefer the book, how many can fight against their training?"

When "Ulysses" was first published, it sold for 150 francs. The wealthy people invariably objected to the price as being too high, but the students never complained, and one was known to have stayed in bed for four days, so as not to arouse an appetite, in order to buy a copy.

Going Contrary to Many Rules

In establishing her shop, Miss Beach has been greatly aided by her friend, Mlle. Adrienne Monnier, who has a bookstore across the street from Shakespeare and Company. It is thus that Miss Beach has been able to avoid all the complications of French red tape. It is doubtful if she could have even rented a place of business without Mlle. Monnier's assistance, as landlords are not fond of renting to foreigners, especially during these days of housing shortage. But now Miss Beach is firmly established and is held in high respect by her neighbors.

It is interesting to note that Mlle. Monnier opened the first lending library in France just a few years ago. It is a great success and today there are two or three others.

Miss Beach is very appreciative of the cooperation that she has received from the publishers in America in allowing her easy methods of purchase and liberality in discounts. The English publishers are much more strict, requiring full payment in advance and only twenty-five per cent discount. French publishers allow a third discount and will deliver books on monthly deposit. The bookseller may return at the end of each month books for which he thinks he has no market.

The duty on books coming into France is not high, being one and one-tenth per cent. But the increased cost of obtaining them is in the time it takes to get them thru the customs. Sometimes it is necessary to wait in line for several hours and then to take the books home by taxi for lack of other means of transit. Miss Beach's only assistant, a little Greek girl, spends easily half her time in these formalities.

One of the first things that struck me on entering the shop was that no prices are marked in any of the books. When someone wishes to buy a book, Miss Beach figures out the price from the American or English price on the basis of current rates of exchange. If the price were already marked in the book, the purchaser might feel that it was rather high without realizing that it was the home price translated into francs.

The high rate of exchange makes the purchase of American books prohibitive for many over here, but on the other hand the favorable exchange is drawing more and more Americans to Paris, many of whom sacrifice other things that they may have around them the books they need and love. Shakespeare and Company is a unique bookshop, going contrary to many of the principles laid down for the "successful bookseller," but it is making a success, slowly but surely, just the same. And that success will have in it something much finer than the mere sale of books. It will have given aid and encouragement to many writers who might otherwise have been lost in the shuffle, and will have given to many readers a new angle on the personality and intimacy of books and their authors.

Appendix II

BEACH'S LETTER OF PROTEST AGAINST THE
PIRATING OF *ULYSSES* (FEBRUARY 2, 1927)

Paris, 2nd February 1927.

It is a matter of common knowledge that the ULYSSES of Mr. James Joyce is being republished in the United States, in a magazine edited by Samuel Roth, and that this republication is being made without authorization by Mr. Joyce; without payment to Mr. Joyce and with alterations which seriously corrupt the text. This appropriation and mutilation of Mr Joyce's property is made under colour of legal protection in that the ULYSSES which is published in France and which has been excluded from the mails in the United States is not protected by copyright in the United States. The question of justification of that exclusion is not in issue; similar decisions have been made by government officials with reference to works of art before this. The question in issue is whether the public (including the editors and publishers to whom his advertisements are offered) will encourage Mr Samuel Roth to take advantage of the resultant legal difficulty of the author to deprive him of his property and to mutilate the creation of his art. The undersigned protest against Mr Roth's conduct in republishing ULYSSES and appeal to the American public in the name of that security of works of the intellect and the imagination without which art cannot live, to oppose Mr Roth's enterprise [with] the full power of honorable and fair opinion.

(signed)

Lascelles Abercrombie	Léon-Paul Fargue
Richard Aldington	E.M. Forster
Sherwood Anderson	François Fosca

René Arcos
M. Arcybacheff
Ebba Atterbom
Azorin
C. du Baissauray
Léon Bazalgette
Jacinto Benavente
Silvio Benco
Julien Benda
Arnold Bennett
Jacques Benoist-Méchin
Konrad Bercovici
J.D. Beresford
Rudolf Binding
Massimo Bontempelli
Jean de Bosschère
Ivan Bounine de l'Academie Russe
Robert Bridges
Eugène Brieux de l'Académie
Française
Bryher
Olaf Bull
Mary Butts
Louis Cazamian
Jacques Chenevière
Abel Chevalley
Maurice Constantin-Wéyer
Albert Crémieux
Benjamin Crémieux
Benedetto Croce
Ernst Robert Curtius
Francis Dickie
H.D.
Norman Douglas
Charles Du Bos
Georges Duhamel
Edouard Dujardin
Luc Durtain
Albert Einstein
T.S. Eliot
Havelock Ellis

Gaston Gallimard
Edward Garnett
Giovanni Gentile
André Gide
Bernard Gilbert
Ivan Goll
Ramon Gomez de la Serna
Cora Gordon
Jan Gordon
Georg Goyert
Alice S. Green
Julian Green
Augusta Gregory
Daniel Halevy
Knut Hamsun
Jane Harrison
H. Livingston Hartley
Ernest Hemingway
Hugo von Hofmannsthal
Sisley Huddleston
Stephen Hudson
George F. Hummel
Bampton Hunt
Bravig Imbs
Holbrook Jackson
Edmond Jaloux
Storm Jameson
Juan Ramon Jimenez
Eugene Jolas
Henry Festing Jones
Georg Kaiser
Hermann Keyserling
Manuel Komroff
A Kouprine
Réné Lalou
Pierre de Lanux
Valery Larbaud
D.H. Lawrence
Emile Legouis
Wyndham Lewis
Ludwig Lewisohn

Edouard Estaunié de l'Académie
Française
Archibald MacLeish
Brinsley MacNamara
Maurice Maeterlinck
Thomas Mann
Antonio Marichalar
Dora Marsden
John Masefield
W. Somerset Maugham
André Maurois
D. Merejkovsky
Régis Michaud
Gabriel Miro
Hope Mirrlees
T. Sturge Moore
Paul Morand
Auguste Morel
Arthur Moss
J. Middleton Murry
Sean O'Casey
Liam O'Flaherty
Jose Ortega y Gasset
Seumas O'Sullivan
Elliot H. Paul
Jean Paulhan
Arthur Pinero
Luigi Pirandello
Jean Prévost
Marcel Prévost de l'Académie
Française
C.F. Ramuz
Ernest Rhys
Elmer E. Rice
Dorothy Richardson
Jacques Robertfrance
Lennox Robinson
John Rodker
Romain Rolland
Jules Romains
Bertrand Russell

Victor Llona
Mina Loy
André Spire
Th. Stephanides
André Suares
Italo Svevo
Frank Swinnerton
Arthur Symons
Marcel Thiébaut
Virgil Thomson
Robert de Traz
R.C. Trevelyan
Miguel de Unamuno
Laurence Vail
Paul Valéry de l'Académie Française
Fernand Vandérem
Fritz Vanderpyl
Francis Viéle-Griffin
Hugh Walpole
Jacob Wassermann
H.G. Wells
Rebecca West
Anna Wickham
Thornton Wilder
Robert Wolf
Virginia Woolf
W.B. Yeats

George W. Russell "A.E."
Ludmilla Savitzky
Jean Schlumberger
May Sinclair
W.L. Smyser
E. OE. Somerville
Philippe Soupault

Yale University, Beinecke Rare Book and Manuscript Library (box 1, folder12)

Appendix III

BEACH'S UNSENT LETTER TO JAMES JOYCE
(APRIL 12, 1927)

12 April 1927

Dear Mr. Joyce,

I see that I owe the English publishers over two hundred pounds. The 15th is the date on which they must be paid. I have not a sufficient provision in the bank to meet all the bills and shall try to get some of the more lenient publishers to wait a fortnight, but it makes business relations very unpleasant. There are a lot of American bills too. I never try to borrow from my family. They are too poor. From what you tell me, you have only a few thousand francs left, the balance of your royalties for *Ulysses* will barely cover your rent on the 15th. You will get a big price for the manuscript of *Dubliners,* but I imagine that Rosenbach will pay only a small part of the sum down. The rest he will settle up later. Meanwhile I am afraid I and my little shop will not be able to stand the struggle to keep you and your family going from now till June, and to finance the trip of Mrs Joyce and yourself to London "with money jingling in your pocket." It is a very terrifying prospect for me. I already have many expenses for you that you do not dream of, and everything I have I give you freely. Sometimes I think you don't realize it, as when you said to Miss Weaver that my work was "easing off." The truth is that as my affection and admiration for you are unlimited, so is the work you pile on my shoulders. When you are absent, every word I receive from you is an order. The reward for my unceasing labour on your behalf is to see you tie yourself into a bowknot and hear you complain. (I am poor and tired too) and I have noticed that every time a new terrible effort is required from me, (my life is a continual 'six hours' with sprints every ten rounds) and I manage to accomplish the task that is set me you try to see how much more I can do while I am about it. Is it human?

With kindest regards
Yours very sincerely
Sylvia Beach

James Joyce Collection, University at Buffalo (SUNY) (manuscript)

Appendix IV

BEACH'S SPEECH FOR THE INSTITUT RADIOPHONIQUE D'EXTENSION UNIVERSITAIRE

SPEECH BY MISS SYLVIA BEACH OF SHAKESPEARE
AND COMPANY, FOR THE INSTITUT RADIOPHONIQUE
D'EXTENSION UNIVERSITAIRE, MAY 24, 1927

* * *

The invitation of the Radio Institute has given me an opportunity to express my love for France and my gratitude for her hospitality. It was a French woman, Mlle. Adrienne Monnier, founder of the first literary book-shop in Paris, who gave me the idea of opening a library where French readers might become acquainted with the modern literature of England, and particularly of America. Such a library was completely lacking in Paris at that time. During the War I discovered Mlle. Monnier's "Maison des Amis des Livres" where writers and readers met, undisturbed by the bombs. M. Paul Claudel expressed the sentiment of those who frequented the shop when he inscribed in one of his books: "a Adrienne Monnier, notre camarade a tous." She advised me to start a library similar to hers, but of English and American books, which I did with her help, in 1919. Americans are supposed to be capable in business matters; in this case an American girl would have been lost in her first attempts to run a bookshop, had she not been guided by the experience and wisdom of her French friend. I called my shop "Shakespeare and Company". Side by side on the shelves were Sherwood Anderson and Charlotte Brontë, Beowulf and Bennett, James Joyce and Ben Jonson, Macaulay and McAlmon, Hardy and Hemingway, Samuel Richardson and Dorothy Richardson. There was a great deal of Poetry. A large number of French people came to the shop as soon as it was opened. One of the great French writers, M. Valery Larbaud, accepted the post of godfather to Shakespeare and Company. An English writer, Mr. Arnold Bennett, I think, said of M. Larbaud that his knowledge of English literature would put to shame any Englishman. Walt Whitman, Walter Savage Landor, Coleridge, Samuel Butler, and James Joyce are some of our writers with whom he has made French readers familiar. I received much encouragement also from M. Andre Gide and M. Paul Valéry, and from the leading authorities on English letters: MM. Legouis, Cazamian, Charles Du Bos and Abel Chevalley. At least half of the members of my library are French. Some of them are Professors at the Lycees, who read all our modern books up to the very latest American ones, slang and all. Students generally borrow the Classics, which are too expensive for their purses, and difficult to obtain from the Sorbonne Library, many needing the same book at the same moment.

Shakespeare and Company immediately became a center for young American writers who had had to flee from persecution in our country. Their post-War need of freedom of expression had come in contact with American post-War restrictions, and the spirit of independence inherited from their ancestors, drove them to take refuge in France. One of them, Robert McAlmon, founded the Contact Publishing Co., which brought out books by Ernest Hemingway, William Carlos Williams, Bryher, Mina Loy, Emmanuel Carnevalli, Gertrude Stein, McAlmon, and others. Another publishing house, The Three Mountains Press, was founded by William Bird, a young American, the author of a book on French Wines that met with the approval of even the most learned French specialists on the subject.

The most important event in the life of Shakespeare and Company was the publishing of ULYSSES. One evening at the house of the well-known poet, M. Andre Spire, I met the great Irish writer, James Joyce. After years of wandering, he had come to France to finish his book, ULYSSES. It was appearing as a serial in the Little Review in New York. Now we have an organization in America called "The Society for the Suppression of Vice," founded by a man named Comstock. This Society removes paintings of the nude from art gallery windows, and forbids the circulation of Rabelais, though, for some reason, passing over the Bible, Shakespeare, and Swift. The attention of the Society was called to ULYSSES. In James Joyce's book life is expressed with perfect frankness, as for example, in Shakespeare's Hamlet. So the Editress of the Little Review, Miss Margaret Anderson, was brought up for trial, and condemned for publishing an immoral book, and her review was suspended. Mr. Joyce then consented to let Shakespeare and Company bring out ULYSSES. The importance of this work in our literature is so great, and its suppression in America was of such universal interest that as soon as a complete edition in Paris was announced, letters enquiring about it came pouring in from all over the world. My shop was beseiged by impatient subscribers. After many months passed and all the difficulties had been overcome, ULYSSES appeared on Mr. Joyce's birthday, February, 1922, and, as everyone knows, was a tremendous success. The first edition was immediately swallowed up. It is now in its 9th edition. It is still forbidden in America and in England as well. M. Valery Larbaud introduced James Joyce to the French public in a lecture at the "Maison des Amis des Livres" in December, 1921. The lecture appeared in the Nouvelle Revue Francaise and was the first article on ULYSSES. The English and American critics soon followed suit, and have been writing about it ever since. The young writer, M. August Morel, aided by M. Laurbaud, is engaged in a French translation of ULYSSES.

A year ago a Whitman Exposition was opened at Shakespeare and Company. The committee that organized it was presided over by Mr. Viele-Griffin. Many interesting manuscripts, early editions, photographs, etc., were loaned, particularly by M. Leon Bazalgette, the translator of Walt Whitman. The first person who came to do honour to our American Poet, was the great French poet, M. Paul Valery.

A new point of contact between French and Americans is the review, "Transition" recently founded here by Mr. Eugene Jolas and Mr. Elliott Paul, both Americans. In every number of "Transition" there are, besides the works of our writers, translations by Mr. Jolas from the French. He is devoting himself to making the best French writers known in America. On the other hand, French reviews and publishing houses are becoming more and more hospitable to American writers. I hope that Shakespeare and Company has contributed its share in the work of bringing the French and American people to a better understanding of one another.

Sylvia Beach Papers, Department of Rare Books and Special Collections,
Princeton University Library (typed speech) / SBP (box 179, folder 2)

GLOSSARY OF CORRESPONDENTS

Antheil, Elizabeth "Böske" Markus (1902–1978). Niece of the Austrian author and playwright, Arthur Schnitzler, and wife of the American composer, George Antheil.

Antheil, George (1900–1959). American composer, pianist, author, and inventor. In the 1920s, he became the first avant-garde American composer recognized in Europe, thanks mainly to his 30-minute *Ballet mécanique*. While in France he befriended many expatriate artists, including James Joyce and Ernest Hemingway. He and his wife Böske rented the apartment above Shakespeare and Company.

Beach, Cyprian (Eleanor Elliot) (1891–1951). Sylvia Beach's younger sister. During her career as a film actor, she changed her name from Eleanor to Cyprian. She later settled in Pasadena, California, with her partner, the silent film star Helen Jerome Eddy.

Beach, Eleanor Orbison (1864–1927). Daughter of missionaries to India and the wife of Sylvester Woodbridge Beach, she was the mother of Holly, Sylvia, and Cyprian Beach.

Beach, Holly (Mary Hollingsworth Morris) (1884–1973). Sylvia Beach's elder sister. She organized the American Junior Red Cross in southern Italy during World War I and was active throughout her life in the American Red Cross. She married American businessman Frederic Dennis and settled in Greenwich, Connecticut.

Beach, Sylvester Woodbridge (1852–1940). Father of Holly, Sylvia, and Cyprian Beach. A graduate of the Princeton Theological Seminary, he was the pastor of the First Presbyterian Church in Princeton.

Bird, William (1888–1963). American publisher and journalist. His small press in Paris, Three Mountains, brought out experimental modernist works, including an initial version of Ernest Hemingway's *in our time.*

Briggs, Carlotta Welles (1889–1979). American friend of Sylvia Beach. During the First World War, she worked in the anti-typhoid vaccine lab at Val-de-Grace Military Hospital in Paris. Her husband, Jim Briggs, served in the military in France during World War I.

Bryher (Annie Winifred Ellerman) (1894–1983). Poet, memoirist, novelist, and magazine editor. She wrote under the pseudonym Bryher. Bryher offered financial backing to writers, including James Joyce and Edith Sitwell, and she contributed to the financial stability of Shakespeare and Company. Married for short periods to Robert McAlmon and Kenneth Macpherson, Bryher's most lasting romantic relationship was with Hilda Doolittle (H.D.).

Carlos Williams, William (1883–1963). American poet (and pediatrician). He was involved in both the Imagist and modernist movements.

Cody, Morrill (1901–1987). American diplomat, author, and editor. He worked for the U.S. Foreign Service for more than twenty years, was the deputy director of the United States Information Agency, and managed Radio Free Europe in Paris for nine years. Cody also authored and edited several books.

D'Avout, Bernard (dates unknown). Printer and baron. He succeeded Maurice Darantière as the manager and owner of the printing house Darantière.

Douglas, Norman (1868–1952). British novelist. During his life he was involved in numerous scandals, one involving a teenage boy. He is best known for his novel *South Wind*.

Dudley, Katherine (1884–unknown). American painter who exhibited at the Art Institute of Chicago in 1920. She later moved to Paris and was interned with Sylvia Beach and other American women at Vittel during the Second World War.

Fitzgerald, F. Scott (1896–1940). American expatriate writer and chronicler of the Jazz Age. His most famous novel is *The Great Gatsby* (1925).

Flanner, Janet (1892–1978). American writer and journalist. French Correspondent for *The New Yorker* from 1925 to 1975. In her column, "Letter from Paris," which appeared under the pseudonym Genêt, she introduced notable new Parisian artists, including Picasso and Matisse. Flanner's *The Cubical City* (1926) is her only novel.

Frank, Waldo (1889–1967). American novelist, historian, and critic. He became associate editor of the journal *The Seven Arts* in 1914.

Fraser, Ian Forbes (1907–1969). Director of the American Library in Paris. In 1952 he famously closed the Library's door to Roy Cohn and Joseph Schine, agents sent by Joseph McCarthy to search for anti-American literature.

Friede, Donald (1901–1965). American heir. He was the first vice president of publishing house Boni and Liveright and later formed his own firm Covici, Friede, Inc. He published Steinbeck, Radclyffe Hall, and Theodore Dreiser, among others.

Gaige, Crosby (1882–1949). American theater producer and director. He also authored cookbooks and an autobiography, and served as vice president for the Managers Protective Association.

H.D. (Hilda Doolittle) (1886–1961). American poet, novelist, and memoirist. In 1916, after publishing her first book *Sea Garden*, she became editor of *The Egoist*. In the 1930s she became a patient of Sigmund Freud.

Hemingway, Ernest (1899–1961). American author who lived in Paris during the 1920s. A veteran of World War I, like F. Scott Fitzgerald he has become synonymous with the "Lost Generation." In 1953 he won the Pulitzer Prize for *The Old Man and the Sea*, and a year later he won the Nobel Prize.

Huddleston, Sisley (1883–1952). British journalist, author, and revisionist historian of World War II, Huddleston wrote primarily about France and war as a columnist for the *London Times* and the *Christian Science Monitor*. In 1944 he was taken prisoner by the Free French for being a Vichy supporter.

Jolas, Eugène (1894–1952). Writer, translator, and literary critic. In 1927, Jolas, his wife Maria, and Elliot Paul founded the literary magazine *transition* in Paris. Jolas met James Joyce in Paris and became an influential force in supporting *Finnegans Wake*.

Jolas, Maria McDonald (1893–1987). Wife of Eugène Jolas and co-founder of *transition*. A strong proponent of peace, she was the president of the Paris American Committee to Stop War, and vehemently opposed the U.S. war with Vietnam while she was living in Europe. She translated numerous French works into English, including *The Poetics of Space* by Gaston Bachelard.

Joyce, Helen Fleischman (1894–1963). American divorcee who married James Joyce's son, Giorgio Joyce.

Joyce, James (1882–1941). Irish writer whose works include *Dubliners* (1914), *A Portrait of the Artist as a Young Man* (1916), *Ulysses* (1922), and *Finnegans Wake* (1939). Beach published *Ulysses* on February 2, 1922.

Joyce, Stanislaus (1884–1955). Brother of James Joyce. He was born in Dublin, but left for Trieste, where he lived with Joyce while working as an English-language teacher. In 1950 he published *Recollections of James Joyce* and assisted Richard Ellmann with his milestone biography *James Joyce* (1959).

Knopf, Alfred A. (1892–1984). American publisher. Born in New York City, he founded the publishing house Alfred A. Knopf, Inc., and remained chairman until his death.

Kreymborg, Alfred (1883–1966). American author and editor. He worked in New York City with Man Ray in 1913–14 to produce ten issues of *The Glebe*, the modernist magazine that published Ezra Pound's *Des Imagistes* (the first anthology of the Imagist movement). In 1921 he moved to Paris to co-edit the journal *Broom, An International Magazine of the Arts*.

Loeb, Harold (1891–1974). American co-editor of the literary journal *Broom*. Having boxed while attending Princeton University, Loeb was one of Ernest Hemingway's sparring partners and later became a model for the character Robert Cohn in *The Sun Also Rises* (1926).

Léon, Paul (1893–1942). Russian exile who moved to Paris in 1918 and was a friend of James Joyce and his family. After Beach gave up the rights to *Ulysses* in 1930, Léon became Joyce's most faithful adviser. He died in Auschwitz.

Matthews, Elkin (1851–1921). British publisher and bookseller. In 1887 Matthews moved from Exeter to London to open a bookshop, The Bodley Head, in a partnership with John Lane. After publishing several works, including *The Yellow Book* (a quarterly literary periodical), Matthews published many prominent writers, including Pound, Joyce, and Yeats.

Mathews, Jackson (1907?–1978). American writer, translator, and editor. In 1963, after gathering several of Beach's letters, typescripts, and other items, he put together a "Hommage à Sylvia Beach" for the literary magazine *Mercure de France*. Mathews' wife, Martheil, translated Bauldelaire's *Flowers of Evil* (1955) and Valéry's collected works alongside him.

McAlmon, Robert (1896–1956). American publisher and writer. Among the first expatriates to frequent Shakespeare and Company. McAlmon assisted Joyce with the editing and typing of *Ulysses* and also provided financial support for the project.

Monnier, Adrienne (1892–1955). French writer, editor, and bookseller. Her bookstore, La Maison des Amis des Livres, provided writers from diverse backgrounds with a place to gather, discuss, and read their work. Monnier founded the French-language review, *Le Navire d'Argent*, which published many American works in translation and helped popularize American writing in France.

Moore, Marianne (1887–1972). American modernist poet and writer. Moore worked as an editor for the magazine *The Dial*. In her capacity as editor she supported younger poets such as Allen Ginsberg and Elizabeth Bishop.

O'Brien, Edward J. (1890–1941). American anthologist, editor, and author known primarily for his popular annual compilations. As an author, O'Brien produced several works, including *White Fountains* (1917) and *The Forgotten Threshold* (1918).

Peter, Marion (née Mason) (dates unknown). Lifelong friend of Sylvia Beach. She helped Beach smuggle published copies of *Ulysses* into the United States, and named her daughter Sylvia after her friend (Sylvia Peter worked as an assistant at Shakespeare and Company in the 1930s). In 1966, Marion Peter gave a collection of her letters to Beach to Princeton University Library.

Pinker, James B. (1863–1922). Founder of James B. Pinker and Son, London literary agents. His agency managed a wide range of influential authors such as Joyce, Oscar Wilde, Joseph Conrad, and Aldous Huxley.

Pound, Dorothy (1886–1973). English artist and wife of Ezra Pound. The daughter of Olivia Shakespear, the novelist and, for a short time, lover of W. B. Yeats. Pound helped facilitate Ezra Pound's friendship with Wyndham Lewis and other painters during the vorticist period.

Pound, Ezra (1885–1972). American poet and critic. Pound edited and contributed to several literary magazines and journals and helped advance the careers of authors such as Marianne Moore, Yeats, Joyce, and Eliot. He also edited and contributed to *Des Imagistes* (1914), the first anthology of the Imagist poetic movement.

Reynolds, Mary (1891–1950). American who worked as a bookbinder in France. Reynolds was involved in both the Surrealist and Dadaist movements and worked alongside Marcel Duchamp and others. She espoused a creative approach to bookbinding.

Slocum, John (dates unknown). First president of the James Joyce Society, founded in February 1947, and co-author of *Bibliography of James Joyce (1882–1941)*, published in 1953.

Stein, Gertrude (1874–1946). American writer and lifelong partner of Alice B. Toklas. Stein moved to Paris in 1903 and, like Beach, was one of the social hubs of Parisian expatriate life.

Tate, Allen (1899–1979). American poet and critic. His writings include the poem "Ode to the Confederate Dead" (1928) and a biography, *Stonewall Jackson: The Good Soldier* (1928). In 1942, Tate worked alongside Andrew Lytle in elevating America's oldest literary quarterly, *The Sewanee Review*, into one of the nation's most prestigious journals.

Titus, Edward (dates unknown). American publisher and owner of the Parisian book room and gallery, At the Sign of the Black Manikin. Beginning in 1926, Titus published twenty-five books, including the English version of Alice Prin's *Kiki's Memoirs*. In 1929 he began publishing and editing *This Quarter* magazine, which contained the writings by artists such as Salvador Dali and Max Ernst, as well as Ernest Hemingway's "The Undefeated."

Toklas, Alice B. (1877–1967). American personality and partner of writer Gertrude Stein. In 1933 Stein published her memoir under the title *The Autobiography of Alice B. Toklas*, and in 1954 Toklas published her own memoir and cookbook titled *The Alice B. Toklas Cookbook*.

Weaver, Harriet Shaw (1876–1961). English editor and patron of Joyce. After financially supporting the literary journal *The Egoist*, Weaver succeeded Ezra Pound as its editor. She fully believed in Joyce's genius, and in 1914 serialized *A Portrait of the Artist as a Young Man* in *The Egoist*. She later founded the Egoist Press in order to publish the book.

Wright, Richard (1908–1960). American writer. In 1946, Wright moved to France and joined the expatriate circle in Paris. His many works include *The Outsider* (1953), *Black Power* (1954), and *White Man, Listen!* (1957).

INDEX

Sylvia Beach is abbreviated SB throughout. Photographs are numbered Fig. 1 through Fig. 30. Locators with an "n" refer to footnotes.

CPSIA information can be obtained
at www.ICGtesting.com
Printed in the USA
LVOW12s0914090318
569263LV00002B/5/P